Enterprise Information Systems Assurance and System Security:
Managerial and Technical Issues

Merrill Warkentin, Mississippi State University, USA

Rayford B. Vaughn, Mississippi State University, USA

IDEA GROUP PUBLISHING
Hershey • London • Melbourne • Singapore

Acquisitions Editor:	Michelle Potter
Development Editor:	Kristin Roth
Senior Managing Editor:	Amanda Appicello
Managing Editor:	Jennifer Neidig
Copy Editor:	Jane Conley
Typesetter:	Sharon Berger
Cover Design:	Lisa Tosheff
Printed at:	Yurchak Printing Inc.

Published in the United States of America by
  Idea Group Publishing (an imprint of Idea Group Inc.)
  701 E. Chocolate Avenue
  Hershey PA 17033
  Tel: 717-533-8845
  Fax: 717-533-8661
  E-mail: cust@idea-group.com
  Web site: http://www.idea-group.com

and in the United Kingdom by
  Idea Group Publishing (an imprint of Idea Group Inc.)
  3 Henrietta Street
  Covent Garden
  London WC2E 8LU
  Tel: 44 20 7240 0856
  Fax: 44 20 7379 0609
  Web site: http://www.eurospanonline.com

Library of Congress Cataloging-in-Publication Data

Enterprise information systems assurance and system security : managerial and technical issues / Merrill Warkentin and Rayford Vaughn, editors.
     p. cm.
  Summary: "This book brings together authoritative authors to address the most pressing challenge in the IT field - how to create secure environments for the application of technology to serve our future needs"--Provided by publisher.
  Includes bibliographical references and index.
  ISBN 1-59140-911-X (hardcover) -- ISBN 1-59140-912-8 (softcover) -- ISBN 1-59140-913-6 (ebook)
  1. Computer security. 2. Computer networks--Security measures. 3. Management information systems. I. Warkentin, Merrill. II. Vaughn, Rayford, 1947-
  QA76.9.A25E5455 2006
  005.8--dc22
                              2005032072

British Cataloguing in Publication Data
A Cataloguing in Publication record for this book is available from the British Library.

Enterprise Information Systems Assurance and System Security: Managerial and Technical Issues

Table of Contents

Section II: Security Implications for Business

Section III: Security Engineering

Section IV: Security Technologies

Section V: Authentication Issues

Preface

Few topics in the *information technology* (IT) field today generate as much interest as security. Interestingly, the IT world has been struggling with security issues for over 30 years, yet many security problems remain unsolved, unaddressed, and serious. As those responsible for securing systems and networks address security issues by a combination of hardware, software, procedures, policy, and the law, intruders and insiders circumvent protection mechanisms, discover new and unpublished vulnerabilities, or find lapses in an organization's policy and procedure in their efforts to damage systems, destroy data, or simply for mischief purposes. The attacker clearly has an advantage in this struggle between those who protect and those who penetrate. While the protector must close all vulnerabilities, the attacker need only find one to exploit.

Security in enterprise computing systems is also not simply a matter of technology and cannot be addressed satisfactorily with hardware and software alone. It is also a matter of managing people, establishing and enforcing strong (and correct) policies, implementing procedures that strengthen security, and periodically checking the effectiveness of the security architecture and making necessary changes. The provision of security in any enterprise must also be tailored to that particular organization. While the principles of computing security and common wisdom in the IT field are important, the actual application of such principles depends largely on a number of factors that often vary from enterprise to enterprise (e.g., confidentiality needs for data, customers, access requirements, volatility of data value, and others). Those individuals responsible for enterprise security must balance the need for security against the need for access to their system (by customers and employees), must be concerned with the cost of the security measures compared to the overall strength of the security architecture being constructed, and must also be cognizant of how well the security perimeter is performing. These are difficult tasks indeed. Success in these tasks requires vigilant attention to many factors, and the successful security manager must constantly re-educate him- or herself and his or her staff.

This book was edited by a management information systems professor and a computer science professor — both of whom believe that a cross-disciplinary approach to the security problem is important and that architected solutions are possible in any enterprise to provide "sufficient" or "adequate" security. The original thought in developing this book was to provide a collection of chapters useful to corporate security staff, government security administrators, and students of security who wish to examine a particular topic in some detail. We sometimes referred to the book as "good airplane reading" because one can read one or two chapters easily on a typical flight. We also considered this book as useful in the classroom. During a typical 16-week semester, students can spend each week discussing a different chapter of interest. Therefore, the reader can feel free to pick and choose chapters to read in any order — depending simply on the reader's interest. Each chapter stands alone, but they have been grouped into five distinct topic areas: security policy and management; security implications for business; security engineering; security technologies; and authentication issues. The mix of authors is interesting, too. We have purposely chosen authors to contribute who represent industry (practicing security engineers) as well as academia, and authors who present an international perspective (e.g., Australia, Finland, Singapore, China). There is a mix of practice and research embedded in the chapters, with the stronger emphasis on practice. As such, the reader may on occasion find conflicts in advice or conclusion between chapters. Given that the practice of security today is not exact, this is a natural result of independent views and writings.

We begin the book with four chapters addressing *security policy and management*. This topic was placed first since one must understand the policies to be enforced and management practices before a security solution can be considered. In Chapter I, Fink, Huegle, and Dortschy address the "role" of IT governance in e-business applications and propose a model framework for such governance activity. Past initiatives to provide IT governance frameworks are included here as well. Warkentin and Johnston build on this theme in Chapter II and discuss the problem of governance and the framework for ensuring that an organization's security policies are implemented over time. They also include a healthy discussion on whether such governance should be centralized or decentralized. Chapter III by Griffy-Brown and Chun presents a real-world case study of implementation of a strong security policy in the automotive industry and the lessons learned in dealing with security policy conflicts with business practices and needs. Finally, in Chapter IV, Sharman, Krishna, Rao, and Upadhyaya discuss procedures necessary to address malicious code. Virus, spyware, and scam spoofs are on the rise today, so no security architecture would be complete without addressing this area.

The second major division is *security implications for business*. Here we placed six chapters that examine specific nuances of small- and medium-sized businesses, e-commerce, and the law. Mishra and Dhillon address the impact of the Sarbanes-Oxley (SOX) Act on IT governance and internal controls in Chapter V. SOX has been highly controversial since its adoption and few large businesses have not been impacted by this legislation. Du, Jiao, and Jiao then provide an international perspective in Chapter VI on the development of a security blueprint for e-business applications, and they include a case study as an example of an implementation. Chapter VII, written by Masood, Sedigh-Ali, and Ghafoor, then discusses the principles of security management for an e-enterprise. These authors include a set of security metrics that the reader will find useful. In Chapter VIII, Weippl and Klemen provide another international view of a set of principles for implementation of IT security in small- and medium-sized enterprises or SME, which are often distinctly different than those that govern security design in large enterprises. Chapter IX continues to examine security implications in e-commerce applications. Here Furnell reiterates some of the same principles previously suggested by other authors, but applies them to the e-commerce practice. Finally, this section concludes with Chapter X addressing a topic made critical by the terrorist attacks of September 2001 — namely, survivability. Here Snow, Straub, Baskerville, and Stucke discuss the need for dispersal of people, technology, and physical assets.

In the third major section, focused on *security engineering*, we chose to include five important chapters. As might be expected, the authors in this section have significant industrial experience and several are practicing security engineers. Chapter XI was authored by Henning, a security engineer with Harris Corporation of Melbourne, Florida. Here she presents some basic tenets of security analysis that can be applied by any systems engineer to ensure early integration of security constraints into the system definition and development process. Ms. Henning's experience over many years of practice adds to the credibility of this work. Chapter XII addresses the issue of product selection and how one evaluates the strength of a product given current government procedures and laboratory analysis. Vaughn discusses this topic and provides some historical background that the reader will find interesting. In Chapter XIII, Murphy provides insights into the development of a robust *demilitarized zone* (DMZ) as an *information protection network* (IPN). Dr. Murphy's many years of experience at EDS and now as the president and founder of Dexisive Inc. are apparent to the reader as he discusses various approaches to implementing a DMZ. Chapter XIV proposes a unification of the process models of software engineering and security engineering in order to improve the steps of the software life cycle that would better address the underlying objectives of both engineering processes. This chapter, by Zulkernine and Ahamed, is based on an academic's view and is a good addition to the practical bent of the surrounding chapters. Last, Chapter XV by Graham and Steinbart addresses wireless security — an area of growing concern today as more enterprises move toward wireless infrastructures.

All security engineers and managers involved in the provision of security for IT systems must, at some point, consider specific *security technologies*, the topic of our fourth major division. We include five chapters here, each of which we found extremely interesting and informative reading. Chapter XVI by Dampier and Siraj provides an overview of what intrusion detection systems are and some guidelines on what to look for in such technologies. In Chapter XVII, Dodge and Ragsdale provide a most excellent treatment of honeypots, an evolving technology useful in many ways. Honeypots (and honeynets) are placed on one's network and designed to be attacked while being closely monitored. Such devices are helpful to determine who is attacking your system, whether or not you have an internal threat, and as a sensor inside a protected network to monitor the effectiveness of the security perimeter, among other uses described in this chapter. Warkentin, Schmidt, and Bekkering provide a description of the steganography problem in Chapter XVIII, where sensitive information may be secretly embedded in apparently innocuous messages or images, and discuss how steganalysis is used to find incidences of this problem. Chapter XIX, by Villarroel, Fernández-Medina, Trujillo, and Piattini, takes a more academic bent and provides ideas on how one might architect a secure data warehouse. Here we have ideas from researchers in Spain and Chile presented. The last chapter in this section, Chapter XX, provides an overview of investigative techniques used to find evidence of wrongdoing on a system. Here Dampier and Bogen present the intricacies of digital forensics and how one might intelligently respond to incidents requiring a digital forensic application.

The area of authentication issues makes up the last major division of the book. Authentication is an important factor in securing IT systems in that policy decisions made by a computer must be based on the identity of the user. We provide three distinct views here — one academic, one international, and one industrial and government combined. In Chapter XXI, Taylor and Eder provide an exploratory, descriptive, and evaluative discussion of security features in the widely used Windows and Linux operating systems. This is followed in Chapter XXII by a contribution from Finland, where Pulkkis, Grahn, and Karlsson provide an excellent taxonomy of authentication methods in networks. As an academic contribution, they also provide some research efforts in which they are involved. Last, we have a chapter on the important topic of identity management. In Chapter XXIII, Hollis (U.S. Army) and Hollis (EDS) provide the reader with an excellent discussion of what comprises identity management, what technologies are useful in building this capability, and how one makes a return on investment argument for such a capability.

We hope that you find this book useful, and we would enjoy hearing from its readers.

Acknowledgments

The authors would like to acknowledge the efforts of the many contributors to the work contained within this book. Without their willingness to participate in this endeavor, there would be no book. Their hard work in developing the manuscripts, revising them as necessarily, and editing them for final form constitutes the heart of this project. We also wish to thank all the reviewers who volunteered to provide invaluable input by identifying manuscripts worthy of inclusion in the book and who also supplied important guidance into the improvement of each chapter during revisions.

The authors also wish to thank Jordan Shropshire, whose hard work and diligence in assisting us with the administrative processing of submissions, revisions, author information, and communications were important contributions to the success of this project. We also wish to acknowledge the support of Idea Group Inc., especially Kristin Roth, whose facilitation of the activities at each stage of the process and prompt response to our many questions helped make the process a smooth one.

Merrill Warkentin, Mississippi State University, USA
Rayford Vaughn, Mississippi State University, USA

* * * * *

I wish to thank my wife, Kim Davis, whose suggestions and general support provide me with the opportunity to pursue my professional goals. Kim has collaborated with me on security-related investigations and has frequently provided interesting professional perspectives on my various projects. But most importantly, her constant personal support provides the foundation for all my endeavors.

I also wish to thank Harold and Rosena Warkentin, who as parents and as teachers provided me with the motivation and desire to pursue my dreams, to work hard, and to always ask "why?"

Finally, I would like to thank the Center for Computer Security Risk (CCSR) at Mississippi State University (Ray Vaughn, Director) for its continuing support for my IA research and for that of my doctoral students.

Merrill Warkentin

* * * * *

I would also like to acknowledge my wife, Dianne Vaughn, for being supportive of me while I spent so much time at the office and at home working on this and other projects that seem to occupy much of my life. I would also like to acknowledge the Computer Science and Engineering Department at Mississippi State University for providing support and encouragement during the production of this book.

Rayford Vaughn

Section I:

Security Policy
and Management

Chapter I

A Model of Information Security Governance for E-Business

Dieter Fink, Edith Cowan University, Australia

Tobias Huegle, Edith Cowan University, Australia

Martin Dortschy, Institute of Electronic Business —
University of Arts, Germany

Abstract

This chapter identifies various levels of governance followed by a focus on the role of information technology (IT) *governance with reference to information security for today's* electronic business (e-business) *environment. It outlines levels of enterprise, corporate, and business governance in relation to IT governance before integrating the latter with e-business security management. E-business has made organisations even more reliant on the application of IT while exploiting its capabilities for generating business advantages. The emergence of and dependence on new technologies, like the Internet, have increased exposure of businesses to technology-originated threats and have created new requirements for security management and governance. Previous IT governance frameworks, such as those provided by the IT Governance Institute, Standards Australia, and The National Cyber Security Partnership, have not given the connection between IT governance and e-business security sufficient attention. The proposed model achieves the necessary integration through risk management in which the tensions between threat reduction and value generation activities have to be balanced.*

Introduction

Governance has gained increasing attention in recent years, primarily due to the failures of well-known corporations such as Enron®. The expectations for improved corporate governance have become very noticeable, especially in the United States, where the Sarbanes-Oxley (SOX) Act of 2002 aims to restore investor confidence in U.S. markets by imposing codes of conduct on corporations. The concept of corporate governance is much quoted as "the system by which companies are directed and controlled" (Cadbury, 1992, p.15). The corporate governance structure, therefore, specifies the distribution of rights and responsibilities among different participants in the corporation, such as the board of directors and management. By doing this, it provides the structure by which the company objectives are set and the means of attaining those objectives and monitoring performance.

Corporate governance includes concerns for information technology governance because without effective information management, those charged with corporate responsibilities would not be able to perform effectively. *eWeek* (2004) make the case for IT professionals to take a leading role in corporate governance since they have control over the processes underpinning governance activities. They mention the example of the human resource database providing information about employees' compensation which, if the information is properly monitored, could provide an early indication of malpractice. This means that IT functions need to be secure so that "business data is not altered by unscrupulous hands" (*eWeek,* 2004, p. 40). With business increasingly utilising modern digital technology in a variety of ways, effective information security governance has, therefore, become a key part of corporate governance.

In this chapter, the role of corporate governance in relation to the security of information technology and *information and communications technology* (ICT) will be examined. Current developments and models such as those offered by the IT Governance Institute and Standards Australia will be outlined and the current lack of model development in extending the governance concept to information security in today's world of e-business will be identified and discussed. The purpose of the chapter is thus to develop a model that aligns IT governance with security management in an e-business environment through a review of existing approaches and synthesis of concepts and principles.

Need for Governance

The case of Enron® exemplifies the need for effective corporate governance. Enron®'s downfall was brought about, as described in broad terms by Zimmerman (2002) in USA TODAY®, by "overaggressive strategies, combined with personal greed." He believes that there were two main causes for this failure: first, breakdowns caused by ignored or flawed ethics, and second, "Board of directors failed their governance." He recommends that in order to keep this from happening again, corporate governance should no longer be treated as "soft stuff," but rather as the "hard stuff" like product quality and customer service. He quotes *Business Week®* of August 19-26, 2002 when he concludes that "a company's viability now depends less on making the numbers at any cost and more on the integrity and trustworthiness of its practices." In other words, good corporate governance.

The term corporate governance is often used synonymously with the term enterprise governance since they are similar in scope as can be seen from the following definitions. They both apply to the role and responsibilities of management at the highest level in the organisation. An example of a framework for enterprise governance is one that is provided by the *Chartered Institute of Management Accountants* (CIMA) and the *International Federation of Accountants* (IFAC) (2004):

> *[Enterprise governance is] the set of responsibilities and practices exercised by the board and executive management with the goal of providing strategic direction, ensuring that objectives are achieved, ascertaining that risks are managed appropriately and verifying that the organization's resources are used responsibly.*

The term corporate governance is used by the *Organisation for Economic Co-operation and Development* (OECD) (Brand & Boonen, 2003) and understood to be:

> *the system by which business corporations are directed and controlled. The corporate governance structure specifies the distribution of rights and responsibilities, among different participants in the corporation such as board, managers, shareholders and other stakeholders and spells out the rules and procedures for making decisions on corporate affairs. By doing this, it also provides the structure by which the company objectives are set and the means of attaining those objectives and monitoring performance.* (pp. 15-16)

The above definitions not only reveal commonality but also emphasize two dimensions, namely, conformance and performance. Conformance focuses on structure such as the existence of the board and executive management, who in turn communicate their perceptions of corporate objectives. Performance, on the other hand, provides expectations about the achievement of corporate objectives and is associated with activities such as risk management, resource utilisation, and performance measurement. It could be argued that the former has a greater corporate orientation as it has a leadership role, unlike the latter that is linked to the execution of business activities and has more an operational orientation and could be termed business governance.

IT systems contribute to the performance dimension of the organisation as they support the organisational processes by delivering IT services. They are, therefore, most closely linked with the business governance component of the above dichotomy. However, as IT is increasingly becoming an integral part of business, the responsibility for IT becomes part of the responsibility of the board of directors, and thereby also very much part of

Figure 1. IT governance and enterprise governance

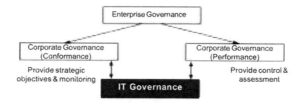

the conformance aspects of governance. The latter is much broader in scope, implying greater strategic and diligence responsibilities on the part of the board and executive management.

Figure 1 shows how the enterprise governance framework extends to IT governance through the influences of corporate and business governance as outlined above. The two levels interact with IT governance as follows: the key role for corporate governance is to provide strategic objectives and their monitoring, while business governance provides control and assessment of the operational activities of IT. Both are required to make IT play its intended role for the organisation.

The following section provides a more detailed examination of IT governance by examining the perspectives of a professional, government, and research body. This will explain in more depth the interaction between IT governance with the higher levels of governance as well as the scope of IT governance itself. With regard to the latter, attention will be given to IT security within IT governance in line with the objectives of the chapter.

IT Governance

Perspectives on IT governance from three significant institutions in this field are examined below: they are the IT Governance Institute, *Standards Australia* (SA), and National Cyber Security Partnership. The analysis focuses on the activities of IT governance and the integration of IT security in the respective frameworks in order to synthesis these views later into a model of information security governance.

ITGI* (2001) argued that executives are getting more and more dependent on information technology to run their businesses. Hence, IT governance is defined by the Institute (2003) as:

*the responsibility of the board of directors and executive management. It is
an integral part of enterprise governance and consists of the leadership and
organisational structures and processes that ensure that the organization's
IT sustains and extends the organization's strategies and objectives.* (p.10)

According to ITGI®, IT governance has as its main purposes the achievement of strategic
alignment, value delivery, risk management, and performance management. The question
of IT security is addressed by providing emphasis to risk management, as it is realised
that with IT's benefits and opportunities comes greater risk. Mechanisms, therefore, are
required to exercise control over the use of IT in order to cope with these risks. Risk
management is perceived as the appropriate management of threats relating to IT,
addressing the safeguarding of IT assets, disaster recovery, and continuity of operations.

SA (2004), an Australian federal government department, recently developed a detailed
approach for ICT governance to guide senior officeholders in evaluating, directing, and
monitoring the operations of ICT systems. They defined the governance of ICT as:

*the system by which the use of ICT is controlled. It involves evaluating and
directing the plans for the use of ICT to support the organisation and
monitoring this use to maintain that plan. It includes the strategy and
policies for using ICT within an organisation.* (p. 6)

SA identified seven key principles of ICT governance, namely establishing clearly
understood responsibilities for ICT, planning ICT to best support the organisation,
acquiring ICT in a cost-beneficial manner, ensuring ICT is of the required quality,
performs when required, conforms with formal rules, and respects human factors.

The principle "ensure ICT is of the required quality" refers to different tasks that are part
of IT security management, such as ensuring system availability and security from attack,
theft, and misuse of crucial business data. This also includes the preparation of disaster
recovery plans to ensure business continuity. Additionally, it is suggested that the
organisation is able to monitor and report all security breaches, including attacks and
fraud. Finally, accurate procedures for the measurement of the effectiveness of security
measures have to be in place. SA advocates risk management methods for the identification of security risk, its evaluation, and mitigation. It is essential for the well-being and
legal compliance of the organisation that upper management is informed about security
risks and their implications while making decisions.

The Corporate Governance Task Force of the National Cyber Security Partnership (2004)
argued that although information security is often considered a technical issue, it is also
a governance challenge that involves risk management, reporting, and accountability
and, therefore, requires the active engagement of executive management. The managerial
aspect of security management is defined as *information security governance* (ISG), a
subset of an organisation's overall governance program. Within ISG, risk management,
reporting, and accountability are considered key policies.

The *National Cyber Security Partnership* (NCSP) made the topic of IT security contemporary by including cyber security for effective ISG. It made a number of recommendations for the adoption of ISG in the U.S. using the IDEAL framework (initiating, diagnosing, establishing, acting, and learning). Appendices of the NCSP report provide extensive information on functions and responsibilities, organisation and processes for implementation, and ISG assessment tools.

While the above approaches provide an overview of IT governance and an acknowledgment of its responsibilities with respect to information security, they do not go as far as providing prescriptions on how best to integrate security issues into governance. Guidance in this respect is desirable as IT security has become more complex with the emergence of the e-business phenomenon.

E-Business and Security

E-business has been defined by McKay and Marshall (2004) as:

> *a business that creatively and intelligently utilises and exploits the capabilities of IT and Internet technologies to create efficiencies, to achieve effectiveness gains such as flexibility and responsiveness, and to create strategic opportunities through competitive uses of IT to alter markets and industry structures.* (p. 5)

This type of business is a development of e-commerce, a system that uses the Internet to provide a new channel to conduct trade with customers and suppliers. Further integration of ICT into the business itself enabled value chains to be developed with customers and suppliers. Inside the organisation, enterprise resource planning (ERP) software provided integration with new applications, such as supply chain management, and between existing applications, such as accounting and finance. With e-business, organisations have become even more dependent on the utilisation of ICT to create and maintain business advantages, albeit using technologies that are different from previous ones (e.g., the Internet).

The e-business environment can be contrasted from the traditional IT environment in three major ways (Fink, 2004). First, under the new approach, systems are open while previously they were considered closed. In other words, globally networked systems are more accessible and open to attack than systems kept strictly in-house without Internet access. Second, assets are now more virtual than tangible and more difficult to track as networks of cooperating organisations emerge. The assets of such organisations largely lie in intellectual property rather than in "bricks and mortar." Third, in the past, emphasis was placed on developing systems with the objective of meeting users' expectations, while now operations are critical since organisations are dependent on the continued functioning of their IT systems. For example, business is lost should the Web site on the Internet cease to function and customer may never return to the site.

The new environment has created new sets of technological risks. Technological risks, despite the name, are largely brought about by the actions of humans. They attract the greatest attention when brought about maliciously. Methods of attack are numerous and include viruses that can be introduced through data obtained from the Internet. The opportunity for hacker attacks is provided since the Internet enables others sharing the network to penetrate information systems in an unauthorised manner. Data and messages being forwarded on this network are potentially subject to interception and modification while being transmitted. Systems themselves can be brought down by denial-of-service attacks designed to prevent services requests to specific services such as accessing a Web application on the Internet.

In response to these concerns, e-business should implement a system of security measures. These measures include those that ensure the availability of systems (to prevent system outages), integrity (so that data can be relied upon for decision making), confidentiality (to prevent unauthorised disclosure of information), and authenticity (verifying that users are who they claim to be). In addition, an organisation should implement broad security approaches, including the use of security policy, contingency planning, and disaster recovery. These will ensure that the e-business continues to operate efficiently and effectively.

Model for Information Security Governance

The preceding sections provided an overview of enterprise governance and highlighted the importance of IT governance at the corporate (conformance) and business (performance) levels. An overview was also provided of three perspectives on IT governance itself. The three approaches describe IT governance as an executive management task in which IT activities at the highest level are strategically managed in order to gain maximum alignment between IT and business. At a more operational level, the role of IT is perceived to be one of generating value for the organisation, ameliorated by the need to practice effective risk management in order to secure the organisation from new and complex technological and human threats.

This section proposes a model for information security governance, shown in Figure 2. It consists of two major components, namely, information security governance and e-business security management. Within the former are strategic high-level processes (e.g., setting objectives) as well as lower-level operational processes (e.g., IT value delivery) that were identified in previous discussions. However, it does not include risk management, which performs the special function of integrating the two major components as seen in Figure 2. The e-business security management component deals with security issues, again at a high level (e.g., developing a security policy) and at a lower level (e.g., implementing security to ensure system availability).

The approach adopted to develop the above model was a methodical and structured one since the objective was to achieve overall effective information security management as

Figure 2. Integration of IT governance and e-business security management

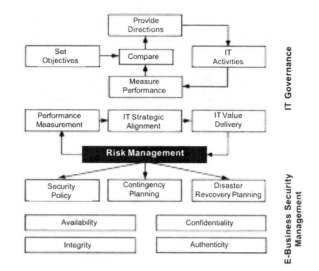

part of IT governance. The random introduction of security software, tools, and techniques is likely to be ineffective, as information can not be protected without considering all the activities that impinge on security. The holistic point of view that is required is within the broad objectives of IT governance, since "IT governance provides the processes to develop, direct, and control IT resources" (Korac-Kakabadse & Kakabadse, 2001, p. 1). Therefore, effective IT governance processes and mechanisms are seen as the enablers of a structured approach to IT management and thus are a precondition to effective information security governance for e-business.

IT Governance

At the highest level, IT governance does not differ from what would be expected to take place within enterprise governance. The governance process starts with setting objectives for the enterprise's IT, thereby providing the initial direction. From then on, a continuous loop is established for measuring IT performance, comparing outcomes to objectives, and providing redirection of activities where necessary and a change to objectives where appropriate. To be effective, an iterative process is most appropriate (ITGI®, 2003).

At the more detailed level, the key missions of IT need to be accomplished. The IT Governance Institute (2003) states that the purpose of IT governance is to direct IT endeavours and to ensure that IT's performance meets the following objectives: strategic alignment, value delivery, risk management, and performance measurement. Strategic alignment refers to the leveraging of IT into business activities, while value delivery is the exploitation of business opportunities and the maximization of benefits by the use of IT. The two activities are closely connected (ITGI®, 2003), since benefits will emerge if IT is successfully leveraged into business activities. The performance of IT has to be managed according the motto "What you can not measure, you can not manage," and hence a system of performance measurement metrics is required.

As discussed in a later section, risk management plays a significant integrating role in the proposed model, as shown in Figure 2. Basically, risk management integrates the management of security measures in the governance processes of an organisation, and consequently it can be seen as the connecting link between IT governance and e-business security management.

E-Business Security Management

To mitigate risk at the highest level requires the establishment of an information security policy, contingency planning, and the development of a disaster recovery plan (Hong, Chi, Chao, & Tang, 2003). The purpose of a security policy is to articulate management's expectations of good security throughout the organisation. Polices should be achievable and encourage employees to follow them rather than viewing them as another odious task to be performed. Contingency planning and the disaster recovery plan should prevent an IT disaster from becoming catastrophic. The latter ensures that there is an arrangement to resume normal operations within a defined period of time after a disaster has struck.

Underpinning the high-level management approach is a system of security measures that should ensure that the organisation's assets — particularly its information — are protected against loss, misuse, disclosure, or damage (ITGI®, 2001). More specifically, Braithwaite (2002) states:

> *E-business security represents an accumulation and consolidation of information processing threats that identify the need to protect the integrity and confidentiality of information and the need to secure the underlying support technologies used in the gathering, storage, processing, and delivery of that information.* (p. 1)

Measures are required to assure high levels of availability, integrity, confidentiality and authenticity of business critical information (Halliday, Badenhorst, & v. Solms, 1996).

- **Availability**: this implies a number of requirements, such as ensuring continuing access to systems by users and the continued operation of the systems. The use of a firewall gateway will ensure that the internal, trusted systems are secured from attacks originating in outside, untrusted systems.

- **Integrity**: measures to ensure the completeness and unaltered form of data being processed in the organisation. Strong organisational controls, such as the hiring of competent staff and their supervision, and application controls, such as reconciling balances between different business applications as transactions are processed, are required.

- **Confidentiality**: this ensures that data can be read only by authorized people. In an e-business environment, all sensitive and confidential data should be encrypted while it is being transmitted over networks and as it is stored in the organisation's databases.

- **Authenticity**: e-business systems enable participants of the extended organisation (like suppliers, employees and customers) to be connected (Rodger, Yen, & Chou, 2002). User identification and authentication via digital signatures and certificates are therefore a specific requirement for this networked business environment (Wright, 2001).

When aligning governance with security, a number of issues emerge. They essentially focus on incorporating governance practices into security via effective risk management and reconciling the conflicting objectives of value delivery and security.

Risk Management

As observed in the preceding discussions, effective risk management is a key objective of IT governance (ITGI®, 2004; Standards Australia, 2004) and is required to minimise the IT risks associated with operating an e-business. In the proposed model, it can furthermore be seen as an integrating force, linking IT governance processes with e-business security management. It can also be viewed as a way of integrating security into the processes of an organisation — an important but also a very challenging task (McAdams, 2004).

Greenstein and Vasarhelyi (2002, p. 251) define risk as "the possibility of loss or injury" and risk management as a methodology, which assesses first "the potential of future events that can cause adverse affects," and second, the implementation of strategies that mitigate these risks in a cost-efficient way. Eloff, Labuschagne, and Badenhorst (1993) propose a risk management life cycle and define it as a process of risk identification, analysis, assessment, resolution, and monitoring.

The elements of the traditional risk management life cycle are important for e-business, but due to e-business' inherent needs for flexibility and responsiveness (e.g., to react to emerging customer demands), an ongoing and more dynamic risk management approach is required (Mann, 2004). This implies the capability to quickly adapt IT structures, including security, to business conditions while being able to adequately monitor the changing risk environment. Furthermore, Internet-based technologies are subject to rapid change in an increasingly complex threat landscape. This may require the deployment of a real-time risk management approach in which risks are identified and reported as transactions are processed in real-time (see Labuschagne & Eloff, 2000).

Fink (2004) reviewed existing risk management methodologies as to their suitability for the Internet environment and found significant shortcomings among some well-known products. He recommended that an effective methodology should be able to meet the following criteria:

- **Comprehensive**: the methodology must cover both the technological (e.g., Internet) and business (trading partners) scenarios of an e-business.

- **Inclusive**: the methodology must cover all types of assets (physical and virtual) and all types of vulnerabilities and threats that can be encountered in an e-business environment.

- **Flexible**: it must offer a variety of techniques (quantitative and qualitative) that can be applied across all types of e-business models (e.g., supply chain management, ERP).

- **Relevant**: the application of the methodology should lead to the identification and successful implementation of security measures relevant to e-business (e.g., digital signatures and certificates for trading partners).

A key aspect of risk management is making trade-offs. For example, the greater the desired level of security, the more administration and control are required and the greater the tendency to reduce the ability to access data and information. Consequently, more security comes along with an increased cost and a reduction in the initiatives that employees are allowed to use in creating opportunities for their organisation. Hence, e-business security might conflict with the objective of value delivery in IT governance.

Some, however, have argued that security can be seen as value itself. McAdams (2004, p. 38), for example, states that "an organization could embrace security as a core value much like customer service rather than merely as an adjunct support activity." Indeed, the previously discussed objectives of e-business security management (availability, confidentiality, integrity, and authenticity) are connected with positive outcomes for the organisation. However, the value resulting from security measures is finite, as eventually additional efforts for security are not rewarded with additional value for the business. Hence, it is important to determine the required level of security during risk management so as to ensure that costs of security are balanced by resultant benefits.

In practice, this task is difficult, as the cost of security is either unknown or difficult to measure. This problem is demonstrated by a recent study of Forrester Research (2004). The survey "How much security is enough" was conducted in August 2003 among 50 security executives at organisations with more than $1 billion in revenue. The results are illustrative of the problem: 40% of the respondents stated that their organisation's security spending was improperly focused, and 42% stated that it was inadequate for 2003. However, 60% of respondents said that they did not even know how much security incidents cost their businesses every year. Thus, determining the right level of security is difficult but crucial in order to achieve benefits from IT while adequately managing security.

Guidelines for Implementation

While the above discussions provide the theoretical background and rational for the proposed information security model, this section provides guidelines for the organisation on how such a model can best be implemented.

- A clear understanding needs to exist within the organisation on the responsibilities of governance at the enterprise level and how IT governance integrates into this. The approach recommended for the information security model is two-pronged, namely, ensuring conformance via corporate governance and performance through business governance.

- For an e-business, information security has become an important consideration. The organisation has to understand the nature and significance of current and possible future threats and risks as well as the counter measures that are available to an e-business. Risk in this environment can be of a business nature (e.g., unresponsive trading partners) and technological nature (e.g., malicious attacks via the Internet). Risk is complex and specialist advice may be required from professionals such as IT security analysts and IT auditors.

- Risk management plays the key role in balancing what appears to be conflicting objectives when applying ICT, namely, value realisation and security. A suitable risk management methodology needs to be acquired that recognises these two competing functions of ICT and takes into account the characteristics of e-business. The criteria for such a methodology were outlined in an earlier section.

- A program of education to raise competence and awareness should be implemented across all levels of management to ensure that the requirements for effective information security governance are well understood. Such a program should be delivered in stages, as the concepts are complex, and regularly reviewed in response to changes in technology and the business environment. By being systematic and structured, organic management behaviour is encouraged.

- It is recommended that an adaptable and flexible attitude be adopted during implementation in that the model needs to integrate into the existing ICT, and organisational and management structures. Current organisational culture and resource constraints need to be taken into account to achieve the best fit possible and to manage any resistance to change successfully. For example, a new ethos in support of governance may have to emerge.

- Lastly, implementation progress should be reviewed and monitored on a regular basis applying the well accepted feedback loop. It is recommended that a project sponsor from senior management be identified to guide implementation and to ensure that the model receives strong commitment from executive management.

Conclusion

This chapter has shown the need for governance and suggested a concept for the integration of IT governance with enterprise governance. It then identified three major approaches to IT governance and their management of IT security. The latter was shown to be critical for the operation of an e-business. Hence, a framework was developed in which IT governance and e-business security operate together in an integrated, structured, yet holistic manner. The proposed model recognises that IT governance aims to optimise the value delivery of ICT while e-business security ensures that identified risks are controlled in an efficient manner. This model emphasizes the importance of risk management as the method that links IT governance and e-business security and thereby resolves the often conflicting objectives of security and value delivery.

References

Braithwaite, T. (2002). *Securing e-business systems: A guide for managers and executives*. New York: John Wiley & Sons.

Brand, K., & Boonen, H. (2004). *IT governance - A pocket guide based on COBIT*. The Netherlands: Van Haren Publishing.

Cadbury, A. (1992). *Report of the committee on the financial aspects of corporate governance*. London: The Committee on the Financial Aspects of Corporate Governance.

CIMA/ IFAC. (2004). *Enterprise governance: Getting the balance right*. Retrieved January 3, 2005, from http://www.cimaglobal.com/downloads/enterprise_governance.pdf

Eloff, J. H. P., Labuschagne, L., & Badenhorst, K. P. (1993). A comparative framework for risk analysis methods. *Computers & Security, 12*(6), 597-603.

eWeek (2004). The governance edge. *21*(42), 40.

Fink, D. (2004). Identifying and managing new forms of commerce risk and security. In M. Khosrow-Pour (Ed.), *E-commerce security advice from experts* (pp. 112-121). Hershey, PA: CyberTech Publishing.

Forrester Research. (2004). *How much security is enough*. Retrieved September 6, 2004, from http://www.forrester.com/

Greenstein, M., & Vasarhelyi, M. A. (2002). *Electronic commerce: Security, risk management, and control* (2nd ed.). Boston: McGraw-Hill.

Halliday, S., Badenhorst, K., & v. Solms, R. (1996). A business approach to effective information technology risk analysis and management. *Information Management & Computer Security, 4*(1), 19-31.

Hong, K.-S., Chi, Y.-P., Chao, L. R., & Tang, J.-H. (2003). An integrated system theory of information security management. *Information Management & Computer Security*, *11*(5), 243-248.

ITGI® - IT Governance Institute. (2001). *Information security governance*. Retrieved September 6, 2004, from www.ITgovernance.org/resources.htm

ITGI® - IT Governance Institute. (2003). *Board briefing on IT governance*. Retrieved September 6, 2004, from www.ITgovernance.org/resources.htm

ITGI® - IT Governance Institute. (2004). *IT control objectives for Sarbanes-Oxley*. Retrieved September 6, 2004, from www.ITgovernance.org/resources.htm

Korac-Kakabadse, N., & Kakabadse, A. (2001). IS/IT governance: Need for an integrated model. *Corporate Governance*, *1*(4), 9-11.

Labuschagne, L., & Eloff, J. H. P. (2000). Electronic commerce: The information-security challenge. *Information Management & Computer Security*, *8*(3), 154-157.

Mann, D. (2004). *A life-cycle approach to risk management*. Retrieved October 10, 2004, from http://www.computerworld.com/securitytopics/security/

McAdams, A. (2004). Security and risk management: A fundamental business issue. *Information Management Journal*, *38*(4), 36.

McKay, J., & Marshall, P. (2004). *Strategic management of eBusiness*. Milton, Queensland, AUS: John Wiley & Sons.

National Cyber Security Partnership (2004). *Information security governance - A call to action*. Retrieved October 26, 2004, from http://www.cyberpartnership.org/InfoSecGov4_04.pdf

Rodger, J., Yen, D., & Chou, D. (2002). Developing e-business: A strategic approach. *Information Management & Computer Security*, *10*(4), 184-192.

Standards Australia. (2004). *Corporate governance of information and communication technology - Draft for public comment*. Retrieved April 20, 2004, from http://www.standards.com.au

Wright, A. (2001). Controlling risks of E-commerce Content. *Computers & Security*, *20*(2), 147-154.

Zimmerman, J. W. (2002, November). Is your company at risk? Lessons from Enron®. *USA TODAY®*, *1*, 27-29.

Tradmark Notice

- ITGI® is a registered trademark of Information Systems Audit and Control Association, Inc. / IT Governance Institute (ITGI).

- USA TODAY® is a registered trademark of Gannett Co. Inc.

- Business Week® is a registered trademark of the McGraw-Hill Companies, Inc.

- Enron® is a registered trademark of Enron Corp.

Chapter II

IT Security Governance and Centralized Security Controls

Merrill Warkentin, Mississippi State University, USA

Allen C. Johnston, University of Louisiana-Monroe, USA

Abstract

Every enterprise must establish and maintain information technology *(IT) governance procedures that will ensure the execution of the firm's security policies and procedures. This chapter presents the problem and the framework for ensuring that the organization's policies are implemented over time. Since many of these policies require human involvement (employee and customer actions, for example), the goals are met only if such human activities can be influenced and monitored and if positive outcomes are rewarded while negative actions are sanctioned. This is the challenge to IT governance. One central issue in the context of IT security governance is the degree to which IT security controls should be centralized or decentralized. This issue is discussed in the context of enterprise security management.*

Introduction

Information system security management goals can only be achieved if the policies and procedures are complete, accurate, available, and ultimately executed or put into action. Organizations must be conscious of the hazards associated with the diffusion of technology throughout the firm and must reflect this awareness through the purposeful creation of policy. Furthermore, it is prudent that organizations take the appropriate measures to maximize the transfer of policy into effective security management practices. This can only happen with an effective organizational design or structure and with adherence to proper information assurance procedures. Stakeholder compliance is only possible with the enforcement of internal controls to ensure that the organization's policies and procedures are executed.

The goals of IT security are to ensure the confidentiality, integrity and the availability of data within a system. The data should be accurate and available to the appropriate people, when they need it, and in the appropriate condition. Perfect security is not feasible — instead IT security managers strive to provide a level of assurance consistent with the value of the data they are asked to protect.

It is within their structures and governance procedures that organizations are able to address the issues of responsibility, accountability, and coordination toward the achievement of their purpose and goals. As organizations evolve to position themselves appropriately within their domains of interest, their governance posture evolves. These changes are reflected in the IT component of the organization as well. Within this mode of flux, however, one thing remains constant — a desire to obtain and maintain a high level of information assurance. In this context, the roles of IT governance and organizational design in fulfilling the security management commitment are presented and presented.

Policies-procedures-practice. An organization's information security is only as good as the policies and procedures designed to maintain it, and such policies and procedures must also be put into practice (or executed). If managers, developers, and users are not aware of such policies and procedures, they will not be effectively executed. Of critical importance to the assurance of information security is the establishment of an enterprise training program with verifiable training protocols to ensure that all personnel (new and existing) are fully aware of such polices and procedures so that they can be put into practice on a daily basis.

Figure 1. Security policy — procedure — practice

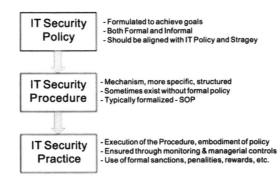

IT Governance

Governance encompasses those activities that ensure that the organization's plans are executed and its policies are implemented. *Planning* leads to *strategies* that are embodied in *policies* that are translated into *procedures*, which are executed and enforced through the *governance* process. One might say that governance is the method to ensure that policies and procedures are put into practice.

To support the goals of corporate governance, there must be a formalized process to guide the acquisition, management, and utilization of all strategic corporate assets, including its information resources. **IT governance describes the distribution of IT decision-making responsibilities within the firm and focuses on the procedures and practices necessary to create and support strategic IT decisions.**

The IT Governance Institute (2003) states that the purpose of IT governance is to direct IT endeavors and to ensure that IT's performance meets the following objectives: strategic alignment, value delivery, risk management, and performance measurement. Risk management ensures the appropriate management of IT-related risks, including the identification and implementation of appropriate IT security measures. Activity and performance monitoring and measurement are critical to ensure that objectives are realized, but require feedback loops and positive measures to proactively address deviation of goals.

The *IT Governance Institute* (ITGI®) (http://www.itgi.org/) has established the *Control Objectives for Information and related Technology* (COBIT) to facilitate in conducting all audits. This methodology is especially helpful in establishing the scope and plan for IT audits, and can guide managers in identifying appropriate controls and selecting effective infrastructure processes. This methodology of IT governance and control can also aid in maintaining compliance with the Sarbanes-Oxley Act and other applicable legislation. It can help a firm to establish assessment criteria for automated controls within key business processes and to gauge the performance of their application support activities (ITGI, 2003). Furthermore, it is designed to help ensure alignment between technology investments and business strategies. (For an expanded discussion of COBIT, see Dhillon and Mishra (2006).)

IT Architecture

IT governance can be effective only if the enterprise organizes its information technology (hardware, software, procedures) in a manner consistent with its organizational and technical requirements. There are numerous formalized approaches to establishing an appropriate configuration for the organization's information resources. Such configurations are termed the "IT architecture" and are intended to efficiently and effectively support IT governance mandates as articulated in policy and procedure and enacted in practice.

The *Institute of Electrical and Electronic Engineers* (IEEE) describes an architecture as a dynamic structure of related components, whose design and maturation are governed by an established set of principles and guidelines. In building construction, the blueprint establishes the design, and the building is the actual embodiment of that design. In IT, the architecture establishes the design of the infrastructure, whereas the actual hardware and software installation is the embodiment of that design.

Information Systems Centralization

For any enterprise function (whether production, billing, R&D, or others), there are various trade-offs in terms of the degree of centralization of managerial control. Certain functions (such as supply-chain management and purchasing) are subject to greater scale economies and are always operated more efficiently if they are highly centralized. Other organizational functions (such as customer support) may operate better when the function is decentralized for greater flexibility and attention to individual needs of the constituents. However, most functions exhibit some level of trade-offs between highly centralized and highly decentralized control. Information systems or IT functions are also subject to this continuum.

The components of an organization's *information system* (IS) include hardware (such as storage servers), software components (application servers, etc.), data resources (often maintained in data servers), and personnel who build and maintain the system. These resources may be highly centralized in one IT department, highly decentralized (in the control of all the organization's departments), or somewhere along the continuum between the two extremes. The degree to which the IS is centralized or decentralized comprises one of the most fundamental characteristics of a firm's IT architecture or structure. A key role of IT managers is determining the IT architecture for the organization's information system, and one of the most important aspects of the architecture is the degree of centralization. The focus of this chapter is primarily on control and decision-making centralization, rather than on the physical location of IT assets.

Centralized Information Systems

In centralized information systems, the information resources and decisions regarding their acquisition and control are concentrated in one particular business unit that provides IT services to the whole firm. The main characteristics of a centralized approach include control, efficiency, and economy. Some centralized IS have always been centralized, while others have resulted from a cost-saving regrouping of an organization's IS to one particular location.

The primary advantage of centralized systems is centralized control using established technology and vendors (Kroenke & Hatch, 1994). Hardware and software standards save time and money in purchasing, installation, and support, and enable greater inter-operability of systems and sharing of data between divisions and departments. *Enterprise resource planning* (ERP) and other enterprise-class applications require seamless intra-organizational data exchange.

This uniformity is built on a formal assessment of technology requirements and a professional evaluation of various technology choices, resulting in lower technical risks.

Approved system components will typically function together more easily, with few surprising system compatibility issues. Centralized IT departments are typically staffed by highly trained and qualified IT professionals who employ structured systems design and maintenance procedures, leading to highly reliable systems. Professional IT managers often excel at selecting superior IT staff members.

Further, centralization enables efficiency gains that include reduced duplication of effort, resources, and expertise. Savings are realized through joint purchasing procedures and sharing of system resources (such as storage solutions, output devices, etc.). Further efficiencies are realized from the enterprise-wide administration of contracts and service agreements, licenses, and asset management.

There are other advantages of highly centralized IS architectures. Training costs can be minimized when the IT staff can specialize in a small set of hardware and software components. Planning is easier when all IT resources are under one group's control, and IT alignment can be more easily accomplished. An organization can afford key niche IT professionals with specialized skills within a large IT division more easily than if IT staff is dispersed throughout the enterprise with smaller budgets.

However, centralized systems may entail an initial cost disadvantage (Kroenke & Hatch, 1994), given the high salaries of systems professionals, the added bureaucracy, and the inflexibility of such systems, which can cause costs to escalate (Robson, 1997). Because of their propensity to command large budgets, centralized centers may be perceived within the organization as cost centers (rather than profit centers). Centralized operations may also slow various tasks when contrasted with decentralized systems where each business unit has its own autonomous system for local tasks (Robson, 1997). Autonomy to perform IT-related functions is synonymous with decision-making authority and can provide expedited responses to pressing matters. Reliance on single central components (servers, etc.) may increase the vulnerability of the entire system should any of those central components fail. Furthermore, central systems are isolated from customers and real business concerns, leading to a lack of responsiveness and personal attention to individual groups. Relationships between the centralized support unit and other business units within the same organization become more formalized and less flexible. Anytime decision-making authority is taken away from the departments and given to the organization, disparities between the goals of decision-making activities and their resultant outcomes may occur. This is because the knowledge of the unique requirements of the departmental or individual elements is either absent or undervalued.

Decentralized Information Systems

Decentralized systems provide the individual units with autonomy over their own IT resources without regard to other units. The primary advantages of the decentralized approach are the added flexibility and empowerment of individual business units. Response times to business demands are often faster. The proximity to the users and their actual information requirements can lead to closer fit, and the added involvement of end users in system development can lead to superior systems designs.

Start-up costs are relatively low in decentralized information systems (Kroenke & Hatch, 1994). Furthermore, it is far easier to customize and scale system components to individual departmental needs. There is increased autonomy (Hodgkinson, 1996), leading to increased flexibility and responsiveness. This enables far greater motivation and involvement of users as they perceive a sense of ownership (Robson, 1997). The redundancy of multiple computer systems may increase the reliability of the entire system — if one component fails, others may fill the gap. Finally, a decentralized approach reduces the conflicts that may arise when departments must compete for centralized IT resources.

Obviously decentralized IT management is more appropriate for organizations comprised of highly diverse business units that operate in very different marketplaces with very different business needs. If each unit is subject to different regulations, competitive pressures, and technology environments, then a centralized system may severely limit each unit's effectiveness. But a decentralized approach (which can still achieve information sharing through networking) will allow each unit each unit to react to its unique environment.

Because the locus of decision making is at the point of impact, decentralized systems typically have increased accountability, motivation, and management responsiveness (Hodgkinson, 1996). The increased understanding and customer focus is not without its costs, however. The lack of centralized control can lead to conflicts and policy clashes — sourcing from multiple vendors can certainly create incompatible systems, and inefficiencies can result from a high degree of duplication of resources, effort, and expertise. Additionally, the autonomous actions of the individual units (and perhaps the users within the units) can have disastrous results if the motivation or efficacy for compliance with the policies and procedures of the organization is missing. In other words, the facilitation of autonomy through decentralized managerial control may present a scenario in which increased decision-making authority and IT support activities are necessitated, but the desire or expertise necessary to adequately fulfill the requirements is lacking.

Centralization in IT Security Management

There are numerous information assurance mechanisms that may be deployed and managed in manner consistent with a desired level of centralization. For instance, firewall protection can be administered at the enterprise level by one administrator or a single unit within the organization. Alternatively, decentralized firewall protection, in which the individual user maintains a personal firewall solution, may be appropriate for environments characterized by a highly autonomous end user community. Another example of a security technology that can be deployed and managed in either a centralized or decentralized manner is an antivirus solution. While most organizations would probably choose to integrate antivirus protection into their enterprise level protection strategies, it is possible to deploy antivirus protection at the end-user level. In fact, for many organizations that allow mobile computing or remote connectivity, reliance on end users to appropriately manage an antivirus solution is commonplace. The same scenario is repeated for those security technologies that have not yet matured to the level of an enterprise-level solution, such as antispyware technology.

Currently, it is difficult to argue that the centralized IT security management strategy is undeniably more effective in providing the best protection to all organizations. When considered from the standpoint of prevention, detection, and remediation, it could be argued that each of these lines of defense could be addressed more immediately and precisely at the individual level. Unfortunately, there are no definitive answers to this problem because of the element of the human condition and its associated complexities. While many solutions may appear on the surface to be best suited for enterprise-level management, issues of culture, competency, and/or politics may force individual level management.

Case Study

A comparative case study of two units within one enterprise (Johnston et al., 2004) compares the results of malware exposure under two types of IT security governance. The first, TechUnit, can be characterized as a centralized organization in terms of its IT environment, including its IT security governance. MedUnit, however, has a highly decentralized structure in which individual users maintain a high degree of control over their IT resources, including the responsibility for security-related activities. See Table 1 for details of the key differences.

The practice of centralized IT security management provided TechUnit with a highly effective framework from which to address issues specific to the Blaster and Sobig.F worms. As stated by the director of IT, "All of our PCs have antivirus software and multiple layers of protection and, in terms of the worms (Sobig.F and Blaster), it was all hands-off to the users" (Johnston et al., 2004, p. 8). This is a consistent theme among the other IT personnel. The only actions taken by TechUnit IT personnel to deal with the worms were slight modifications to their firewall and e-mail server filter. There were only a few observations of Blaster or Sobig.F worm activity in TechUnit's computing environment. These instances were identified and resolved solely by IT personnel with no impact in terms of cost, time, philosophy, or credibility (user confidence). The IT director noted, "If we have done our job properly, the impact is minimal, if at all felt, to the user community." Perhaps the minimal amount of end-user interaction required by TechUnit's IT personnel to deal with the worms could help to explain the notable absence of specific knowledge of the worms' functionality. Notably, the level of specific knowledge of the Blaster and Sobig.F worms increased as the level of management decreased and the degree of user interaction increased.

A decentralized approach to IT security management is one in which there is a high level of autonomy for end users in dealing with the security of their respective computing resources. The IT environment of MedUnit is highly reflective of such an approach. Although certain protection mechanisms are deployed in a manner consistent with centralized IT security management, such as the use of virus protection software, the majority of IT security management practices are decentralized described as follows.

MedUnit's users dictate IT security management policy and procedures. As explained by the MedUnit systems analyst, "While we have some end users that are technically savvy, it makes supporting those that aren't, very difficult. [End users] dictate what is

Table 1. Categories of threats to information systems (Source: Johnston et a.l, 2004; Adapted from Whitman, 2003)

Protection Mechanism	"TechUnit" (centralized)	"MedUnit" (decentralized)
Password	The centralized password management policy requires end users to maintain a single userid and password for access to all systems. Additionally, end users are required to adhere to specific password standards.	The decentralized password management approach allows users to establish their own unique password schemes. There are no specific requirements.
Media backup	IT management personnel are solely responsible for initiating and monitoring all data redundancy procedures.	IT personnel, as well as end users, actively participate in media backup efforts.
Virus protection software	Antivirus activities are initiated and supported for all end users and computational systems by IT personnel only.	IT personnel, as well as end users, actively participate in antivirus efforts.
Employee education	Formal training programs such as workshops and Intranet support webs are developed and implemented by IT personnel only.	End users are responsible for handling their specific training requirements.
Audit procedures	IT personnel monitor all relevant system and network logs.	End users are asked to monitor their respective systems for inappropriate activity.
Consistent security policy	IT personnel establish security policy for the entire FBU.	End users are instrumental in the establishment of security policy. Each unit within FBU #2 may have its own security policy.
Firewall	IT personnel maintain a single firewall for the entire FBU.	End users are asked to maintain personal firewalls for their respective systems.
Monitor computer usage	IT personnel are solely responsible for the monitoring of computer usage and resource allocation.	End users may monitor computer usage for their respective systems.
Control of workstations	Only IT personnel have administrative rights to computing resources. End user access is restricted.	End users have either Power-User or Administrator accounts on their respective workstations depending on their requirements.
Host intrusion detection	IT personnel are solely responsible for host intrusion detection.	End users are asked to maintain their own host intrusion detection mechanisms, such as ZoneAlarm®.

going to happen. If several [end users] want something to happen, it's going to happen" (Johnston et al., 2004, p. 9). When faced with a malicious epidemic such as Blaster and Sobig.F, this approach to security management is not effective in the discovery or eradication of the worms. "We were hit pretty hard. It just hit us all of a sudden. For about two weeks, we could expect to come to work every morning and patch systems" (p. 9).

Conclusion and Future Research

In the current climate, the security of information systems needs to be properly managed in order to ensure availability of resources. Organizations planning their IT security management strategies can benefit from the findings of this research. While the decentralized approach and federal governance architecture facilitate meeting end-user requirements, security may need to be increasingly centrally managed. This is not necessarily contradictory to improving functionality for end users, since under the decentralized approach, end users are expected to take an active role in activities such as auditing and intrusion detection. This takes time and effort, and an end user's failure to practice these functions can potentially compromise the whole network for all users. Users may consider high IT activity in security breach remediation as a positive sign of service, but this may not last with repetitive loss of network availability. If MedUnit is indicative of security management under a decentralized approach, we expect a shift towards more centrally managed security in the future, considering the increasing external security threats. Further research is necessary to examine how to combine adequate security with realistic expectations regarding end-user involvement in security practices. This study examines two polar opposites of centralization and decentralization in IT security management. Future research endeavors can include varying levels of centralization across a larger number of FBUs.

References

Hodgkinson, S. (1996). The role of the corporate IT function in the Federal IT organization. In M. Earl, *Information management: The organizational dimension*. Oxford, UK: Oxford University Press.

IEEE Std. 1471.2000. *Recommended practice for architectural description*. New York: IEEE.

ITGI®- IT Governance Institute. (2003). *Board briefing on IT governance*. Retrieved September 6, 2004, from www.ITgovernance.org/resources.htm

Johnston, A. C., Schmidt, M.B., & Bekkering, E. (2004, April). IT security management practices: Successes and failures in coping with Blaster and Sobig.F. *Proceedings of the 2004 ISOneWorld International Conference*, Las Vegas, NV (pp. 1-12).

Kroenke, D., & Hatch, R. (1994). *Management information systems*. Watsonville, CA: McGraw-Hill.

Mishra, S., & Dhillon, G. (2006). The impact of the Sarbanes-Oxley (SOX) Act on information security governance. In M. Warkentin & R. Vaughn (Eds.), *Enterprise information security assurance and system security: Managerial and technical issues* (pp. 62-79). Hershey, PA: Idea Group Publishing.

Robson, W. (1997). *Strategic management and information systems: An integrated approach*. London: Pitman Publishing.

Whitman, M. E. (2003). Enemy at the gate: Threats to information security. *Communications of the ACM, 46*(8), 91-95.

Chapter III

A Case Study of Effectively Implemented Information Systems Security Policy

Charla Griffy-Brown, Pepperdine University, USA

Mark W. S. Chun, Pepperdine University, USA

Abstract

This chapter demonstrates the importance of a well-formulated and articulated information security policy by integrating best practices with a case analysis of a major Japanese multinational automotive manufacturer and the security lessons it learned in the implementation of its Web-based portal. The relationship between information security and business needs and the conflict that often results between the two are highlighted. The case also explores the complexities of balancing business expedience with long-term strategic technical architecture. The chapter provides insight and offers practical tools for effectively developing and implementing information security policies and procedures in contemporary business practice.

Introduction

John Fisherman, *chief information officer* (CIO) at Akamai Motor Corporation[1] (Akamai), was just beginning to breathe easy again, but he lacked time. Six months earlier, his division, the *Information Systems Division* (ISD), created and implemented a Web-based portal called FieldWeb to provide front-end access to Akamai and Genki[2] (the performance luxury division of Akamai Motor Corporation) dealership data and to increase the efficiency of the company's *dealership sales managers* (DSMs) by over 18.16%. Following this implementation, the ISD intended to implement the Web portal in seven other areas of the organization. The company's security concerns had been addressed, but Fisherman knew that dealing with information security was an ongoing process, not a destination. His goal was to ensure that policies, processes, and procedures were in place to ensure that Akamai remained secure.

In order to protect information assets, firms must first clearly articulate management's expectations regarding information system security and ethics. Documented policies are the foundation upon which security architecture is built. This chapter provides insight and practical tools for effectively developing and implementing information security policies and procedures in contemporary business practice. In order to demonstrate the real-world struggle with best practices, this chapter centers on a case study analysis of a Web-portal implementation at Akamai. This Web-portal implementation was the first time Akamai opened up its back-end systems to the risk of the Internet. Consequently, the company had to carefully consider how to proceed with its portal implementation and to proactively rethink its information security policies while undertaking this large-scale deployment. The end result was the design of a secure system and the implementation of a new learning process to proactively and continuously develop security system policies.

Policy Development Doesn't Have to Be Painful

Conventional wisdom holds that designing and maintaining security policy often gets bogged down in a bureaucratic inefficiency and seemingly never-ending wrangling. Otherwise, such policy is a carefully guarded document preserved on the security officer's computer. Some firms adhere to what is often referred to as the unwritten "primordial network security policy" (Watchguard, 2004), which states, "Allow anyone in here to get out, for anything, but keep everyone out there from getting in here."

The reality is that developing and maintaining security policy does not need to be shrouded in such extreme secrecy. Furthermore, security policy does not have to be perfect. However, it should be consistently reviewed and refined given the ongoing changes in business technology and circumstance (Baskerville & Siponen, 2002; Hong, Chi, Chao, & Tang, 2003). Regardless of organization size, companies must have articulated security policies in order to remain competitive and secure (Siponen, 2000).

Figure 1. Survey of managers and employees (Source: Harris Interactive Inc., Rochester, NY, May 2003)

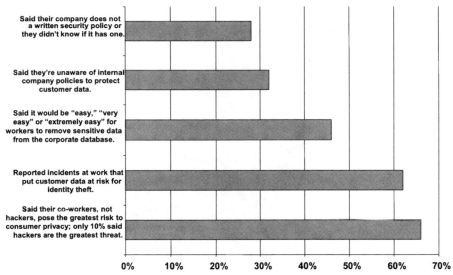

Survey of Managers and Employees

* *Survey of 500 US workers & managers who handle sensitive customer information at work*

This section briefly outlines a few simple steps for developing the first draft of a security policy. Subsequent sections will provide a bird's-eye view of the development of security policy in a real-world business case.

As defined by the *Computer Security Institute* (CSI) (http://www.gocsi.com) and the *Systems Administration and Networking Security Institute* (SANS), security policies should indicate "purpose, scope, a policy statement, standards, action, and responsibilities." Policies should be written simply and clearly to minimize the effort in maintaining them. It is wise initially to refine the "purpose, scope, and policy statement" section so that it will not need to be changed, whereas the "standards, action, and responsibility" sections often require periodic modification. Also important to keep in mind is that system-specific policies are generally written with a specific technology in mind (e.g., Windows 2000, Linux, Solaris, etc.). In contrast, program policies are broader in scope and generally apply industry standards, such as ISO 17799 (Kwok & Longley, 1999). For program policies, such industry guidelines provide a considerable head start in security policy development.

Security policies are first and foremost about people, not technology. A recent survey by Harris Interactive (Figure 1) showed that while 65% of workers recognize that employees pose the greatest security risk, more than a quarter of companies surveyed had no written policy. Furthermore, more than 30% of employees said that they were

Figure 2. Types of attacks or misuse detected in the last 12 months (by percent) (Source: CSI/FBI Survey, 2004)

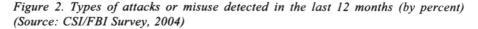

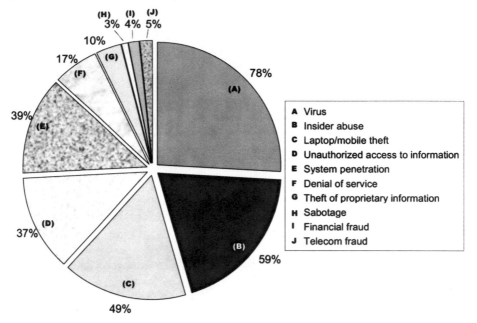

unaware of internal company security policies. Assertions that people constitute a critical link in rendering systems secure are confirmed by the CSI/FBI 2004 survey, which showed that the largest form of security attack or misuse was through viruses (largely avoidable through education/training) and that 49% of problems were due to insider abuse (Figure 2).

The process of developing security policies, affecting their distribution, and raising awareness among employees must, therefore, be top priorities. This doesn't mean that developing the first draft has to be complicated. In fact, the usual process involves assembling a small team of several people responsible for drafting the first document in order to keep the committee formation itself from halting the policy creation process. The committees that are formed and their fit within the organization vary depending on the business.

Before writing the policy, it is important to determine business requirements (Tryfonas, Kiountouzis, & Poulymenakou, 2001) and to ask fundamental questions such as the following:

•   What services are required?

•   Does the business require everyone to access the Web?

•   Do users need remote access to the internal network?

•   What are the priorities and risks associated with security policy creation?

The first document to be drafted is usually the *root security policy* (RSP), which delineates the basic security framework and specifies the initial list of subordinate polices that should be produced. These policies, like the basic questions asked above, should be organizationally specific, but typically will include key terms such as the following: acceptable computer use, passwords, e-mail, Web blogging, Web, Internet, wireless, servers, incident response plan, and the like. The root security policy specifies:

- the company name (Does the policy apply to the entire company?);

- the purpose of the policy (What is it for?); and

- the individuals responsible for carrying out the policy (Who enforces policy?).

The RSP should also indicate specific penalties for breaking the policy, the persons or entities who enforce the policy, all who must abide by the policy, any documents referred to or listed in the policy, ways to request policy changes, and the frequency of policy review.

The rest of the policy-making procedure involves making lists and asking questions. For example, all of the assets to be protected (such as servers, desktop computers, laptop computers, PDAs, etc.) must be listed and described. In addition, the following questions should be asked regarding each asset:

- Who administers the asset?

- Who uses it?

- How critical is the asset to the mission of the enterprise?

- How is the asset to be protected?

A few additional areas of policy need greater and unique clarification, such as incident response and disaster recovery. For example, a clear plan for security triage needs to be laid out, along with an escalation procedure indicating specifically when and whom to call in the event of a security breach. Accountability is also very important (Kwok & Longley, 1999). Firms must clearly identify individuals or teams who are to be responsible and held accountable for recovery following security disasters. Because any mention of a security incident outside the organization can have detrimental consequences, it is also important to articulate who is authorized to discuss company security with outsiders.

As indicated in Figure 2, it is important to note that the most technically secure systems can be completely vulnerable to "social engineering" practices, such as conning people into revealing sensitive personal or company data such as passwords or codes that need "clarification," or merely by an act as simple as opening a virus-laden e-mail. Therefore, one of the most critical areas of policy development is security policy distribution and training of personnel. Security professionals often claim that the weakest link in network security is the user. Therefore, security policy should address not only security enforcement, but also the provision of periodic employee education and awareness programs and the distribution of the security policy itself.

Finally, it is important to remember that securing the network is not the goal of the security policy — the goal is to secure the *business*. In this context, anything that threatens the confidentiality, integrity, and availability of corporate assets should be considered and guarded against within the security policy framework. Information security policy development is ongoing and is never 100% complete, so the policy documents should state how often they will be reviewed and revised and which committee or team of employees will have that responsibility. The policy document should also indicate the security life cycle, including network vulnerability assessments.

Although security policy development doesn't have to be painful, the reality is that typically there are "pains" due to business pressures. The security landscape and business needs by their very nature change rapidly. Thus, information systems security policy involves constant learning and may not always go as planned (Slay, 2003; Tryfonas et al., 2001). In this context, the current literature provides a number of approaches to information system security and policy. The primary approach is threat awareness tracking the "front-line" in the information system security battle (Freeman, 2000; Slewe & Hoogenboom, 2004; Symantec, 2003). Another approach is to focus on management perspectives of risk assessment (Conway, 2003; Farahmand, Navathe, Sharp, & Enslow, 2005). Few approaches focus on policy. Furthermore, the policy research establishes stylized concepts about policy, such as the important notion that successful policy must be federated and emergent (Baskerville & Siponen, 2002).

To better highlight these needs, we provide an example of a real-life security process implementation to illustrate how emergent and federated security policy development must be considered. Next, we take an in-depth look at Akamai's successful but bold move to the Internet to demonstrate the security challenges faced by a typical business and to offer a generalizable process for dealing with these challenges.

Web-Portal Implementation
at Akamai

Akamai's information systems environment. The *information system* (IS) applications that Akamai implemented were primarily developed and implemented by the employees of the local business environment. The different divisions of Akamai (i.e., Akamai Automobile, Genki Automobile, Motorcycle, Power Equipment, etc.) operated as autonomous divisions. As a result, many of the IS applications were developed within each division specifically to support the unique needs of that division. Within the ISD at Akamai were approximately 240 application servers. In a transaction-oriented system that had over 185 functions to allow Akamai and Genki dealerships access to sales information, dealerships accessed these servers via the *interactive network* (IN) and generated approximately 74,000 users.

Using portals to access dealership sales information. *District sales managers* (DSM) were responsible for managing regions of Akamai and Genki automobile dealership sales. There were 61 Akamai and 23 Genki DSMs in the United States. On average, each DSM met with 20 automobile dealership owners and focused discussions on the prior month's sales performance and consulting services (such as marketing, operations, services, or customer service issues). On a monthly basis, DSMs spent between four and eight hours per dealership using their laptops to gather and analyze dealership sales information from 12 autonomous IS applications. A DSM recalled:

> *Gathering information for dealership meetings was frustrating. Downloading or capturing sales information was like a 12-step process. Each particular type of information was captured from different mainframes, PC applications, printed hard copy of reports ...Every DSM had his own unique way of capturing and analyzing information when he prepared for dealership meetings ...There was no standard or easy way of acquiring the dealership sales information for our meetings.*

DSMs could access the 12 IS applications through internal or external connections to the Akamai network. Internal to the company, DSMs accessed the Akamai network from their desktop computers, which was a part of the company's IS infrastructure. However, the DSMs were often traveling in the field visiting dealerships and were frequently required to access the Akamai network and IS applications using dial-up modems. The speed and access to the Akamai network was consequently limited by the connection speed available in hotel rooms.

The topics of discussion during the dealership sales meetings changed from week to week. Factors such as dealership sales incentives, marketing promotions, and customer loyalty programs made it difficult for DSMs to predict their agendas for their dealership sales meetings. A DSM recalled:

> *If the DSMs went to a dealership for a meeting and found out that they were missing information, they had to borrow a telephone line from the dealer to connect with [Akamai]. The dealers had to unplug their faxes so the DSMs could plug into the dealer's lines and dial into [Akamai's] systems. This didn't make us look good, period.*

Three-Phase Framework of Portal Implementation

This chapter presents a three-phase framework that details key events and factors contributing to developing and implementing a Web-based portal at Akamai (Figure 3). The three phases include: (1) recognizing opportunity, (2) making it happen, and (3) delivering results/sharing the wealth. This same framework will also be used to examine securing Akamai's systems.

Phase 1: Recognizing Opportunity

Akamai's CIO (hereafter, John) realized that Web-based portals were becoming an important tool to access information from autonomous IS applications. However, using

Figure 3. A process model for implementing the FieldWeb portal

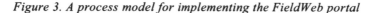

Identifying Opportunity	Making It Happen	Delivering Results & Sharing the Wealth	
Nov. '01 CIO and E-Bus. Mgt. identified need to Implement FieldWeb.

Feb. '02 eBus/ISD joint presentation:
- Fieldstaff and tech. requirements.
- Obtained Exec. Mgt. approval.

Keith identified as champion from eBusiness.

David identified as champion from ISD.

April 2002 FieldWeb project kicked off.

25 ISD employees identified for FieldWeb Portal Team.

FieldWeb goals set: single sign-on.

Sept. 08, 2003 set as target implementation date because of DSM convention. | Apr. 12 – Jun. 7, 2002 FieldWeb team scoped & identified high level requirements.

Surveys and interviews conducted.

FieldWeb team worked with a few DSMs to understand technology needs.

Jose facilitated discussions with AAM to understand their process of deploying portal with their suppliers.

Epicentric selected as the technology of choice. FieldWeb Team selects .NET technology.

Phase 1: client-based application (dealer contact reports) implemented.

Phase 2: Web enable access to the same information.

September 2003: FieldWeb rolled out to DSMs at convention. | DSM's dealer visit preparation time reduced 1.45 hours; resulting in a 18.1% efficiency gains and $1.4 M immediate cost savings.

DSM Survey:
- 96% overall satisfaction.
- 88% significant gain in DSM productivity.

FieldLink rolled out to additional segments of the business:
1. Genki Auto Sales.
2. Parts & Services.
3. National Sales
4. Zone Sales
5. Motorcycle
6. Power equipment
7. Associates (future). | Synchronizing Organizational Resources and Establishing Dynamic Capabilities |

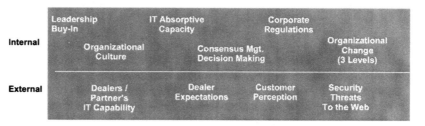

Internal	Leadership Buy-In	IT Absorptive Capacity	Corporate Regulations	
	Organizational Culture	Consensus Mgt. Decision Making		Organizational Change (3 Levels)
External	Dealers / Partner's IT Capability	Dealer Expectations	Customer Perception	Security Threats To the Web

Web-based portals to access corporate internal applications and systems had never before been implemented at Akamai because the company was often reluctant to expose itself to any types of security risks.

In November 2001, John set out to implement a portal that would serve as one secure point of access for all of the IS applications and to provide a common process for acquiring and utilizing field sales information. John noted:

> *The district sales managers spent an enormous amount of time pulling information from reports that came from all over the place. They spent time*

consolidating the information to get the right information, so that when they went to the dealerships for sales meetings, they could talk intelligently ... With all of these electronic reports sitting on 12 autonomous applications, why not let technology consolidate the data for you instead of having a person do that work? The DSM was trying to help the dealer with the business rather than spending all of the dealer's time pulling and consolidating data.

John identified two champions to lead the portal implementation. One champion came from within the ISD (hereafter referred to as David) and the other from the e-business division (hereafter, Keith). Prior to joining the e-business division, Keith had spent four years as a DSM. On April 2002, David and Keith headed a team of 25 ISD employees (hereafter, FieldWeb Team) to lead the implementation and development of a portal, FieldWeb. One of the primary goals of FieldWeb was to provide DSMs with a single sign-on point of access for the 12 autonomous IS applications. Through a single sign-on point of access, FieldWeb provided the ability to capture and deliver information from the internal IS applications and to populate user-friendly portal fields for the DSMs.

The FieldWeb Team set September 23, 2003, as the portal implementation date because it wanted to simultaneously deploy the portal and train all 84 Akamai and Genki DSMs at an annual Akamai sales conference.

Phase 2: Developing and Implementing the Portal

The FieldWeb Team worked with the e-business and the automobile sales division to establish key deliverables and to understand the requirements for the portal. The team spent eight weeks (April - June 2002) examining and identifying high-level requirements for FieldWeb. The team spent time conducting surveys and interviews with key DSM, ISD, e-business, and sales executives to better understand the strategic objectives, requirements, and directions of their respective divisions. An ISD manager recalled the Team's findings:

The process of the DSMs gathering sales information was rather slow ... They [DSMs] had to sign on and wade through all these sales reports in order to find the section of the report that was important to them. These reports existed on the mainframe, and we needed to easily pass the report files to our servers as text files, so there was a built-in process to do that. And once the text files arrived, we essentially needed to pass them out to XML and to display them as PDF files. Conceptually this wasn't very difficult to do. Often those reports exist at different levels for dealers, for the district, for the zone, or for the national office.

Furthermore, while the team attempted to understand the business and information processing needs of the portal, a manager mentioned that the technology needed to establish a good balance between business needs and technology development, while establishing a solid shared vision of where the company wanted to be in two, four, five years from now.

After understanding the needs of the DSMs and identifying requirements, the team identified four main objectives for the FieldWeb portal: (1) to improve the efficiency of DSMs by decreasing the number of steps needed to access information from the autonomous IS applications; (2) to improve sales communications by optimizing the information and knowledge flow to DSMs; (3) to improve the DSMs access to and speed of information, to expand the accessibility to more locations and devices, and to simplify navigation to information and applications; and (4) to strengthen Akamai and the dealership relations by improving the effectiveness of dealership visits.

Since the development and implementation of portal technologies was new to the general automobile manufacturing business environment, David and Keith asked that the FieldWeb Team learn from the *Akamai Automotive Manufacturing* (AAM) division, who had implemented a portal a year earlier to aid in accessing information related to the automobile manufacturing processes. AAM was viewed as an internal champion who initiated and led many of the IS implementation and adoption projects. In the event of security threats, AAM served as the hub for all Akamai divisions and was responsible for tracking, notifying, and relaying information from the local American cities and to its global sites.

After evaluating and experimenting with different portal hardware and software, the FieldWeb Team decided to duplicate the same portal architecture hardware and software technology (Epicentric and .NET, respectively) used within AAM. For six months (April to September 2003), the team developed FieldWeb portal.

Phase 3: Delivering Results and Sharing the Wealth

At the annual Akamai dealership sales convention in September 2003, the team introduced and delivered FieldWeb portal to all DSM employees and sales managers. It took only 10 minutes for ISD to present, train, and spread knowledge about the portal. As a result of the FieldWeb's implementation, the team reported that DSMs reduced their dealer sales preparation time by 1.45 hours, resulting in an 18.1% efficiency gain and an immediate $1.4 million cost savings.

Keith recalled:

> The DSMs now don't have to spend as much time on locating, downloading, and acquiring information that they need for their dealership meetings. ... Now, they have one point of access for multiple sources of sales information ...The information that they acquired through the portal is up-to-date and accurate ...The DSMs can now spend more of their time analyzing the business sales operations and consulting with the dealers on process improvements.

On March 2004, the FieldWeb Team conducted a follow-up implementation satisfaction survey and found that 96% of the DSMs were satisfied with the FieldWeb portal; 88% had experienced a gain in productivity while gathering sales information.

Information Systems Security Management and Ongoing Policy Development

In order to demonstrate the ongoing policy development in the context of the portal roll-out, the same three-phase framework is applied (Figure 4).

Figure 4. A process model for implementing security in the Field WebPortal

Identifying Opportunity	Making It Happen	Delivering Results & Sharing the Wealth
April 19, 1999: Team of 14 Akamai employees gathered in Japan to reflect on security issues affecting Akamai's network. Global Securities Policy created and established as corporate standard. AAM established as the central point of security coordination and efforts. ISO 17799 established in Oct. 2002, becoming the reference point for Akamai's security evaluation. Dec. 2002 External securities evaluator contracted to conduct vulnerability assessment. John and peers form from Security Operations Committee (SOC). Exposure at the dealership identified with portal log-on and keystroke traceability.	Champion from E-Bus. leads to evaluation of security issues. Security's objective to balance stability, security, and costs with flexibility, convenience, and business needs. Internet Access Security Issues presented to Sales Vice President, June 2002. FieldWeb Team identified the hard-token (EncryptoCard) as FieldWeb access security solution of choice. Central management of firewalls. Time limit for portal log off initially set to 30 minutes. FieldWeb team establishes security procedures; 10 minute training conducted at DSM convention; DSMs signs security conformity form. ISO 17799 implemented after FieldWeb deployed.	Scaling the security to other parts of the organization. FieldWeb rolled out to additional segments: 1. Genki Auto Sales. 2. Parts & Services. 3. National Sales 4. Zone Sales 5. Motorcycle 6. Power equipment 7. Associates. **Synchronizing Organizational Resources and Establishing Dynamic Capabilities**

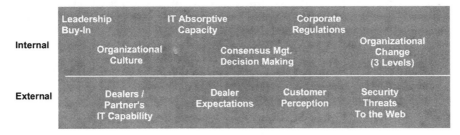

Internal	Leadership Buy-In	IT Absorptive Capacity	Corporate Regulations	
	Organizational Culture	Consensus Mgt. Decision Making		Organizational Change (3 Levels)
External	Dealers / Partner's IT Capability	Dealer Expectations	Customer Perception	Security Threats To the Web

This framework illustrates that while the processes for security development were proactive, they were not always linear. Although security was a significant priority and the leadership was proactive about it, the development of policy was a learning process requiring organizational change. For example, initial risks were identified and mitigated, but after an initial vulnerability assessment, it was determined that a broader committee needed to be put into place and that local as well as headquarter concerns needed to be escalated. In addition, in parallel with the roll-out of the Web portal were the development and adoption of international standards (ISO17799). Akamai was proactive enough to be able to incorporate these standards into the ongoing development of its security policy and was able to adopt new procedures and processes as needs arose. The following analysis reviews these issues in detail.

Addressing Security Issues

The development and implementation of the Akamai's IS applications were governed by the Akamai global securities regulations. Every division within Akamai was responsible for its own profitability, and each established its own IS, business processes, and security measures. The primary focus of security was twofold: (1) intrusion prevention, and (2) incidence response. Prior to 1999, the security of all IS applications within the different divisions at Akamai was managed by the divisions who implemented the technologies. In 1999, Akamai's executives formed a group of high-level managers to form the Global Securities Task Force and commissioned that group to coordinate and better understand the corporate global security issues. The task force's main objectives were to identify security issues that affected Akamai's network and to provide solutions to protect the company from external threats. The Global Securities Task Force created the *Akamai Global Network System Policy Handbook,* which defined the basic security policies of the Akamai network and systems objectives. The document initially was distributed only to a few tasked with network integrity.

Operating on this new imperative, the executive management team at Akamai also formed a regional security organization called the *Security Operations Committee* (SOC). Akamai's CIO and his peers from various Akamai companies in North America — Akamai Research Group, Akamai Canada Manufacturing, Akamai Canada, Akamai Sales and Distribution, Akamai Manufacturing, Power Equipment — formed the SOC. The SOC convenes on a quarterly basis to discuss issues related to IT and business and to map out regional IT strategy.

One of the foremost security risks that the FieldWeb Team faced as it developed the portal was related to the functionality of browsers. The team was concerned that unauthorized users could access information or would use keystrokes capturing software to retrieve temporary files without the DSMs' knowledge. A manager recalled:

> *When the DSM visited a dealer, he often used a computer that wasn't controlled by [Akamai]. We had to make sure that there wasn't information left there that would be usable by someone who came along behind ... A*

static ID and password was not going to be good enough in the dealership environment ... The technology we implemented required the DSMs to carry around an encrypto card that changed the password every 60 seconds to two minutes. When a DSM leaves, he has a certain degree of comfort that someone can't come behind him and gain access to the system.

Balancing and Evaluating the Benefits and Risks of Web Portals

While implementing FieldWeb, the team realized that FieldWeb needed to protect sensitive information as mandated by local and international standards. In the midst of the deployment, ISO 17799 was adopted, thereby necessitating new best practices. Because of the recent introduction of the Web-based portal technology to the general business environment, ISD initially did not possess expertise in the technology and its security implications. A manager noted, "... Because businesses were just being exposed and introduced to Web-based portal technology, we were challenged by being able to balance getting the data out fast versus ensuring good levels of security."

Given the pressures on the ISD and the economic environment it faced, it was difficult to justify a larger architectural redesign for future growth because of the related expense. This situation posed a security challenge because the team had to develop short-to-medium-term security solutions, and it realized that the entire information architecture should change, thereby making these systems obsolete. Many of the elegant short-term security measures employed were not scalable. The broader solution was to focus on policies and procedures, with knowledge that the technical solutions would change significantly over time. The Web-portal team continued to increase awareness through a long-term single architectural solution that enabled future expansion.

At Akamai, the process of constantly reevaluating IT projects was a series of trade-offs between security, stability, cost and business needs, convenience, and flexibility (Figure 5). Every project affected the alignment of the scales, and managers needed to decide the trade-offs involved in achieving balance. The Web-portal project brought this reality to the forefront in IT decision making at Akamai.

Figure 5. Balancing the trade-offs in securing IT projects

Identifying Security-Related Solutions

When ISO 17799 was adopted in October 2002, John asked the FieldWeb Team to work with an outside consulting firm to conduct a vulnerability assessment to better understand the security of Akamai's North America Division's internal IS applications. The team found security vulnerabilities and recommended that ISD needed to develop appropriate countermeasure tools to close the security gaps. The team determined that it was important to develop a multifactor security solution, to educate and train the DSMs on security risks, and to enforce DSMs' accountability on security policies and procedures.

Akamai also realized that there was a greater need for policy transparency, where the original global security document was made readily available to anyone requesting the document. A manager recalled:

> *The [Global Securities Policy] security handbook was more important as a concept than as an actual document. The document aided us in getting the appropriate accountability in place and developing specific standards based on ISO 17799 and other international/national standards ...Since we did not have any security standards in place, we relied on this document to guide our security evaluation.*

Akamai recognized that policies and procedures had to be more readily available to employees within the organization, as security had become highly reliant on employee awareness. Additionally, formal procedures needed to be put in place to ensure that there was a life cycle of reviewing, updating, and disseminating information on the company's security policies.

Vulnerability Assessment Life Cycle

After delivering the FieldWeb portal to the DSMs in December 2003, the FieldWeb Team was asked to conduct a second vulnerability assessment to discover other risks. The team used the British Standard and ISO 17799 as its evaluation framework. Following this assessment, the ISD teamed up with an industry security expert to evaluate the susceptibility of the FieldWeb portal. The evaluation of the portal infrastructure passed with no significant problems.

The FieldWeb-portal project enabled the ISD to re-engineer the traditional processes associated with gathering, capturing, and analyzing data from the automobile sales process. The FieldWeb implementation provided an opportunity to tackle the tedious issue of gathering information across autonomous IS applications prior to the monthly DSM dealership meetings. In doing so, the FieldWeb project enabled DSM managers to re-engineer the traditional business processes associated with meeting with the dealerships. FieldWeb's implementation still complied with the company's IT governance regulations and the constraints specified by its Japanese parent company.

John and the FieldWeb Team intend to share their portal implementation success with seven other divisions at Akamai. The FieldWeb Team realized that the implementation of the portal would be challenging, since each additional implementation held unique challenges. A senior manager commented on the benefits and risks of implementing the portal:

> *Intrusion prevention is the largest concern with implementing a WebPortal at [Akamai]. Within [Akamai], we actually lose $3M every day that we are down. Losing $3M a day is the figure that we can count. No one knows the amount of losses that we can't count.*

Conclusion

Information security is an ongoing process, where the goal is to secure the business, not the networks. When business needs change, the technology required to facilitate those needs and the business processes also change. For Akamai, the Web-portal project highlighted the reality that, in the new digital marketplace, firms must have processes in place for evaluating the trade-offs among security, cost, and business needs.

Prior to this project, Akamai had a global security policy, but it was not widely accessible. There was also a need to implement robust policies and to enforce procedures for creating, maintaining, and disseminating policy. This project compelled Akamai to position itself for ongoing challenges, as the trade-offs mentioned earlier were continually balanced. Because of this constant "rebalancing," the key to a robust information systems security policy is getting started and developing a team of professionals who are equipped with the appropriate resources, time, and tools for dealing with ongoing policy development. Given the scope required for policy distribution and awareness, this mandate ultimately involves the entire organization. To ensure that these security policy efforts work, management must mandate the responsibility to a designated team.

Akamai is a vivid, real-life example of how information security happens in practice. The example also illustrates how firms struggle to ensure that security implementation is done well. This company's experience also demonstrates the critical human side of the policy-making process in a dynamic environment. The specific security challenges of Akamai may not apply to all companies. However, the three-phase framework for dealing with new deployments and feeding new security understanding back into policy and procedure development does.

The struggle between implementing a short- and long-term IT security solution is not unique to Akamai. Short-term projects are relatively easy to justify in corporate budgets, but often come with security solutions that are usually project-specific. Long-term enterprise architecture solutions carry a hefty price tag, but offer potential long-term savings, reduced complexity, and often enhanced system performance. The success of Akamai provides insight into real policy making under time pressure and the complexity of new technology environments. Policy making is difficult, features constant change and adaptation, and is not always perfect. Akamai's experience provides business managers, security professionals, and students with valuable insight into the importance of policy making, as well as a vivid example of the process in practice.

References

Baskerville, R., & Siponen, M. (2002). An information security meta-policy for emergent organizations. *Logistics Information Management, 15*(5), 337-346.

Conway, P. (2003). Storage security: Issues and answers. *Computer Technlogy Review, 23*(10), 27.

CSI/FBI Computer Crime and Security Survey (2004). North Hollywood, CA: Computer Security Institute Publications.

Farahmand, F., Navathe, S., Sharp, G., & Enslow, P. (2005). A management perspective on risk of security threats to information systems. *Information Technology and Management, 6*(2), 203-225.

Freeman, D. H. (2000). How to hack a bank. *Forbes.* Retrieved April 30, n.d., from www.forbes.com/asap/00/0403/056.htm

Hong, K., Chi, Y., Chao, L., & Tang, J. (2003). An integrated systems theory of information security management. *Information Management and Computer Security, 11*(5), 243-248.

Kwok, L., & Longley, D. (1999). Information security management and modeling. *Information Management and Computer Security, 7*(1), 30-40.

Siponen, M. (2000). A conceptual foundation for organization information security awareness. *Information Management and Computer Security, 8*(1), 31-41.

Slay, J. (2003). IS security, trust and culture: A theoretical framework for managing IS security in multicultural settings. *Campus-Wide Information Systems, 20*(3), 98-104.

Slewe, T., & Hoogenboom, M. (2004). Who will rob you on the digital highway?. *The Communications of the Association for Computing Machinery, 47*(5), 56-61.

Symantec (2003). *Internet security threat report.* Cupertino, CA: Symantec Corporation World Headquarters. Retrieved October 12, 2003, from https/www.ses.symantec.com/content/ESRC.cfm?EID=0

Tryfonas, T., Kiountouzis, E., & Poulymenakou, A. (2001). Embedding security practices in contemporary information systems development approaches. *Information Management & Computer Security, 9*(4), 183-197.

Watchguard (2004). Primordial network security policy. Retrieved June 24, 2004, from http://www.watchguard.com

Endnotes

[1]   Due to the provisions of a confidentiality and non-disclosure agreement, a pseudonym has been assigned to the firm name. The firm, a major Japanese automotive manufacturer, will therefore be referred to as Akamai.

[2]   Due to the provisions of a confidentiality and non-disclosure agreement, a pseudonym has been assigned to the firm name and its divisions. The performance luxury division of this Japanese automotive manufacturer will be referred to as Genki.

Chapter IV

Malware and Antivirus Deployment for Enterprise Security

Raj Sharman, State University of New York at Buffalo, USA

K. Pramod Krishna, State University of New York at Buffalo, USA

H. Raghov Rao, State University of New York at Buffalo, USA

Shambhu Upadhyaya, State University of New York at Buffalo, USA

Abstract

Threats to information security are pervasive, originating from both outside and within an organization. The history of computer security is dotted with the tales of newer methods of identification, detection, and prevention of malware, only to be followed by a new set of threats that circumvent those safeguards. The explosive growth of the Internet and wide availability of toolsets and documentation exacerbates this problem by making malware development easy. As blended threats continue to combine multiple types of attacks into single and more dangerous payloads, newer threats are emerging. Phishing, pharming, spamming, spoofing, spyware, and hacking incidents are increasing at an alarming rate despite the release of breakthrough security defense products. A multi-layered, integrated approach using different security products in conjunction with well-defined security policies and antivirus software will form the foundation for effective enterprise security management.

Introduction

Enterprise deployment refers to uniform distribution, operation, administration, and maintenance of a common solution across all departments in a given organization. The strategies and teachings from this chapter apply to all organizations, large and small, as long as an enterprise deployment solution is used. The increased use of the information superhighway has been accompanied, inevitably, by a commensurate increase in the incidence and impact of malware outbreak. A malware attack is more pernicious than other forms of *information security* (IS) vulnerabilities in that its impact is generally not confined to one or a few entities; rather, it is normal for a large number of organizations to be affected at once, to a substantial degree. The scale of impact determines the scale of damage. Deployment strategies are therefore crucial, not only to prevent attack, but to also contain the spread of impact once vulnerability at some point has been maliciously exploited. Antivirus software has evolved over the last decade to become, along with firewalls, one of the main defenses against malware invasion and a primary tool in the maintenance of information security. To be sustainable, security must be aligned with business practices and priorities, as well as with the overall corporate IS policy. This chapter begins with a brief introduction and discussion on the history of viruses and of the emergence of antivirus software. Later sections present an approach to protection against malware, integrating antivirus software, firewalls, IDS, and other security applications into a practicable framework. Finally, the chapter concludes with a detailed discussion on the mechanics of malware and of antivirus software.

Malware and Its Impact

Malware is short for malicious software and is typically used as a catch-all term to refer to the class of software designed to cause damage to any device, be it an end-user computer, a server, or a computer network. Among the many forms malware can assume are that of a virus, a worm, a Trojan, spyware, or "backdoor," among others.

Malware on the Internet is not only massive in sheer quantity but also prorate. In August of 2003, McAfee, an anti-malware software manufacturer, identified fewer than two million malware products on the Internet; less than a year later, in March of 2004,; as many as 14 million such products were detected by the same company (Argaez, 2004). This rate of increase is expected to continue in the foreseeable future. The damage caused by all this malicious software is humungous. Table 1 enumerates ten malware programs and the estimate of the damage caused by them to businesses worldwide.

Malware today is not merely the result of the deviance of the traditional hacker; discontented employees, political activists, and other disgruntled elements are increasingly among those taking advantage of technology advancements to damage companies and commit acts of industrial espionage. The threat of malware increases business risk, results in reduced productivity and serious losses in terms of consumer confidence, time effort, and business opportunity. The annual CSI/FBI Computer Crime and Security

Table 1. Cost to businesses due to malware outbreak (Source: Mi2g, 2004)

Name of malware	Cost to businesses
Sobig	$37.1 billion
MyDoom	$22.6 billion
Klez	$19.8 billion
Mimail	$11.5 billion
Yaha	$11.5 billion
Swen	$10.4 billion
Love bug	$8.8 billion
Bugbear	$3.9 billion
Dumaru	$3.8 billion
SirCam	$3 billion

Survey (CSI/FBI, 2004) provides information on the estimated losses, in U.S. dollars, resulting from instances of breach of enterprise security and also the about the prevalence of the security technologies in today's corporate world. These statistics contradict the widely prevalent perception that installation of an antivirus system is adequate defense against virus attack. Clearly, Antivirus systems, whether stand-alone or flanked by a firewall, are grossly inadequate by themselves; there is need to adopt an integrated approach to dealing with malware. Knowledge of the origins and development of malware is essential to the development of an effective defensive model. We present a brief overview of the history of malware in the next section.

History of Malware

The first computer virus was recorded on an IBM PC in 1986 and was called the Pakistani "Brain" Virus. It was one of a class of early viruses — the boot sector viruses — that spread through the use of floppy disks. However, the first malware to seriously alarm information system users of the era was the MERRY CHRISTMAS worm (Capek, Chess, & White, 2003), which spread in December 1987 through the early Internet. The Internet was then a network that comprised only of the *European Academic Research Network* (EARN), the BITNET, a co-operative U.S. university network, and the IBM corporate network. Though it was not designed to cause any harm, the worm choked these networks. It was an innocuous Christmas greeting, but had been programmed to replicate once opened and send itself to everyone in the user's address list, without the knowledge of the user. Many network administrators reported having millions of copies of the e-mail clogging their networks. Even in the limited scope of the Internet of the day, replication evidently ensued on a scale normally characteristic of an epidemic. Within two days, the first countermeasures, being a primitive form of antivirus software, were released. Perhaps the best known among the early Internet worms was the *denial-of-service* (DoS) attack in November 1988, by the "Morris worm," named after its creator, Robert Morris, Jr. The DOS attack generally floods targeted networks and systems with transmission of data that regular traffic is either slowed or completely interrupted. The scale of impact was unprecedented; 10% of the systems connected to Internet were brought to a halt, and the world realized the potency of this incipient threat (Dacey, 2003). In the early 1990s, new and more complex viruses, such as polymorphic viruses, emerged. Subsequently, viruses also began taking the form of OS executables, followed in the mid-1990s by the debut of macro-enabled viruses. The late 1990s saw the emergence of Network worms that used network protocols and commands to infect the system. And in the first half of this decade, more sophisticated attacks called "blended threats" become popular. These combine two or more of the malicious code categories, resulting in powerful attack tools.

This trend of increasing technological sophistication has been accompanied by a perceptible reduction in the amount of time taken by a virus attack to "peak" in terms of the number of systems infected. In the mid-1990s, the number of machines infected by a virus tended to peak 11 to 13 days after the incipience of that virus, a period that is now down to between three and four days. This phenomenon may be attributed to various factors, such as increased sophistication of the virus itself, rapid growth of the Internet, and improvement in of "seamless interconnectivity" between geographically dispersed offices of business firms. The data tabulated in Table 2 illustrates this general trend.

Another trend is the drastic decrease in the time elapsed between the identification of a vulnerability by software vendors and the development of code by hackers to exploit the same. The time between vulnerability disclosure and exploitation has dropped from around 9-10 months in the mid-1990s to less than 6-7 days by mid-2004. Many security experts believe that "zero-day" threats are imminent. A zero-day blended threat would exploit the vulnerability even before the vulnerability is announced and a patch is made public. This demands greater proactivity from IT-support teams and the need to equip them with a conceptual framework that will enable them to take independent action.

Table 2. Time taken by Virus to become prevalent over years (Source: Orshesky, 2002)

Name of malware	Year of creation	Type	Time taken to spread
form	1990	boot sector virus	3 years
concept	1995	word macro virus	4 months
Melissa	1999	e-mail enabled word macro	4 days
Love Letter	2000	e-mail enabled script	5 hours
Slammer	2003	SQL worm	10 minutes

Life Cycle of a Virus

Antivirus software has been the chief defense mechanism since the proliferation of viruses started. Most antivirus solutions are comprehensive security solutions that can be centrally monitored. They can also be configured to remove administrative rights from client machines. Antivirus programs normally manage the life cycle of viruses in four steps:

1.   Prevention of virus outbreak;

2.   Containment of virus outbreak;

3.   Restoration of the affected nodes; and

4.   Reporting and alerting all the complementing perimeter security systems.

Antivirus Solution: The Layered Approach

The inherent complexity of enterprise networks demands a common security framework for all the entities involved in such a network, as has been discussed in the earlier sections. Furthermore, it is essential that deployment strategies include a comprehensive plan to evolve, distribute, operate, administer, and maintain these security policies across the organization. We present a generic three-layered approach:

1.   Layer 1: Gateway and content security

2.   Layer 2: Intranet servers

3.   Layer 3: Desktops and user community

The illustration of this layered approach is portrayed in the Figure 1.

Layer 1 — Gateway Security and Content Security

This layer deals with the Internetvisible servers as well as the DMZ network of an organization. It can be further subdivided into (a) gateway traffic, and (b) content security.

Gateway Traffic

The antivirus solution in the gateway security layer (GSL) complements the protection provided by of the firewall and DMZ configuration. Typically this layer has firewall and e-mail servers that are exposed to the public Internet. The choice of operating system and specialized e-mail tools plays an important role in ensuring the security in these inbound

Figure 1. Three-layer defense in enterprise network

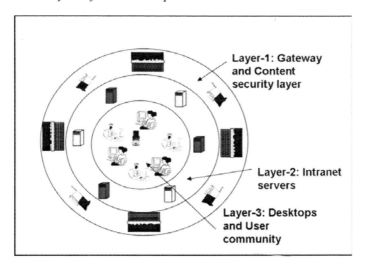

e-mail platforms exposed to the public Internet. These inbound e-mail servers can be configured to blacklist mail-abuse services and *simple mail transfer protocol* (SMTP) sources of virus and spam identified by the intrusion detection system. Based on organizational policies and defined security levels, this layer can be configured to deny *post office protocol* (POP) and *Internet message access protocol* (IMAP) access to external servers and to Web-based e-mail servers. It is imperative for an organization to configure firewall access filters to deny access to non-organization SMTP servers from user e-mail clients. Similar access controls on POP, IMAP, and SMTP can be placed on the border routers of the intranet of the organization. Filtering at this layer can also be configured to block *server message block* (SMB) Windows share access, *P2P* (peer-to-peer) network access, and *instant messaging* (IM).

Layer 1 features "firewall logs" that play a significant role in antivirus deployment. Malware is frequently aimed at exploiting certain ports in the target machine and using them to broadcast itself, and these Firewall logs in Layer 1 can be "parsed" for such attempts (Banes, 2001). This security management control process could be customized based on past experience and current activity (Stowe, 2002).

Content Scanning

The other major focus of this layer is on scanning the content of files and messages, primarily those exchanged with the public Internet. The content-scanning function of Layer1 processes e-mail attachments, scans e-mails for specific text, identifies spam based on e-mail content, and provides blacklisting services that were not included in the firewall filters. The scanning function is not confined to incoming traffic — malware originating within the organization is also addressed by the content scanning function of Layer 1.

Scanning of e-mails is discernibly an important function, given the sheer volume of malware designed to proliferate through this medium. Antivirus solutions that work with different technologies of the e-mail recipient servers in Layer 1 and the intranet e-mail servers in Layer 2 are available. E-mail scanning solutions typically combine antivirus and anti-spam protection into a single product. E-mail attachments in such an implementation are selected for scanning based on their suffixes and on other criteria defined based on the level of security desired by the organization. One critical security management decision in this function is whether notification is sent to the sender or the recipient of an infected e-mail attachment. Factors to be considered in this connection include: (1) the implications of sending such notifications to spoofed origination addresses; and (2) the fact that an external party might be using such information to map the capabilities of an antivirus deployment. Notifications to the intranet community should specify the course of action expected of the recipient of the notification, such as isolating the infected file.

The scanning of non-e-mail traffic employs a different procedure. Inbound traffic is scanned for infected files and malicious code using specialized proxy servers capable of scanning specific kinds of traffic, such as ftp transfers. Outbound traffic from an organization's Web and ftp servers or user file transmissions also has to be scanned for malicious code. This service is typically integrated with the firewall and is often focused on specific technologies like Active X and Java applets.

Layer 2 — Intranet Servers

The previous layer dealt with e-mail and proxy servers placed in the DMZ network. We now address the next layer in the security of the enterprise — e-mail servers, file servers, and proxy servers hosted on the organizational intranet. Given that the major medium of virus propagation is e-mail, antivirus solutions for e-mail servers demand special attention.

Antivirus software should be installed on both e-mail servers and client machines, and should be selected based on the e-mail software used. Most organizations now provide remote-access capability to Layer 2 e-mail servers, either through a *virtual private network* (VPN), a *remote access server* (RAS), or Webmail. Some VPN gateways can be configured to verify the existence of selected antivirus solutions on the remote computer. Access to POP and IMAP services should be made available only after proper authentication. There are some products that provide "integrated solutions" on a single platform, allowing one to combine layers, usually the e-mail aspect of Layers 1 and 2. However, if resources permit, different antivirus products in Layers 1, 2, and 3 should be used, as this strengthens the viability of the enterprise antivirus software deployment (Stowe, 2002). The antivirus solution on fileservers addresses a factor entirely different from all the above: minimizing the risk of users accessing infected files and of the distribution of such files. The storage capacities have grown rapidly in the last decade with the *storage area network* (SAN) and *network-attached storage* (NAS) technologies achieving many breakthroughs. With this tremendous increase in the storage space, the completion of a virus scan in the allotted time has also become a concern. When a user attempts to copy or save a file, the antivirus agent will attempt to open the file, triggering a scan by the antivirus software. Scanning protects the users in real-time when files are written to the storage system, plugging security holes that exist with older on-demand or scheduled scanning methods. Newer technology allows for the use of load distribution across several servers, ensuring optimum performance at all times.

Layer 3 — Desktop and User Community

The final and innermost layer is the one that has traditionally received maximum attention. The scanning issues for file servers in Layer 2 hold good for desktops as well, thanks to the increase in storage space and processing speed. The use of Webmail, instant messaging tools, peer-to-peer file sharing, shared permissions in the intranet, and downloads from the Internet are all possible sources of virus infection. Access to such services should be addressed while formulating the organization's security policy. It is highly desirable that automated scans be configured for user machines and that administrator privileges on those machines be unavailable to lay users. This helps ensure that critical antivirus programs are not uninstalled and that the user does not install any new programs or tools.

The user community is critical to any anti-malware deployment strategy. IT administrators and policymakers should never underestimate the value of educating users about IT security policies and guidelines. Although automation has in recent years reduced the need for manual intervention, employees still need to adhere to the guidelines and IS policies of the organization. An astute observation by Melinda Varian of the Princeton University Computer Center shall ever be worth citing in this context. In a 1987 letter to an IBM employee about the "Christmas worm," she wrote that "our networks exist on the goodwill of the users" (Chess & White, 2003). The worms and denial-of-service attacks that plague our networks today illustrate exactly this truism — a network's functionality still depends on the exemplary deportment of the users and on their adherence to defined guidelines.

Patch Deployment in
Enterprise Network

The staggering increase in reported information system vulnerabilities and vulnerability exploitation is growing unabatedly every year. Automated attacks are successfully exploiting such software vulnerabilities, as increasingly sophisticated hacking tools become more readily available and easier to use. In this context, preemptive and proactive plugging of the vulnerabilities forms a good defensive strategy. Effective patch management includes several critical elements, such as top management support, standardized policies, dedicated resources, risk assessment, testing, distribution of patches, and monitoring the effectiveness of patch deployment (Dacey, 2003). Let us look at some facts illustrating the seriousness of the current situation:

- According to the FBI and Carnegie Mellon University, more than 90% of all security breaches involve a software vulnerability caused by a missing patch that the IT department already knows about (Neray, 2004).

- On January 25, 2003, the Slammer worm triggered a global Internet slowdown and caused considerable harm through network outages and other unforeseen consequences. Some of the reported incidents due to its impact were: shutting down of a 911 emergency call center, cancellation of airline flights, failure of ATMs, and disruption of important systems at nuclear power plant facilities. The patch for the software vulnerability exploited by Slammer was released by Microsoft in July 2002 (Dacey, 2003).

- During the summer of 2003, the Blaster threat appeared a full 27 days after the associated vulnerability was announced through a critical security bulletin by Microsoft and a patch was made available by that company. Clearly, had this time been used in simple patch-deployment, much of the impact of that worm could have been mitigated.

Patch Management — Common Mistakes and Solutions

Patch management has become expensive and time-consuming for most enterprises. The failure to patch systems constitutes a considerable threat and leaves the enterprise network vulnerable to malware attack. Some of the factors that serve to undermine the effectiveness of the patching process are (Robinson, 2003):

1. System managers often fail to recognize that a certain patch or alarm is relevant to their machines.

2. Even after such recognition, many vulnerable systems remain un-patched due to neglect.

3. Patches themselves may be defective and may not protect comprehensively against the vulnerability they are targeting.

4. Patches may themselves cause new vulnerabilities if their functionality and the fact that installing them has no other impact on the machine is not ascertained.

Points (3) and (4) above make it clear that merely the automation of patch deployment is not enough in an enterprise environment. Patches have to be tested thoroughly before being deployed to ensure that they do not compromise other aspects of information security. Furthermore, the increase in the number and type of patches (for example, OS patches, database patches, network equipment patches, firewall patches, Web services application patches, etc.) being released by software vendors itself creates a management problem. Another challenge to IT teams is the presence of multiple operating systems and applications in an enterprise network. Sometimes patches may be version-specific, requiring care before blanket deployment.

Several services and automated tools are available to assist entities in performing the patch management function, including tools designed to be stand-alone patch management systems. In addition, systems management tools can be used to deploy patches across an entity's network. Patch management vendors also offer central databases of the latest patches, incidents, and methods for mitigating risks before a patch can be deployed or a patch has been released. Some vendors provide support for multiple software platforms, such as Microsoft, Solaris, and Linux, while others focus on certain platforms exclusively, such as Microsoft or Solaris.

Patch management tools can be either scanner-based (non-agent) or agent-based. The scanner-based tools are better suited for small organizations, while the agent-based products are better suited for large organizations. Though the scanner-based tools scan a network, check for missing patches, and allow an administrator to patch multiple computers, they lack capabilities to serve a large number of users without breaking down or requiring major changes in procedure. Another difficulty with scanner-based tools is that part-time users and turned-off systems will not be scanned. Agent-based products place small programs, or agents, on each computer, to periodically poll a patch database — a server on the network — for new updates, giving the administrator the option of applying the patch. Agent-based products require upfront work to integrate agents into the workstations and in the server deployment process, but generate less network traffic and provide a real-time network view. The agents maintain information that can be reported when needed. Finally, some patch management tools are hybrids, allowing the user to utilize agents or not (Dacey, 2003). This trade-off in risk versus time and its economic impact due to early/late patch deployment (both tangible and intangible) is difficult to measure. The determination of the best time for the patch deployment based on the optimal uptime for its enterprise network is a recommended technical approach.

Antispyware in Enterprise Network

Symptoms and Impact of Spyware

This emerging class of malware has risen quickly from obscurity to near ubiquity. A recent survey conducted by analyst firm IDC Inc. (IDC, 2004) estimates that 67% of consumers' personal computers are infected with some form of spyware. This has created a new set of challenges that are as significant as better known ones such as viruses and worms. The common symptoms of the infection of spyware are:

- unauthorized pop-up advertisements making Web browsing difficult;

- sudden change in the performance of the computer slowing it down considerably;

- appearance of new and unwanted toolbar on the browser without installation; and

- increased crashing of operating systems, Web browsers, and other common applications.

The business impact of spyware includes (Piscitello, 2005):

1. loss of productivity;
2. increased IT support costs;
3. theft of intellectual property;
4. liability associated with privacy violations;
5. premature information disclosure; and
6. loss of credibility and damage to the organization.

Antispyware for Enterprise Network

Spyware is fast emerging as a major concern, and new enterprise anti-spyware tools are helping network security managers eradicate this malware. Advanced anti-spyware tools targeted at the enterprise market typically feature centralized management tools and automatic update services. Furthermore, many antivirus providers have announced plans to incorporate anti-spyware functionalities into their products.

Mechanics of Malware and Antivirus Software

This section attempts to provide an understanding of the mechanics of the working of a virus and of antivirus software. A real-life example may be salutary to this purpose. We will consider the example of a recent virus named W32/Gobi to understand how a virus affects a machine and how the antivirus software works against such threats. We consider this specific example because it poses a formidable challenge to antivirus software makers with its unique combination of a *portable extension* (PE) file infector virus, backdoor capabilities, advanced polymorphism, entry-point obscuring, and retro- and anti-debugging features (Perriot, 2004). The various virus types and their antivirus detection techniques are explained briefly in chronological order of their debut.

Pattern Recognition

This was the earliest method of virus detection used in the first generation of antivirus scanners. Pattern file recognition examines key suspect areas and uses the virus pattern file to compare and detect viruses.

Integrity Checking (Check-Summing)

This is another old method in which the antivirus program builds an initial record of the status (size, time, date, etc.) of all the files on the hard disk. It then uses check-summing programs to monitor changes to the status of the files. If a change is found, the integrity checker warns the user of a possible virus. The biggest drawback of this technique was that it raised a lot of false alarms, such as when legitimate programs make changes to files in normal process routines. Furthermore, it warns the user only after the file is infected and cannot help prevent infection proactively.

X-Raying

This is a method of virus detection that uses a set of techniques that enables us to see a picture of the virus body, seeing through the layer of encryption. This detection method may be employed if the encryption algorithm used by a virus presents certain weaknesses. Let us illustrate this by choosing an XOR function as the encryption method. Then each byte of the encrypted text ("ciphertext") is derived from one byte of the clear text ("plaintext") by XORing it with a fixed byte value between 0 and 255 (the "key"). If we are presented with this ciphertext C, given that it uses an XOR function to attain encryption, we can guess the value of key K based on the first byte of the ciphertext C_0. Thus we can apply the guessed key K to other bytes and decrypt them too (Ferrie, 2004).

32-Bit Viruses and PE File Infectors

This class of virus appeared with the advent of Windows 95, which introduced the 32-bit operating system and a new format for executable files. The standard *portable executable* (PE) file, featured in that and all succeeding versions of the Windows operating systems, reads information from each of its different headers and begins running the program from a set position, called "the entry point." PE file-infectors work in various ways to run themselves each time the host file gets executed. One method is to create a new section within the file, insert the viral code or "signature" into it, and change the entry point to that specific section. This enables the viral code to be executed before the host program is and to thus activate its destructive payload.

Entry Point Obscuring

The *entry point obscuring* (EPO) technology uses a different technique. The virus does not affect the file at its entry code, but places a "Jump-to-Virus" instruction somewhere in the middle of the file code section. As a result of this code placement, the virus is activated only if the affected program's branch where the code resides receives control, and this makes the detection and disinfection procedures more complex (Kaspersky & Podrezov, 2001). Another similar file infection method inserts the viral code in some unused space in the file sections and modifies the entry point to point to the viral code. The distinguishing feature of this method is that it doesn't change the file size. The major threat of PE viruses is that they have no built-in technical limitations and run like a real program, which makes it harder to be detected and eradicated. There remains a threat of file corruption, and PE infectors' uses different methods, from polymorphism, which enables a virus to constantly change its form to evade detection by signature scanners, to stealth, and even routines targeting specific antiviruses.

Encrypted Virus

These feature the encryption technology in virus writing that hides the fixed signature by encrypting the scrambling virus, making it unrecognizable to the antivirus software. An encrypted virus consists of a virus decryption body routine and the encrypted virus body. Once the infected program is launched, the virus decryption routine gains control, decrypts the virus body, and transfers control to it. This could make the detection extremely difficult, but the decryption routines used by the viruses remained the same for long time, enabling antivirus software makers to develop methods to search for the sequence of bytes that identified specific decryption routines.

Polymorphic Viruses

A polymorphic virus features a scrambled virus body, a decryption routine of encrypted viruses, and a third component called a "mutation engine" in encrypted form. A mutation engine generates randomized decryption techniques each time the virus infects a new program. This creates no fixed signature and no fixed decryption routine, and, further-more, no two infections look alike. This poses a formidable challenge to antivirus software makers. Tequila and Maltese Amoeba were the first polymorphic viruses to be created. Dark Avenger, the author of "Amoeba," distributed the mutation engine, also called MtE, to other virus authors to create new and advanced polymorphic viruses (Symantec, 1996).

Polymorphic Detection

Antivirus researchers tried to create decryption routines that detect each polymorphic virus, one by one. But this approach was time consuming and costly, as mutation engines could provide billions of variations. This led virus researchers to develop a new method called "generic decryption." A scanner, using generic encryption techniques, loads the file being scanned into a self-contained virtual container created in the *random access memory* (RAM). The scanner monitors and controls the program file as it executes, but an infected program cannot cause any damage as it is being executed in isolation from the real computer. When an infected file is executed, the decryption routine executes, and the virus decrypts itself, exposing the virus body to the scanner, thus enabling the latter to precisely identify the virus signature. If no virus is found in the file, the scanner removes the program file from the virtual computer and proceeds to scan the next file. The problem with generic decryption is speed, and it has limited practical use. To overcome this problem of speed, virus researchers developed the heuristic-based generic decryption technique.

Heuristic-Based Generic Decryption and Emulation

This enhancement of generic decryption employs "heuristics," a generic set of rules that helps differentiate non-virus from virus behavior. A typical virus program exhibits inconsistent behavior compared to a non-infected program, and heuristic-based generic decryption looks for such inconsistencies that could indicate the presence of an infected file. Such indication prompts a scanner to keep the file running inside the virtual computer for a longer period, allowing it to decrypt and expose the virus body, a process sometimes referred to as "emulation." Virus authors came up with anti-emulation and anti-debugging to defeat antivirus scanners (Symantec, 1996).

Anti-Emulation

As described in the previous section, a virus under emulation will be allowed to run just enough inside a virtual computer to decrypt itself and reveal its code for either a straightforward scan or a generic heuristic scan. Anti-emulation is the technique used by viruses to defeat this. Viruses use anti-emulation techniques to defeat the generic heuristics detection process by themselves detecting if emulation is in progress. Some anti-emulation systems are incorporated into the decryptor of a virus so that it does not decrypt properly and hence will not reveal its code.

Anti-Debugging

Anti-debugging techniques are small pieces of code that have no overall effect on the virus when it is run under conditions bereft of antivirus scanning techniques. However, it causes the virus to malfunction or crash when it is run under a debugging environment, thus preventing the detection of the virus (MidNyte, 2000).

Retrovirus

Retrovirus is a computer virus that specifically tries to bypass or hinder the operation of antivirus programs. The attack may be generic or specific to a known product, is also known as anti-antivirus (Hyppönen, 1994). Retroviruses attempt to subvert the antivirus scanners mostly using the following approaches: (1) by modifying the code of an antivirus program file; (2) hiding itself when it detects that the antivirus program is activating, or by stopping the execution of the program or triggering a destructive routine; (3) by altering the computing environment in a way that affects the operation of an antivirus program; (4) by using methods in the virus code that cause problems for antivirus programs; (5) by exploiting a specific weakness or a backdoor in an antivirus program; or (6) by using generic methods that generally make it difficult or potentially dangerous to detect, identify or disinfect the virus (e.g., the GoldBug virus).

Backdoor

A program that surreptitiously allows access to a computer's resources (files, network connections, configuration information, etc.) via a network connection is known as a backdoor or remote-access Trojan. Note that such functionality is often included in legitimate software designed and intended to allow such access, but virus writers exploit and uses this to spread malware. Let us illustrate this in detail. Hackers use scanners to search the Internet for computers that are vulnerable to a backdoor break-in. Most often, personal computers connected to the Internet are prone to these, as security levels are far lower than the rigidly protected enterprise systems. Hackers download scripts onto these machines, essentially hijacking them, and then use them to launch a denial-of-service attack. Due to the script planted in these computers through the backdoor, these machines become slave computers called zombies. Following a command from the master computer, zombies (also called botnets) simultaneously send out requests for information, called IP packets, that bombard the victim network and eventually shut it down. An advantage of this type of distributed denial-of-service attack is that it is almost impossible to trace the actual hacker, as the DOD attack comes from many sources.

Virus Infection Cycle of W32/Gobi

The virus W32/Gobi is a PE file infector written in assembly language. It has backdoor capabilities and virus body is 29KB long. It has a twofold infection strategy: (1) direct action; and (2) registry hooking. The direct action method works the following way. As soon as the virus runs on the machine, and if the username is different from the one recorded in the virus body, Gobi infects up to seven ".exe" or ".scr" files in the Systems and Windows directory. Then it hooks the "HKCR\exefile\ shell\open\command" registry key. Once any executable is launched from Windows Explorer, the virus is invoked. This is achieved by directing control from the registry key to an infected program — either "runonce.exe" (on Windows 9x systems) or a copy of "taskman.exe" (on Windows NT-derived systems). Once the registry hook is done, Gobi infects programs launched from Windows Explorer before letting them run. Gobi was written to avoid infecting certain file types (Windows System File Checker [SFC], WinZip self-extractors, and UPX-packed files) and carries a list of 117 file names belonging to antivirus and other security products. It also chooses only files that are between 8,000 bytes and 4,000,000 bytes in size. We have organized the discussion on the mechanics of infection of Gobi into five steps to bring better clarity to the discussion (Perriot, 2004).

- **Step 1:** Once these conditions are met, the Gobi starts the infection by carrying out the entry point obscuring routine. This routine directs control flow from the host code to the virus decryptor, which is located at the original end of the last physical section of the file. The virus attempts to locate five consecutive CCh bytes in the section and records their position if it finds them. CChs are often found in programs written in high-level languages and are commonly used as alignment padding by compilers. Next, Gobi searches for FF15h and FF25h patterns corresponding to indirect calls and execute "jmps" instruction, the most common instructions used to perform import calls. Then, the indirect branch pointing to the Import Address Table entry of the selected exit API is modified to transfer control to the virus decryptor. Gobi replaces the first four CCh bytes with the virtual address of the decryptor, and changes the memory reference of the indirect branch to point to the location of the CChs if they were found. If no CChs were found earlier, the six-byte jump or call is simply replaced with a snippet of code of equal length that inserts the virtual address of the decryptor and returns to it.

- **Step 2:** In the next step, the polymorphic engine is called to generate the decryptor and the encrypted body of the virus; the virus code is written to the host, and the PE header is modified accordingly. Gobi has a complex polymorphic engine that is 9KB long. The junk instruction generator of Gobi supports a wide variety of opcodes: data transfer operations, arithmetic and logic operations, and rotations with capabilities to generate additional Byte, word, and dword variants. The virus carries a traditional decryption loop relying on "XOR" as the basic encryption operation. The parameter of the "XOR" is a sliding key, and it is modified between three and 16 times per loop iteration, making W32/Gobi very difficult to detect by the x-raying method. The decryption of the virus may be backward or forward, and once the polymorphic engine produces a decryptor, Gobi uses it to encrypt its virus body.

- **Step 3:** In this step, Gobi carefully takes necessary precautions to avoid being detected by the Integrity-checking method. It saves and restores file attributes and times across an infection, and if there was originally a non-zero checksum in the PE header, it is recalculated using the CheckSumMappedFile () function. W32/Gobi uses an array of anti-debugging techniques to avoid detection by scanners. Gobi calls the IsDebuggerPresent () function, and it either resolves or directly reads the DebugContext field of the Thread Information Block at fs: [20h]. Gobi exits if it senses that it is being debugged. It also features a three-second timeout per file infection and, on reaching timeout, it triggers an exception to end its execution. The virus also carefully zeros out the decrypted virus body before exiting and finishes by calling the exit() function of msvcrt.dll. This final self-mutilation prevents the activation of any "goat" program that may be written to detect virus. "Goat" or "bait" files are dummy program files that are being monitored for change in status for infection by antivirus scanners.

- **Step 4:** Gobi is also a retrovirus and actively attacks the antivirus products. In a period of four hours after the registry hook, Gobi uses the list of 117 names in its retro routine. It terminates the process and patches the corresponding executable file, replacing the entry point of the file with a "ret" instruction (opcode C3h) followed by up to 127 random bytes.

- **Step 5:** Gobi installs a backdoor on the infected host after the four-hour period. The UPX-packed executable, dropped into the temporary directory under the filename "DABACKDOOR.EXE" has backdoor functionality. Once run, the backdoor component registers itself under "HKLM\...\Run" in order to ensure that it is run every time Windows is started. The backdoor listens on port 666/tcp and its access is password-protected. It possesses standard remote-control features of file upload and download, remote file system manipulation, file execution, remote process killing, password-stealing, keylogging (performed by an external DLL dropped to disk), and certain remote desktop interaction functionalities. It also notifies the hacker by e-mail when it starts, sending such information about the compromised system as the username, computer name, and local time.

Antivirus Engine and Database

Antivirus scanners generally include an *antivirus* (AV) engine and a virus-detection database. These two components are normally integrated into a single unit. However, in some antivirus software products, the engine only serves as a loader for the database, and it is here that all the functionality is implemented. In other cases, the engine serves as a library of commonly used functions, and the database simply exercises these functions to perform the task of finding a virus. For detection of new viruses, the updating of the engine is as important as the updating of the database (Muttik, 2000).

Conclusion

The year 2004 bustled with serial computer virus outbreaks. It also saw an increase in bot programs and the incidence of spam and phishing, as well as in spyware and adware generation, indicating the determination of hackers to invade and undermine every popular Internet application and device and exploit every available security loophole. Outdated forms and methods of attacks have been promptly replaced with newer, more effective methods that can ensure greater reach and effectiveness, and thus larger profits. Based on the general trend of malicious code and Internet-based attacks, some of the future forecasts regarding malware are:

- Smarter blended threats are increasingly wreaking havoc and will continue to present a challenge to enterprise security.

- Spam mails, phishing will continue to be a major concern in e-mail usage, while newer malware like pharming viruses are emerging.

- *Internet relay chat* (IRC), *peer-to-peer* (P2P) communication will continue to be weak security links and new file-swapping technologies continue to raise new concerns.

- Social engineering is emerging as one of the biggest challenges, as there is no technical defense against the exploitation of human weaknesses.

- The time between vulnerability disclosure and release of malware exploiting the vulnerability continues to get shorter, requiring more proactive assessment tools and constant vulnerability assessment of the enterprise networks.

More information about the attack methodology of W32/Gobi virus can be obtained from Virus Bulletin publication (Perriot, 2004).

We have provided an overview of the types of malware, integrated approach to antivirus software implementation in enterprise, patch management, mechanics of virus and antivirus. As organizations find themselves having to defend a mobile and geographically disperse workforce, they have to adopt more proactive and innovative security strategies in combating malware.

References

Argaez, E. D. (2004). *How to prevent the online invasion of spyware and adware.* Retrieved Janaury 10, 2005, from Internet World Stats Web site at http://www.internetworldstats.com/articles/art053.htm

Banes, D. (2001). *How to stay virus, worm and Trojan free - without anti-virus software.* Retrieved May 20, 2005, from http://www.giac.org/certified_professionals/practicals/gsec/0747.php

Capek, P. G., Chess, D. M. , & White, S. R. (2003,). Merry Christmas: An early network worm. *Security & Privacy Magazine, IEEE, 1*(5), 26-34.

CSI/FBI. (2004). *9th CSI/FBI Annual computer crime and security survey.* CSI Institute. Retrieved from http://gocsi.com

Dacey, R. F. (2003, September 10). Information security: Effective patch management is critical to mitigating software vulnerabilities. Testimony Before the Subcommittee on Technology Information Policy, Intergovernmental Relations, and the Census, House Committee on Government Reform. U.S. GAO-03-1138T.

Ferrie, F. P. a. P. (2004, September 8-9). *Principles and practise of x-raying.* Paper presented at the Virus Bulletin Conference, Jersey, UK.

Hyppönen, M. (1994). *Retroviruses - How viruses fight back.* Paper presented at the 1994 Virus Bulletin Conference, Jersey.

IDC. (2004, December 1). *IDC Market Analysis: Worldwide Spyware 2004-2008 Forecast and Analysis: Security and System Management Sharing Nightmares.* Press Release. Framingham, MA.

Kaspersky, E., & Podrezov, A. (2001). *F-Secure virus descriptions: MTX.* Retrieved May 20, 2005, from http://www.f-secure.com/v-descs/mtx.shtml

Mi2g. (2004). *Economic impact of worms.* Retrieved March 13, 2005, from http://www.wholesecurity.com/threat/cost_of_worms.html. Original source from http://www.mi2g.com

MidNyte. (2000). *An introduction to encryption.* Retrieved March 12, 2005, from http://web.textfiles.com/virus/enciii.txt

Muttik, I. (2000, September). *Stripping down an AV engine.* Paper presented at the 2000 Virus Bulletin Conference, Orlando, Florida.

Neray, P. (2004, October 14). Beyond Patch Management. *COMPUTERWORLD,* Retrieved February 10, 2005, from http:www///computerworld.com

Orshesky, C. M. (2002). Survival of the fittest: The evolution of computer viruses. Cornell University, original source, True Secure Corporation. Retrieved May 23, 2005, from http://www.cit.cornell.edu/computer/security/seminars-past/virus-june02/survival/sld013.htm

Perriot, F. (2004, June). Ship of the desert. *Virus Bulletin*. Retrieved January 29, 2005, from http://www.virusbtn.com/issues/virusbulletin/2004/06.pdf

Piscitello, D. (2005, January 10). How to keep spyware off your enterprise Network. *SecurityPipeline*.

Robinson, C. (2003). Patch deployment best practices in the enterprise. *CSO Online*.

Stowe, M. (2002). *Security management view of implementing enterprise antivirus protection*. White paper dated 12/23/2002, accessed from InfoSec reading room, SANS Institute.

Symantec. (1996). Understanding and managing polymorphic viruses. *The Symantec Enterprise Papers, 30*. Retrieved January 18, 2005, from http://securityresponse.symantc.com/avcenter/reference/striker.pdf

Section II:

Security Implications for Business

Chapter V

The Impact of Sarbanes-Oxley (SOX) Act on Information Security Governance

Gurpreet Dhillon, Virginia Commonwealth University, USA

Sushma Mishra, Virginia Commonwealth University, USA

Abstract

This chapter discusses the impact of Sarbanes-Oxley (SOX) Act on corporate information security governance practices. The resultant regulatory intervention forces a company to revisit its internal control structures and assess the nature and scope of its compliance with the law. This chapter reviews the organizational implications emerging from the mandatory compliance with SOX. Industry internal control assessment frameworks, such as COSO and COBIT, are reviewed and their usefulness in ensuring compliance evaluated. Other emergent issues related to IT governance and the general integrity of the enterprise are identified and discussed.

Introduction

Accounting scandals at some of the big corporations like Enron, HealthSouth, Tyco, and WorldCom had a devastating impact on investor confidence. Clearly, it was possible to engage in frauds of such magnitude because of the inability of auditors to detect early signs of such possibilities. In the case of Enron, an accounting loophole allowed the company to use gross instead of net value to calculate profits from energy contracts (Ackerman, 2002). Many shareholders lost their confidence in corporate reporting of company financial statements and generally in the integrity of the auditors. Issues such as lack of independence of auditors providing higher margin consulting services to audit clients, limited independence by corporate directors, increased use of stock options as a means of compensation, and inadequacy of the *generally accepted accounting principles* (GAAP) came to the fore.

The resultant crisis in the financial markets and massive media coverage of the frauds created a situation where government's interference was inevitable. The main reason cited, leading to such a situation, was a lack of accountability of top management to government and shareholders. Measures like assessment of internal controls on the part of corporations to restore investor confidence did not seem enough (Agarwal & Chadha, 2004). Investor protection needed radical changes in the legal system as form of assurance. Thus, the U.S. government intervened by passing the Sarbanes-Oxley Act in 2002.

This chapter reviews the impact of legal controls on *information technology* (IT) governance practices, especially in the case of the SOX Act. The chapter is organized into four sections. The first section describes the concepts of corporate governance, IT governance, and internal controls. A review of the definitions is followed by a rationale for good corporate governance practices. The next section discusses specific titles of SOX Act that impact IT governance practices. Interpretations of those areas of SOX that relate to increased importance of IT Governance are then presented and emerging issues associated with compliance with this law are identified and addressed. The concluding section presents a discussion of the future challenges and implications.

Corporate Governance and IT Management

Corporate governance, as defined by the *Certified Information Systems Auditor* (CISA) Review Manual (2004), is ethical corporate behavior by directors or others charged with governance in the creation and presentation of wealth for all stakeholders. The ethical issues of an organization are fostered through corporate governance practices. The practice of corporate governance is further defined by the *Organization for Economic Cooperation and Development* (OECD, 2004) as:

> *the distribution of rights and responsibilities among different participants in the corporation, such as board, managers, shareholders and other stakeholders, and spells out the rules and procedures for making decisions on corporate affairs. By doing this, it also provides the structure through which the company objectives are set and the means of attaining those objectives and monitoring performance.* (in CISA Review Manual, p. 52)

Thus, corporate governance lays the ground for all other types of management functions focused on different areas of specialization, for example, IT governance.

Information Technology Governance

IT governance is a structure of relationships and processes to direct and control the enterprise to achieve its goal by adding value while balancing risk and return over IT and its processes (ISACA, 2004). The amount of investment in IT projects is seemingly high today. It has become increasingly important to clearly define the value derived from these investments and present justification to the shareholders. Effective management of IT and good IT governance practices do not necessarily have the same purpose. Though both these functions cater to the effectiveness of IT in an organization, there lies a subtle difference in the domain of each.

IT management has a much narrower focus and ensures effective supply of the IT products and services for operational efficiency. It is primarily concerned with the management of IT operations. IT management could be looked upon as a subset of the IT governance process. Successful implementation of a strategic IT project to meet the objectives of an enterprise is an example of good IT management techniques (Haes & Grembergen, 2004).

The domain of IT governance is much broader and concentrates on envisioning the IT requirements of the business in the future for strategic advantage and better performance. Deciding upon a strategic IT project to meet business goals, defining implementation techniques, and allocating optimal resources for effective management of IT projects could be examples of effective IT governance in use.

The objective of IT governance is to plan how the organization could meet its goals in the future through optimal use of IT resources. IT governance is concerned with objectives that focus on areas such as: alignment of IT with business, assessment of the value and benefit that IT provides to business, management of the risks associated with IT, and performance measures for IT services to the business (Anantha, 2004). This can be achieved by setting up IT governance frameworks with practices best suited for an organization. Corporate governance can be effectively implemented by having strong IT governance and a method of objective assessment and implementation of internal controls in a company. IT is the backbone of effective internal controls. Hence, internal controls play an important role in achieving a healthy corporate governance culture in an organization.

Role of Internal Controls

The importance of identifying, establishing, and maintaining the integrity of internal controls has been felt by organizations for a rather long period of time. It was the *Committee of Sponsoring Organizations of the Treadway Commission* (COSO) that first introduced a framework for assessing internal controls in 1992. Subsequently, other frameworks, such as *Control Objectives for Information and related Technology* (COBIT), were developed and are now being extensively used by businesses.

Internal Control Objectives

Internal controls are a means to provide reasonable assurance that an organization will achieve its business objectives while avoiding undesired risks. Internal controls are policies, procedures, practices, and organizational structures put in place to reduce risks. At the heart of internal controls lies routinization of organizational processes. Any problem in the company ought to be corrected based on compliance or management-initiated concerns. Internal control activities and supporting processes are either manual or supported by computers. They operate at all levels in an organization and help in reducing risks involved at various stages of the operation, thus helping the organization reach its business objectives.

In 1992, the American Institute of Certified Public Accountants, the Institute of Internal Auditors, the American Accounting Association, the Institute of Management Accountants, and the Financial Executives Institute issued a jointly prepared statement. This authoritative document identified the fundamental objectives of any business unit (General Masters, Inc., 2004). Accordingly, objectives of internal control have to be achieved in three broad areas:

- Economy and efficiency of operations, including safeguarding of assets and achievement of desired outcomes. This comprises an entity's basic business objectives, along with performance and profitability.

- Reliability of financial and operational data and management reports.

- Well-guided compliance efforts directed to all laws and regulations.

The responsibility of implementing and monitoring these controls lies with the management of the firm. The board of directors and the senior executives of the organization establish an appropriate culture in workplace where each individual takes part in the control process. This can be achieved through effective and explicit communication of internal control objectives.

The internal control objectives are a statement of the desired result or vision that is to be achieved by implementing the control procedures in a particular activity. These objectives vary with functionalities implementing it. Some of the examples of these objectives could be:

- **Internal accounting controls**: These are primarily concerned with accounting operations, such as safeguarding assets and reliability of financial records.

- **Operational controls**: These objectives are directed at the daily operations, functions, and activities that ensure operations are meeting the business objectives of the firm.

- **Administrative controls**: These are concerned with operational efficiency in a functional area and adherence to management policies. They support the operational controls.

The effectiveness of internal control has been an ongoing debate across industries. Yet, there is no consensus on a common definition of the term among business executives, auditors, or regulators. Due to this prevalent ambiguity, executives have been able to define internal controls in manner convenient to them.

COSO

It is indeed difficult to assess the effectiveness of internal controls of different organizations, as each has its own standard definition. Organizations are different in many aspects: size, business philosophy, nature of the industry to which they belong, and corporate culture, to name a few. With combination of such factors, each organization has a unique environment and thus different measures for effectiveness of its internal controls. To overcome these problems, the Committee of Sponsoring Organizations of the Treadway Commission framework was developed. Effectiveness of internal controls in business processes must be measured and evaluated to identify obstacles to success and quality. The COSO framework describes a unified approach for evaluation of the internal control system that a management designs to provide reasonable assurance of achieving the fundamental business objectives. The original COSO framework contains five control components that assure sound business objectives. These are:

1. **Control environment:** The control environment defines the tone of an organization and the way it operates, providing both discipline and structure. Organizations with effective control environments set a positive example from the "top management" and try to create integrity and control consciousness. The management sets formalized and clearly communicated policies and procedures, encouraging shared values and teamwork. This objective primarily provides the ethics, direction, and philosophy to the organization. It focuses on the integrity of the people in the organization and their competence. Management, through its human resources development practices, conveys these values. The standard set by the management is reflected in the ways in which it assigns responsibility and authority to employees. Basically, if the employees can align their value system with that of the organization and see their future with it, then management is successful in passing down its core values to employees. As Ramos (2004) puts it, "The control environment is the foundation for all other components of internal controls and provides discipline and structure" (p. 29).

2.   **Risk assessment:** Through the process of risk assessment, management identifies the potential threats that can prevent it from meeting business objectives. Management should be aware of the possible risks involved in business, identify them, and analyze the likelihood and impact of these risks on the business. It is management's discretion to decide how risk averse it is and also to determine how these tolerance levels can be achieved. Organizations are vulnerable to various kinds of risks because they are in a state of flux in a dynamic environment. Thus they need mechanisms to identify and deal with risks resulting from such changes. An organization is anchored to its mission and goals through objective setting.

3.   **Control activities:** These include the operationalization of policies and procedures that are created and established to show management's intention of addressing all the risk elements. Such activities cover the entire organization, at different levels and different functionalities. These could include activities like approvals, authorizations, verifications, and segregation of duties, to name a few. Essentially, these activities fall under any one of the three objectives: operational, financial reporting, and compliance. Whatever the nature of the activities, there has to be awareness and responsibility among the people who undertake the tasks. Ethical consideration of these responsibilities cannot be documented. These activities are usually less formal or structured in small organizations, and in some cases, there may be no need for certain activities due to the direct involvement of the manager, owner, or CEO. Nevertheless, the intent of such activities is that these must exist to provide the system of checks and balances necessary for effective internal control.

4.   **Information and communication:** Computer-based systems are required to run an enterprise because they produce reports containing operational, financial, and compliance information. These systems contain internally generated data as well as information about external events, developments, and conditions required for informed decisions. Surrounding the control activities, there should be systems in place that can capture and communicate relevant information in a timely manner and help in ensuring integrity of the internal controls. Information thus obtained could be critical to the processes of conducting, managing, and controlling the operations of the organization. To facilitate the communication process, there should be adequate open channels for information flow. These channels are needed to reinforce the message to personnel that internal control responsibilities are a priority and should be taken seriously (Steinberg & Tanki, 1993). It is the responsibility of the management to clearly articulate the role of each individual in the internal controls system and the way it impacts other activities in the company.

5.   **Monitoring:** In today's Internet age, the pace and rate of change of information needs of an organization is fast. Thus to perform effectively all systems must be evaluated to ensure that they are performing as intended, particularly internal control systems. This kind of monitoring can be accomplished either by ongoing checks and balances that occur during normal operations or through separate evaluations by management, often with the assistance of the internal audit function. The extent of ongoing monitoring usually determines the need for separate evaluations. When deficiencies in internal control are discovered, they should be reported immediately to higher management levels in the organization, including the board of directors if the need arises, for appropriate remedial action

to be taken. In such cases, management should obtain input from third parties, such as the external auditor or those not part of the internal control systems.

A detailed understanding of the COSO framework does not guarantee that a complete assessment of effective internal controls system would be possible. The COSO framework, however, does highlight the importance of identifying and managing risks across the enterprise. A newer version of the COSO framework is now available that consists of eight components. In addition to the existing five controls, three new controls have been added. These are: objective setting, event identification, and risk response.

Measuring the effectiveness of internal control is a difficult task since it is an ongoing process. Three primary business objectives and the eight COSO components needed to achieve those objectives constitute the internal control framework. To evaluate the effectiveness of the controls, it is necessary to know the intent of having a control in the first place. "Elements of controls that should be considered when evaluating control strength include whether the controls are classified as preventive, detective, or corrective in nature" (ISACA, 2004, p. 30). Given the particular nature of the control, its effectiveness can be determined.

COBIT

Strong IT support is required to effectively manage the internal controls. Even though companies realize the importance of the general IT controls, they need formal guidelines for effective IT governance. To address this requirement, Control Objectives for Information and related Technology have been created. It is a rich, robust, and the most widely used IT governance framework. This framework is considered a standard across industries for developing and maintaining IT controls. It is positioned to be more comprehensive for management, as it is at a higher level than technology standards for information systems management.

The idea behind the COBIT framework is that information is needed to support business objectives and requirements. Companies should be able to assess the nature and extent of IT controls required to integrate their internal control objectives. Basically, it is important for a company to demonstrate how its IT controls support COSO and whether IT controls are appropriately documented in all COSO components.

In COBIT, control objectives are defined in a manner consistent with COSO. It is a process-oriented framework following the concept of business reengineering. COBIT is comprised of four domains, 34 IT processes or high-level control objectives, and 318 detailed control objectives. A control objective has been identified and the rationale to link the document to business objectives has been provided at all identified processes and domains. It is a comprehensive framework for managing risk and control of information and related technology. COBIT 3rd edition, released in 1996, is the latest version available.

COBIT was developed to align IT resources and processes with business objectives, quality standards, monetary controls, and security needs. COBIT is composed of four domains:

Figure 1. Relationship between COSO components and the COBIT objectives (Source: Fox, 2004)

COBIT Control Objectives	Control Environment	Risk Assessment	Control Activities	Information and Communication	Monitoring
Plan and Organize (PO)					
Define a strategic IT plan.		•		•	•
Define the information architecture.			•	•	
Determine technological direction.					
Define the IT organization and relationships.	•			•	
Manage the IT investment.					
Communicate management aims and direction.	•			•	•
Manage human resources.	•			•	
Ensure compliance with external requirements.			•	•	•
Assess risks.		•			
Manage projects.					
Manage quality.	•		•	•	•
Acquire and Implement (AI)					
Identify automated solutions.					
Acquire and maintain application software.			•		
Acquire and maintain technology infrastructure.			•		
Develop and maintain procedures.			•	•	
Install and accredit systems.			•		
Manage changes.			•		
Deliver and Support (DS)					
Define and manage service levels.	•		•		•
Manage third-party services.	•	•	•		•
Manage performance and capacity.			•		
Ensure continuous service.			•		•
Ensure systems security.			•	•	•
Identify and allocate costs.					
Educate and train users.	•			•	
Assist and advise customers.					
Manage the configuration.			•	•	
Manage problems and incidents.			•	•	•
Manage data.			•	•	
Manage facilities.			•		
Manage operations.			•	•	
Monitor and Evaluate (M)					
Monitor the processes.				•	•
Assess internal control adequacy.					•
Obtain independent assurance.	•				•
Provide for independent audit.					

1. **Planning and organization:** This domain covers the strategic importance of IT and assesses how IT would be best able to meet business objectives. It reaffirms the importance of planning and organizing effectively for the company's strategic vision to be realized. To achieve this, a proper technological infrastructure is required.

2. **Acquisition and implementation:** In this domain, the importance of methods and tools to bring strategic goals to the operational level is highlighted. IT solutions have to be developed or acquired to meet the objectives and integrated with the business process. Continuous improvement in existing systems and its maintenance is the goal in this domain.

3. **Delivery and support:** This domain considers the delivery of required services for proper functioning of the systems as its core function. To deliver services, necessary support processes must be set up to help in processing data or support application controls.

4. **Monitoring:** This domain monitors all IT processes for their quality and compliance with control requirement. Continuous monitoring ensures that all the controls are in place and working effectively. It also addresses any oversight on behalf of management in control process.

Each of these domains has a series of sub-domains that extensively cover all the control points for governance. The relationship of COSO with IT-control guidelines like COBIT has to be understood properly to achieve the goals of effective internal control. Figure 1 shows the relationship between COSO and COBIT objectives.

COBIT assumes three levels of IT efforts when considering the management of IT resources. At the lowest level, there are activities and tasks required to achieve measurable results. The next level is defined by processes, which are a series of joined activities or tasks where controls can be placed. At the highest level, processes are naturally grouped together to form domains. These domains are in alignment with the management cycle or life cycle applicable to IT processes. This conceptual framework of three levels can be approached from three vantage points: information criteria, IT resources, and IT processes.

The Sarbanes-Oxley Act

The Sarbanes-Oxley Act is the popular name for the *Public Company Accounting Reform and Investor protection Act*. By a nearly unanimous vote in July 2002, the U.S. Congress passed this law, which has been termed as most radical redesign of federal securities laws since the 1930s. This 131-page law is intended to protect investors by improving the accuracy and reliability of corporate disclosures and plugging loopholes in existing stocks and securities laws. SOX was enacted in response to public anger at accounting fraud and corporate governance failures. It mandates that companies use stringent policies and procedures for reporting financial information accurately and timely. These mandates break new ground in the fight against corporate fraud and require a wide variety of information technologies to sustain compliance in perpetuity. To ensure compliance, violators of any rule of the U.S. *Security and Exchange Commission* (SEC) issued under this act may face civil or criminal sanctions.

Even though SOX is a U.S. law, it has international implications. International companies with offices in the U.S. must comply with its requirements (Nash, 2003). SOX impacts European companies, many of which are dually listed on exchanges in Europe and the U.S. or have subsidiaries headquartered in the U.S. Specifically, Section 106 of the Act states that its jurisdiction includes any foreign public accounting firm that prepares or furnishes an audit report to a publicly traded U.S. company. Volonino, Kermis, and Gessner (2004) note:

> *Key to achieving sustainable compliance with SOX is an IT infrastructure that satisfies mandated levels of internal control, corporate governance, and fraud detection. Compliance will require seamless integration of properly implemented and documented* information systems *(IS). Data passed from events and transactions to financial statements must be controlled — and preserved so as to not destroy the details.* (p. 1)

The Security and Exchange Commission rule for SOX Section 404 mandated that a company's internal control over financial reporting should be based upon a recognized internal control framework. The SEC recommends COSO as the model of choice for ensuring that proper internal controls are in place.

The Act called for the formation of a powerful *Public Company Accounting Oversight Board* (PCAOB). It significantly alters corporate and accounting requirements in six important areas: (1) auditor oversight, (2) auditor independence, (3) corporate responsibility, (4) financial disclosures, (5) analyst conflicts of interest, and (6) civil and criminal penalties for fraud and document destruction (Anderson & Black, 2002).

Auditor oversight has often been cited as a common source of error in accounting records. This act does not allow companies to get away with such mistakes. Auditor involvement at every stage of assessment of business effectiveness is mandatory according to SOX. Auditors' independence has also been emphasized in this act. Companies should check the internal controls and report as part of compliance.

Firms must be able to produce unaltered e-records and other documents in a timely manner when summoned by PCAOB (Patzakis, 2003).

The corporation is responsible for assuring that ethical practices are followed by the corporation and that information shared with outsiders is accurate and trustworthy (Coates, 2003). The financial disclosures made by companies should be checked, verified by auditors, and attested by top management. Endorsement of the reports by top management is a unique feature of this act, and this exercise is intended to increase investor confidence in the financial reports of the company. Any endeavor to manipulate data or transactions by analysts, therefore, is under the direct scrutiny of top management. This reduces analysts' conflict of interests and they are forced to present correct and accurate picture of the company's finances. Any negligence in financial reporting could result in criminal or civil charges against the company. This helps to ensures ethical practices.

Sarbanes-Oxley Sections Impacting IT

Internal Controls: Title III–Corporate Responsibility

Section 302. Corporate Responsibility for Financial Reports applies to financial statements and related financial information. It requires CEOs and CFOs to certify ("sign") the following in each annual and quarterly report filed with the SEC:

• that the report has been reviewed; and

• that, to the best of their knowledge, the report does not contain an untrue statement or omit any material fact.

This means that the report fairly presents the issuer's financial condition and results of operation. The CEOs are responsible for establishing and maintaining internal controls and have designed *disclosure control procedures* (DCP) in such a way that all material information relating to the issuer and its consolidated subsidiaries is made known to them during the reporting period. The section ensures that the CEOs have evaluated the effectiveness of internal DCP within the 90 days prior to the report and that the report reflects their conclusions about the effectiveness their DCP as of that date.

It implies that they have disclosed to the company's auditors and to the audit committee all significant deficiencies in the design or operation of internal controls, as well as any fraud–whether or not material–that involve management or other employees who have a significant role in the issuer's internal controls. It also implies that there have been no significant changes in internal controls that could affect statements in the future. If there are such changes, then the type and importance of such changes must be reported (Coffee, 2002).

Internal Controls: Title IV–Enhanced Financial Disclosures

Section 401. Disclosures in Periodic Reports requires the company to disclose "all material off-balance sheet transactions, arrangements, obligations (including contingent obligations) and other relationships" that might have a "material current or future effect" on the financial health of the company. As per this section, each annual report of the company must include management's opinion regarding the effectiveness of the issuer's internal control procedures and a description of management's role in establishing and maintaining those procedures.

Section 401 restricts the use of pro forma information. This section states that information contained in a public company's reports must be "presented in a manner that reconciles it with the financial condition and results of operations of the issuer under generally accepted accounting principles."

Section 404. Management Assessment of Internal Controls is another primary thrust of SOX. Most companies focus on Section 404 because it requires that CEOs and CFOs certify the effectiveness of the financial controls they have in place (Hoffman, 2003). It requires a new disclosure document referred to as an *internal control report*. An internal control report, which is also included in every annual report, must "state the responsibility of management for establishing and maintaining an adequate internal control structure and procedures for financial reporting" [Section 404(a)]. Management assessment of "the effectiveness of the internal control structure and procedures of the issuer for financial reporting," which the audit firm must "attest to and report on" [Section 404(b)], should also be included.

Section 404 addresses the design and operational effectiveness of financial reporting controls of the organization by making it mandatory that internal control processes, procedures, and practices must be documented and tested. The SEC maintains that the purpose of Section 404 is to provide investors and others with reasonable assurance that companies have designed processes to help ensure that transactions are properly authorized, recorded, and reported (Gallagher, 2003), and that assets are safeguarded against unauthorized or improper use. As such, the intent of Section 404 is to prevent fraud and demonstrate adequate control.

Section 409. Real Time Issuer Disclosures requires companies to disclose any event that may have a material impact on their financial condition or operations on a "rapid and current basis." While what is meant by *timely* has yet to be defined, it might be as soon as 48 hours after an event. This section states that disclosure may need to "include trend or qualitative information and graphic presentations, as the Commission determines . . . is necessary or useful for the protection of investors and in the public interest."

Corporate Governance: Title IX–White Collar Crime Penalty Enhancements

Section 906. Corporate Responsibility for Financial Reports holds CEOs, CFOs, and corporate directors both accountable and liable for the accuracy of financial disclosures. In contrast to Section 302, Section 906 penalties apply only if the officer knows of the problem or error when certifying a report. According to this section, certifying a report while being knowledgeable that it does not meet the requirements of this section results in a fine of up to $1,000,000, or imprisonment for not more than 10 years, or both. Willfully certifying a statement not meeting the requirements results in a fine of up to $5,000,000, or imprisonment of not more than 20 years, or both.

Fraud and Records Retention: Title VIII – Corporate and Criminal Fraud Accountability

Section 802. Criminal Penalties for Altering Documents applies to the retention and protection of corporate audit documents and related records, including e-records. This section establishes new criminal penalties for document alteration and destruction. Section 802 imposes a fine and/or imprisonment of up to 10 years for noncompliance of any accountant who conducts an audit of a publicly traded company. Auditors are required to maintain all audit and review work papers for at least five years.

Procedures for preserving e-records that comply with SOX requirements are needed since they will be subject to greater scrutiny. This legislation demands proper e-records management, particularly when they could be used for electronic evidence

.

Emergent Issues

SOX came into effect in 2004, with the larger companies having to show compliance by November 2004. The issues that arise from enactment of the law are manifold. The primary challenge to IT companies today is driven by SOX compliance. The Act is exerting tremendous pressure on IT organizations to attest to the control of IT processes related to financial reporting. Only recently has the daunting scope of these requirements become apparent to them, and a majority of IT organizations are struggling to cope with these overwhelming compliance demands. These new responsibilities add significant effort to the already daunting IT business management challenges — pressure on IT to drive more business value, lower costs, and maintain high-service levels. The IT approach to SOX compliance could typically include the following actions:

- The IT division of the company should work with the CFO or Sarbanes Steering Committee to understand the specific business processes determined to be within Sarbanes' scope.

- The IT team should identify the related computerized applications directly impacting the business processes. This would lead to a proper documentation of the processes.

- Management should also understand the control requirements of the firm's external financial attestation auditors on what is called the "acceptable IT general controls."

- IT managers should identify the specific IT general control components that impact the significant computerized applications (i.e., security).

- Management should identify and document those control techniques that achieve the objectives of the IT general controls components.

- The IT division should identify deficiencies in the control environment and/or compensating controls on the business process end to enhance the control environment as needed.

- IT managers should test the IT controls identified to ensure their functionality and operating effectiveness.

The requirements of the act, such as enhanced disclosure of off-balance sheet items and necessity for companies to present pro forma "operating" earnings reconciled to GAAP earnings, are necessary steps toward eliminating some of the techniques that unscrupulous corporate executives have used to mislead investors. While useful, these provisions are only patching holes in the financial reporting process rather than dealing with any underlying structural issues. The commitment of the directors to the financial issues of the company in ways that are ethical and moral is important for the success of SOX.

The act commissions the study of potential impact of a shift from rules-based to principles-based accounting standards. Rules-based accounting standards are filled with specific details in an attempt to address as many potential contingencies as possible. This has made standards longer and more complex. Under these standards, there is provision for arbitrary criteria for accounting treatments that allows companies to structure transactions to circumvent unfavorable reporting. Thus companies can present financial reports in a way desirable to them.

Principles-based accounting is inherently more flexible. It provides a conceptual basis for accountants to follow instead of a list of detailed rules. It is expected that it would better enable financial reporting to evolve and keep pace with new financial instruments and techniques. It would require more judgment calls by auditors and management, as it is well known that investors' desire for a more consistent application of accounting principals is what led to the proliferation of transaction-oriented rules to provide implementation guidance to management. GAAP is a principles-based system. In addition, principles-based accounting standards allow accountants to apply professional judgment in assessing the substance of a transaction. This approach is substantially different from the "checkbox" approach common in rules-based accounting standards.

The Sarbanes-Oxley Act will create new avenues of concern for organizations having to cope with pressures to improve the quality of information for the sake of compliance in the coming years. The tools for automatic control mapping, evaluating online and real-time control functioning will greatly facilitate compliance. It will fuel further research to meet the demands of the law. There are numerous research issues emerging from these challenges, including behavioral factors for facilitating collaborative policy development and technological factors for automating data flows (Volonino et al., 2004). Some of these avenues could be: process simplification and standardization, data simplification and standardization, technology standardization and integration. The Act can impact various aspects of IT, and thus many emergent issues would have to be dealt with as the understanding of the legislation improves with time. Some of the areas that would need attention in future by the companies could be:

- **Data integrity and electronic records retention policy:** SOX links e-record management accountability between internal and external record managers in a supply-chain fashion — as electronic data interchange (EDI) and e-commerce link data, documents, and records in commercial transactions. "This chain-of-accountability imposes several requirements" (Volonino et al., 2004, p. 6). Some of these responsibilities could be deployment of e-record storage methods to make sure that organizational knowledge is documented and preserved. The companies are required to develop more reliable and verifiable means for e-record management and retrieval techniques than are available today. This could be a potential area of concern for companies in future.

- **Integrity of communications:** In order for the compliance objectives to be effective, there has to be a better way of communicating faster and reliably through electronic medium. This could help in faster reporting of problems in data security, thus helping to prevent future frauds. Research into how to reduce exposure of critical data and how to prepare to respond to e-record requests (or demands) by the oversight board is urgently needed. This area needs further exploration.

- **Process/work flows:** Real-time update of information could be a challenge for the companies. Recording each and every transaction and retrieving the information at a short notice would need a lot of system planning and reorganizing. Creating reports from transactions and showing quarterly compliance is also a daunting task. Thus interdependencies among transactions and processes (including where transactions start and stop) must be identified. Technologies are needed to specify what can go wrong in data processing, where controls are needed, how to prevent and detect control problems, and who is responsible for monitoring the controls. Section 404 of the Act requires organizations to test and document processes and procedures designed to prevent fraud and demonstrate adequate control. This area needs future attention from companies showing compliance.

- **Disaster recovery practices and security policies:** Information security assurance policies in companies would be a critical area to look into in the future. Disaster recovery policies need to be made transparent to outsiders who can become potential stakeholders of the company. To show compliance, companies need to develop and deploy effective information security threat response and investigation policies. Those policies will require collaboration between corporate IT security teams and IT auditors. Methods to identify policy requirements and facilitate collaboration need to be devised.

- **Improved anti-fraud techniques across industries:** Data integrity has been a main thrust of SOX. Systems employed to control, record, and report data have to ensure that no manipulation has been done. New systems to meet this demand have to be developed. "Data passed from events and transactions to financial statements must be controlled — and preserved so as not to destroy the details essential for fraud detection" (Volonino et al., 2004, p. 6). In order to detect fraud, the computer systems of the company must be capable of linking both the sales estimates and sales reality to the financial function. If we simply look at historic accounting information, it will be difficult to detect fraud, much less detect it before another financial report is issued. Methods for IS integration and fraud detection are needed, as well as an understanding of the nature and warning signs of fraud. This could be a potential area of concern and has to be addressed by the corporations.

- **Rigorous checking for effectiveness of internal controls:** Managers should address the design and operating effectiveness of internal controls. In doing so, internal controls will be tested. Top management should encourage this practice. The nature of testing that has to be done to check the effectiveness of internal controls depends on the computer-based systems of the company and type of control being validated. It is important to note that testing must be done to establish a basis for management's conclusion. Simply asking whether controls are adequate is not sufficient. This suggests an active role for senior management in evaluating IT and audit processes. Involvement of top management will revive research into systems to facilitate horizontal and vertical communication throughout the organization.

- **Cost of compliance:** The cost of compliance to companies is overwhelming. In an annual survey of compliance in IT by businesses, the estimated cost of compliance for the year 2006 is more than $6.0B, almost equal to the amount spent in 2005 which was $6.1B (Hagerty & Scott, 2005). This could be detrimental for small companies since they will be unable to justify the benefits of the act against the cost of compliance. Some of the small publicly traded companies have gone private just to avoid this cost. Besides the monetary aspects, other cost in terms of time invested by company personnel or effort (in form of traveling and explaining control areas in their branch offices all across the globe) are placing significant demands on the resources of companies. This could be a concern if the companies have to keep paying so much for compliance.

Conclusion

SOX has created challenges and set new standards for IT governance in companies. To fully comply with the law, companies will need to improve information quality to insure transparency and reliability. Investors (individual or institutional) are outsiders for the most part and can only rely on the good faith of corporate insiders for insight into effectiveness of the companies. To protect such investors, SOX attempts to legislate ethics and integrity into the public management process.

Government's determination to increase corporate responsibility has ushered in new legislation that impacts IT directly. With increased disclosures, new enforcement schemes, and emphasis on corporate accountability, SOX delivers significant reforms and places significant demands on IT. The Sarbanes-Oxley Act has the potential to reshape the role of IT in business. The role of IT governance, within the broader context of corporate governance, demands new attention and efforts on the part of the executives, shareholders, and government.

Improvement in technology to meet the requirements would be a driving factor to make the law successful. Technology, such as enterprise resource planning systems, has the potential to meet such demands. Other upcoming technologies like XML, especially the XBRL and XBRL-GL derivatives, could provide firms with the possibility of cost-efficient, online, real-time systems (Alles, Kogan, & Vasarhelyi, 2004). These facilities could help in posting the financial statements on the Web as soon as they are completed. The last recorded corporate transactions, contracts, and commitments in process could be made available to public through the company's Web site even prior to their realization in traditional accounting.

Compliance with legislations like SOX would appear to be a necessary condition for corporate responsibility, but it is insufficient. Public policy merely addresses the manifestations of corporate social pathology. Top executives will have to set an example to other employees in the company by sticking to good corporate practices. A law cannot make people moral or ethical in behavior.

In today's scenario, the organizational dynamics have reasonably changed from what they were even 20-25 years ago, and the dependency of the organizations on technology has been accelerating. Management practices have to be flexible in terms adopting new technologies. Making use of new technologies for corporate governance practices is cost effective for the companies in the long run. Currently, there is much apprehension about this legislation and it would not be surprising if SOX, like many other complicated laws, has unforeseen results that will dampen the spirit of introducing this law (Alles et al., 2004).

Sarbanes-Oxley was created to restore investor confidence in public markets. This Act has literally rewritten the rules for accountability, disclosure, and reporting of good corporate governance. Ethical practices are no longer optional. The responsibility of making this Act a success lies with the managers and auditors of each and every firm. Such legislation can act as a watchdog, but morality cannot be legislated.

References

Ackman, D. (2002, January 15). Enron the incredible. *Forbes.com*. Retrieved February 22, 2004, from http://www.forbes.com/2002/01/15/0115enron_print.html

Agrawal, A., & Chadha, S. (2004). Corporate governance and accounting scandals. AFA 2004 San Diego Meetings. *Journal of Law and Economics* (forthcoming 2005).

Alles, M., Kogan, A., & Vasarhelyi, M. (2004). The law of unintended consequences? Assessing the costs, benefits and outcomes of the Sarbanes-Oxley Act. *Information Systems Control Journal, 1*, 17-20.

Anantha, S. (2004). Auditing governance in ERP projects. *Information Systems Control Journal,* (2), 19.

Anderson, P. J., & Black, A. R. (2002, October 23). Accountants' liability after Enron. *S&P's: The Review of Securities & Commodities Regulation, 35*(18), 227.

Coates, B. E. (2003). Rogue corporations, corporate rogues & ethics compliance: The Sarbanes-Oxley Act, 2002. *Public Administration and Management, 8*(3), 164-185.

Gallagher, S. (2003, August 1). Gotcha! Complying with financial regulations. *Baseline Magazine*. Retrieved November 29, 2005, from http://www.baselinemag.com/article2/0,3959,1211224,00.asp

General Masters, Inc. (2004). *COSO framework and Sarbanes Oxley* [Electronic Version]. Retrieved July 2, 2005, from http://www.gmasterinc.com/coso/cosomain.htm

Haes, S., & Grembergen, V. (2004). IT Governance and its mechanisms. *Information Systems Control Journal, 1*.

Hagerty, J., & Scott, F. (2005). SOX spending for 2006 to exceed $6B. *AMR Research*. Retrieved November 29, 2005, from http://www.amrresearch.com/content/view.asp?pmillid=18967

Hoffman, T. (2003). Users struggle to pinpoint IT costs of Sarbanes-Oxley compliance. *Computerworld,* December 1. Retrieved November 29, 2005, from http://www.computerworld.com/managementtopics/management/itspending/story/0,10801,87613,00.html

Information Systems Audit and Control Association (ISACA)(2004). *CISA Review Manual, 2004 Edition.* Rolling Meadows, IL: ISACA.

La Porta, R. et al. (2000). Investor protection and corporate governance. *Journal of Financial Economics*, 58, 3-27.

Nash, E. (2003, November 7). Compliance must be top of your agenda. *Computing,* 33.

Organisation for Economic Cooperation and Development (OECD) (2004). *Principles of corporate governance.* Paris: Organisation for Economic Cooperation and Development.

Patzakis, J. (2003, Spring). New accounting reform laws push for technology-based document retention practices. *International Journal of Digital Evidence, 2*(1), 1-8.

Ramos, M. (2004, September/October). Just how effective is your internal control? *The Journal of Corporate Accounting and Finance*, 29-33.

Steinberg, R., & Tanki, F. (1993). Internal control-integrated framework: A landmark study. *The CPA Journal Online.* Retrieved November 29, 2005, from http://www.nysscpa.org/cpajournal/old/14465853.htm

Volonino, L., Kermis, G., & Gessner, G. (2004, August 5-8). Sarbanes-Oxley links IT to corporate compliance. In *Proceedings of the Tenth Americas Conference on Information Systems.* New York: Association for Information Systems.

Chapter VI

A Security Blueprint for E-Business Applications

Jun Du, Tianjin University, China

Yuan-Yuan Jiao, Nankai University, China

Jianxin (Roger) Jiao, Nanyang Technological University, Singapore

Abstract

This chapter develops a security blueprint for an e-business environment taking advantage of the three-tiered e-business architecture. This security blueprint suggests best practices in general. It involves (1) security control by layers — from physical access, to network communication, to operating systems, to applications, and (2) different stages of the management process, including planning, deployment, administration, and auditing. Also reported is a case study of the implementation of the proposed security blueprint in a Singapore multinational corporation. Such issues as security control analysis, management process analysis, and cost-benefits analysis are discussed in detail.

Introduction

The Internet has created huge opportunities for new companies and new business for those established organizations formerly bound by a saturated market. E-business is defined as the conduction of business with the assistance of telecommunications and telecommunication-based tools, mainly over the Internet (Clarke 1999), including *busi-*

ness-to-business (B2B), *business-to-customer* (B2C), and intra-organizational commerce (Siau & Davis, 2000). Security is essential and very critical to e-business applications. The importance of information privacy to e-business has been recognized for some time (Agre & Rotenberg, 1997; Bingi, Mir, & Khamalah, 2000; Lichtenstein & Swatman, 2001), with the Gartner Group (2002) nominating information privacy as the greatest impediment to consumer-based e-business through 2006.

However, when building up a secure environment for e-business applications, there are no industry standards for people to follow on their design or implementation jobs. All that can be referred is from the security product manufacturers and system integrators. The truth is that security systems can only provide a certain level of protection to an e-business environment. Therefore, security protection must be in place at different layers, and the management process must be carried out at different stages. From the authors' viewpoint, security is not a by-product; it is a combination of managing technologies and security processes, rather than "put the firewall here, put the intrusion detection system there."

This chapter develops a security blueprint for a typical e-business environment based on the discussion of the major components in three-tiered e-business architecture. This security blueprint includes general security control layered from physical access, network communication, operating system, to application; and security management processes staged from planning, deployment, administration, to auditing.

Typical E-Business Environment

Originally, business computing was carried out as a point task, without any real concept of a networked operation. All the business processes are run on a single platform or single tier. Later, many systems evolved to a two-tiered approach, also known as client/server architecture, where most of the business process runs on the server and the client is mainly concerned with presentation and only holds a limited amount of user-specific data. Today, more and more e-business applications are deployed as a three-tiered architecture owing to its increased performance, flexibility, maintainability, reusability, and scalability, while hiding the complexity of distributed processing from the user. After this, things get more complicated, with additional applications running in different tiers, which is so-called multi-tiered architecture. However, multi-tiered architectures have arisen not necessarily because great thought was given to this choice of architecture; in truth, they are more the result of trying to make the best of what was there.

This section will describe a typical three-tier e-business environment and identify the major components from system architecture perspectives.

Three-Tier E-Business Architecture

When it comes to an e-business environment, usually, these three tiers (layers) can be described as the *presentation* layer, *business* logic layer, and *data* layer. These tiers are

Figure 1. A typical e-business environment

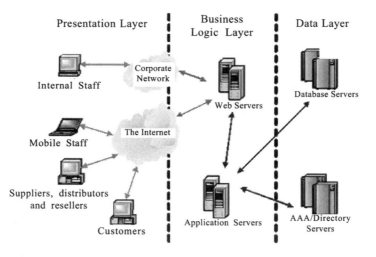

logical, not physical. One machine can run several business tiers and tiers can be distributed across several machines. A typical three-tiered e-business architecture is shown in Figure. 1.

Major Components in an E-Business Environment

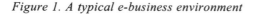

In the three-tiered e-business architecture, the major components can be identified as a Web browser, a Web server, an application server, a database server, an AAA/directory service, a corporate network, and the Internet, as illustrated in Figure 2.

Figure 2. Major components in an e-business environment

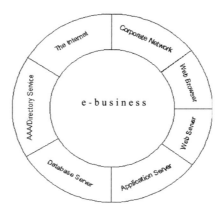

A Security Blueprint

A secure e-business environment must prevent most attacks from successfully affecting valuable e-business resources. While being secure, the e-business environment must continue to provide critical services that users expect. Proper security and good functionality can be provided at the same time. A secure e-business environment must also be resilient and scalable.

This section will develop a security blueprint for an e-business environment based on a three-tiered e-business architecture and major components described in the previous section.

Security Blueprint Overview

This security blueprint emulates as closely as possible the functional requirements of the typical e-business environment discussed in the previous section, which can help people to build or maintain a secure e-business environment for e-business applications.

As illustrated in Figure 3, this security blueprint consists of four security control layers, starting from physical access, network communication, operating system, to application. As part of this security blueprint, to maintain a secure e-business environment, the major security management processes included and staged are planning, deployment, administration, and auditing.

Security Control Layers

As part of the security blueprint for e-business environment, the security control layers cover all major components identified in a typical three-tiered e-business environment,

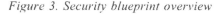

Figure 3. Security blueprint overview

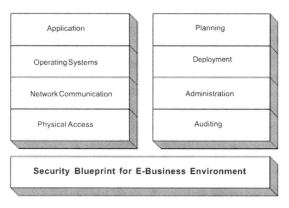

including physical access, network communication, operating system, and application layer.

Physical Access Layer

The security control for physical access is an extremely important part of keeping all sensitive devices and data secure in an e-business environment. In the typical e-business environment discussed previously, all components of the business logic layer and data layer are considered as critical devices from a security perspective, as illustrated in the Table 1. It is necessary to put all critical devices into a separate space (data center, computer room, and even server racks) and maintain very strict control over who can enter it, then use card key or keypad systems, log books, and human security to limit unauthorized access.

Network Communication Layer

The corporate network and the Internet are the major components that fall into this layer, as illustrated in Table 1. These components perform specific roles in an e-business environment, and thus they have specific security requirements. Network attacks are among the most difficult attacks to deal with because they typically take advantage of an intrinsic characteristic of the way the corporate network operates. Hence, most security technologies are applied at this layer to analyze the network traffic and eliminate malicious threats, including router access control, switch access control, firewall, intrusion detection system, virus detection system, virtual private network, and secure sockets layer.

Operating System Layer

As the most likely target during an attack, the operating system layer presents some of the most difficult challenges in an e-business environment from a security perspective. In a typical e-business environment, the major components, such as the Web browser, Web server, application server, database server, and AAA/directory service, are all running on top of various operating systems like Unix, Linux, Windows, and the like, as illustrated in the Table 1.

Meanwhile, for various reasons, these operating systems provide strong functionality to support different application services while numerous system holes or bugs remain. Because of this vulnerability, operating systems are the most frequently attacked components in an e-business environment.

To secure these operating systems, careful attention must be paid to each of the components in the e-business environment. Here are two important guidelines to reinforce operating system layer: (1) keep any operating system up-to-date with the latest patches, fixes, and so forth; and (2) lock down any operating system by disabling unwanted service.

Table 1. Major components in security control layers

Components / Layers	Web Browser	Web Server	Application Server	Database Server	AAA/ Directory Service	Corporate Network	Internet
Physical Access Layer		✓	✓	✓	✓	✓	
Network Communication Layer						✓	✓
Operating System Layer	✓	✓	✓	✓	✓		
Application Layer	✓	✓	✓	✓	✓		

Application Layer

Most components of a typical e-business environment, such as a Web browser, Web server, application server, database server, and AAA/directory service, fall into this layer, as illustrated in the Table 1.

As we know, applications are coded by human beings (mostly) and, as such, are subject to numerous errors. These errors can be benign (e.g., an error that causes a document to print incorrectly) or malignant (e.g., an error that makes the credit card numbers on a database server available via an anonymous FTP). It is the malignant problems, as well as other more general security vulnerabilities, that need careful attention. Similar to the operating system layer, care needs to be taken to ensure that all applications within an e-business environment are up-to-date with the latest security fixes.

Management Process Stages

To maintain a secure e-business environment, numerous security management processes of the daily operations of e-businesses are involved. As part of the security blueprint for an e-business environment, the management processes have been organized into four stages, planning, deployment, administration, and auditing.

Planning Stage

The most important stage of security management is planning. It is not possible to plan for security, unless a full risk assessment has been performed. Security planning involves three processes: *asset identification*, *risk assessment*, and *action planning*, as illustrated in Figure 4.

Asset identification is used to identify all the targets of the actual e-business environment. Risk assessment is used to analyze the risks for each asset and determine the category of the cause of the risk (natural disaster risk, intentional risk, or unintentional

Figure 4. Processes at the planning stage

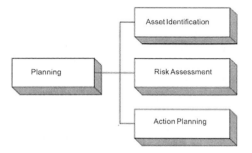

Figure 5. Processes at the deployment stage

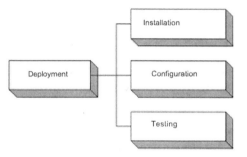

risk). Action planning is used to describe the security guidelines and present a security architecture using the enabling security technologies.

Deployment Stage

The deployment stage is relatively simpler than the planning stage. At this stage, the action plan developed at planning stage will be implemented accordingly. This stage includes three key processes: *installation, configuration,* and *testing,* as illustrated in Figure 5.

Administration Stage

After the deployment stage, a "secure" e-business environment has been built. However, it is not really secure without a proper security administration. This is true because

Figure 6. Processes at the administration stage

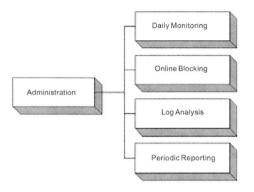

Figure 7. Processes at the auditing stage

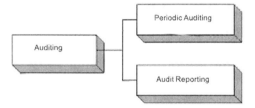

most assets need to be maintained daily to ensure that they have no proven vulnerabilities. In addition, security systems (such as firewall, IDS, antivirus) keep generating alerts, events, and logs that require adminito strators take necessary actions.

The administration layer consists of four major processes, including *daily monitoring*, *online blocking*, *log analysis*, and *periodic reporting*, as illustrated in Figure 6. These processes are not only applied to security systems, but also to other assets in the actual e-business environment.

Auditing Stage

The auditing stage provides the formal examination and review of the established e-business environment. This layer contains two major processes, *periodic auditing* and *audit reporting*, as illustrated in Figure 7. These processes can be carried on by either internal staff or external parties. In an e-business environment, an annual security audit conducted by external party is recommended.

Case Study

Company XYZ, with its operational headquarters in Singapore and branch offices in the U.S., Japan, India, Thailand, Malaysia, and Hong Kong, is a telecommunications service provider that provides end-to-end networking and managed services to *multinational corporations* (MNC) and *small and medium enterprises* (SME) across Asia.

The company has *points-of-presence* (POP) located in 17 cities across 14 countries. Technical support is available 24 hours a day and 7 days a week. The company has built an *Internet data center* (iDC) in Singapore to provide e-business hosting services as part of its managed services. Of course, its own e-business applications, such as *customer portal system*, *billing system*, and *trouble ticketing system*, are running on this iDC as well.

This section will discuss the applicability of the developed security blueprint using the Singapore-based MNC company as a case study.

Established E-Business Environment

An Internet data center is defined as a service provider offering server outsourcing, hosting, and collocation services, as well as IP and broadband connectivity, *virtual private networks* (VPNs), and other network and transport services. It needs to be physically secure against physical intrusions and equipped with fire suppression, uninterrupted power supply, and disaster recovery systems.

As a telcom provider and managed services provider, the company's iDC has a complex architecture and multiple functions. However, the authors just intend to discuss the environment related to e-business hosting service in this chapter. The simplified e-business environment is shown in Figure 8. This established e-business environment is mainly made up of core routers (two Cisco 7513 routers), distribution switches (two Cisco Catalyst 6509 switches), firewalls, access switches, and other necessary devices. All those critical devices are configured as duplex to provide redundancy to ensure the continuous operations of e-business applications.

The corporate LAN of this company is connected into distribution switches, thus allowing internal staff to access the company's e-business applications such as the customer portal, billing system, and trouble ticketing system for daily jobs. Putting these e-business applications into iDC will take advantage of the established e-business environment while saving money on the security protection for the corporate network.

Security Control Analysis

Applying security control to the e-business environment is critical for building a trust relationship between e-business owners and the company.

Figure 8. A case study for security blueprint

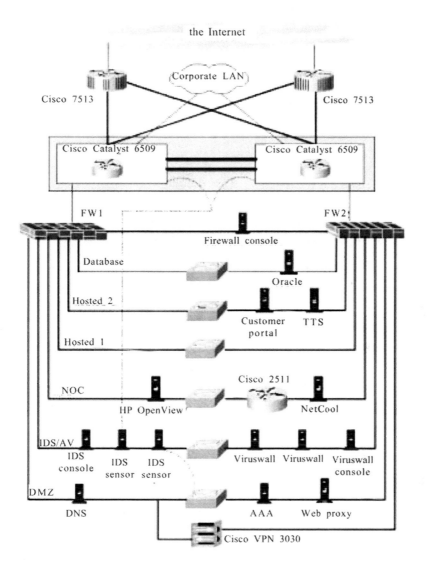

Physical Access Layer

In order to prevent unauthorized people from getting into the company's iDC, which keeps all the network devices, application servers and important data, the company has implemented very strict physical access control systems, including biometrics HandKey II system, access card control system, lifetime CCTV recorder system, multi-level password restriction, centralized UPS system, and standby power generator. Besides these systems, the iDC is also monitored by on-shift engineers all the time. In addition, all equipment (network devices and hosts) are put into server racks and locked, while all network cables are put under the floating floor or within server racks. Authorized personnel must sign in and out at memo books to obtain the rack keys.

Additionally, to protect the data backup against fire, theft, and other natural risks, the company has an agreement with another managed service provider for off-site backup, which allows both companies to store data backup media for each other. The data backup media will be duplicated monthly.

Network Communication Layer

As most attacks come from the Internet and corporate network, the company has employed industry-standard security systems in place to eliminate risks at the network communication layer. These include firewall cluster, gateway antivirus cluster, *intrusion detection system* (IDS), AAA system, reverse Telnet access, and VPN access. In addition to the security systems, all network devices including routers and switches are locked down, and *access control list* (ACL) is applied for better security control.

All network devices and hosts are also configured to send *simple network management protocol* (SNMP) traps and logs to HP OpenView and NetCool systems for monitoring purpose. HP OpenView shows a graphic diagram of the health status of the e-business environment, while NetCool collects all logs and SNMP traps from network devices and hosts. On-shift engineers keep monitoring this information to ensure the network health and security protection is in place.

Operating System Layer

The company uses various operating systems to implement its services, such as SUN Solaris, HP-UX, and Windows NT/2000. As required by the corporate security policy, all operating systems must be hardened and kept updated with the latest security patches from their manufacturers.

Application Layer

The security control for this layer is mainly to keep security patches and service packs for commercial applications up-to-date (for example, CheckPoint Firewall-1 service pack 6, Radiator RADIUS patches, virus pattern for TrendMicro InterScan Viruswall, attack signature for RealSecure IDS, etc.).

For customized e-business applications, such as a customer portal system, billing system, and trouble ticketing system, the software development team is responsible to review program logics and coding to avoid any system holes and backdoors.

Management Processes Analysis

In addition to the four layers of security control implemented at iDC, the company has also installed security management processes to continuously maintain a secure e-business environment. A security team has been formed by the engineers from different departments (IT, network operations, network planning, and software development) and is led by a security specialist who reports directly to the *chief technology officer* (CTO).

This section discusses the related security management processes in the established e-business environment using a real e-business application — a Web-based *trouble ticketing system* (TTS).

The TTS enables customers to report fault and check status online, and allows engineers to enter the troubleshooting progress and sales to understand the troubleshooting procedure. It couples with the customer portal and billing system to provide a single-point solution to corporate customers. The TTS consists of one Web server, one application server, and one database server. Both the Web server and the application server are running at one physical server box, while the database server is running at another server box.

Planning Stage

Three processes are executed at this stage, including asset identification, risk assessment, and action planning.

When running the asset identification process, the major assets for TTS will be identified as follows: Web and application server, database server, and TTS data.

Following the risk assessment process, the major risks to those identified assets are listed as follows: physical attack to the server boxes and network devices; network attack to the operating systems, Web server, application server, database server, and TTS application; and attack or damage to the TTS data either physical or remotely.

Once the above asset and risks have been identified, the following actions are developed to eliminate those risks to the assets: (1) physically locate those server boxes and network devices into iDC and lock them to server racks; (2) deploy the Web and application server boxes according to the database segment; (3) utilize the firewall cluster to block most remote attacks with certain firewall policies; (4) utilize each IDS sensor located at distribution switches to monitor potential attacks and intruders; (5) utilize the gateway antivirus cluster to scan and clean viruses contained in HTTP traffic; (6) lock down the operating system for Web and application server boxes and allow only Web and application services to run; (7) lock down the operating system for the database server boxes and allow only database services to run; (8) examine the TTS program code to prevent any system holes and back doors.

Deployment Stage

Following the action planning, the installation process will be carried out to setup physically all server boxes and access switches if any, and install the operation system and software such as Web server, application server, oracle server, and TTS application. The configuration process will go through the lock-down procedures for operation system and application software, and tunes up parameters for better performance. Sometimes, since misconfiguration may cause more risks and even bring the server down and crash application services, the testing process will ensure that deployment is in compliance with the action plan.

Administration Stage

The security team coupled with the on-shift operation team carries out all processes defined at this stage at any time. Daily monitoring includes the following tasks: network diagram view from HP OpenView, SNMP traps from NetCool, firewall console, IDS console, antivirus console, and syslog window.

Online blocking will be carried out once a remote attack has been identified. The security team will do the log analysis every day and generate security reports every week and every month.

Auditing Stage

The security team will carry out an internal audit every half year to determine the effectiveness of existing security controls, watch for system misuse or abuse by users, verify compliance with corporate security policies, validate that documented procedures are followed, and so on. An audit report will be generated after the auditing and given to management for review and further action.

Table 2. Cost analysis for e-business environment

Cost (SG$)	Acquisition & implementation	Operation	Ongoing changes & growth	Total	% of Total
IDC features	280K	12K	0	292K	18%
Security systems	350K	36K	15K	401K	25%
Network & communication	420K	168K	27K	615K	39%
Maintenance staff	0	240K	50K	290K	18%
Total	1050K	456K	92K	1598K	-
% of Total	65%	29%	6%	-	100%

Cost-Benefit Analysis

The cost of building a secure e-business environment involves not only the one-time hardware/software/project expenses but also the recurring cost for users, operations, and ongoing changes. For the company's established e-business environment, the cost analysis can be done via four areas, including iDC features, security systems, network and communications, and maintenance staff.

The physical construction, including a floating floor, CCTV camera system, biometrics handkey system, server racks, UPS, and power generator, together form the iDC features.

Security systems consist of the firewall cluster, gateway antivirus cluster, IDS console and sensors, Cisco VPN concentrator, and various monitoring and logging systems.

Network and communication cost refers to the expense of the Cisco router 7513, Cisco switch 6509, network cabling, Internet bandwidth subscription, and access switches for individual network segments behind the firewall cluster.

Maintenance staff means internal skilled manpower needed to maintain this established e-business environment for fulfilling operation and security requirements. This mainly refers to the company's security team and on-shift operation engineer team.

In this study, the acquisition and implementation cost is a one-time charge and takes a very huge percentage (65%), while expenses for operation costs and ongoing changes and growth are estimated on an annual basis, assuming there are no big changes required on the e-business environment. Table 2 shows the summarized implementation cost and other estimated costs.

Although the cost may be high to SMEs, it is indeed cost-effective for large organizations and e-business providers, due to the great benefits obtained from the secure e-business environment. These benefits include shared bandwidth, shared security protection, scalability, reliability, and total ownership cost saving.

Conclusion

Building a secure e-business environment is very critical to e-business applications. The chapter develops a security blueprint for an e-business environment based on the analysis of a three-tiered architecture and provides general best practices for companies to secure their e-business environments. Also discussed is the applicability of this security blueprint based on the case study of a Singapore-based MNC. This case study shows that the security blueprint for e-business environment is suitable and cost-effective in particular for large companies like *multi-national corporations* (MNC).

References

Agre, P. E., & Rotenberg, M. (1997). *Technology and privacy: The new landscape.* Cambridge, MA: MIT Press.

Bingi, P., Mir, A., & Khamalah, J. (2000). The challenges facing global e-commerce. *Information Systems Management, 17*(4), 26-34.

Clarke, R. (1999). *Electronic commerce definition.* Retrieved July 30, 2004, from http://www.anu.edu.au/people/Roger.Clarke/EC/ECDefns.html

Gartner Group (2002). Retrieved May 20, 2003, from http://www.zeroknowledge.com/business/default.asp

Lichtenstein, S., & Swatman, P. M. C. (2001, June 25-26). Effective management and policy in e-business security. In B. O'Keefe, C. Loebbecke, J. Gricar, A. Pucihar, & G. Lenart (Eds.), *Proceedings of Fourteenth International Bled Electronic Commerce Conference*, Bled, Slovenia. Kranj: Moderna organizacija.

Siau, K., & Davis, S. (2000). Electronic business curriculum-evolution and revolution @ the speed of innovation. *Journal of Informatics Education & Research, 2*(1), 21-28.

Chapter VII

Security Management for an E-Enterprise

Ammar Masood, Purdue University, USA

Sahra Sedigh-Ali, University of Missouri-Rolla, USA

Arif Ghafoor, Purdue University, USA

Abstract

Enterprise integration is the key enabler for transforming the collaboration among people, organization, and technology into an enterprise. Its most important objective is the transformation of a legacy operation into an e-enterprise. In an e-enterprise, the tight coupling between business process and the underlying information technology infrastructure amplifies the effect of hardware and software security failures. This accentuates the need for comprehensive security management of the infrastructure. In this chapter, the challenges posed by fulfilling myriad security requirements throughout the various stages of enterprise integration have been outlined. To better categorize these requirements, the set of security domains that comprise the security profile of the e-enterprise have been specified. The set of security metrics used to quantify various aspects of security for an e-enterprise are also identified. The chapter concludes by describing the details of the proposed security management strategy.

Introduction

Enterprise integration (EI) is the integration of people, organization, and technology in an enterprise (Fox & Gruninger, 1998). One of the objectives of EI is transforming a legacy operation into an e-enterprise, which is defined as an enterprise where business practices are tightly coupled with the underlying *information technology* (IT) infrastructure (Hoque, 2000). This coupling heightens the effect of hardware and software security failures and underscores the need for comprehensive security management of the infrastructure, including configuration management, user activity monitoring, patch management, and integration of security mechanisms (I3p, 2003).

In this chapter, the focus is on the integration problem; namely, how to integrate the diverse security mechanisms and requirements implemented at various levels of the infrastructure into a coherent framework for supporting enterprise security (I3p, 2003). The challenges posed by fulfilling myriad security requirements throughout the various stages of enterprise integration are outlined. To better categorize these requirements, the set of security domains that comprise the security profile of the e-enterprise are specified. The security policy of the e-enterprise is in turn used to determine the requirements for each functional unit.

After determining the security requirements for the identified domains, descriptions are provided for security management techniques used to ensure that these requirements are met. These techniques rely heavily on the use of software metrics, which are used to provide qualitative assessments or quantitative measurements, or both, for the software infrastructure (Fenton, 1991). Metrics provide an integral link from detailed plans at the lowest level of implementation to the highest levels of planning. Security metrics are useful in expressing the cost, benefit, and impact of security controls with respect to economic, technical, and risk perspectives (I3p, 2003). They are useful in guiding both product selection and secure composition (I3p, 2003). In providing security to an e-enterprise, metrics are used to extract information from the operational model of the

Figure 1. E-enterprise security management

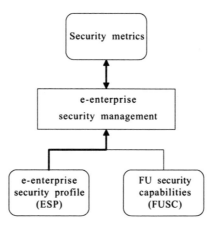

enterprise and to guide and assess security management efforts throughout the course of integration.

The processes involved in the security management of an e-enterprise are shown in Figure 1. The e-enterprise security profile and security capabilities of *functional units* (FUs) are used as input by the security management technique to ensure that every security requirement is fulfilled during all the stages of enterprise integration. As previously discussed, these techniques rely on the utilization of security metrics. These metrics are evaluated at every stage of integration to determine the security stature of the e-enterprise. Security metrics are also used to guide the integration process by guiding the selection of suitable alternatives that achieve the required security posture for the e-enterprise.

The organization of the rest of the chapter is as follows. In the beginning, the background for the chapter is provided, including a discussion of related literature in enterprise security management. The security domains used for profiling the e-enterprise are discussed in the next section and are followed by deliberations on the set of security metrics used in security management. The proposed security management methodology for enterprise integration is discussed next. Future trends in enterprise security management are subsequently described. The chapter is concluded by summarizing the findings and proposing avenues for future research.

Background

EI has been considered a key technical enabler for transforming the business processes of an organization with the goal of realizing benefits of e-business (Lam & Shankararaman, 2004). The *EI methodology* (EIM) presented in Lam and Shankararaman divides the overall EI project into six phases while considering the three key management aspects of process, deliverables and risks in each phase. The presented EIM technique is tailored toward business process-oriented integration of the enterprise and does not consider the security management problem during integration.

An approach for developing the enterprise security architecture with the aim of providing the conceptual design of the network security infrastructure, related security mechanisms, and policies and procedures has been presented by Arconati (2002). This study considers the security policy, security domains, trust levels, and tiered networks as major elements of the security architecture. The security domains help partition the enterprise network into logical entities. Trust levels allow for evaluation of the security needs of each domain, whereas tiered networks provide a model for physically partitioning the enterprise network as per the enterprise security policy. This approach, however, does not consider the integration problem.

A definition of enterprise security infrastructure, along with its objectives, has been given in Maley (1996). The infrastructure presented is of limited scope, as it only considers the infrastructure required to support public key technology in an enterprise.

Security and privacy issues in e-commerce systems have been discussed by Antón and Earp (2001). Scenario management and goal-driven assessment have been considered the key enablers in providing security and privacy support to e-commerce systems. The presented policy specification strategies are focused towards e-commerce systems and may not be directly applicable in general e-enterprise architecture.

The organizational aspects involved in the implementation of an enterprise system have been presented by Strong and Volkoff (2004). Their work presents an informal roadmap for enterprise system implementation by highlighting the key processes involved and by identifying the challenges that need to be managed in the course of implementation. Our proposed security management strategy can be coupled with the roadmap introduced in their work to provide a formal framework for enterprise integration.

The problem of secure composition of systems has been addressed in McDermid and Shi (1992); however, the only security property considered in the composition is information flow, which seriously limits the scope of this approach.

The matrix-based representation of security metrics is based on previous work by the authors, Sedigh-Ali, Ghafoor, and Paul (2002), in modeling and prediction of software test coverage.

Security Domains and the E-Enterprise Security Profile

As enterprise security is a very broad term, security domains have been used to formally classify the security attributes of an e-enterprise into multiple categories. Each security domain thus represents a logical collection of interrelated security attributes. The following security domains are used for profiling the security of an e-enterprise: *auditing*, *authentication*, *access control*, *cryptography*, *system protection*, *intrusion detection*, and *perimeter protection*. Each will be discussed separately.

Auditing

The security of information systems requires the ability to trace all actions on sensitive objects back to the subjects originating these actions. This is accomplished by ensuring that all requisite security-related information is properly logged. Auditing is defined as the analysis of log records, with the goal of presenting information about the system in a clear and understandable manner (Bishop, 2002). Auditing seeks to establish accountability for all security-related events, which can be helpful in reconstruction of larger-scale activities (I3p, 2003). The strength of auditing mechanisms depends upon various factors, such as the extent of logged data, analysis algorithms, and protection of the audit trail. Auditing requirements are usually application-dependent; for example, an application such as an electronic funds transfer, which requires strong controls for access to sensitive objects, would prefer to log a greater volume of data and have stronger analysis algorithms as compared to another application, for example, an electronic library, which deals with less sensitive objects.

Authentication

By definition, "authentication is the binding of an identity to a subject" (Bishop, 2002, p. 309). Authentication mechanisms are used to verify the identity of subjects and thus ensure that the claimed identity is correct. Authentication mechanisms could be based simply on user name and passwords or can be more advanced and based on digital credentials, biometrics, or the like. The existence of separate authentication mechanisms for each individual functional unit of an enterprise may impede its transformation; thus, it may be desired to provide a single entry point to users through *single sign-on* (SSO) functionality. SSO is a mechanism whereby the single action of user authentication and authorization can permit enterprise-wide user access. The identification of subjects is more problematic in distributed as compared to centralized applications. The strength of authentication support directly impacts the security of an enterprise, as weak authentication mechanisms can allow access to sensitive information by unauthorized subjects. Authentication services are also essential to ensure proper accountability of events by the auditing mechanisms.

Access Control

The security requirements for an e-enterprise also include protection against unauthorized access to or modification of information. Access control is used to restrict access of subjects to the objects as per well-defined rules. The access control mechanisms are closely linked with authentication services as the extent of access granted to a subject is dependent on the subject's identity. Examples of different access control policies used in an enterprise are *discretionary access control* (DAC), *mandatory access control* (MAC) (Sandhu & Samarati, 1994) and *role-based access control* (RBAC) (Ferraiolo, Sandhu, Gavrila, Kuhn, & Chandramouli, 2001). In DAC, the basic premise is that subjects have ownership of objects of the system and can, at their discretion, grant or revoke access rights on the objects they own to other subjects. In MAC, the access is governed on the basis of subject and object classifications. The subjects and objects are classified based on some predefined sensitivity levels. RBAC is a more flexible approach as compared to DAC and MAC.

Cryptography

Cryptography mechanisms allow secure communication between integrating units. Cryptographic mechanisms not only help in restricting access of secure information to unauthorized subjects, but also provide support to ensure data integrity (e.g., via digital key). Cryptographic controls also allow strong association of data with its resource, thus providing support for non-repudiation. Two major cryptographic schemes in use today are symmetric (private key-based) key and asymmetric (public key-based) key schemes. The main problems in the symmetric key system are key management and key exchange, which limits the utility of such systems for distributed applications. Asymmetric key cryptography systems use a complementary pair of keys, which greatly simplifies the key management. The *Data Encryption Standard* (DES) (NBS, 1993) and *Rivest-Shamir-Adleman* (RSA) (Rivest, Shamir, & Adleman, 1978) cryptosystems are examples of symmetric key and asymmetric key systems, respectively. The cryptographic requirements of an e-enterprise depend on the sensitivity of data flow between the communicating parties; for example, communication of financial information between two units would require stronger encryption as compared to transmission of less sensitive data.

System Protection

This domain includes mechanisms that are used to protect the integrity of the system and data. They not only ensure that the system and its resources are not corrupted, but also provide support for remedying an integrity breach. System protection ensures that underlying assumptions about the security functionality of the enterprise modules always hold true. Data integrity ensures that critical data, such as passwords or digital signatures, have not been compromised and modified. Examples of mechanisms that provide system protection include virus-detection systems and mechanisms to block mobile code transfer. The degree of system protection requirements depends upon the functionality and criticality of the resources of the enterprise. As an example, within an enterprise, the system protection requirements would be stronger for a financial entity as compared to an administrative entity.

Intrusion Detection

The goal of these systems is simple — to detect intrusions. Intrusions may be determined through the identification of unexpected patterns in system usage or by monitoring a sequence of actions that can cause a breach of security. The efficiency of such systems depends on both the availability of reliable and complete system data and the effectiveness of detection techniques utilizing that data. Anomaly detection and misuse detection are two common intrusion-detection techniques. As compared to misuse detection, which requires a model of normal system usage, anomaly detection has the advantage of not requiring a priori knowledge of the system.

Perimeter Protection

Such mechanisms are used to restrict unauthorized information exchange across the logical or physical system boundary. Their primary objective is to monitor all information entering and leaving the system to ensure that information flow conforms to the defined security policy. Firewalls are the most common example of such systems. They provide protection against many types of attacks, including unauthorized internal access, compromise of authentication, unauthorized external access, spoofing, session stealing, tunneling, and flooding (Anderson, Brand, Gong, & Haigh, 1997). Two commonly used firewall technologies are application-level firewalls and filtering firewalls. The filtering

Table 1. E-enterprise security domains

Security Domain	Description
Auditing	Logging and analyzing events relevant to security
Authentication	Verifying the binding of subjects to their identity
Access Control	Allowing or preventing actions by users based on a set of criteria
Cryptography	Allowing secure communication between integrating units
System Protection	Ensuring that the system and resources are not contaminated
Intrusion Detection	Detecting events that represent attempts to breach security
Perimeter Protection	Preventing unauthorized information exchange at boundaries

firewall performs access control based only on packet attributes, as compared to the application-level firewall that also considers the contents of packets. The application-level firewall is more powerful in filtering unwanted contents, but this strength comes at the expense of increased complexity. These security domains are summarized in Table 1.

These security domains help in establishing the security profile of the e-enterprise through categorization of its security requirements for all functional units of the enterprise in terms of various security domains. In addition, they allow for documenting the existing security capabilities of the FUs. The *e-enterprise security profile* (ESP) and *FU security capabilities* (FUSC) matrices that depict this information are defined as follows.

Definition 1

The e-enterprise security profile is defined as a matrix, ESP, consisting of n + 1 rows and m columns, where:

$n = Total\ number\ of\ FUs\ requiring\ integration$

$m = Total\ number\ of\ security\ domains$

The value of ESP $[i,j]$ ($1 \leq i \leq n$, $1 \leq j \leq m$) denotes the security requirements for the ith FU of the enterprise for the jth security domain.

The $n + 1^{th}$ row depicts the security requirements for additional centralized control, if required to provide centralized security mechanisms such as single sign-on.

Definition 2

The FUs security capabilities is defined as a matrix, FUSC, consisting of n rows and m columns, where n and m are as given in Definition 1.

The value of FUSC [i, j] $(1 \leq i \leq n, 1 \leq j \leq m)$ *denotes the security capability of the ith FU of the enterprise for the jth security domain.*

The following example clarifies the difference between ESP and FUSC.

Example 1

Consider a company, ABC Co. that consists of two FUs, the *operations FU* (OFU) and the *accounting FU* (AFU). At present, both FUs incorporate independent security mechanisms to meet the company security policy. In order to better achieve its strategic goals, ABC Co. has decided to implement *business-to-business* (B2B) and *business-to-consumer* (B2C) electronic applications, for which it is required to integrate the current FUs. The integration needs to ensure that the FUs continue to interoperate and that the security requirements of the applications are met. For simplicity, we limit this discussion to the three security domains of authentication, access control and cryptography.

ABC Co. has identified the following security requirements for its FUs to support the transformation. In order to support the applications, the OFU is required to have *temporal RBAC* (TRBAC) for access control and the DES symmetric key encryption scheme for cryptography. The requirements for the AFU are temporal and context aware RBAC, that is, GTRBAC for access control and RSA public-key encryption for cryptography. Authentication support will be provided by an additional centralized *control FU* (CFU) to provide single sign-on functionality. The planned e-enterprise security profile is given as the following ESP matrix:

$$ESP = \begin{matrix} & Auth & AC & Crypto & \\ & \begin{pmatrix} null & TRBAC & DES \\ null & GTRBAC & RSA \\ SSO & null & null \end{pmatrix} & & \begin{matrix} OFU \\ AFU \\ CFU \end{matrix} \end{matrix}$$

The existing security capabilities of the FUs are given by the FUSC matrix below:

$$FUSC = \begin{matrix} & Auth & AC & Crypto & \\ & \begin{pmatrix} DS & TRBAC & DES \\ DC & MAC & DES \end{pmatrix} & & \begin{matrix} OFU \\ \overline{AFU} \end{matrix} \end{matrix}$$

In the above, DS and DC refer to digital signatures and digital certificates, respectively.

Security Metrics

Security metrics provide a framework for measuring the cost and effectiveness of complex security systems. Security improvement begins by identifying metrics that quantify various aspects of security for the e-enterprise. These metrics are then used during all stages of the enterprise integration to select suitable alternatives. The following metrics have been considered to be of particular importance in quantifying the security of an enterprise: *survivability*, *privacy*, *confidentiality*, *integrity*, *availability*, *accountability*, *reliability*, and *non-repudiation*. Each will now be discussed individually.

Survivability

Survivability is defined as the as "the capability of a system to fulfill its mission, in a timely manner, in the presence of attacks, failures, or accidents" (Ellison et al., 1997, p. 2). The survivability metric for an e-enterprise thus quantifies the degree to which it can function after disruption. It depends on the strengths of the system protection, perimeter protection, and intrusion-detection domains. An enterprise with a stronger intrusion-detection system but weak perimeter protection may be able to detect a disruption earlier, but may not be able to survive the disruption due to compromise of security-critical data. It is thus important to consider all contributing domains in quantifying the survivability attribute.

Privacy

While EI allows the enterprise to further its potential through B2C and B2B applications, it also creates a need for stronger controls to protect the privacy of individually identifiable information. Information privacy is profoundly affected by organizational functions such as e-commerce, database management, security, telecommunications, collaborative systems, and systems implementation (Earp & Payton, 2000). The privacy metric is used to quantify the extent of privacy support provided by the e-enterprise. This support directly depends upon the strengths of the authentication, access control, cryptography, system protection, and perimeter protection domains, all of which will impact the computation of the privacy metric.

Confidentiality

Confidentiality is used to quantify the degree to which the information or resources of the e-enterprise are concealed. The transformation of the enterprise heightens the need for strong protection of all such information or resources, which can now be accessed more easily via the underlying IT infrastructure. The confidentiality measure of the enterprise can differ for different types of information or resources. For example, it is more important to restrict unauthorized exposure of customer credit card information stored within the enterprise database than it is their e-mail addresses. It could be more important to hide even the existence of data for cases where the mere existence of information can jeopardize the information that needs to be protected. The confidentiality metric is evaluated as a function of the authentication, access control, and cryptography domains.

Integrity

In order to establish trust in the transformation, it is essential to ensure that the e-enterprise data or resources are not altered or destroyed in an unauthorized manner. The integrity metric is used to quantify the trustworthiness and correctness of enterprise data or resources. Integrity not only includes data integrity (trust in information content), but also includes resource integrity (trust in the source of data). Integrity is evaluated as a function of the access control, system protection, and cryptographic domains. A higher value for the integrity metric may be required for financial data as compared to maintenance data

Availability

Availability quantifies "the alternation between proper and improper service, and is often expressed as the fraction of time that a system can be used for its intended purpose during a specified period of time" (Nicol, Sanders, & Trivedi, 2004, p. 49). The transformation of the enterprise opens new avenues for attackers to disrupt operations through *denial-of-service* (DoS) attacks by compromising the underlying IT infrastructure. The availability metric measures the ability to use information or resources as desired. Its evaluation depends upon the strengths of the intrusion detection, system protection, and perimeter protection domains.

Accountability

Accountability signifies the extent to which activities in the e-enterprise are traceable to their sources. The transformation of the enterprise results in more open access to its resources, and this in turn can potentially result in increased violations of the enterprise security policy. It is therefore important to quantify the degree of available support for accountability to ensure that the enterprise is always able to maintain its stated security posture. The accountability metric captures this information as a function of the strength of the auditing domain.

Reliability

Reliability is the capability of the enterprise to perform consistently and precisely according to its security specifications. The reliability metric captures this information as the probability that the e-enterprise perform the specified operations, as per its security policy, throughout a specified period of time. The concept of system failure is central to traditional reliability theory; its analogue in reliability for security would be a security breach (Littlewood et al., 1993). The reliability metric is evaluated as a function of the system protection and perimeter protection domains.

Non-Repudiation

Non-repudiation quantifies the extent of an enterprise to accurately associate data with its resources. It thus determines the e-enterprise ability to prevent false denial of actions by users involved in data handling/processing. The transformation of the enterprise would result in increased electronic transactions between intra-enterprise FUs and inter-enterprise systems, thus intensifying the need for accurate assessment of non-repudiation. It is evaluated as a function of the authentication, auditing, and cryptographic domains.

The identified metrics would normally be expressed as a vector of attributes, where each attribute quantifies the relevant metric for a particular environment or e-enterprise subsystem. For example, if only the confidentiality metric is considered, and it is assumed that the e-enterprise has three different types of data/resources — financial, operational, and customer data, then the confidentiality metric would be:

$$Confidentiality\ (C) = \{C_{financial},\ C_{operational},\ C_{customer}\} \qquad \text{Equation 1}$$

Furthermore, if it is assumed that under the present configuration of the e-enterprise the confidentiality of financial, operational, and customer data/resources have been determined to be high, medium, and low, respectively, then the confidentiality metric will be:

$$C = \{high,\ medium,\ low\}.$$

Security Management Methodology

As evident from Figure 1, the e-enterprise security profile and functional unit security capability matrices provide direct input to the proposed *security management methodology* (SMM). They determine the security profile deficiencies (i.e., absence of required capabilities) and FU capability excesses (i.e., presence of non-required functionality) in the enterprise. The concepts of functional deficit and functional excess used in Jilani and Mili (1998) are borrowed here to define the *security profile deficit* (SPD) and *FU capability excess* (FUPX). The binary difference (-) operator is first defined as follows.

Definition 3

The difference between $ESP[i, j]$ and $FUSC[k, l]$ elements, is denoted by $ESP[i,j] - FUSC[k, l]$ or $FUSC[k,l] - ESP[i,j]$ and is defined as:

$$ESP[i,j] - FUSC[k,l] = \begin{cases} ESP[i,j] & \text{if } ESP[i,j] \neq FUSC[k,l] \wedge ESP[i,j] \neq null \\ null & otherwise \end{cases}$$

and similarly:

$$FUSC[k,l] - ESP[i,j] = \begin{cases} FUSC[k,l] & \text{if } FUSC[k,l] \neq ESP[i,j] \\ null & otherwise \end{cases}$$

Definition 4

The security profile deficit signifies the deficiencies in ESP with respect to FUSC and is defined as:

$$SPD = \begin{cases} ESP[i,j] - FUSC[i,j] & (1 \leq i \leq n, 1 \leq j \leq m) \\ ESP[i,j] & (i = n+1, 1 \leq j \leq m) \end{cases}$$

Definition 5

The FU capability excess (FUPX) signifies the excesses in FUSC with respect to ESP and is defined as:

$$FUPX = \{FUSC[i,j] - ESP[i,j] \, (1 \leq i \leq n, 1 \leq j \leq m)\}$$

For the ESP and FUSC matrices given in Example 1, the values of *SPD* and *FUPX* are:

$$SPD = \begin{matrix} & \text{Auth} & \text{AC} & \text{Crypto} & \\ \begin{pmatrix} null & null & null \\ null & GTRBAC & RSA \\ SSO & null & null \end{pmatrix} & \begin{matrix} \text{OFU} \\ \text{AFU} \\ \text{CFU} \end{matrix} \end{matrix}, \quad FUPX = \begin{matrix} & \text{Auth} & \text{AC} & \text{Crypto} & \\ \begin{pmatrix} DS & null & null \\ DC & MAC & DES \end{pmatrix} & \begin{matrix} \text{OFU} \\ \text{AFU} \end{matrix} \end{matrix}$$

The SPD matrix computed above highlights that the e-enterprise security profile requirements for the GTRBAC-based access control and RSA encryption scheme for the second FU are not achievable directly by the current capabilities. The FUPX matrix identifies the current excess capabilities of both FUs from the perspective of the desired e-enterprise security profile. As an example, the authentication domain of the second FU is determined to have an extra capability of handling digital certificates, where null is desired.

The computed SPD and FUPX matrices thus allow formal identification of the integration requirements for the enterprise. The following three types of relations can exist between the elements $SPD[i,j]$ and $FUPX[i,j]$ (except for $i = n + 1$ and for the cases where both $SPD[i,j]$ and $FUPX[i,j]$ are null); that is, the elements in the same row and column of both the SPD and the FUPX matrices, corresponding to the same security domain and the same FU:

- **Type A:** For the security profile deficiencies identified by $SPD[i,j]$ the corresponding $FUPX[i,j]$ is null, thus the security profile deficiencies can only be fulfilled by adding more capabilities to the jth security capability of the ith FU through addition of an integration mechanism $INT[i,j]$ to $FUSC[i,j]$.

- **Type B:** For the FU excess security capabilities identified by $FUPX[i,j]$ the corresponding $SPD[i,j]$ is null, thus excess security capabilities can be eliminated only by restricting the jth security capability of the ith FU through addition of the integration mechanism $INT[i,j]$ to $FUSC[i,j]$.

- **Type C:** The security profile deficiencies identified by $SPD[i,j]$ and the FU excess security capabilities identified by $FUPX[i,j]$ are both non-null and thus can be fulfilled and eliminated respectively only by both addition to and restriction of some of the jth security capabilities of the ith FU through the addition of the integration mechanism $INT[i,j]$ to $FUSX[i,j]$.

The integration matrix, INT, computed in this way can thus be able to identify integration requirements for achieving the desired security profile of the e-enterprise. It is to be noted that the $(n+1)^{st}$ row of INT and ESP (and even the SPD) matrices will be the same, and moreover all non-null integration mechanisms in this row have to be of Type A.

The INT matrix for Example 1 will be:

$$INT = \begin{pmatrix} Int_{11} & null & null \\ Int_{21} & Int_{22} & Int_{23} \\ SSO & null & null \end{pmatrix} \begin{matrix} \text{OFU} \\ \text{AFU} \\ \text{CFU} \end{matrix}$$

Auth AC Crypto

where SSO is an integration mechanism of type A, Int_{11} and Int_{21} are integration mechanisms of type B, and Int_{22} and Int_{23} are integration mechanisms of Type C.

While applying the proposed SMM, it is assumed that a number of choices are available for selection of an integration mechanism corresponding to each non-null entry of the

Table 2. Integration mechanism choices for INT corresponding to Example 1

Integration Mechanisms	Choices
Int_{11}	A_{11}, B_{11}
Int_{21}	A_{21}
Int_{22}	A_{22}, B_{22}
Int_{23}	A_{23}
SSO	SSO_1

INT matrix. The e-enterprise SMM then guides the selection of suitable integration mechanisms by computing the value of the security metrics for each possible combination of these mechanisms. This process can either terminate upon achievement of predefined values for the security metrics, or it can iterate for all combinations and select the combination corresponding to the best value of the security metrics. The proposed SMM thus ensures the achievement of the desired value of security metrics within the constraint that all e-enterprise security requirements are fulfilled.

In order to illustrate the proposed SMM, consider that for the INT matrix of Example 1, a number of choices are available for each integration mechanism, as shown in Table 2. Thus there are a total of four combinations of integration mechanisms possible for this example, where the selection of the best configuration is decided by the evaluation of security metrics for each configuration. For simplicity, evaluation of only the confidentiality metric (C) of Equation 1 is considered for each configuration. Based on the results given in Table 3, configuration Number 4 is finally selected, as it provides the best value of C. It is to be noted that by virtue of the procedure used in construction of the *INT* matrix, the selected integration mechanisms are also able to fulfill the security requirements of the given e-enterprise.

Table 3. Integration configurations and corresponding value of C

Config. No	Configuration	Value of C
1	$A_{11}, A_{21}, A_{22}, A_{23}, SSO_1$	*{high, low, low}*
2	$A_{11}, A_{21}, B_{22}, A_{23}, SSO_1$	*{high, medium, low}*
3	$B_{11}, A_{21}, A_{22}, A_{23}, SSO_1$	*{low, high, low}*
4	$B_{11}, A_{21}, B_{22}, A_{23}, SSO_1$	*{high, high, medium}*

Future Trends

In this chapter, security metrics have been primarily considered in the context of enterprise integration; however, in the future, security metrics are also expected to be utilized for defining the enterprise risk posture. The risk posture is defined in terms of threats (intrusion, insider attack, etc.) and undesirable consequences (loss of confidential information, etc.) that concern the enterprise (I3p, 2003). The sustained assessment of the risk posture can be used as input by enterprise managers to identify security-critical areas. This would also allow enterprise managers judicious allocation of limited enterprise resources for providing the required security solutions.

There is an increased trend of dynamic collaboration between enterprises — collaboration in which participating entities join and leave the collaboration at any time. In such environments, the security concerns become very important because of the interdependencies and varying level of trust between collaborating entities. Another issue of concern in such environments is the inability to precisely identify the security boundaries of participating entities. In order to handle these issues, a unified mechanism is required to enable collaborative entities to manage security in a comprehensive and consistent manner.

Conclusion and Future Work

The dependence of e-enterprises on the underlying information structure greatly magnifies the impact of even minor security violations. It is, therefore, very important to carefully plan and carry out enterprise integration in a manner that guarantees the complete achievement of high-level security goals. The objective of this chapter was to provide a security management framework for enterprise integration. This objective is achieved by categorization of security requirements through security domains and application of security management techniques based on security metrics. The propagation of security constraints from the enterprise level to the infrastructure level helps in minimizing redundancy in secure integration of the enterprise. The proposed security management strategy for the complex process of enterprise integration not only ensures consistency between the enterprise security policy and its implementation, but will also facilitate the quantification of enterprise security attributes.

In the future, the plan is to conduct various experiments to verify the efficacy of the proposed approach. The intent is to model and investigate the relationship between integration cost and achieved security metrics. This study will help in identifying the economic impact of different integration approaches, as metrics can be used to provide guidelines for allocation of resources vis a vis the risk involved. Another future plan is to study issues concerning the integration of security management techniques with organizational management practices.

References

Anderson, J. P., Brand, S., Gong, L., & Haigh, T. (1997). Firewalls: An expert roundtable. *IEEE Software, 14*(5), 60-66.

Antón, A. I., & Earp, J. B. (2001). Strategies for developing policies and requirements for secure e-commerce systems. In A. K. Ghosh (Ed.), *Recent advances in e-commerce security and privacy* (pp. 29-46). Boston: Kluwer Academic Publishers.

Arconati, N. (2002). One approach to enterprise security architecture. *SANS Infosec Reading room*. Retrieved September 8, 2004, from http://www.sans.org/rr/whitepapers/policyissues/504.php

Bishop, M. (2002). *Computer security, art and science* (1st ed.). Reading, MA: Addison-Wesley.

Earp, J. B., & Payton, F. C. (2000). Dirty laundry: Privacy issues for IT professionals. *IT Professional, 2*(2), 51-54.

Ellison, R. J., Fisher, D. A., Linger, R. C., Lipson, H. F., Longstaff, T., & Mead, N. R. (1997). Survivable network systems: An emerging discipline. *Technical Report CMU/SEI-97-TR-013*. Pittsburgh, PA: CMU Software Engineering Institute.

Fenton, N. (1991). *Software metrics: A rigorous approach* (1st ed.). New York: Chapman and Hall.

Ferraiolo, D. F., Sandhu, R., Gavrila, S., Kuhn, D. R., & Chandramouli, R. (2001). Proposed NIST standard for role-based access control. *ACM Transactions on Information and System Security, 4*(3), 224-274.

Fox, M. S., & Gruninger, M. (1998). Enterprise modeling. *AI Magazine, 19*(3), 109-21.

I3p. (2003). Cyber security research and development agenda. *Institute for Information Infrastructure Protection*. Retrieved August 8, 2004, from http://www.thei3p.org/about/2003_Cyber_Security_RD_Agenda.pd

Jilani, L. L., & Mili, A. (1998, December 8-10). Estimating COTS integration: An analytical approach. In *Proceedings of the 5th Maghrebian Conference on Software Eng. and Artificial Intelligence,* Tunis, Tunisia (pp. 33-47).

Lam, W., & Shankararaman, V. (2004). An enterprise integration methodology. *IT Professional, 6*(2), 40-48.

Littlewood, B., Brocklehurst, S., Fenton, N., Mellor, P., Page, S., & Wright, D. (1993). Towards operational measures of computer security. *Journal of Computer Security, 2*(2-3), 211-229.

Maley, J. G. (1996, June 19-21). Enterprise security infrastructure. In *Proceedings of the 5th Workshop on Enabling Technologies: Infrastructure for Collaborative Enterprises* (pp. 92-99). Stanford, CA: IEEE Computer Society Press.

McDermid, J. A., & Shi, Q. (1992, November 30 - December 4). Secure composition of systems. In *Proceedings of the IEEE 8th Annual Computer Security Applications Conference,* San Antonio, TX (pp. 112-122).

National Bureau of Standards (NBS). (1993). Data encryption standard. *National Bureau of Standards FIPS PUB 46-2*. Retrieved September 8, 2004, from http://www.itl.nist.gov/fipspubs/fip46-2.htm

Nicol, D. M., Sanders, W. H., & Trivedi, K. S. (2004). Model-based evaluation: From dependability to security. *IEEE Trans on dependable and Secure Computing, 1*(1), 48-65.

Rivest, R. L., Shamir, A., & Adleman, L. M. (1978). A method for obtaining digital signatures and public-key cryptosystems. *Communications of the ACM, 21*(2) 120-126.

Sandhu, R., & Samarati, P. (1994). Access control: Principles and practice. *IEEE Communications, 32*(9), 40-48.

Sedigh-Ali, S., Ghafoor, A., & Paul, R. A. (2002, December 26-29). Temporal modeling of software test coverage. In *Proceedings of the IEEE 26th Annual Computer Software and Applications Conference* (pp. 823-828). Oxford, UK: IEEE Computer Society Press.

Strong, D. M., & Volkoff, O. (2004). A roadmap for enterprise system implementation. *IEEE Computer, 37*(6), 22-29.

Chapter VIII

Implementing IT Security for Small and Medium Enterprises

Edgar R. Weippl, Vienna University of Technology, Austria

Markus Klemen, Vienna University of Technology, Austria

Abstract

Small and medium enterprises *(SMEs) increasingly depend on their* information technology *(IT) infrastructure but lack the means to secure it appropriately due to financial restrictions, limited resources, and adequate know-how. For many managers in SMEs, IT security in their company is basically equivalent to having a firewall and updating the antivirus software regularly. Strategic policies, information theft, business continuity, access controls, and many other aspects are only dealt with in case of security incidents. To improve security in a company holistically, four levels (organizational level, workflow level, information level, and technical level) need to be addressed. Parts of existing standards are useful to address issues on the organizational level; Pipkin's approach is especially useful for SMEs. Modeling of business processes and taking security/dependability into account can improve reliability and robustness of the workflow level. On the information level, role-based access control is state-of the art. On the technical level, basic security measures (antivirus software, firewalls, etc.) need to be addressed and aligned with a corporate security policy.*

Introduction

In most countries, small and medium-sized enterprises employ far more people than large corporations and are an important and often underestimated economic factor. For both large companies and SMEs, business success depends increasingly on reliable IT infrastructure. That said, new e-commerce technologies offer great opportunities and chances, especially for SMEs, but they also pose novel IT-related risks that so far have not been addressed with the necessary vigilance. In this context, we define "SMEs" as companies employing not more than 400 employees.

In comparison to large corporations, SMEs typically have fewer resources and less expertise in strategic and operational IT security policies and tasks. Their IT infrastructure is either maintained by one or very few employees, usually with limited know-how regarding IT security, or by small IT service companies, most of which are not accustomed to even consider using information security standards — such as Control Objectives for Information and related Technology (COBIT) or Common Criteria — due to various reasons. We will address this problem later in this chapter.

According to Avizienis, Laprie, Randell, and Landwehr (2004), security encompasses the aspects of availability, confidentiality, and integrity. The main attributes of dependability are availability, reliability, safety, integrity, and maintainability. In this chapter, we will address security and some aspects of dependability on all four layers mentioned before. On the organizational level, security strategies are developed and a corporate security culture has to be established. The second level is the workflow level. Day-to-day core business processes need to be aligned with the company's security strategy. In addition, IT administrators need this guidance to know which information and technical infrastructure needs to be secured. Protecting information against unauthorized access is addressed on a logical level, the information level. Security on the technical level encompasses aspects such as network security, antivirus software and hardware dependability.

Figure 1. A holistic approach to security encompasses four levels within SMEs

Security Layer	Security-related Research Areas
1. Organisational Level	Decision-making processes under uncertainty, IT-Security strategies, Corporate Security Culture, Risk Management
2. Workflow Level	Security Workflows: Integration of standardized security workflow methodologies; Development of secure business processes
3. Information Level	Access Control, User Rights, Federal Identity (Single-Sign-on)
4. Infrastructure Level	Classical Security Aspects : Secure Networks, Hardware, Tempest, Sniffer, Trojans, viruses, vulnerabilities

SME Compared to Large Companies

In highly competitive global markets, SMEs usually are only successful if they provide highly customized solutions for their customers. SMEs generally cannot easily create revolutionary new products or services because they have neither the financial means for long-term research and development nor the power to push their products and services into global markets. Their competitive advantage is their intimate knowledge of their customers' needs and requirements and often a highly specialized know-how in a very focused area.

The knowledge of their customers is also emphasized by the management style of many SMEs. Many SMEs are operated as family businesses managed by their founders or their descendants. Even though the management usually knows a lot about their customers and their core business, they often lack a systematic approach of organizing their business processes. An ad-hoc management style based mainly on intuition certainly offers benefits as companies can quickly adapt to customer requirements. However, as a consequence, strategic concepts and especially strategic IT security policies are rarely developed. It is obvious that ad-hoc security measures and safeguards are only of limited effect and often overlook important threats and security aspects, which are not adequately addressed.

In many cases, the management of SMEs does not see their company as a likely target for hacker attacks or intruders. Therefore, they deem IT security low priority. This is a very dangerous misconception of the evolving threats to modern IT infrastructure. More and more, criminal organizations discover the financial potential of abusing computers connected to the Internet, for example, for spamming, credit card fraud, or distribution of illegal videos, images or software (CT, 2004). Therefore, hackers care less and less about the target profile and more about how to make quick money by abusing hacked systems for their illegal activities. Since SMEs are less protected than large corporations but have more powerful server systems and better broadband connections than private households, they are becoming an interesting target for these activities.

Another aspect, which is often underestimated, is industrial espionage. Since know-how is the most important asset of SMEs, proper safeguards have to be taken to protect this asset from intruders as well as from malicious or disgruntled employees or former employees. This fact becomes even more evident as the IT infrastructure used by many SMEs offers services similar to large companies, such as Internet access on every work desk, remote access for home workers or traveling salesmen, distributed databases, or simple ERP and CRM systems. However, as SMEs usually spend less money — both in absolute and relative figures — on IT management and information security, they are much less prepared for potential attacks from outside or inside. Many of these threats can already be mitigated by organizational safeguards, which are discussed in the next section.

Organizational Level

Since unclear responsibilities would render large corporations unmanageable, management usually maintains organizational charts to keep a clear picture of the organizational structure. Additionally, policies and IT security policies in particular provide an important strategic guideline for the IT department.

While large companies often invest a large amount of resources in the organizational aspects of IT security, the management of small- and medium-sized companies usually ignores these areas. This is a serious problem, because despite the smaller hierarchy and manageable organizational structure, a missing strategy and proper documentation leaves many important questions unasked. A corporate security culture would be an important strategic guideline for the day-to-day operational security-related decisions of IT administration personnel, who otherwise have to make decisions in an ad-hoc manner and without a coherent strategy.

In contrast to large companies, SMEs rarely develop strategic policies; written IT security policies and even system documentation are often nonexistent. Therefore, a clear strategic guideline that would help administrative personnel to properly assess the role and importance of IT security as seen by senior management is missing.

As mentioned above, many medium-sized businesses create their main competitive advantages from know-how. For these companies, a secure IT Infrastructure that is not only prepared to handle every day viruses and worms, but that also considers hackers, disloyal employees, and other intruders as potential threats is of paramount importance. IT security standards can assist in developing a systematic approach.

IT Security Standards for SMEs

Established Standards

Information security frameworks, like Common Criteria, COBIT[1], MARION[2], *IT Infrastructure Library* (ITIL)[3], ISO/IEC 17799:2000[4], its predecessors *British Standard* (BS) 7799[5], and *Code of Practice* (CoP), *Guidelines on the Management for IT Security* (GMITS) ISO/IEC 13335, or the German IT Baseline Protection Manual[6], were originally developed either for large corporations or governmental institutions to establish or keep a certain level of service quality and security. The *Information Assurance Technical Forum* (IATF)[7] incorporates the Common Criteria and encompasses the three main areas — people, technology, and operations. The IATF serves more as a tutorial than a reference checklist. Therefore, SMEs have to invest considerable amounts of effort in defining and implementing actual tasks.

Due to their complexity and extent — the Baseline Protection Manual consists of more than 2.400 pages — they are difficult to adapt for SMEs. Often, administrators and system operators are overwhelmed by the sheer size of the handbooks and guides and postpone their security strategy planning indefinitely.

Figure 2. Overview of classification of the most relevant information security standards

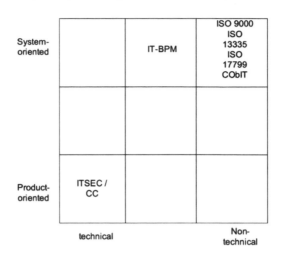

Therefore, a more pragmatic approach is needed that covers all necessary areas that need to be addressed, but which is still feasible for companies with low IT budgets. We will, therefore, introduce an adopted approach that we deem most suitable for this purpose in the next section.

A Pragmatic Approach for SMEs

Donald Pipkin (2000) developed an interesting approach that — with a few modifications — is very suitable for smaller companies, even though it was originally developed for large corporations. Pipkin suggests an Information Security process model consisting of five aspects: (1) inspection, (2) protection, (3) detection, (4) reaction, and (5) reflection. We present an approach based on this model, adapted to the special requirements of smaller companies.

Aspect 1: Inspection

The most important tasks in developing an information security policy are to determine which key processes and corporate functions are essential, the capabilities they require, and their interaction with one another. The inspection aspect plays and important role in evaluating the security needs of a company and assessing its current status and level of preparedness. This aspect contains of five steps:

1. **Resource inventory** consists of a thorough inventory of a company's resources and assets. After identifying these assets, appropriate ownership has to be assigned to establish proper responsibilities. The determination of the value of the inventory is the last part of this step.

2. **Threat assessment** identifies what threatens the identified assets. This step can be facilitated by classifying threats into five major categories: human error, natural disasters, system failures, malicious acts, and collateral damage.

3. **Loss analysis** addresses the question of how a threat might develop, after getting a clearer picture about the potential threat categories. Potential angles are denial-of-service attacks, theft of resources, deletion of information, theft of information, disclosure of information, corruption of information, theft of software, theft of hardware, or disruption of computer-controlled systems. The loss analysis step is one of the most difficult and important parts of the Inspection phase. Putting numbers at the potential costs of bad events is challenging and notoriously erroneous; however, having established a rudimentary framework not only helps developing and realizing a reasonable IT security policy but also facilitates to "sell" security to the management — being confronted with the potential costs in case of emergencies, managers are more willing to invest in their security infrastructure.

4. **Identification of vulnerabilities**: After the threats and their potential outcomes have been defined by Steps 2 and 3, these must be mapped against potential vulnerabilities. Where are weaknesses in the company? These might be technical (security design flaws, incorrect implementation, innovative misuse) or organizational weaknesses (e.g., social engineering).

5. **Assignment of safeguards**: Basically, four categories of safeguards exist: *avoidance* or *mitigation* (by applying technical or organizational improvements), *transference* (e.g., by insuring against the threat), or *acceptance* (in case that neither improving the protection of the asset nor insuring is a viable solution, usually due to high insurance costs).

6. **Evaluation of current status**: After the first five steps have been conducted, the results should be re-assessed and tested.

Aspect 2: Protection

For this aspect, important decisions are made with regard to the objects that need protection, the required level of protection, and how to reach this level by creating a comprehensive security design. The aspect consists of five steps. The security policy should already indicate which of these five steps need to be addressed in what level of detail.

1. **Awareness** is a much underappreciated step toward achieving a secure IT system. Awareness training, which can help to raise the organizational security level significantly, does not have to be longer than one to two hours but should be conducted regularly, for example, once a year. This training can help to reduce the probability of successful virus attacks by user errors (e.g., opening malicious e-mails or following links to infected Web sites) and social engineering attacks.

2. **Access** considerations to company resources are of utmost importance. These considerations should cover physical access as well as logical access (network access control). Therefore, all access methods should be examined closely. Weaknesses may not only exist in form of actual vulnerabilities (e.g., due to a faulty

118 Weippl & Klemen

software module), but also in the form of simple logical errors in the access control concept. In most cases, employees are granted too many user rights for too many areas, since this is simpler to handle and less of a hardship for administrators – at least in the short term.

3. **Authentication and authorization:** The development of proper authentication and authorization models and the handling of authentication management is the focus of this step. The potential subversion of authentication and authorization safe-guards must be kept to a minimum, for both employees and external personnel. Most SMEs make insufficient use of modern operating systems' capabilities, lest using additional technology, like cryptographic tokens. It is usually already a big leap forward if the authentication and authorization concepts are reevaluated and improved by making use of existing access control technologies integrated into today's operating systems, like Kerberos, Active Directory, or similar concepts.

4. **Availability:** SMEs typically do not possess highly redundant server systems due to the high investment costs. Therefore, thorough consideration should be put into "what-if" scenarios. Developing and updating outage emergency plans may alleviate this disadvantage for SMEs compared to large companies, which can afford redundant systems and highly secure data processing centers. The classi-fication of availability models can help to find a suitable mix of economic reasonable safeguards.

5. **Confidentiality:** Confidentiality concerns are important even for the smallest company. Most companies keep their competitive advantage due to some kind of information asymmetry. Information is by far the most important asset of compa-nies, with very few exceptions. Therefore, proper methods of ensuring confiden-tiality must be established to prevent information loss and fraud, even in small companies.

Aspect 3: Detection

Aspect 3 includes processes that intend to minimize the losses from a security incident that could interrupt the core business processes. This aspect includes methods to detect misuses by examining potential attackers, available and known attack vectors, and countermeasure technologies. There are three main steps:

1. **Classify intruder types:** Who is likely to attack from outside? How tough is the competition in the company's branch? Did the resource inventory process identify assets that are of special interests for certain outsiders?

2. **Enumerate intrusion methods:** After potential intruder types have been identified, their most probable intrusion methods and the corresponding process should be evaluated. This is the groundwork for the development of proper intrusion detection and intrusion prevention methods. It should be remarked that these first two parts require a highly sophisticated know-how of intrusion technologies and intrusion detection. It is unlikely that — despite self-assessments of IT personnel — the necessary expert knowledge exists in an average SME. Therefore, consulting specialists for this step is highly recom-mended.

Copyright © 2006, Idea Group Inc. Copying or distributing in print or electronic forms without written permission of Idea Group Inc. is prohibited.

3. **Assess intrusion detection methods:** *Intrusion detection systems* (IDS) or *intrusion prevention systems* (IPS) are often expensive and personnel-intensive — they require 24 x 7 monitoring by employees, making them much too expensive for smaller enterprises. SMEs can still tackle this problem by improving the logging capabilities of their existing hardware infrastructure. Most modern network devices support the SNMP protocol, which — although not entirely secure itself — makes it fairly easy to monitor the network centrally. All modern operating systems (as well as back-office applications like database systems or mail server) provide detailed logging mechanisms, which can also be collected centrally. Designing a sound centralised monitoring center, which is an excellent basis for intrusion detection, is not beyond the financial or technological capabilities of SMEs. Due to a higher administrative efficiency, these safeguards can even reduce the administrators' day-to-day work load significantly, if implemented diligently.

Aspect 4: Reaction

Aspect 4 determines how to respond to security incidents. It must define the process of reacting to certain threat scenarios. To be effective, the response must be selected, documented, and tested before there are actual incidents so that the responsible people know what to do in case of an actual attack or problem. The incident response plan is a critical part of business continuity, which actually most SMEs do not care to develop. The areas to address in this aspect consist of:

1. **Develop response plan:** Based on a scenario analysis, a response plan and an incident containment strategy must be developed. The administrative personnel must have guidelines on how to proceed in case of emergency. These guidelines must be management-approved, so that the administrators do not hesitate to react to threats according to the threat and not according to the pressure by the users ("I just need to finish that, please stay online!"). In case of emergency, time is an extremely critical factor; therefore, containment strategies should be set into motion right away, despite the momentary inconvenience for users.

2. **Assessing the damage:** After a threat is contained securely, the damage must be assessed thoroughly. This is a challenging phase for administrative personnel. Users are pressuring to get the systems back online due to deadlines or increasing work loads; management wants detailed reports of what has happened; and administrators are pressured to work as quickly as humanly possible. But speed kills diligence. Therefore, the administrators should allow themselves to assess the damages thoroughly before starting the recovery procedures. Otherwise, the administrator may worsen the situation even more, or the system may still be compromised when normal operations resume due to hasty decisions, and a forensic analysis of what really happened may be impossible.

3. **Incident recovery procedures:** In accordance with the prior steps, recovery procedures should be defined, management-approved, and tested. This last requirement is extremely rare in smaller companies. The reason for this is that many recovery procedures cannot be tested easily during normal operations or tests may be risky themselves. For example, a complete backup restore of an important server (e.g., by restoring a server disk image) might turn out to be fatal if the image proves

to be faulty during the restore process. Large companies can afford the luxury of maintaining test systems that are identical to those in use, but this is usually not feasible for SMEs. On the other hand, without testing the recovery procedures, they might turn out to be insufficient or faulty in case of a real emergency, also with dire consequences.

Therefore, appropriate considerations are necessary to overcome these limitations. For example, instead of maintaining a complete second test server, it may be sufficient to invest in a backup storage system of the server. The restore process can then be tested on the backup hard disks on a weekend without compromising the existing storage system. Similar solutions can usually be found for other areas of the IT system.

Aspect 5: Reflection

After security incidents are handled, follow-up steps should be taken to put the incidents behind and continue normal operations. If the incident led to the identification of issues that have not yet been addressed, they should be dealt with appropriately. Improvements should be evaluated and checked for potential interaction with other areas of the IT security policy. The aspect consists of one main step:

- **Incident documentation and evaluation:** Documentation of the IT system is often marginal as it is, but the documentation of incidents is usually even worse.

  Administrators are usually glad that everything is back to normal and quickly switch back to day-to-day work. However, it is crucial that the whole incident is documented properly and discussed with partners or colleagues. The incident response should be evaluated and if improvements seem necessary, they should be added to the incidence response plans.

  Working through this approach is a realistic goal even for smaller companies. It might require the time and work efforts of one employee for a couple of weeks, but

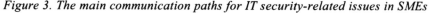

Figure 3. The main communication paths for IT security-related issues in SMEs

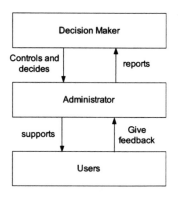

the effort will be beneficial in the long run, as the frequency and impact of future security incidents will be significantly reduced.

- **Stakeholders:** IT security policies in SMEs must consider not only the requirements of information security from a technical perspective, but also psychological and social factors (Anderson, 2001), which influence the role of information security policies in companies.

The main stakeholders in an established, typical SME can be identified as follows:

1. Decision maker (upper management or owner)
2. IT administrator
3. User
4. External consultants

Within the company, the most important stakeholders are the decision maker, the IT administrators, and the IT users. Their main communications paths can be described as follows:

- **The decision maker:** The main decision maker of a SME — usually either the owner of the CEO — is in a difficult position:

1. He or she has to trust the administrator or administrators.
2. He or she has to design a security policy or at least evaluate proposals for one without having a proper technical back ground.
3. He or she has to take the responsibility for the policies.
4. He or she has to balance the power between administrators and users.
5. He or she has to define trust relationships and enforce them.

Therefore, every decision maker needs to develop his or her own personal strategy on how to cope with these problems. The decision maker must find ways to balance the power between the stakeholders and must implement a trust concept on which he or she can rely and which does not make the decision maker too dependent on a single employee or a single IT service company. We will therefore suggest a concept that complies with these basic requirements.

IT Administrator

In SMEs, administrators are responsible for almost all technical issues. Changing laser printer toner, assigning and modifying user rights in operating systems, setting up and maintaining Internet connections, and in many cases even designing the Web pages of the corporate Web site are often among their responsibilities.

Since administrators have so many responsibilities, they often neglect security. Security is not easily visible and therefore often not rewarded appropriately by management; engagement in security is sometimes even hindered or at least ridiculed. Usually security aspects receive higher priority only after the company has been hit by a serious incident.

An important task of IT personnel in addition to the operational day-to-day work has to be tactical planning and conceptual design of the IT infrastructure. In many cases, the necessary resources — even if mainly some of the employees' time — are something for which the administrator must actively fight. Still today, many decision makers in SMEs deem conceptual work a waste of time and money.

Regarding the amount of available IT personnel resources, the following three scenarios are most common:

1. **No dedicated administrator:** One of the employees manages the IT network in addition to his or her normal duties. This scenario is usually characterized by a fuzzy assignment of responsibility, missing policies, and minimal security safeguards. Financial investments in IT security are only considered after major incidents like a hacking attack or a loss of data due to non-existing backup strategies.

2. **One dedicated administrator:** This maximizes management's dependency of the administrator. The same problem basically applies to a scenario in which an external administrator or IT service company is assigned to fulfill the necessary IT administration tasks.

3. **More than one dedicated administrator:** This reduces the dependency of a single administrator and allows mutual controlling and overlapping responsibilities.

IT User

An estimated 77% of information theft is caused by company employees (Cox, 2001). In SMEs, access control and logging mechanisms are generally less strict and the threat of information loss due to insiders is often neglected.

The introduction of substantial restrictions of user privileges like Web surfing, private e-mailing, or individual desktop settings like backgrounds, cursors, or sounds, at once is usually not an appropriate step to increase the level of IT security in a company. On the contrary, this can induce passive resistance of the employees to security safeguards and thereby even reduce the overall security level. Therefore, even after a major security incident, new restrictions should be applied with care. The reasons for the restrictions should be communicated to the employees. Getting a sense of the threats that are addressed by new restrictions might help to develop a better understanding and support of the employees. In the end, it is usually user interaction that opens the door for external intruders — for example, clicking to open an attachment containing dormant malicious code, following links to a hacker's Web site or downloading a Trojan horse. Therefore, gaining employee understanding and support for an improved IT security policy is paramount to increase the overall IT security level significantly. This human factor is much too often overlooked or neglected.

Figure 4. Integrating a trusted third party

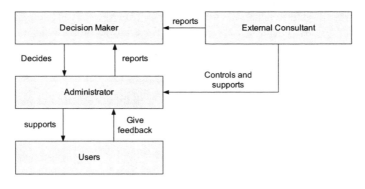

External Consultant

Consulting external security experts and arranging security audits can be viable schemes to reduce the potential risks from only having one or few IT administrative personnel or being supported by a single IT service company.

Since external consultants can be easily perceived as a sign of management distrust of its employees, it is important to achieve the administrators' goodwill for the consultants' engagement. That said, combining the introduction of external consultants with training programs for the employees can reduce the risk of internal resistance to an external auditing program. Also, the results of an audit always have to be presented as suggestions for enhancement and not as criticisms of the personnel's achievements.

Having security audits on a regular basis, for example, once or twice a year, can significantly and effectively reduce the dependability of the IT administrators. Another advantage to this is the ability of the auditing company to help out in case of a sudden drop-out of a key employee, e.g., due to a car accident, sudden illness, or resignation on short notice. This might otherwise put the company in a difficult and vulnerable state for quite a long time.

Changes in the IT administration staff present perfect opportunities to introduce a trusted third party into the IT security policy of a company. A new employee is not yet accustomed to the company and will, therefore, accept a controlling and consulting authority easier.

A concrete scheme for realizing the integration of a trusted third party is as follows: the administrators receive all the necessary user rights to fulfill all their tasks in the role of system operator. Some rights are revoked, especially those that would facilitate the manipulation of logging mechanisms. In Windows 2000/2003, for example, this can be achieved by creating auditor accounts[8], as suggested by Cox and Sheldon (2001).

Auditor accounts must be able to trace all activities of users and administrators and have access to all system logs. Administrators must not have access to these auditor accounts. In Windows 2000 or 2003, for example, the administrator account should be used as the auditor account. This account, similar to the root user in all UNIX® flavors, generally has all system rights. All system operators must be moved to other groups with fewer system rights. They must not be part of the administrators and server operators group and be reassigned to custom management groups that do not have the right to change and delete the audit logs. The following six steps must be performed:

1.   Assign the auditor roles (at least two persons).

2.   Rename administrator account to auditor account or something similar.

3.   Move all existing administrators from the administrator group to a modified group that does not possess rights for changing or deleting log files.

4.   The Windows administrator account properties are opened and a new password is set.

5.   The first auditor types in his or her personal segment of the password. This segment is also written on a card that is put into an envelope kept by the CEO.

6.   The other auditors and system operators repeat Step 5.

Like a multi-key lock, no auditor can log on using the auditor account without the other auditors. This may seem cumbersome, but it is cheap, easy-to-implement, and distributes the responsibility evenly. Hiring external consultants for at least one auditor role reduces the risk of social engineering attacks (Anderson, 2001). This concept also fulfills the "need-to-know" principle developed by Saltzer and Schroeder (1975).

Workflow Level

Large corporations make more and more use of workflow management tools to optimize their core business processes. Today, even small- and medium-sized businesses are increasingly process oriented. Despite their ad-hoc way of addressing upcoming problems, most businesses explicitly or implicitly define their main business processes. In the context of security, we have two major aspects of workflows: security and dependability of workflows; and security and dependability workflows. The former is concerned with security *of* workflows — such as availability of customer care, whereas the latter focuses on workflows of managing security — for example, installing security updates on servers or evaluating log files.

Security and Dependability of Workflows

Systems that implement business processes evolve over time. This evaluation can be organized in a simple two- life cycle consisting of a *development phase* and a *use phase*. During the development phase, the following entities have to be taken into account to ensure dependability: the physical world, human developers, development tools, and test facilities. The use phase is influenced by the physical world, administrative personnel, users, service providers, infrastructure, and unauthorized outsiders.

Security and Dependability Workflows

Workflows that deal with security (such as hardening of servers, installing patches, updating security policies) need to be adapted for SMEs. There are many standard workflows that administrators in SMEs need to follow. Large companies have the resources to adapt existing standards and define their procedures accordingly.

Since the IT infrastructure but not the core business of many SMEs is very similar, it makes sense to standardize security workflows. When modeling workflows with appropriate tools, such as Adonis (Figure 5 and Figure 6) or Aris, cost estimates can be easily calculated. Evaluation models such as SooHoo's model (SooHoo, 2000) can then be used to automatically determine an optimum set of cost-effective measures.

Figure 5. Server maintenance can be performed on several levels

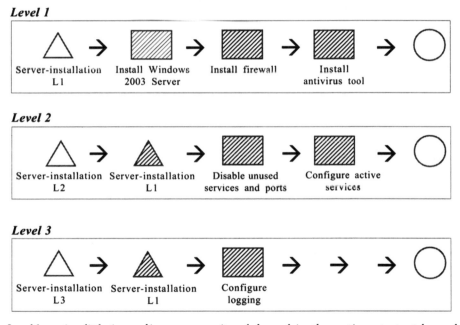

Level 1 requires little time and improves security only by applying the most important patches and updates. Additional tasks (Levels 2 and 3) further improve security but also require additional resources. The levels are processed cumulatively. Higher levels include lower levels (subprocesses).

Figure 6. Level 1 contains only the basic security measures for installing a server

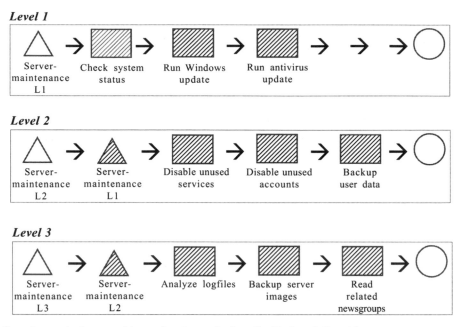

Security can be increased by performing tasks described in Levels 2 and 3.

In Figure 5, different levels of sophistication of the process "server maintenance" are shown. Level 1 encompasses the most fundamental aspects only, such as installing new patches and updating the antivirus software signatures. The second level includes additional tasks, such as disabling unused services and accounts and creating and executing a backup plan. The third level improves security and dependability even further. It is the job of management to decide which level is required, depending on how mission-critical the availability and protection of their core processes is for the survival of the company. These decisions need to be based on solid models and probable scenarios.

The simulation of the workflows can establish an adequate foundation. In Figure 6, the process of installing servers is modeled. Again, there are different levels showing what administrators need to do for basic protection (Level 1) and advanced security (Level 3).

Information Level

Access control mechanisms are a well-established concept of protecting data against unauthorized disclosure and modification. In military settings and large companies, *mandatory access control* (MAC) models such as Bell LaPadula (Bell & LaPadula, 1975, 1996) or Biba (1977) have been used for many years — either by using native MAC systems or by implementing their features using other techniques (Osborn, Sandhu, & Munawer, 2000). Discretionary access control was useful for personal computers and very small company networks; however, maintenance requires so much effort that they are hardly used today. Innovative concepts, such as the Chinese Wall model (Brewer & Nash, 1989), implement the dynamic nature of access control — especially in business consultancies that deal with sensitive data of many client companies. However, today's best practice for SMEs is clearly the model of *role-based access control* (RBAC) (Sandhu, 1996; Sandhu, Ferraiolo, & Kuhn, 2000).

One of the fundamental security concepts of role-based access control is separation of duty. It provides enhanced capabilities to specify and enforce enterprise policies compared to existing access control standards (Sandhu et al., 2000). RBAC has static and dynamic aspects. The user-role membership is static; role activation refers to roles that may be activated dynamically at runtime.

First, *static separation of duties* (SSD) is based on user-role membership (Gavrila & Barkley, 1998). It enforces constraints on the assignment of users to roles. This means that if a user is authorized as a member of one role, the user is prohibited from being a member of a second role. Constraints are inherited within a role hierarchy.

Second, *dynamic separation of duties* (DSD) is based on role activation. It is employed when a user is authorized for more roles that must not be activated simultaneously. DSD is necessary to prohibit a user to circumvent a policy requirement by activating another role (Figure 7) (Essmayr, Probst, & Weippl, 2004).

Figure 7. Constraints in RBAC allow the implementation of separation of duty

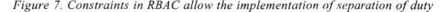
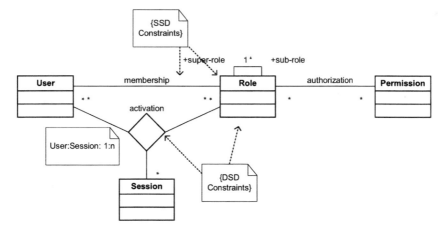

Securing Infrastructure

In this section, we only provide a very brief overview since security is usually addressed adequately at the technical level, even in SMEs. For a couple of years now, viruses, worms, and Trojan horses are omnipresent; hence, most companies have installed antivirus software and firewalls. Administrators are usually knowledgeable about basic technical security safeguards.

SMEs often provide solutions for large companies. As IT solution providers, they face two challenges. First, they need to secure their own infrastructure. This is necessary because customers need to trust that their data is well protected. SMEs have special requirements because of their limited capabilities, which we already described in detail. Second, they need to secure the solutions they install at client sites. Depending on their clients, the solution providers have to be able to credibly address issues of large corporations and SMEs. The main difficulty for small IT solutions providers is to prove that they are able to implement large-scale solutions that reach a security level exceeding their own; moreover, they need to show that they can deal with the complex organizational issues of their clients better than large competitors would.

Conclusion

Security needs to be addressed at four levels (organizational level, workflow level, information level, and technical level). SMEs differ from large companies in many aspects. These differences explain why IT security is usually not that well addressed in SMEs, even though SMEs increasingly depend on their IT systems as much as large companies do. Additionally, SMEs may be more often attacked in the future, as large companies become increasingly difficult to hack. In this chapter, we provided insight into security measures for each of the four levels.

References

Anderson, R. (2001). *Security engineering: A guide to building dependable distributed systems*. New York: John Wiley & Sons Inc.

Avizienis, A., Laprie, J.-C., Randell, B., & Landwehr, C. (2004). Basic concepts and taxonomy of dependable and secure computing. *IEEE Transactions of Dependable and Secure Computing, 1*(1), 11-33.

Bell, D., & LaPadula, L. (1975). *Secure computer system: Unified exposition and multics interpretation*. ESD-TR-75-306, Technical Report MTR-2997. Bedford, MA: Mitre Corporation.

Bell, D., & LaPadula, L. (1996). Secure computer system. Mitre Technical Report 2547. *Journal of Computer Security, 4*(2), 239-263.

Biba, K. J. (1977). *Integrity considerations for secure computer systems.* Technical Report ESDTR-76-372, ESD,/AFSC, MTR 3153. Bedford, MA: Mitre Corporation.

Brewer, D., & Nash, M. (1989, May 1-3). *The Chinese wall security policy.* Paper presented at the 1989 IEEE Symposium on Security and Privacy, Oakland.

Cox, P., & Sheldon, T. (2001). *Windows 2000 security handbook.* Berkeley, CA: Osborne/McGraw-Hill.

CT. (2004). Remote-controlled spam armies, proven: Virus writers supply spam infrastructure. *ct Magazin für Computertechnik.* Retrieved from http://www.heise.de/ct/04/05/006 (in German)

Essmayr, W., Probst, S., & Weippl, E. R. (2004). Role-based access controls: Status, dissemination, and prospects for generic security mechanisms. *International Journal of Electronic Commerce Research, 4*(1), 127-156.

Gavrila, S. I., & Barkley, J. F. (1998). Formal specification for role-based access control user/role and role/role relationship management. Paper presented at the *Proceedings of the 3rd ACM Workshop on Role-Based Access Control*, Fairfax, VA.

Osborn, S., Sandhu, R. S., & Munawer, Q. (2000). Configuring role-based access control to enforce mandatory and discretionary access control policies. *ACM Transactions on Information and System Security, 3*(2), 85-206.

Pipkin, D. L. (2000). *Information security.* Upper Saddle River, NJ: Prentice Hall.

Saltzer, J. H., & Schroeder, M. D. (1975, September). Protection of information in computer systems. In *Proceedings of the IEEE, 63*(9), 1278-1308.

Sandhu, R. S., Ferraiolo, D., & Kuhn, R. (2000, July). *The NIST model for role-based access control: Towards a unified standard.* Paper presented at the *Proceedings of 5th ACM Workshop on Role-Based Access Control*, Berlin, Germany (pp. 47-63). ACM.

Sandhu, R. S., & Samarati, P. (1996). Authentication, access control, and audit. *ACM Computing Surveys, 28*(1), 241-243.

Schneier, B. (2000). *Secrets & lies: Digital security in a networked world.* New York: John Wiley & Sons, Inc.

SooHoo, K. (2000, June). *How much is enough? A risk-management approach to computer security.* Consortium for Research on Information Security and Policy (CRISP). Stanford University, Stanford, CA.

Endnotes

[1]   COBIT has been developed and is maintained by the Information Systems Audit and Control Association (ISACA)—http://www.isaca.org

[2]   CLUSIF—Club de la Sécurité des Systèmes d'Information Français, https://www.clusif.asso.fr/index.asp

[3]   Office of Government Commerce, http://www.ogc.gov.uk

[4]   The ISO 17799 Directory can be found at http://www.iso-17799.com

[5]   Internal Audit and Risk Management Community,
      http://www.knowledgeleader.com/

[6]   Federal Office for Information Security (Germany) (BSI) http://www.bsi.de/english/
      index.htm

[7]   http://www.iatf.net/

[8]   Some operating systems, like Novell Netware, already have auditor roles pre-
      defined.

Chapter IX

E-Commerce Security

Steven Furnell, Network Research Group, University of Plymouth, UK

Abstract

This chapter considers the requirements for security in business-to-consumer e-commerce systems. Experience to date has revealed that these services are potentially vulnerable to a wide range of Internet-based threats. Some of these, such as data streaming and phishing, can be closely tied to the e-commerce domain, whereas others (such as malware, denial-of-service attacks, and Web site defacement) represent more generally applicable problems that nonetheless assume additional significance in an e-commerce context. The existence of the threats demands a variety of safeguards. Technical measures can be used to ensure the confidentiality and integrity of transactions and to support authentication of the parties involved. In addition, supporting measures are considered valuable to raise consumer awareness of security and boost confidence in e-commerce services. It is concluded that e-commerce represents an area of continued growth, and potential threats are likely to grow rather than diminish. As such, appropriate attention by service providers is crucially important.

Introduction

Among the most significant requirements for the success of e-commerce are security and trust on the part of both the consumers and the businesses offering services. This chapter addresses the topic of e-commerce security from the *business-to-consumer*

(B2C) perspective, based upon the variety of services that have arisen in parallel with the commercialisation of the Internet and the Web. Although many such services incorporate protection, ample evidence suggests that security incidents are an increasing threat to the e-commerce domain.

The chapter begins by identifying the growth of e-commerce services and the consequent requirement for trust on the part of the consumers and businesses involved. This discussion draws upon survey findings from recent years, revealing that security is unsurprisingly one of the main concerns that surround the wider scale acceptance of consumer-focused e-commerce. Leading on from this, attention is given to a variety of the threats to which such systems are exposed, supported by examples that have occurred in practice. Awareness of these threats may naturally affect consumers' willingness to utilise the services, which brings consequent challenges for service operators in gaining their confidence. As such, the chapter then proceeds to discuss safeguards that can be used to provide the necessary protection and reassurance. This begins with consideration of technical measures and identifies a number of security protocols and services that have arisen specifically to serve the demands of online payments and e-commerce. This is followed by an examination of supporting measures that can be used to foster consumer trust and security awareness. The chapter concludes with brief consideration of future trends in online commerce that are likely to increase the requirement for security still further. It should be noted that the discussion does not aim to provide a tutorial or "how to" guide for actually implementing the safeguards but rather to raise awareness of relevant issues pertaining to both consumers and merchants in order to provide a starting point for interested readers.

Background

Within a relatively short time, electronic commerce services have risen to become a core element of the Internet and Web environment. The success has primarily been driven by the advantages for the consumer, such as increased convenience and choice, combined with the reduced cost of the products and services being offered. Findings published by Forrester Research have indicated that online retail sales in the United States exceeded $100 billion in 2003 (Johnson, Walker, Delhagen, & Wilson, 2004), representing a 38% increase over the previous year. The U.S. is by no means alone in this respect, and the signs point towards continued growth in other regions as well (Fortune, 2004).

In addition to increasing in volume, B2C e-commerce offerings have evolved considerably since the early days of the Web. The initial use of commercial Web sites was effectively as an electronic "shop window" where visitors could see product and service availability, but could not purchase them directly. Today's sites have, of course, moved well beyond this — which in turn serves to increase the requirement for security, as sensitive personal and financial details are regularly provided during the course of transactions.

Given that e-commerce is thriving, one may be tempted to assume that security aspects must have been addressed and that the resulting environment is trusted one. Unfortu-

Figure 1 . Incidents of Internet fraud (IFCC, 2004)

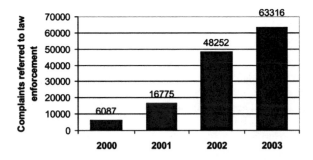

nately, however, the evidence suggests that as the use of e-commerce increases, so too does the number of users who are encountering problems with it. As an illustration of this, Figure 1 depicts findings from the *Internet Fraud Complaint Center* (IFCC)(2004) and shows that the number of complaints received by that organisation and referred to law enforcement has escalated significantly in recent years.

Although e-commerce is forging ahead in spite of these problems, survey results also suggest that a sizable proportion of non-purchasers are being put off by security-related fears. Some indicative examples of such findings are listed below.

- 2003 findings from PaymentOne (2003) revealed security concerns to be far and away the prime reason preventing consumers from shopping online — accounting for 70% of responses.

- A 2003 survey of 1,212 consumers, sponsored by TRUSTe (2003), revealed that 49% limited their online shopping because of fears over the misuse of their personal information.

- A 2004 study conducted by MailFrontier (2004) suggested that 29% of Internet users in the U.S. would avoid online shopping during the festive season as a result of phishing scams.

In addition to those users who are put off entirely, it would be naïve to assume that all of those already using e-commerce services are doing so with complete confidence. For example, further survey findings have suggested that over 90% of users who shopped online were doing so in spite of having some form of security concern (Furnell & Karweni, 2000). Although this particular study is now several years old, there is little doubt that many consumers would give similar responses today, and the growth of e-commerce has had more to do with factors such as the cost and convenience than the perceived improvements in protection.

Of course, the risk of a security incident is not only a concern for potential consumers. The issue also presents itself as a concern for reputable businesses wishing to trade online, and the provision of e-commerce services is a reality for an increasing proportion of businesses. As an illustration of this, the 2004 Information Security Breaches Survey, from the UK Department of Trade & Industry (DTI, 2004), revealed that 73% of respondents claimed to have a transactional Web site — up from just 13% in the previous version of the same survey two years earlier. This is particularly significant from a security perspective, in that the earlier survey had also posed the question of whether e-commerce systems are more or less of a target for attack than other systems. A substantial 61% of respondents considered them more likely to be targeted, with only 7% considering there to be less likelihood (the remaining respondents felt the threat was unaltered) (DTI, 2002). These opinions are borne out by the practical evidence. An analysis of Internet threats by Symantec suggested that e-commerce sites were the most frequently targeted victims in the first half of 2004. The analysis distinguished between random attacks and those that were perceived to be specifically targeted, and determined that e-commerce sites accounted for the largest proportion (16%) of incidents. The corresponding percentage for 2003 was just 4%, with the increase potentially suggesting that attackers are becoming increasingly motivated by the prospect of financial gain (Symantec, 2004).

Suffering a security breach of any kind is clearly not good news for the victim organisation, but the ramifications of the incident may go beyond the direct impact. An obvious example of this is the potential for longer term damage to image and reputation. In this respect, survey results have shown that publicised incidents can adversely affect customer opinions, and cases have indeed been reported in which competitors have explicitly tried to take advantage of this by mentioning that their rivals have suffered security breaches in order to lure away customers (Schultz, 2004).

As a result, online retailers are very much aware of the problem that security represents for their business. A 2000 survey from CommerceNet (2000) asked merchants to identify the main barriers to B2C e-commerce. In the resulting "top ten" list, based upon answers from 1,000 respondents in six countries, the issues of "security and encryption" and "trust and risk" occupied the highest positions.

E-Commerce Threats

Having established that e-commerce services are attractive targets for attack, the discussion now proceeds to consider the nature of the problems that may be encountered. The chart in Figure 1 has already shown that fraud has found an opportunity to flourish within the Internet environment. However, operators of e-commerce services have a number of threats to be concerned about — and fraud-related issues are just part of the story. Other potential problems include malicious code, various forms of hacker attack, and issues arising from insufficient attention to security. While some of these issues are generic to all types of Internet-based systems, others are more likely to be specifically targeted against e-commerce sites. However, even those threats of a more general nature have the potential to deliver more significant impact in the context of e-commerce services, as they may result in damage to customer trust and goodwill. An outline of some of the most significant issues is provided in the sub-sections that follow.

Malware

Worms, viruses, and other forms of *malicious software* (malware) represent the biggest threat to networked systems in general (Gordon, Loeb, Lucyshyn, & Richardson, 2004), and thus are certainly issues that e-commerce operators cannot afford to ignore. An infection may affect the availability of services, causing lost revenue for their providers. Malware is also an issue from the customer perspective, in the sense that it could compromise security during their use of e-commerce services. A good example of this was the Bugbear worm from September 2002, which had keystroke logging capabilities and thus put the user's personal details at risk of being captured if he or she initiated a transaction from an infected system (Liu & Sevcenco, 2002).

Denial of Service

Denial-of-service (DoS) attacks involve the intentional impairment or blocking of legitimate access by an unauthorised party (e.g., by flooding the victim site with spurious traffic). DoS has risen to become one of the most significant threats facing Internet systems. As an illustration of this, the 2004 version of the CSI/FBI's annual Computer Crime and Security Survey reveals that DoS attacks were the second-most costly type of incident reported, accounting for $26M from the 269 respondents that were willing and able to quantify their losses (Gordon et al., 2004). Although the experience of DoS incidents is by no means limited to e-commerce sites, the impact in these cases has the potential to be felt particularly strongly, in the sense that unavailability of the site directly equates to a halting of business operations. For example, one of the most widely publicised DoS incidents dates back to February 2000, when a Canadian teenager operating under the alias "Mafiaboy" initiated a series of distributed DoS attacks against numerous popular sites, including commerce-oriented services such as Amazon.com and eBay. The impact was significant — for example, when the Amazon.com Web site was targeted on February 8, it became 98.5% unavailable to legitimate users (Arent & McCullagh, 2000). This situation lasted for around 30 minutes, and legitimate visitors to the site had to wait about five minutes to get to Amazon's home page. It is easy to imagine that many people would have given up in this time, resulting in potential lost revenue for the company if they then went elsewhere rather than returning later.

Web Site Defacement

Given that the Web site is often the shop window for the e-business, it is important to ensure that it conveys the correct information and the best impression. With this in mind, vandalism of a site and alteration of its content is clearly unwelcome. Unfortunately, defacement has become a significant problem, and sites running unpatched Web server software represent a relatively easy target, even for novice hackers. If known vulnerabilities remain unresolved, they provide an opportunity for attackers to gain entry and then replace or modify site contents. As such, one group of potential perpetrators here may be external hackers arbitrarily attacking the site simply because it is vulnerable. Alternatively, attacks may result from more targeted actions by competitors or disgruntled employees.

As with DoS attacks, defacement incidents are by no means confined to e-commerce sites, and a look at statistics from a defacement archive (such as http://zone-h.org) will reveal all manner of targets, from government sites to academic institutions. However, the potential impact for an e-business could again be greater than for a site that is purely providing information services. For example, encountering a defaced site has the potential to cause lasting damage to the customer's impression of the business and in particular to the perception of its security (e.g., if the business cannot even protect its own shop window, why should I trust it with my data?).

Data Streaming

Data streaming is one of the threats that is more likely to explicitly target the e-commerce domain and involves the bulk theft of personal data such as payment card details by individuals or groups hacking into related systems. Although consumers may instinctively consider that their data requires protection against interception as it travels across the network, the evidence shows that it is far more likely to be vulnerable at the remote destination, where hackers may break in and steal it en masse. Such opportunities may exist as a result of badly configured or inadequately maintained systems that are vulnerable to hacker exploits, as well as poorly designed systems that have not separated the storage of sensitive customer details from the public-facing Web server. A notable example occurred in early 2000, when a hacker calling himself "Curador" began hacking into small e-commerce sites to steal payment card details. Beginning in late January and continuing through into early March, he penetrated nine sites, located in Britain, U.S., Canada, Japan, and Thailand, stealing between 750 and 5,000 card numbers each time (it was estimated that 26,000 cards were compromised in total). Having stolen the card data, Curador also set up Web sites to share the details with others (the site registrations naturally being paid for using stolen card numbers). The FBI estimated losses exceeding $3 million, taking into account the cost of closing down Curador's sites and issuing new cards.

Phishing

Another of the types of attack that is more likely to specifically target the e-commerce domain, phishing tries to trick users into divulging sensitive data through messages and Web sites that purport to be from legitimate sources such as banks and online retailers. Although phishing incidents can be traced back to the mid-90s, there has been a notable surge in the last year or so, as perpetrators have found ways to apply the techniques for financial gain. Players in the e-commerce domain have therefore become desirable targets for impersonation, and the November 2004 report from the Anti-Phishing Working Group reveals that, from 8,459 unique phishing messages, over 80% had targeted companies in

Figure 2. PayPal phishing (a) e-mail, and (b) bogus site

Dear PayPal user,

PayPal is constantly working to increase security for all our users. To ensure the integrity of our payment network, we periodically review accounts.

Your account will be placed on restricted status. Restricted accounts continue to recieve payments, but are limited in their ability to send or withdraw funds.

To lift this restriction, you need to complete our credit card verification process. At least one credit card in your account has been unconfirmed, meaning that you may no longer send money with this or any other card until you have completed the credit card confimation process. To initiate the credit card information, please follow this link and fill all necessary fields:

http://ww.paypal.com/cgi-bin/webscr?cmd=_rav-form

Thank you,

The PayPal Account Review Department

(a)

the financial services or retail sectors (APWG, 2004). An example of this type of attack is presented in Figure 2, showing an e-mail message purporting to have come from the PayPal service, and the bogus site that users are subsequently led to if they believe the message and attempt to act upon it. As can be seen from the screenshot, the site requests a whole range of sensitive information (including PIN code and social security number), and users gullible enough to provide it all could find themselves at significant risk of both financial loss and identity theft.

Phishing differs from the other threats listed here in the sense that avoiding it requires vigilance on the part of the consumer rather than the e-business (albeit with the business being able to do its bit to alert its customers to the issue). This, however, does not mean that the e-business is unaffected by the problems. Quite the contrary in fact — the impersonated companies often experience escalating costs as a result of increasing volume of calls to their customer support lines (Savage, 2004), and as with other security incidents, the adverse publicity could reduce trust in the affected brand.

Poorly Administered Systems

Although not an attack in itself, a badly administered system is a definite threat that can increase the vulnerability to some of the other problems already discussed. Such systems may be vulnerable because they have not been kept up-to-date (e.g., failure to apply the latest patches, leaving systems open to hacker exploits and malware), or because they have been badly configured in the first place. For example, in June 2000, a UK-based Internet service provider was hacked by an IT consultant who claimed that he wished

Figure 2. PayPal phishing (a) e-mail, and (b) bogus site (cont.)

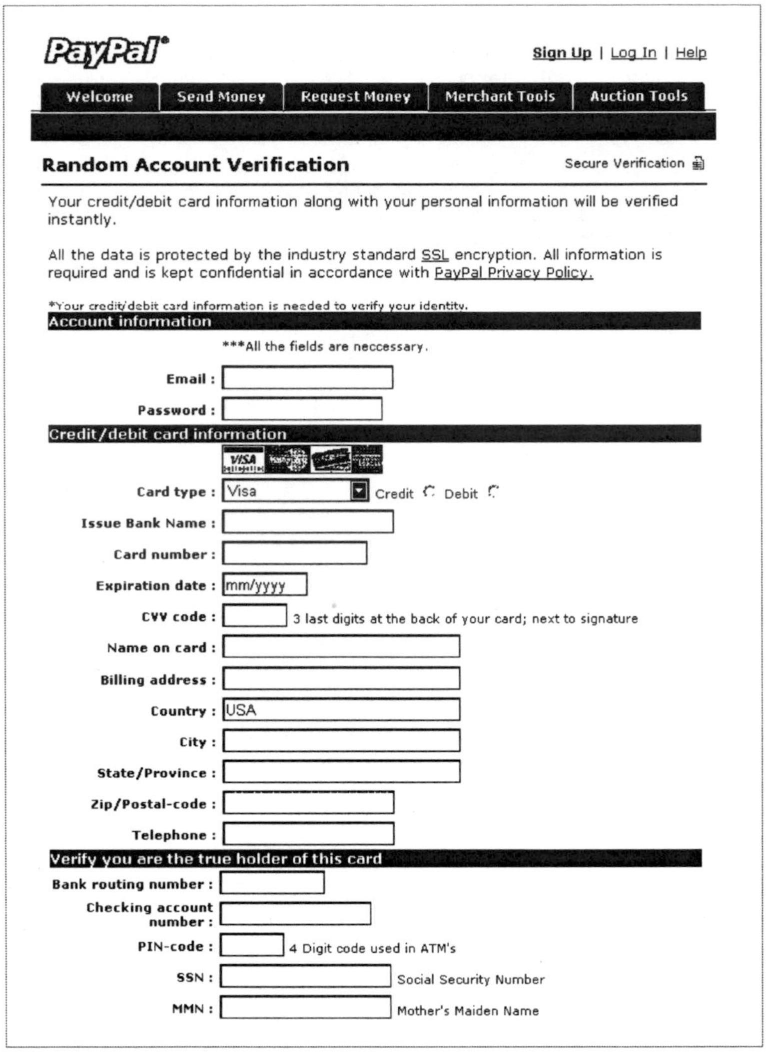

PayPal

Sign Up | Log In | Help

Welcome | Send Money | Request Money | Merchant Tools | Auction Tools

Random Account Verification Secure Verification

Your credit/debit card information along with your personal information will be verified instantly.

All the data is protected by the industry standard SSL encryption. All information is required and is kept confidential in accordance with PayPal Privacy Policy.

*Your credit/debit card information is needed to verify your identity.

Account information

***All the fields are neccessary.

Email :

Password :

Credit/debit card information

Card type : Visa Credit Debit

Issue Bank Name :

Card number :

Expiration date : mm/yyyy

CVV code : 3 last digits at the back of your card; next to signature

Name on card :

Billing address :

Country : USA

City :

State/Province :

Zip/Postal-code :

Telephone :

Verify you are the true holder of this card

Bank routing number :

Checking account number :

PIN-code : 4 Digit code used in ATM's

SSN : Social Security Number

MMN : Mother's Maiden Name

(b)

to expose its security holes. Having compromised its site, the attacker was allegedly able to access the customer database — containing details of more than 24,000 subscribers, including credit card information (Chittenden, 2000). In a properly designed system, this should not have been possible, with a physical separation between public-facing Web server and the system holding sensitive data. As it stood, the configuration of the system had left it vulnerable to a data streaming incident.

The examples presented here provide a clear demonstration that e-commerce faces real security issues. Each of these can cause significant impact and from a commercial perspective, one of the most fundamental risks is that knowledge of the threats could undermine the trust of potential users. As such, it is relevant to consider the approaches that e-commerce providers may pursue in order to reduce their vulnerability, and ensure that their customer base remains intact.

Solutions and Safeguards

Most customers will have some basic expectations for the security of an e-commerce service that can be clearly related to the standard principles of protection:

- **Confidentiality:** Customers will expect that personal details and transaction data will be protected against unauthorized disclosure during both transmission and any subsequent storage.

- **Integrity:** This relates to the expectation that both customer and merchant data will be protected against accidental corruption or deliberate modification. From the perspective of customer data, threats would include alteration of transaction details, while from the merchant perspective, they would include unauthorized changes to Web site details.

- **Availability:** While some downtime is tolerable in the eyes of most users, the general expectation is that a site will be available for use. As such, experiencing unavailability on a frequent or prolonged basis could result in damage to reputation or loss of custom.

The issue of addressing the threats can be approached at several levels. The most direct approach is to provide safeguards via the use of security technologies. However, important contributions can also be made via confidence-boosting and awareness-raising initiatives that target potential consumers. Elements related to all of these approaches are considered in the sections that follow.

Technology Safeguards

The discussion assumes a context in which payments are received and processed directly by the merchant, but it is worth noting that other scenarios may exist that serve to alter the provision and responsibility for security. For example, if the merchant has entrusted payment processing to a service bureau (e.g., the PayPal service), the protection of the related details then becomes its responsibility.

The discussion of threats has already identified that certain generic problems can assume increased significance in an e-commerce context. Similarly, there are a number of security administration activities that can be regarded as baseline good practice, irrespective of whether an Internet system supports e-commerce or not. For example, issues of firewall protection, data backup, use of up-to-date antivirus software, and timely vulnerability patch management can all be viewed as important contributions to network security. However, there is ample evidence to suggest that they are neglected in many systems, and it is vital that e-commerce providers give them suitable attention.

In addition to these general aspects, there are a number of specific provisions that an e-commerce site should expect to make for the protection of transactions:

- **Encryption** — to ensure that transaction data is protected in transit.

- **Peer Authentication** — to verify the legitimacy of both the customer (e.g., the genuine cardholder) and the merchant (e.g., to safeguard against users being duped by bogus sites).

- **Message Authentication** — to ensure that messages are received correctly and cannot be forged or tampered with in transit.

The de facto solution for the majority of e-commerce sites is provided by the *secure sockets layer* (SSL) protocol. Originally developed by Netscape, SSL has also been released as a specification from the Internet Engineering Task Force under the name *transport layer security* (TLS) (Dierks & Allen, 1999). The protocol provides communications privacy over the Internet, fulfilling the above requirements as follows (Freier, Karlton, & Kocher, 1996):

- Ensuring that the connection is private, with an initial handshaking protocol being used to establish a secret session key that can be used to encrypt data with a symmetric method such as *Data Encryption Standard* (DES) or *Rivest Cipher 4* (RC4).

- Enabling the identity of communicating parties to be authenticated via asymmetric cryptographic schemes, such as *Rivest-Shamir-Adleman* (RSA) and *Digital Signature Standard* (DSS).

- Preserving the integrity of message content, using secure one-way hash functions, such as *Message Digest 5* (MD5) and *Secure Hash Algorithm* (SHA), to calculate message authentication code values.

SSL is actually an application independent protocol, and thus its use is not specifically confined to e-commerce scenarios. However, it is within this context that it has received its most significant use. The protocol itself is composed of two layers:

- **SSL handshake protocol** — This is used to establish the secure connection between client and server systems. During this phase, both sides may be authenticated, and they also establish the algorithms to be used for message encryption and integrity services, and the keys that will be used for later protection.

- **SSL record protocol** — This is the lowest level of SSL, and uses the algorithms agreed upon during the handshaking phase to provide protected communications between the client and server. The record protocol can be used to encapsulate a variety of higher level protocols, and thus can provide security for a range of different applications. In the e-commerce context, the server will encrypt requested pages and send them to the browser, which then performs decryption and integrity checking before presenting them to the user.

The general process of establishing an SSL/TLS session is illustrated in Figure 3. Following the initial connection request from the customer's system (the client) the server responds with a copy of its digital certificate in order to enable it to be authenticated. This authentication is performed using the public key of the certification authority, and typically requires no user intervention because the public keys of popular issuers, such as VeriSign, come preloaded into most browsers (if the certificate has been signed by an unknown authority for which the browser does not have the key, the user will receive a warning message and be asked how to proceed). Optionally, the server may also request client authentication, in which case the client must respond with a copy of its own certificate. When the necessary authentication has been achieved, the two sides negotiate the algorithms to be used for encryption and computation of the *message authentication codes* (MACs) for data integrity (a MAC can be regarded as a fingerprint of a message that has been digitally signed by the sender, thus providing a means of confirming both the content and origin). Having done this, the client provides a session key, which can be used for encryption of subsequent communications within the session. In order to prevent eavesdropping, this session key is itself encrypted using the server's public key. Subsequent to this initial handshaking procedure, the client and server are able to exchange messages in a secure manner using the aforementioned SSL record protocol.

The operation of SSL is one of the few aspects of a merchant's security provision that will be visible to the end users, and it is consequently one of the signs that a customer may use to help distinguish a secure site from one that is unprotected and potentially bogus (further possible indicators are considered in the next section). Specifically, when an SSL session is established, a number of indications may be visible at the Web browser level, as illustrated by the prompts and status bar symbol in Figure 4 (in this case, the

Figure 3. SSL handshaking process

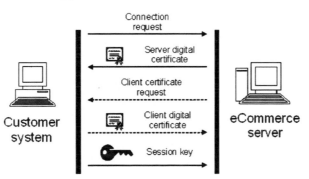

Figure 4 . Connection status indicators in Web browser

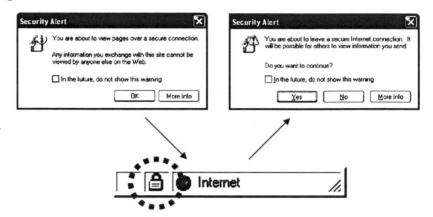

examples are taken from Internet Explorer, but other browsers convey similar details). In some cases, the dialog boxes may not be shown to indicate the start and end of the secure connections (i.e., users may have ticked the box not to show the warnings), but the padlock symbol (or equivalent) is a definite indicator that will remain regardless of the user's preferences. In addition, the URL in the browser address bar will begin with "https" instead of the normal "http."

Although the safeguards of SSL are good from the consumer perspective, there is a notable omission from the merchant perspective in that they cannot, by default, perform a reciprocal confirmation of the consumer's identity (SSL supports it as part of the handshake protocol, but requires the consumer to have a certificate installed — which the vast majority will not have). As a consequence, an honest merchant could receive orders from a stolen or forged credit card. Of course, other administrative safeguards can provide protection here, but this does not mean that suitable safeguards could not be incorporated at the technology level. Indeed, a more substantial alternative to SSL has already been developed that provides considerably more protection — namely, the *secure electronic transaction* (SET) standard.

Unlike SSL, which arose as a security mechanism for general application, SET was specifically designed to provide safeguards for card payments over open networks such as the Internet. It was announced back in 1996 and was a collaborative effort between Visa, MasterCard, and a number of leading technology companies (including Microsoft, IBM, RSA, and VeriSign) (Stallings, 2002). The scheme uses a combination of digital certificates and digital signatures to ensure privacy and confidentiality among the main participants in a transaction: the customer, the customer's bank, and the merchant. When compared to the SSL approach, the most significant difference from the consumer perspective is that credit card details themselves are not divulged to the merchant. This immediately reduces the potential for threats such as data streaming, as merchant systems no longer hold repositories of card details. It also offers advantages to the merchant, in the sense of being able to authenticate the customer. However, in spite of its more comprehensive level of protection, SET has not found its way into widespread use. The main reasons for this are the complexity of the approach, and the resultant demands that it places upon consumers and merchants — both of whom would be required to install specific software to support the mechanism. Faced with this choice, versus the option of using the SSL functionality that is built into Web browsers and servers as standard, it is perhaps unsurprising that the latter has prevailed.

In the absence of consumer-side digital certificates, verifying the legitimacy of those logging into the site and attempting to make purchases and payments remains an important consideration. Baseline customer authentication on many sites simply relies upon a username (or e-mail address) and password combination as the only barrier to accessing user accounts (and making use of any personal/financial information that is pre-stored there). However, this is not the only option. Online banking sites have for some time utilised a somewhat more substantial challenge-response process, requiring the user to enter personal information such as date of birth along with randomly selected digits from a secret security number (thus reducing the possibility of someone capturing the information — for example, via a keystroke logging worm — and then being able to repeat it for a subsequent successful login). The downside, of course, is that this process may be perceived as too time-consuming or complex by potential customers. Indeed, many sites do operate successfully with basic password-based authentication, and users may be willing to tolerate this if the site is not maintaining sensitive personal data (e.g., if the customers are not obliged to store contact and billing details on the site and can instead provide it on a per-transaction basis).

A more tangible demand for effective customer verification comes when a customer attempts to provide card details in order to make payments. Many sites are willing to accept orders on the basis of cardholder name and address, along with the card number and expiry date. Unfortunately, this can leave both the merchants and legitimate cardholders vulnerable to fraudulent transactions. Names and card numbers could have been acquired via data streaming, and although some sites additionally request the verification code printed on the back of the card, even this would be vulnerable if the card itself has been stolen. As a result, the only safeguard in some cases is that the merchant will only deliver to the address associated with the card.

In order to provide additional protection against misuse of card details, major card operators have developed schemes that can be incorporated into e-commerce sites in order to verify that the legitimate cardholder is present at the time of the transaction. Examples of such schemes are Visa's "Verified by Visa" (Visa, 2004) and MasterCard's SecureCode (MasterCard, 2005). Both approaches work on the principle that whenever an online purchase is made using a particular card number, the user must verify that his or her use of the number is legitimate by providing a password (which is then verified by the card issuer). Thus, the standard card details alone are no longer sufficient to authorize a transaction. The approaches require both consumers and merchants to register for the service, and having done so, merchants can then use the logo on their site, providing an additional indication of security for consumers (a theme that is discussed further in the next section).

Such approaches go some way towards providing the additional features that SET already incorporated (e.g., ensuring authentication of the customer for the merchant). However, there are still notable aspects (which SET also dealt with) that remain unresolved — principally the fact that the card details are still provided as part of the transaction and could therefore be vulnerable to interception. Of course, this is not a problem if all retailers use the MasterCard or Visa scheme, because the card number alone will not enable a transaction to be made, but at the moment, there are many sites that do not incorporate the protection. There are also potential compatibility problems, in the sense that the verification windows in which users enter their passwords may get blocked if the user has installed software to block pop-up windows. Getting around this problem obliges users to temporarily disable one aspect of their protection in order to use another. Such issues are indicative of the fact that the technology aspect of e-commerce security has yet to mature to the desirable degree.

Supporting Measures

When considering the security requirements of an e-commerce service, it is important to realise that technology solutions alone are not sufficient. One important reason for this is that, aside from the user authentication and use of SSL, much of it simply will not be visible at the consumer level. For example, by default, the customer will have no idea whether firewalls, antivirus, and software vulnerabilities are being appropriately managed at the host end. Moreover, users cannot be expected to have a technical background, and most would not understand such information even if a merchant was to provide it. As such, it is important for merchants to consider additional measures that serve to provide reassurance in ways that are meaningful to users.

As a starting point, an important realisation for many merchants is that, again by default, their potential customers cannot be sure whether they, or their Web site, are credible or not. With the increasingly sophisticated methods that are now being employed by scammers, consumers cannot simply rely upon surface issues, such as professional appearance, to give them a meaningful assurance. Merchants must therefore consider additional measures to boost confidence of potential users and realise that more security-conscious users may actively look for such signs before electing to make a purchase online.

An increasingly common approach is for sites to achieve an endorsement from a third party and then display visible indicators that the site complies with recognised security and privacy standards. The clear advantage here is that customers no longer need to make a judgment about the credibility of an individual site, but instead only need to assure themselves of the credibility of the certifying party. Some examples of the seals that can commonly be seen on e-commerce sites are shown in Figure 5 (including those relating to the Visa and MasterCard approaches mentioned in the previous section).

Displaying such a seal demonstrates that a site complies with the recognised best practices of the sponsoring organization. As such, those aiming to offer e-commerce services should seek to utilise such seals in order to provide reassurance to prospective customers.

Of course, these approaches would have no credibility if the decision to display a particular seal was to rest entirely with the merchant. As such, issuing organizations will typically have a range of requirements that need to be met before the right to use their

Figure 5. Privacy and security seals

 VERIFIED by **VISA**   **MasterCard** SecureCode

seal is granted. For example, in order to be granted the right to utilize the TRUSTe seal a site must make the following provisions (TRUSTe, 2005):

- user controls, such as functionality to enable personally identifiable information to be updated, and to limit the sharing of it with outside parties;

- security measures, to ensure that pages collecting sensitive information are encrypted using SSL or a comparable technology;

- a complaint resolution process; and

- a privacy statement, addressing issues such as the nature of the personally identifiable information that is collected, and how it will be used.

Similarly, the VeriSign seal is not handed out lightly. Only after the following steps have been completed will a certificate be issued, and the merchant able to use the VeriSign seal on its site to enable verification (VeriSign, 2003):

- Confirmation that the organization named in the certificate has the right to use the domain name included in the certificate;

- Confirmation that the organization named in the certificate is a legal entity; and

- Confirmation that the individual who requested the SSL certificate on behalf of the organization was authorized to do so.

Although the use of seals is a valuable contribution, it still demands a level of awareness on the part of potential customers. Specifically, it requires them to understand how the seals are supposed to work and then to be aware enough to spot bogus use. For instance, the VeriSign Secured seal shown in Figure 5 provides a means of verifying the level of security used by the site concerned (as well as implicitly proving that the seal has appeared on the site legitimately). For example, clicking upon the seal from VeriSign's own site yields the verification details shown in Figure 6.

However, if the customer is not aware of how the seal is meant to work, then a scammer might still find it possible to dupe the customer into a false sense of security by merely taking the image of a seal and displaying it on his or her site. Luckily, the longevity of such scams would very likely be limited, as issuing organizations are keen to safeguard the credibility of their seals and provide a means for such misuse to be reported.

The issue of customer awareness can be taken further than this, and correct attention to the issue could go some way to allaying the fear of purchasing online. Relevant

Figure 6. Verifying the legitimacy of a site

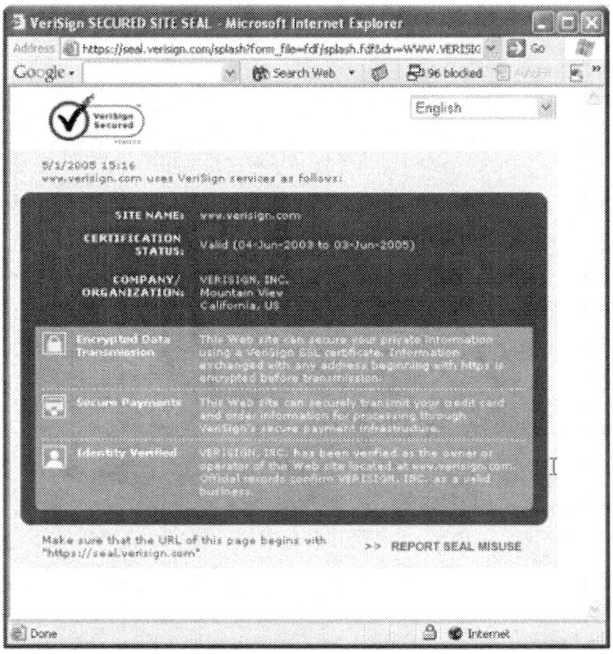

contributions can be made from several perspectives. For example, in addition to demonstrating the credibility of their own site, merchants can help raise their customers' awareness of good practices by promoting tips for safe online shopping. These will not only apply to the use of the merchant's own site and will help to provide transferable knowledge that users can apply in other contexts. Such advice points could usefully include:

- Take note of appearances. Although users should not trust a site merely because it looks professional, they *can* be advised to be cautious about sites that are crudely designed, riddled with spelling mistakes, and the like.

- Look for evidence of credibility, such as third-party seals, and read a site's policies for security and privacy.

- Look for signs of a secure session (e.g., the SSL padlock symbol or something similar) before proceeding to provide sensitive details.

- Pay by credit card in order to take advantage of the protection offered by the card provider (see as follows).

Merchants can also assist with the process by warning about specific threats. For example, those who find phishing scams being operated in their name ought to take a responsible stance and take steps to alert and inform potential victims (e.g., by putting details on their own legitimate Web site and providing an e-mail address through which bogus messages can be reported).

Customer awareness can also be raised by card providers. For example, many cardholders are afraid of their credit card number being stolen, but may not realise that their card provider protects them in this scenario by removing their liability — provided that they have not been negligent in protecting their card or its associated details. In addition, there is evidence to suggest that the scale of the problem is overestimated. For example, although findings from the Association for Payment Clearing Services (APACS, 2004) have suggested that fraud through e-commerce channels is increasing (estimated at £45m in the UK during 2003), the majority relates to the use of card details that have been fraudulently obtained in the real world — the proportion relating to data actually stolen from websites is described as "very low."

Conclusion and Future Trends

E-commerce is a domain with significant promise for the future. As time goes on, the growth of domestic Internet access and the increasing involvement of mobile devices (m-commerce) will yield more potential customers. Indeed, global revenues for this sector have been projected to reach $88 billion U.S. by 2009 (Jupiter Research, 2004).

The outlook for threats is not encouraging. Established problems, such as malware, have not diminished in recent years despite a significant subset of the security industry having arisen to provide protection. In addition, new threats such as phishing have risen to significant prominence, with the e-commerce sector proving to be a natural target. As a result, security clearly demands serious ongoing attention on the part of service operators.

While none of the threats are likely to completely prevent e-commerce, they may still impede its development. For example, recalling the survey findings cited earlier in the discussion, it is already apparent that many more customers would participate in online transactions were it not for their security concerns.

In conclusion, it can be observed that e-commerce has already demonstrated its great benefit for both consumers and merchants. As more people gain access to the Internet, the base of potential customers will only increase. However, the issue of security will remain a concern — and for good reason, given the range of potential threats and the limited extent to which suitable precautions are followed in some cases. Although the total removal of risk is as unrealistic here as it is with other aspects of security, attention to the key points raised here will serve to significantly reduce vulnerability to the threats. The onus is upon operators to make appropriate use of safeguards and to assist in improving customer awareness of genuine threats in order to increase their confidence in using the e-commerce services.

References

Anti-Phishing Working Group (APWG). (2004, November). Phishing activity trends report, November. Retrieved November 17, 2005, from: http://www.antiphishing.org/ APWG Phishing Activity Report - November2004.pdf

Arent, L., & McCullagh, D. (2000, February 9). A frenzy of hacking attacks. *Wired News*, 1.

Association for Payment Clearing Services (APACS). (2004, April). Card fraud overview, *Card Watch. APACS Fraud Prevention.* Retrieved January 7, 2005, from http:// www.cardwatch.org.uk/html/overview.html

Chittenden, M. (2000, June 25). Hacker taps into 24,000 credit cards. *The Sunday Times*, p.14.

CommerceNet. (2000). *Barriers to electronic commerce.* Retrieved from http:// www.commerce.net/research/barriers-inhibitors/2000/Barriers2000study.html

Department of Trade & Industry (DTI). (2002, April). Information security breaches survey 2002. UK Department of Trade & Industry. URN 02/318. London: Crown Copyright.

Department of Trade & Industry (DTI). (2004, April). Information security breaches survey 2004. UK Department of Trade & Industry. URN 04/617. London: Crown Copyright.

Dierks, T., & Allen, C. (1999, January). RFC 2246 - The TLS protocol, version 1.0. Network Working Group, Internet Engineering Task Force Retrieved November 17, 2005, from http://www.ietf.org/rfc/rfc2246.txt

Fortune. (2004). Total B2C revenues for US, Europe & Asia, 1999 - 2003 (in USD billions). Statistics for Electronic Transactions. *ePaynews.com.* Retrieved January 7, 2005, from http://www.epaynews.com/statistics/transactions.html#16

Freier, A. O., Karlton, P., & Kocher, P. C. (1996, November 18). The SSL protocol, version 3.0. Internet Draft, Transport Layer Security Working Group. Retrieved November 17, 2005, from http://wp.netscape.com/eng/ssl3/draft302.txt

Furnell, S. M., & Karweni, T. (2000). Security implications of electronic commerce: A Survey of Consumers and Businesses. *Internet Research, 9*(5), 372-382.

Gordon, L. A., Loeb, M. P., Lucyshyn, W. & Richardson, R. (2004). Ninth Annual CSI/ FBI Computer Crime and Security Survey. Computer Security Institute.

Internet Fraud Complaint Center. (2004). IFCC 2003 Internet fraud report, January 1, 2003-December 31, 2003. National White Collar Crime Center and the US Federal Bureau of Investigation. Retrieved November 17, 2005, from http://www.ifccfbi.gov/strategy/2003_IC3Report.pdf

Johnson, C. A., Walker, J., Delhagen, K., & Wilson, C. P. (2004, January 23). 2003 e-commerce: The year in review. *Forrester Research.* Cambridge, MA: Forrester Research.

Jupiter Research. (2004). Global m-commerce revenue projections for 2009, Statistics for Mobile Commerce, ePaynews.com. Retrieved January 7, 2005, from http://www.epaynews.com/statistics/mcommstats.html#49

Liu, Y., & Sevcenco, S. (2002). W32.Bugbear@mm. Symantec Security Response, 30 September. Retrieved November 17, 2005, from http://securityresponse.symantec.com/avcenter/venc/data/pf/w32.bugbear@mm.html

MailFrontier. (2004, November 18). *MailFrontier research survey detects slowdown in online holiday shopping* (Press Release). MailFrontier, Inc.

MasterCard. (2005). Introducing MasterCard® SecureCode™! Retrieved January 7, 2005, from http://www.mastercardmerchant.com/securecode/

PaymentOne. (2003). Factors discouraging US consumers from using a credit card online. Statistics for General and Online Card Fraud, *ePaynews.com*. Retrieved January 7, 2005, from http://www.epaynews.com/statistics/fraud.html#27

Savage, M. (2004, May). This threat could kill e-commerce. *SC Magazine,* 22-25.

Schultz, E. (2004). Security breaches drive away customers. *Computers & Security, 23*(5), 360-361.

Stallings, W. (2002, May 17). Introduction to secure electronic transaction (SET). Retrieved November 17, 2005, *http://www.informit.com/articles/article.asp?p=26857&redir=1*

Symantec. (2004, September). Symantec Internet security threat report – Trends for January 1, 2004 - June 30, 2004, *Volume VI.*

TRUSTe. (2003, December 1). *Identity theft and spam will deter online shopping this holiday season* (Press Release). TRUSTe.

TRUSTe. (2005). *General Web privacy program requirements.* TRUSTe Program Requirements. Retrieved January 7, 2005, from http://www.truste.org/requirements.php

VeriSign. (2003). *How to create an e-commerce Web site: A VeriSign guide.* VeriSign, Inc. Retrieved November 17, 2005, from www.verisign.com/static/003193.pdf

Visa. (2004). *Verified by Visa.* Retrieved January 7, 2005, from https://usa.visa.com/personal/security/vbv/index.html

Chapter X

The Survivability Principle:
IT-Enabled Dispersal of Organizational Capital

Andrew P. Snow, Ohio University, USA

Detmar Straub, Georgia State University, USA

Carl Stucke, Georgia State University, USA

Richard Baskerville, Georgia State University, USA

Abstract

The horrific terrorist attacks carried out on September 11, 2001, and the ensuing aftermath are driving managers to reconsider organizational risk. The collapsing towers moved the hypothetical risk of centralization to the shockingly real. In this new environment, organizations need to see survivability as a critical imperative motivating an updated enterprise risk mitigation strategy that includes new design objectives such as: (1) more geographically distributed organizations, (2) a move from redundant to physically distributed IT capabilities, and (3) more stringent security and survivability demands on enterprise IT infrastructures and network service providers. While individual firms' strategies will vary in the extent and type of physical decentralization, the overall tendency should be toward further dispersal of people, technology, and physical assets. This chapter examines the concepts of risk and decentralization as articulated in the scientific literature and then presents a strong logic for physical decentralization supported by a technical risk analysis.

Introduction

In the aftermath of September 11, 2001 (referred to hereafter as 9/11), managers need to take a fresh look at organizational risk and how *information technology* (IT) needs to adopt new enterprise risk mitigation strategies. These future risk mitigation strategies may result in the implementation of dispersal strategies in organizational design and more geographically distributed organizations. As a result, IT managers will not only need to develop technologies for supporting this overall organizational dispersal, but will also need to reorganize the IT function in a distributed form to increase survivability of the IT organization itself.

In addition, we believe there is a need for IT managers to understand certain basic networking and organizational survivability principles in order to better support senior executives in designing this dispersal. Primarily, these principles must be applied in two forms. First, the *information systems* (IS) architecture will be forced to move its assurance strategy from fully redundant to economically physically distributed IT redundancy capabilities. Second, network survivability principles from the network technology literature can inform organizational dispersal design. Fundamental economic principles in network survivability are necessary to effectively design the organization for survivability without substantially increasing organizational capital (i.e., size in terms of number of duplicate workers, IT equipment, etc.).

The result will be a shift of risk away from more centralized IT organizations to physically distributed IT infrastructures and networks that interconnect geographically disparate sites. Our contribution in this chapter is to explain the survivability principle as a logical and technical design, project it as an economic principle, and then apply this to the organization as a whole.

We pursue the following line of thinking:

- In the wake of 9/11, organizational dispersal is the most viable organizational option for survivability (the survivability principle);

- Dispersal of IT resources and capabilities is a closely related logical inference (also, the survivability principle); and

- Managers must determine the optimal trade-off between risk and cost in these dispersal decisions (a basic economic principle).

Risk and the Centralization-Decentralization Argument

Risk propositions are always tenuous, the classic calculation of risk being the potential dollar impact of an adverse event multiplied by the probability of that event occurring. The problem with such value propositions are that they are often represented by a very large loss number, which everyone can estimate, multiplied by a very small probability number, which no one believes.

In the physical world, we have always known that human artifices have risk associated with them and that they can fail, as attested to, copiously, in official standards documents (Swanson & Guttman, 1996):

> ***Physical and Environmental Security: Structural Collapse****. Organizations should be aware that a building may be subjected to a load greater than it can support. Most commonly this is a result of an earthquake, a snow load on the roof beyond design criteria, or an explosion which displaces or cuts structural members, or a fire that weakens structural members.* (p. 42)

Thus, the threat of airplane fuel-fired heat collapsing the *World Trade Center* (WTC) was always present, but who believed it would happen? Given the terrifying events surrounding the destruction of the WTC, businesses and information systems managers can no longer afford to suspend their disbelief. New circumstances demand new perspectives. With these terrorist attacks, the risk of attack is no longer an abstraction. What is more, the aftermath of the Pentagon and WTC disasters revealed previously unanticipated ways for organizations to be disrupted. To make matters worse, using Anthrax, bioterrorists closed entire buildings for months in the Fall of 2001.

If decentralization is a viable answer to this risk, how far should this go, if, indeed, it is a strategic necessity? Some CEOs in Manhattan today are already institutionalizing: (1) employee dispersal to more disparate geographic sites (Grant & Gasparino, 2001), and (2) virtualization of the firm (Zuckerman, Davis, & McGee, 2001) to reduce perceived risk. Indeed, some IT functions appear to be rapidly physically decentralizing in the wake of 9/11 (Vijayan, 2001).

But not all firms are convinced that physical dispersal of assets is a strategic necessity. Merrill-Lynch has returned 8000 employees to the *World Financial Center* buildings (TenantWise, 2005). In another case, Nomura Securities International, the U.S. securities unit of Japan's Nomura Securities, says that it "would like to move ... our employees in[to] a single main location and we would prefer to return to our offices [in lower Manhattan] ... as quickly as possible" (Grant & Gasparino, 2001). Indeed, Nomura returned to 2 World Financial Center (TenantWise, 2005).

So the situation is, and likely will remain uncertain for some time to come. Distributing electronic and human resources has trade-offs associated with it, like most other things in life, and the optimal mix of distribution and cost control needs to be carefully considered by managers.

Significant pendulum swings between centralization and decentralization have characterized IT architectures since the dawn of the computer age. These swings are no longer justifiable in the post-9/11 era. Considerations of full and rapid disaster recovery of systems must now motivate information systems managers, and this scenario calls for high levels of decentralization and system mirroring and partial recovery capabilities. How far on the swing of the pendulum this takes an individual firm is one matter. But our belief, and line of reasoning, is that the Gestalt of the decision has changed, and thus it will not be wise to return to the centralization side of the pendulum swing for the foreseeable future. On the other hand, there is a sense that it can become equally risky to unnecessarily co-locate massively significant portions of the organizational capital.

Grounding of the Decentralization Argument

What is the intellectual grounding of the macro-level argument for dispersal? The issue is primarily a question of organizational design. At the highest level, executives must decide in how many physical locations the firm will operate, and they must decide on the allocation of resources among these entities. As Eisenhardt (1985) points out, organizational design frequently emphasizes structural alternatives such as matrix, decentralization, and divisionalization. Such decisions are not unrelated to decisions about outsourcing and the extent to which the firm virtualizes its structure (Chesbrough & Teece, 1996). There are numerous trade-offs that must be considered, not the least of which are control versus cost and risk versus opportunity costs (Chesbrough & Teece, 1996).

There has likewise been an ongoing debate with respect for the argument surrounding centralization versus decentralization of the IS function. One issue is whether the structure of the IS organization reflects the structure of the overall organization. Robey (1981) found that there was no evidence in favor of the co-locational strategy, although other researchers have stressed the need for congruence in goals, known as strategic alignment (Barely, 1990; Henderson & Venkatraman, 1991).

Given that the physical structure of the IS function may not have to perfectly match that of the overall organization, what are the key issues specific to this domain? It is possible to trivialize the issue by reducing it to a one dimensional trade-off and then trying to resolve the problem with a single, logically derived or empirically derived solution. But even a glance at the literature indicates that this is not viable. It is quite clearly a multi-dimensional problem with multi-dimensional solutions. Among these problem dimensions are:

1. Efficiency, effectiveness, and cost (Overman, 1985);
2. Economics of emerging technologies (Dearden, 1987);
3. Coordination control (Brynjolfsson, 1994);
4. Flexibility of assets (Brynjolfsson, 1994);
5. Organizational decision-making style (Tavakolian, 1991);
6. Information intensity (Wang, 2001);
7. Organizational form (Tavakolian, 1991);
8. Competitive pressures (Tavakolian, 1991; Wang, 2001);
9. Political control (Bloomfield & Coombs, 1992);
10. Organizational orientation (Tavakolian, 1991);
11. Organizational innovativeness (Wang, 2001);
12. Size (Tavakolian, 1991); and
13. IT importance (Wang, 2001).

Traditionally, solutions to the centralization-decentralization issue have also been complex, reasoning through the set of organizational activities that lead to certain designs (Brown & Magill, 1998). The hybrid or federal organizational model, for example, combines features of centralization with decentralization (Brown, 1997; Lee, Cheng, & Chadha, 1995), and, like a rheostat, can allow the firm to adjust its structure to needs along many planes. This capability is likely why the empirical evidence favors this mode of distribution of IT functions and assets (Hodgkinson, 1992; Nault, 1998).

Even in light of 9/11, there might be excellent reasons, for example, for a firm to continue to centralize IT strategy (Fowler & Wilkinson, 1998). The risk to the organization is that if all knowledge of IT strategy is embodied in a single location and the sources of that knowledge, both human and physical, cease to exist, the organization will be hamstrung for some time to come.

Our analysis of the overriding IT organizational design issue, and our reasoning for much greater decentralization and distribution of assets, takes two forms. First, we present a logic and set of principles for why firms must move toward distribution of IT assets– human, electronic, and physical. Second, we present a technical risk analysis that takes into account the extent and type of distribution within a framework that favors more decentralization. Neither of these forms of argumentation are closed-form solutions. Detailed analyses of individual firms and their needs are still paramount. But it does point decidedly toward directions that must be taken in practice and toward practice-relevant, follow-on research.

Revisiting Decentralization: Organizational Asset Dispersal

What has really changed since 9/11? As noted earlier, an event that was widely perceived to be a rare or inconsequential has occurred. Following heightened media interest in acts of terrorism and prospects for more of the same, the risk — at least the perception risk — has clearly gone up (Rosen, 2001). The media's dissemination of information about past acts of terrorism has also contributed to this perception. Whether the risk is actually higher than it was or not, insurers clearly believe the risk is higher, as a widespread hardening in their markets confirms (McLeod, 2001).

But has the risk of more and momentous terrorist attacks actually gone up? The counter argument is that tighter airline security, increased international governmental activities in law enforcement and the military, and heightened public awareness may, in fact, mean that the actual risk is lower than before 9/11. What is equally clear, though, is that, irrespective of actual risk, entire industries such as the airline and travel industries have been dramatically affected and will likely continue to be so into the distant future. So we cannot ignore perceptions of risk, in this scenario or in many others. Consumers are wary of B2C purchases over the Web, for instance, even when the transaction is well secured with state-of-the-art encryption. The point is that the ultimate effect is lower sales, in spite of the real risk.

Therefore, the probability of an event seems to be inextricably bound with both the past statistical occurrences and perceptions of the event occurring. These perceptions effectively mean that there is greater risk of a terrorist attack on a firm's IT assets today than on September 10, 2001. Given that the WTC was a beehive of organizational activities that included not only trading and risk management, but also the manipulation and processing of these transactions, this is not an unreasonable assumption, we feel.

One way to explore the future risk to enterprises is to examine how organizations could have organized their assets in such a way so as to minimize the damage caused by the WTC disaster. Some trading firms, such as Cantor Fitzgerald, lost significant numbers of their staff (Zuckerman & Cowan, 2001). Others, such as Marsh-McLennan, were minimally affected in a direct way (Zuckerman & Cowan, 2001), even though they lost a high percentage of employees who were located in the Towers. Was there a difference in organizational structuring that accounts for this?

One critical difference in these cases is that Cantor had more heavily concentrated its human, computing, and physical assets in the WTC. Recovery has been extremely difficult because so much was invested in so few places. Even though it lost hundreds of valuable employees, Marsh did not concentrate resources nearly to the extent of Cantor (Oster, 2001). As a consequence, Marsh was able to recover operations quickly and to move ahead rapidly to create new underwriting capabilities that take the evolved risk environment into account (Oster, 2001).

Concentrations of people and technology raise the risk of a company's survival. The technical analysis of this for a network is presented next, but, for the moment, we can extend this logic to two propositions that may be able to guide managers in distributing their assets and researchers in testing the concept.

IT managers have typically taken a *reliability* perspective of IT capability and infrastructure risk, in that fully redundant capabilities offer fault tolerance. In this rubric, if a site fails, a fully redundant site offers 100% of the capacity required. (This perspective is in accord with the principle that there should be no single point of failure in an organization.) Later, we will show conditions where this approach offers false security. In this line of reasoning, we offer a *survivability* perspective where the IT capacity is dispersed. In this rubric, site failures are accommodated by offering, at some point of multiple and widespread failures, potentially less than 100% of capacity. Given site failure(s), an organization providing an acceptable level of capacity (a "maximally estimable" portion of capacity) is a survivable organization.

There are at least two theoretically testable corollaries to the survivability principle that emerge from this discussion:

- **Corollary 1a:**

  Firms that avoid concentrations of essential IT resources are said to embody the survivability principle [NOTE: by essential IT resources, we mean those IT computer resources, personnel resources, and physical resources, whose loss would threaten the firm's existence because recovery would be so difficult].

- **Corollary 1b:**

  Firms that adopt a strategic goal of survivability, a state in which the firm's existence will not be seriously threatened by the loss of a maximally estimable portion of the firm's assets, will demonstrate longevity.

Principles: Reliability and Survivability

The concept for managing loss that is of greatest interest to us is survivability. In network design, survivability implies that loss of one or an estimated maximum number of connections will not threaten the existence of the overall network. In the context of the firm, survivability implies that the firm's existence will not be seriously threatened by the loss of a maximally estimable proportion of the firm's assets. In the standard risk analysis of the ability of a firm to recover from disaster, such estimated maximal proportions are not usually assessed. We feel that this is a crucial oversight.

What is the conventional solution to risk of system failure? Conceptually, a single "redundant" backup strategy has been the standard solution for the vast majority of firms. This is not sufficient, we argue, to fully mitigate the risk in the contemporary setting. Firms will need to move to more "distributed" models, where some combination of distributed nodes can recover all or part of the system capability. Nodes on the firm's internal network need to be able to pick up the slack in the event of outages — not by just one node, but by multiple nodes if failure occurs at more than one site.

What is new about this approach? To date, most firms have not been willing to expend the significant resources required to build sufficiently large-scale distributed systems to support organizational dispersal. The cost to backup throughout one's enterprise data and software, not to mention people and physical plant facilities, is much higher than to hire or own a single IT backup facility. In the November 2001 Business Continuity Readiness Survey conducted by Gartner, Inc. and the *Society for Information Management* (SIM), more than 60% of respondents were unlikely to even redesign their networks to increase survivability (Gartner, 2001).

However, we believe strongly that the costs involved in a multiple-site risk mitigation strategy are worthwhile and even a strategic necessity in the post-9/11 world. Even traditional research and advisory firms such as Gartner, Inc. are recommending movement to dispersed, far-flung, resilient virtual organizations (Morello, 2002).

Figure 1. Simple redundant IT system configuration or central redundant architecture (CRA)

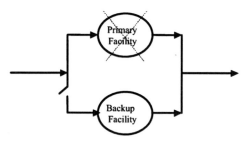

Reliability: Standard Mode of Dispersal

The most common technical solution to survivability is a no-single-point-of-failure reliability that offers 100% redundancy. Under certain conditions, with redundancy, we may be able to achieve a level of fault tolerance that allows complete business continuity in the event of an outage. The concept of a single 100% backup facility is shown in Figure 1. If the primary facility is unable to function, the presence of the fully redundant backup facility may be able to provide for a smooth recovery. We term this architecture a *central redundant architecture* (CRA).

Previously, the rationale for this approach has been compelling because the chance of both facilities failing is much smaller than the chance of one facility failing, as seen in Table 1. The reliability of the redundant configuration (i.e., the chance the configuration will not fail) is derived from the reliability of a single facility:

$$R_r = 1 - (1 - R_s)^2$$

As the reliability of each facility increases separately across the scenarios posed, the possibility of the redundancy method failing is dramatically reduced, from 1% to .01% in this example. This substantially decreases the risk to the enterprise.

However, 9/11 throws into doubt certain critical assumptions to the choice of this architecture. First, there is an inherent assumption in the redundant facility reliability probabilities that the failure events are independent. In the case of the WTC, the terrorists hit several sites at the same time, and some enterprises had both primary and backup facilities in the Twin Towers. Indeed, the infrastructure of the entire lower Manhattan area was seriously disrupted, so even a backup a few blocks away could easily have been inadequate. Imagine the horrific scenario of a large-scale catastrophe for an entire metropolitan region! These co-dependent failure events are why organizational risk has risen so dramatically with 9/11.

Second, the seamless transfer of operations to the backup facility is assumed. If the event that disables the primary site also impedes the ability of the organization to switch to the backup site, this supposedly fault-tolerant architecture is defeated and is no better than a single facility. This defeat can happen in several ways. For instance, the human resources necessary to operate the backup facility may also be destroyed in the event,

Table 1. Comparison of single facility and redundant facility reliabilities

Scenario	Single IT Facility Reliability	Redundant IT Facility Reliability (CRA)
1	0.90	0.9900
2	0.95	0.9950
3	0.99	0.9999

or the transportation system necessary to migrate to the new facility may not available. Both of these scenarios were at issue in the WTC disaster.

Lack of independence clearly undermines current IT solutions to these problems. Survivability forces a higher independence threshold on cold or hot sites, a standard redundant solution to backup and recovery; that is, there must be only a very few and only highly unlikely situations where both facilities can fail.

Going beyond a single backup facility raises the possibility of reconsidering distributed systems arguments that were first evaluated in the eighties and reprised in the nineties with the arrival of the ubiquitous World Wide Web. However, in this reconsideration we must recognize that firms do not want to sell the same airline seat twice from two of their dispersed systems (so dispersed systems must synchronize information and activities) or create cost-inefficient organizations from over-decentralization. Likewise, firms do not want to go out of business because they embraced the known benefits to centralization strategies (e.g., economies of scale, database integrity, etc.). Identifying the optimal position between these two extremes requires more research and is perhaps different for each organization. It is in this spirit that we offer the technical analysis below. The logic is simple and, hopefully, compelling, but exactly how to implement this solution is incomplete. Filling in the missing details is the research challenge we are advocating for the IS field.

Viable Approaches to Redesigning Post-9/11 Information Systems Architectures

There are at least two general approaches that can and should be taken with respect to information architectures:

1.   Strengthen the ability to transfer operations to a backup facility located at a geographically disparate site (R, or the central site plus the backup), or

2.   Implement physically distributed systems of at least R+1 in response to demands for greater risk mitigation.

An example of a distributed organization is shown in Figure 2, where excess capacity is in place to enable an organization to perform 100% of its mission if one site is destroyed or disabled. Here, risk is distributed among a number of smaller sites (N) by enabling each of these sites to recover all or a portion of the firm's IT capabilities. In the event of site(s) failure(s), this architecture delivers some portion of the total capacity.

In this configuration, there is a degree of redundancy to accommodate one site failure, combined with geographic dispersal. More than 100% capacity (C) is required, governed by:

$$C_{Total} = \frac{N}{N-1} \quad \text{and} \quad C_{Site} = \frac{1}{N-1}$$

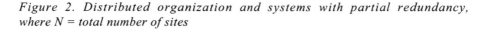

Figure 2. Distributed organization and systems with partial redundancy, where N = total number of sites

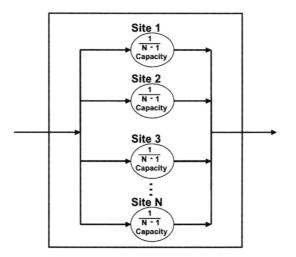

We call such a system a *distributed partially redundant architecture* (DPRA). For example, a DPRA with six sites would require 120% total capacity, each site having 20% capacity. The capacity comparison of N sites with DPRA against the CRA is shown in Table 2.

The strength of such an approach is illustrated for a six-site DPRA in Table 3. Here, we enumerate the chances of different concurrent failure events and show the organizational capacity available under different site failure situations for a six-node distributed organization. Scenarios 1, 2, and 3 correspond to individual site reliabilities of 0.9, 0.95, and 0.99, respectively. Recognize that with zero-site failures we have 120% of organiza-

Table 2. Enterprise capacity requirements

N	Enterprise Configuration	Required Capacity	Capacity Savings Over CRA
2	CRA	200%	0
3	DPRA	150%	50%
4	DPRA	133%	67%
5	DPRA	125%	75%
6	DPRA	120%	80%
7	DPRA	117%	83%

tional capacity available, for a one-site failure we have 100% capacity, and for two-site failures we have 80% capacity. Entries in Table 3 are calculated by:

$$\Pr[x:Fail] = \frac{N!}{x!(N-x)!} R_s^{N-x}(1-R_s)^x \quad \text{and} \quad \Pr[\leq x:Fail] = \sum_{j=0}^{x}\Pr[j:Fail]$$

where x is the number of failed sites, N the total number of sites, and R_s the single site reliability.

If we compare the DPRA probabilities to those of CRA in Table 1, we see that a one-site failure (100% capacity) is still inferior to CRA. However, the DPRA probabilities for two of less site failures (offering a worst case 80% capacity) is superior to CRA for Scenarios 2 and 3. The trade-off is clear—at a capacity savings of 80% (from Table 2), DPRA offers 80% or better capacity performance (from Table 3) at a probability comparable to CRA, which offers 100% capacity. However, if there are further failures, DPRA still offers partial capacity to the enterprise, while the CRA has not survived. So DPRA is resilient to multiple failure situations, while the CRA is not.

This trade-off becomes more obvious in Figure 3, where CRA reliability is compared with DPRA survivability. Figure 3 shows the probability of having two or fewer sites fail for DPRA with three through seven sites, where each site has 95% reliability. Observe that the probabilities are somewhat comparable for CRA with up to one-site failure and the six-site DPRA with up to two-site failures. Also note that if worst case 75% capacity is acceptable, the survivable DPRA is superior to CRA. What is striking is that the point of diminishing returns is achieved at seven sites. This comparison shows the economic trade-off involved in distributed partially redundant architectures and suggests an economic optimization situation.

Note that, for the moment, these calculations assume 100% reliability of the network that interconnects the sites in DPRA. Clearly, moving to a physically distributed enterprise

Table 3. Probabilistic worst case capacity of a six-site distributed organization with 20% redundancy

	Scenario 1 $R_s = .9$	Scenario 2 $R_s = .95$	Scenario 3 $R_s = .99$	Capacity
Pr [= 0 fail]	0.5314410	0.735099	0.9414802	120%
Pr [≤ 1 fail]	0.8857350	0.9672262	0.9985396	100%
Pr [≤ 2 fail]	0.9841500	0.9977702	0.9999805	80%
Pr [≤ 3 fail]	0.9987300	0.9999136	0.9999999	60%
Pr [≤ 4 fail]	0.9999450	0.9999982	1.00000000	40%
Pr [≤ 5 fail]	0.9999990	1.0000000	1.00000000	20%
Pr [≤ 6 fail]	1.0000000	1.00000000	1.00000000	0%

Figure 3. CRA and DPRA survivability and worst case capacity comparison

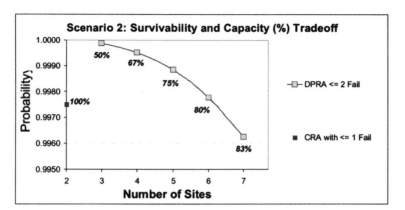

architecture such as DPRA requires highly reliable access and transport networks and shifts a portion of enterprise risk to these networks. Since the carrier networks have had their own reliability and survivability issues (Snow, 2001), some of which were illustrated by the massive concentration of telecommunication data and voice circuits (4.5 million and 300,000, respectively) that suffered long-term outages due to WTC collateral damage to network infrastructure, the sensitivity of the survivability/capacity issue to network reliability is illustrated in Figure 4.

A network reliability of 0.9975 is indicative of redundant network access links (each with a reliability of 0.99) over a resilient transport network with reliability 1.0. In such an

Figure 4. DPRA survivability sensitivity to network reliability

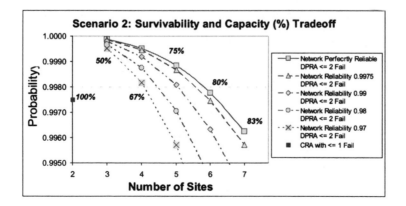

environment, networks would not affect the aforementioned survivability/capacity trade-off, as seen in Figure 4. However, a lower network reliability of 0.98 greatly affects the trade-off. Even when networks can deliver high technical reliability, a physical dispersal shift will require enterprises to negotiate more stringent *service-level agreements* (SLA) with network service providers and increased bandwidth to chosen distributed sites.

Clearly, survivability via a DPRA depends not only on geographic dispersal, but also upon reliable networks. However, this need for resilient networking is felt within other architectures as well (BITS, 2004).

This type of organizational design and IS architecture has several other implications, each of which has serious implications and requires more research:

1. Greater enterprise risk demands will be transferred to the network carriers and vendors — network service providers must respond with highly reliable bandwidth to dispersed site locations;

2. Distributed database capabilities must become available and more reliable;

3. IT security must be effective in spite of the chosen level of decentralization and ubiquitous connection capability; and

4. New organizational methods and procedures need to be deployed, including IT governance.

Organizational Redesign and Distributive Economics

Given this logic, how can executives apply this line of thinking in their organizations? The issue of survivability is, at heart, an economic issue. The question for managers is what level of asset distribution, or how many DPRA sites, are economically viable? The nature of this question is illustrated in Figure 5. As risk drops, the cost of distribution increases.

Overall costs, as illustrated in Figure 5, also include opportunity costs (what you might have done with monies used to construct your distributed environment) and the cost of IT recovery. These costs form a U-shaped curve, with the costs to firm being so high at either extreme that the firm's survival must be seriously compromised. Clearly, costs of losing a single location, designated as "1" in Figure 5, are unbearably high, since the firm would have no back-up, no archives, and hardware, software, or networks to continue business. No responsible firm can be in this position, as its IT capability is not survivable in the event of multiple site failures.

We have argued in this chapter that, post-9/11, a simple redundant or R capability is still a potentially less-than-optimal position for responsible firms. While distributive costs are higher, the opportunity costs are even higher, and could threaten the firm's survivability, as illustrated in Figure 5.

Figure 5. Distributive economics where R is a simple redundant capability (CRA); R+M is an optimal number of distributed sites; and R+N is the largest number of distributed sites possible in a firm

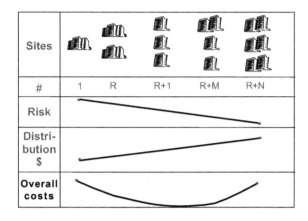

Moreover, distributing one's IT capacity throughout the enterprise would not be a sensible strategy in the cases of larger and/or global firms. The right extreme of the U-shaped curve represents the huge costs of creating recoverable capacity throughout the organization's many locations (for example, all franchises of a large international fast-food chain). These distributive costs could seriously erode the bottom line and, in this way, threaten the firm's economic viability.

This R+M optimal economic choice balances the distributive costs against the risks. Obviously the curves and relationships illustrated in Figure 5 are only hypothetical. To identify an enterprise's specific values, managers must field a risk assessment team including business unit professionals to estimate the costs to their units and the firm for being without systems for certain periods of time and IT professionals to evaluate what would be required to transition to other sites in the event of single and multiple failures, and the costs of establishing and maintaining recoverability at these sites.

These risk-assessment-developed values will more often than not result in an R+M optimal capacity (with M larger than zero).

Guidelines for Managers

The points raised in this chapter logically suggest certain guidelines for managers. Clearly, more research is required regarding organizational design and IS architectures and governance:

1.   If electing a 100% redundant facility, ensure that the ability to carry out that capability is not likely to be compromised by catastrophic personnel or infrastructure loss; or

2.   If electing a physically distributed organization for risk dispersal, develop IT governance strategies that will be effective and place more emphasis on access network reliability and survivability necessary to interconnect dispersed sites.

Enterprise risk assessment and business continuity planning (well-known and well-tested) are the best ways for executives to be as sure as they can that the firm is protected in the event of catastrophe. Ultimately, it helps assure that the firm survives. Naturally, top managers have a duty to their investors to also ensure that this risk mitigation strategy can be executed at the lowest overall cost to the corporation. The DPRA risk mitigation strategy, based on our proposed survivability principle, is an approach that should be seriously considered in the wake of 9/11. IS researchers have a special call to study these issues and to push forward organizational theory that explains how the organization can and should respond to catastrophe and crisis.

References

Barely, S. P. (1990). The alignment of technology and structure through roles and networks. *Administrative Sciences Quarterly, 35*, 61-103.

BITS. (2004). *The BITS guide to business-critical telecommunications services.* Retrieved June 12, 2005, from http://www.bitsinfo.org/downloads/Misc/bitstelecomguide.pdf

Bloomfield, B. P., & Coombs, R. (1992). Information technology, control and power: The centralization and decentralization debate revisited. *The Journal of Management Studies, 29*(4), 459-85.

Brown, C. V. (1997). Examining the emergence of hybrid IS governance solutions: Evidence from a single case site. *Information Systems Research, 8*, 69-94.

Brown, C. V., & Magill, S. L. (1998). Reconceptualizing the context-design issue for the information systems function. *Organization Science, 9*(2), 176-194.

Brynjolfsson, E. (1994). Information assets, technology, and organization. *Management Science, 40*(12), 1645-1662.

Chesbrough, H. W., & Teece, D. J. (1996). When is virtual virtuous?. *Harvard Business Review, 74*(1), 65-73.

Dearden, J. (1987). The withering away of the IS organization. *Sloan Management Review, 28*(4), 87-91.

Eisenhardt, K. M. (1985). Control: Organizational and economic approaches. *Management Science, 31*(2), 134-150.

Fowler, A., & Wilkinson, T. (1998). An examination of the role of the information systems centre. *Journal of Strategic Information Systems, 7*(2), 87-111.

Gartner, Inc., & Society for Information Management (2001). Business continuity readiness survey. Retrieved November 22, 2005, from http://www.conasis.org/expsimbcpsurvey.pdf

Grant, P., & Gasparino, C. (2001, October 27). Lehman Brothers plans to move headquarters out of Wall Street. *Wall Street Journal Interactive (Eastern Edition), C1*.

Henderson, J. C., & Venkatraman, N. (1991). Understanding strategic alignment. *Business Quarterly, 55*(3), 72-78.

Hodgkinson, S. L. (1992). IT structures for the 1990s: Organisation of IT functions in large companies: A survey. *Information & Management, 22*(3), 161-175.

Lee, A., Cheng, C. H., & Chadha, G. S. (1995). Synergism between information technology and organizational structure - A managerial perspective. *Journal of Information Technology, 10*(1), 37-43.

McLeod, D. (2001). Top risk management stories of 2001—1: Terrorism strikes U.S. *Business Insurance, 35*(52), 22.

Morello, D. T. (2002). Building the resilient virtual organization. Retrieved October 1, 2002, from http://www.csoonline.com/analyst/report502.html

Nault, B. R. (1998). Information technology and organization design: Locating decisions and information. *Management Science, 44*(10), 1321-1335.

Oster, C. (2001, November 15). Bouncing back: Insurance companies benefit from Sept. 11, Still seek federal aid — Marsh & McLennan starts new units; Other raise some premiums by 100% — Turning away eager investors. *Wall Street Journal*, A1.

Overman, E. S. (1985). Decentralization and microcomputer policy in state government. *Public Productivity Review, 9*(11), 143-154.

Robey, D. (1981). Computer information systems and organization structure. *Communications of the ACM, 24*(10), 679-687.

Rosen, J. (2001). Bad luck. *The New Republic, 225*(19), 21-23.

Snow, A. P. (2001). Network reliability: The concurrent challenges of innovation, competition, and complexity. *IEEE Transactions on Reliability, 50*(1), 38-40.

Swanson, M., & Guttman, B. (1996, September). Generally accepted principles and practices for securing information technology systems. *National Institute of Standards and Technology Administration Technical Manual*, U.S. Department of Commerce, 42. Retrieved June 15, 2005, from http://csrc.nist.gov/publications/nistpolos/800-14/800-14.pdf

Tavakolian, H. (1991). The organisation of IT functions in the 1990s: A managerial perspective. *The Journal of Management Development, 10*(2), 31-38.

TenantWise. (2005). World Trade Center tenant relocation summary. Retrieved June 12, 2005, from http://www.thenow.com/wtc_relocate.asp

Vijayan, J. (2001). Sept. 11 attacks prompt decentralization moves. *Computerworld, 35*(51), 10.

Wang, E. T. G. (2001). Linking organizational context with structure: A preliminary investigation of the information processing view. *Omega, 29*(5), 429-443.

Zuckerman, G., & Cowan, L. (2001, September 13). At the top: Cantor Fitzgerald took pride in its position at the World Trade Center. *Wall Street Journal*, C1.

Zuckerman, G., Davis, A., & McGee, S. (2001, October 27). In the wake of carnage of terror attacks, The Cantor that was will never be again. *Wall Street Journal (Eastern Edition), A1*.

Section III:

Security Engineering

Chapter XI

Security Engineering:
It Is All About Control and Assurance Objectives

Ronda R. Henning, Harris Corporation, USA

Abstract

Information security engineering is the specialized branch of systems engineering that addresses the derivation and fulfillment of a system's security requirements. For years, security engineering practitioners have claimed that security is easier to build into a system when it is integrated with the system analysis and design. This paper presents some basic tenets of security analysis that can be applied by any systems engineer to ensure early integration of security constraints into the system definition and development process. It sheds light on security requirements interpretation to facilitate the fulfillment of security requirements throughout the system lifecycle.

Introduction

The systems engineering process manages the overall requirements fulfillment and derivation process for a given information system development effort. The specialized branch of systems engineering that supports the fulfillment of information security requirements is the discipline of security engineering. Ideally, information assurance requirements are engineered into a system from the concept definition phase forward. Too often, security is considered an afterthought or a "should" requirement that is optional to the system function and is discarded during early system analysis. Security engineering must support a methodical, repeatable process with measurable, quantifiable results to be considered a scientific pursuit.

Sommerville (2001) characterizes system properties as being functional and non-functional in nature. Functional properties contribute to the achievement of the system objectives. Non-functional properties relate to the behavior of the system in operation and are most often related to the user's perception of the system's value. For example, security is often considered a non-functional property of a system, but if the data is corrupted due to the failure of security mechanisms, it impacts the ability of the system to meet its functional objective.

Koch and Parisi-Presicce (2003) states, "Security requirements are difficult to analyze and model. Security policies are generally specified in terms of highly specialized security models that are not integrated with general software engineering models" (p. 67). Haley, Laney, and Nuseibeh (2004) states, "Expressing specific security requirements is difficult. They tend to be stated as crosscutting concerns that impact many functional requirements" (p. 112). Security requirements are often discarded during early analysis and addressed through the use of separate appliances, such as firewalls, later in the design process.

This chapter presents an approach to security requirement analysis that can be applied during systems analysis. For the broadest application, the chapter does not tie itself to any given development methodology or design technique, nor does it endorse any single standard. Each enterprise tailors its system development artifacts to reflect their unique environments, so this chapter focuses on the content of these artifacts rather than artifacts themselves.

The remainder of this chapter is organized as follows: the security objectives associated with system requirements development are presented. Then, the distinction between security requirements and assurance requirements is described. Sources of security requirements are discussed next. Creation techniques for good security requirements are presented, as are some techniques for tying security requirements into subsequent design phases. Finally, the major cost/benefit analysis factors associated with selecting among alternative security implementations are presented.

Control Objectives

As with other requirement families, information security requirements are normally expressed in terms of their control objectives. For both the *information system* and the *information* it contains, the control objectives provide the foundation for all derivative security requirements. The control objectives are based on three sources (ISO/IEC, 1998):

1. **The environmental context of the information system** — the physical environment associated with the system, in terms of how accessible the system may be to unauthorized personnel.

2. **The information contained within the system** — the value of the information to the organization in terms of the criticality of the information and/or the potential damage to the organization if the information is compromised.

3. **The physical assets of the system** — the actual hardware and software used to implement the system, and their connectivity to other assets.

Objectives associated with information security are usually categorized as security objectives or assurance objectives. Their differences are addressed in the following sections.

Security Control Objectives

Henning (1999) defines five security control objectives, listed in Table 1. Calabrese (2004) defines four security objectives using the acronym *confidentiality*, *authentication*, *integrity*, and *non-repudiation* (CAIN). The question is whether availability is considered an objective or not. For real-time systems, availability is a paramount requirement.

Table 1. The security control objectives

Objective	Definition	Example
Confidentiality	Sometimes called secrecy or privacy, confidentiality is the protection of the assets of a computing system such that the assets are accessible only to authorized parties.	Protection of credit card or personnel privileged information in transit through the network with the use of encryption technologies.
Authentication	Authentication establishes the validity of a user's identity and is fundamentally verified, proven identification of the user to the system. It determines that (1) a user is identified to the system, and (2) is authorized use of the asset.	Validation of identity before acceptance of attack commands or prior to release of funds in the financial community.
Availability	Availability ensures the information and system resources are accessible to authorized system users. A user of the system can be a person or another system that requires a given asset.	Information residing on enterprise servers that is available to traveling users at remote locations.
Integrity	Integrity means that information assets can be modified only by authorized parties in authorized ways.	A user may be authorized to read data from a database but may not modify that information.
Non-repudiation	Non-repudiation is proof of the identity of both the sender and the recipient, preserving the responsibility of both the originator and recipient for their actions.	Validation of a user's signature by the vendor and validation of the vendor by the user prior to acceptance of a credit transaction.

Having the information perfectly secure but delivered too late to take life-critical action does not fulfill the mission of the system.

Assurance Control Objectives

The information assurance control objectives complement the security control objectives and provide the basis for subsequent reasoning about system feature reliability (ISO/IEC, 1998). Information assurance refers to the fact that information is made available to authorized users, when requested, with the expected integrity. In essence, the assurance objectives are subordinate, non-functional objectives supporting the security control objectives.

Information assurance encompasses not only the basic system security properties, but also the policies, procedures, and personnel that are used to maintain the system and its data in a known, secure state. The assurance control objectives are usually considered management functions; they are summarized in Table 2.

Putting the Security and Assurance Objectives to Work

In the traditional sense, systems engineering ends with system development, in that the system requirements have been defined, designed, and implemented. However, when

Table 2. Assurance control objectives

Assurance Objective	Definition	Representative Requirement
Configuration Management	The system that tracks the hardware, software, and firmware configuration of each device.	The system shall be maintained in a known, secure state at all times.
Personnel Management	The personnel practices that support the administration of security functions	The system administration positions shall be considered "positions of trust" in accordance with Directive XYZ.
Vulnerability Management	The maintenance of the system software updates process to ensure all known vulnerabilities are corrected.	The system shall employ a vulnerability scanning and remediation capability.
Software Development Management	The systemic use of software design principles and processes.	Any software developed for the system shall be developed using best commercial practices.
Verification Management	The process of testing and validation used to ensure the system works correctly.	The vendor shall maintain a verification program that includes, at a minimum, unit, subsystem, and system verification procedures.

coupled with the assurance control objectives, security engineering extends beyond the traditional development phase to the operations, maintenance, and decommissioning of a system. Tracing the control objectives throughout the system life cycle becomes essential to the maintenance of the system's assurance posture. From that perspective, security engineering becomes a requirements engineering exercise that emphasizes traceability throughout the system life cycle.

Security Requirements Engineering

Kotoyna and Sommerville (1998) define requirements engineering as "the activities involved in the discovery, documentation, and maintenance of a set of requirements for a computer-based system" (p. 8). Security requirements engineering is specifically concerned with the set of security requirements associated with a computer-based information system.

Sources of Security Requirements

The initial activity of security requirements engineering phase is the identification of the security requirements and their categorization to reflect the control objectives associated with a system. Simply put, a security requirement is a restriction of access to or privileges regarding an object (e.g., facility, equipment, piece of software, piece of data). Security requirements come from multiple sources, some of which are described in the following subsections.

The User's Documentation

The system user or development organization may have had the foresight to develop a detailed set of system requirements. In such cases, the requirements are primarily functional, and probably have omitted security as a separate requirement or included standard boilerplate security requirements. When this occurs, the engineer must search through the requirements specification to derive the system security requirements.

Representative implicit security requirements include:

- The ability to create, read, update, or delete an object in a database;

- The ability to release a message;

- The ability to inhibit an action;

- The ability to create a message; and

- The ability to access operating system services.

These requirements are usually stated as actions to be performed by authorized users or prohibited from execution by certain user groups. By combing through the requirements and user documentation, the implicit security requirements can be transformed into an explicit set of security requirements. The derived requirements should be reviewed with the system's users to ensure a correct interpretation of the concept of operations.

Legacy Systems

In some cases, the best source of requirements may be an existing system. The legacy environment probably embodies the user's current security concept of operations relatively well. When all else fails, active listening in a session with the user walking through how the system is used can be employed to elicit the existing security requirements. Then the "as built" security policy can be compared to the policy "as desired" for the new implementation, and the differences between the two environments can be discerned.

The connectivity and networking implemented in legacy systems also provides clues to the security requirement's implementation. The importance of connectivity countermeasures such as firewalls cannot be over-emphasized during legacy system re-engineering. If these countermeasures are dismissed or neglected, the resulting system could expose the user to more vulnerabilities than the current legacy environment. Users may not think of network infrastructure protections as part of "their" system, but if the users are unaware of the network architecture, important protection measures within the existing implementation may be overlooked.

A Few Words About Security Standards and Maturity Models

Standards documents can be used to provide a "shorthand" notation for security requirements. For example, the Common Criteria uses *evaluation assurance levels* (EALs) to specify the degrees of rigor and correspondence required in the development of an information technology system. A single statement of "the system must support an independent evaluation against EAL3" expands into 5-10 pages of explicit feature statements about the information system. These standards are used to embody best security practices from various user and governmental organizations. The most commonly referenced security standards are described in this section.

The Common Criteria

The *Common Criteria* for information technology security evaluation (CC) (ISO/IEC, 1998) is the result of years of international collaboration to define a standard collection of requirements for security functionality. Originally, the standard was applied to individual products for security and assurance property evaluation (i.e., operating systems, database management systems, etc.). In recent years, the CC has begun to be used for complex system requirements definition activities.

The CC is composed of three primary components (ISO/IEC, 1998; Syntegra, 1998):

1. **Part 1**, *Introduction and general model*, is the introduction to the CC. It defines general concepts and principles of IT security evaluation and presents a general model of evaluation.

2. **Part 2**, *Security functional requirements*, establishes a set of functional requirement statements, defined as components. These components provide the building blocks for the functional requirement specifications

3. **Part 3**, *Security assurance requirements*, establishes a set of assurance components as a standard way of expressing the assurance requirements.

Another perspective on the CC is to consider it a catalog of security and assurance requirements. These requirements can be selected for a given implementation, and the resulting system can be evaluated to determine its compliance with the requirements.

ISO/IEC 17799

The ISO/IEC 17799:2000 standard (ISO/IEC, 2000) addresses security policies and good security practices (NIST, 2002). It is not intended to provide definitive detailed instructions. The document briefly addresses the following major topics:

*   Establishing organizational security policy;

*   Organizational security infrastructure;

*   Asset classification and control;

*   Personnel security;

*   Physical and environmental security;

*   Communications and operations management;

*   Access control;

*   Systems development and maintenance;

*   Business continuity management; and

*   Compliance.

ISO/IEC 17799:2000 does not provide the detailed conformance type of specifications necessary for an organizational information security management program. It can be used as a high-level overview of information security topics that could help senior management understand basic security management issues. Unlike the Common Criteria, ISO/IEC 17799 reflects a business-led approach to best practice on information security management. It describes a number of controls that can be considered as aiding principles providing a good starting point for implementing information security. BS7799 (ISO/IEC, 17799) is primarily used by global organizations with European trading partners to provide a common framework for assurance practices among interconnected enterprises.

The Capability Maturity Model — Integrated (CMMI)

In response to the proliferation of *capability maturity models* (CMMs), the CMMI (Goldenson & Gibson, 2003) was created to provide guidance for process improvement and the ability to manage the development, acquisition, and maintenance of products or services. It is designed to support integration of content from various disparate bodies of knowledge such as systems engineering and software engineering, as well as integrated product and process development activities. The CMMI characterizes process activities in four framework areas, which are further decomposed into process areas (CMMI Author Team, 2002). Within each process area, general and specific goals are further used to provide process characterization granularity.

The System Security Engineering Capability Maturity Model (SSE-CMM)

The SSE-CMM (ISO/IEC, 2002) was written as a companion guide to the various capability maturity models that proliferated in the 1990s. It was formally accepted as ISO/IEC 21827 and is the only such standard dedicated to security engineering practices. It describes the characteristics essential to the success of an organization's security engineering process and is applicable to all security engineering organizations, including government, commercial, and academic. The SSE-CMM addresses:

- Project life cycles, including development, operation, maintenance, and decommissioning activities;

- Entire organizations, including management, organizational, and engineering activities;

- Concurrent interactions with other disciplines, such as system software and hardware, human factors, test engineering, system management, operation, and maintenance;

- Interactions with other organizations, including acquisition, system management, certification, accreditation, and evaluation.

The SSE-CMM establishes a framework for measuring and improving performance in the application of security engineering principles. The SSE-CMM outlines a process-oriented approach to information assurance practices that is gaining acceptance in international circles.

Table 3. Security requirement decomposition — design free and design implicit

Security Sub-policy	Requirement Statement (design free)	Requirement Statement (implied design)
Confidentiality	The system shall preserve the privacy of information between source and destination.	The system shall use the Advanced Encryption Standard (AES) in link encryption mode.
Accountability	The system shall be able to reconstruct a given user's activities	The system shall generate an audit trail that contains the userid, action requested, data files accessed, success/failure of the action, and timestamp of request.
Integrity	The system shall maintain the integrity of the data in transit and at rest	The system shall apply a secure hash algorithm equivalent to SHA-1 protection.
Availability	The system shall be accessible to authorized users at all times.	The system shall deploy intrusion detection and prevention technologies, including anti-virus.

Requirements and Control Objectives

As can be see in Table 3, security requirements can be traced back to the five basic security control objectives. A similar mapping can be conducted for assurance objectives. In the ideal world, the requirements as stated would carry no implicit design decisions with them. Unfortunately, that is not always the case. Table 3 includes both design-free security requirement examples and design-implicit examples for each control objective.

There are a number of reasons why requirements incorporate design decisions. One of them is that there are architectural standards within an enterprise that may specify a given protocol, product, or component configuration. In these cases, ease of administration and cost within the enterprise may outweigh any benefits from an alternate implementation.

Moving Towards System Design

The requirements collected during the systems analysis activities reflect the "should be" state of the system. Pressman (1997) takes these requirements as a baseline and then considers the following additional factors to develop a working set of feasible requirements:

- **Assumptions** — reduce complexity to bound or de-scope the problem.
- **Simplifications** — allow completion within a reasonable period of time.
- **Limitations** — technology limitations that downsize project scope.
- **Constraints** — processing power, availability of resources, and so forth.
- **Preferences** — for the data, functions, and technology used.

When these factors are added to the requirements, a bounded or constrained system architecture can be developed. At this point, a concept of operations and preliminary data flows can be defined and validated with the user organization. Figure 1, adopted from the Common Criteria and Whitten, Bentley, and Dittman (2004) illustrates a process flow that characterizes the process from the initial environmental characterization to the modeling and analysis tasks that occur as part of the systems engineering process.

Optimization of the System Architecture

Based on the validated requirements, factored for Pressman's (1997) list of refinements, the system design can be optimized to reflect a balanced approach to information assurance. In the best of all worlds, architectures would not have to choose between perfect security, optimal performance, and affordable cost. Unfortunately, the world is

Figure 1. A characterization of the security engineering process

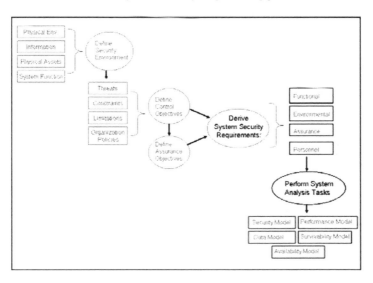

Figure 2. The security alternative tradespace

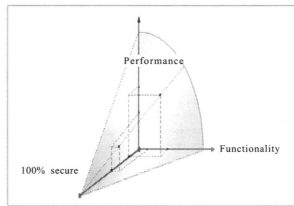

not perfect. Choices have to be made among these parameters to build the best-fit system that provides security with reasonable performance and optimal cost. Figure 2, suggested by O. Sami Saydjari (personal communication, March 30, 1998), illustrates the tradespace of system security alternatives available to the security engineer.

Similarly, it is important to understand the relative cost alternatives associated with various security solutions. Figure 3 graphically illustrates this concept. The security engineer must balance the incremental cost associated with a security or assurance mechanism with the hoped-for incremental improvement in the system's security architecture. This is the concept of "sufficient security" that is described in more detail by Vaughn and Henning (2000). For example, an organization may have a perfectly acceptable burglar alarm and a set of watchdogs. Such an organization may not gain much

Figure 3. The cost of improvement versus the probability of system compromise

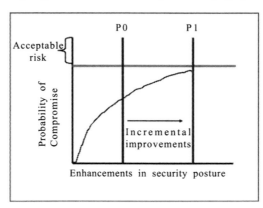

additional protection benefit from further physical security mechanisms. In this case, the probability of compromise would not have a significant incremental improvement. The acceptable risk associated with system operation would not change enough to warrant the investment in the technology.

There are times when previous best practice becomes insufficient. Features that were once incremental improvements in security services may become organizational necessities quite rapidly. For example, personal computers used to have very limited protection mechanisms. Virus protection alone used to be sufficient to protect a personal home computer. Today, serious home computer users have virus protection, firewalls, vulnerability scanning software, and spam filtering in place for "normal" system use.

Any way they are described, security objectives must be met by the system architecture if the system is to have verifiable security properties. Without the definition and specification of system security objectives, there are no functional requirements that can be translated into architectural countermeasures and security services for the architecture.

The Dynamics of Security and Assurance Requirements

Unlike some other system requirements, which are static over the life of the system, the security and assurance requirements may change dynamically depending on the actual threat at a particular moment in time. Factors such as the temporal nature of information (e.g., stock trades), competitor's capabilities, and the importance of the information to an organization all impact the degree of security and assurance needed and the mechanisms chosen to address these requirements. These factors can be discovered by understanding the enterprise, its processes, threats, management philosophy, and its external connectivity and access requirements. If a system design assumes that the security policy of the system never changes, then the users of the system will consider security as an obstacle, not an enabler, to progress.

The information security problem can be reduced to one of risk management based on the assurance measures put in place within the system. As circumstances change, a senior manager should have the ability to take more or less risk–based on judgment, understanding, and knowledge of the organization and with the advice and assistance of the security administrator. Examining a user's security needs and solutions with respect to a given set of environmental conditions and factors affords a higher capability for adaptation of the system as the environmental constraints change.

For example, consider the security requirements of a product design firm in the United States. When a new design is first conceived, it may be stored and managed in a design organization with many other design ideas that may or may not actually be approved for prototyping or production. As a result, the information is "reasonably" protected as proprietary information, but to a much smaller degree than if it were the next generation "must succeed" product for the company. In such a scenario, the protection decisions may change once management decides to move this design into another category for further development and possible prototyping. At this stage, an action has occurred (a management decision) that moved the enterprise to consider a new set of protection mechanisms for the design and perhaps to increase the assurance that it will be effective.

Conclusion

In conclusion, this chapter has presented an overview of the processes involved in security engineering requirements analysis. It presents a departure point for those interested in the security aspects of system engineering. Security requirement derivation becomes easier with practice and as the organizations involved become more comfortable with the notion of security being a functional system requirement. The security engineering practitioner must remember that security is one requirement family within a system architecture, and that the key to a successful security implementation is balance and risk management among the competing engineering and management requirements.

Additional Information

Information about the Common Criteria for Information Technology Systems (the CC) can be found at www.csrc.nist.gov/cc/index.html. The best information about information assurance processes is that incorporated into capability maturity models. The Software Engineering Institute (www.sei.cmu.edu) maintains the definitive archive on the capability maturity model — integrated. For information on the system security engineering capability maturity model, the International System Security Engineering Association (www.issea.org) maintains the SSE-CMM and the SSE-CMM assessment methodology.

References

Calabrese, T. (2004). *Information security intelligence: Cryptographic principles and applications*. Clifton Park, NY: Delmar Learning/Thomson Learning, Inc.

CMMI Author Team. (2002). *Capability maturity model integration, Version 1.1. CMMI for systems engineering, software engineering, integrated product and process development, and supplier sourcing (CMMI-SE/SW/IPPD/SS, V1.1), Staged Representation* (No. CMU/SEI-2002-TR-012, ESC-TR-2002-012). Pittsburgh, PA: Carnegie Mellon University.

Goldenson, D.R., & Gibson, D. L. (2003). *Demonstrating the impact and benefits of the CMMI* (No. CMU/SEI-2003-SR-009). Pittsburgh, PA: Software Engineering Institute.

Haley, C. B., Laney, R. C., & Nuseibeh, B. (2004, March). *Deriving security requirements from a crosscutting threat descriptions.* Paper presented at the Third International Conference on Aspect-Oriented Software Development '04, Lancaster, UK.

Henning, R. (1999, November 29-December 2). Information assurance: The forgotten requirement in modeling and simulation systems. In *Proceedings of Interservice/ Industry Training, Simulation, and Education Conference (IITSEC)* (pp. 298-305). Orlando, FL: IITSEC.

International Standards Organization/International Electrical Commission (ISO/IEC). (1998). *ISO/IEC 15408, COMMON CRITERIA FOR INFORMATION TECHNOLOGY SECURITY EVALUATION.* Washington, DC: U.S. Government Printing Office.

International Standards Organization/International Electrical Commission (ISO/IEC). (2000, March 1). ISO/IEC 17799 Code of practice for information security management. Retrieved May 30, 2005, from http://www.iso.ch/iso/en/ISOOnline. openerpage

International Standards Organization/International Electrical Commission (ISO/IEC). (2002). *ISO/IEC 21827: 2002-10-01(e) Information technology — Systems security engineering capability maturity model (SSE-CMM).* Washington, DC: International System Security Engineering Association.

Koch, M., & Parisi-Presicce, F. (2003, October 30). *Formal access control analysis in the software development process.* Paper presented at the ACM Conference on Formal Methods in Software Engineering '03, Washington, DC.

Kotonya, G., & Sommerville, I. (1998). *Requirements engineering: Processes and techniques.* West Sussex, UK: John Wiley & Sons.

National Institute of Standards and Technology (NIST). (2002, November). *International Standard ISO/IEC 17799:2000 Code of practice for information security management: Frequently asked questions.* Retrieved May 29, 2005, from www.nist.gov.csrc

Pressman, R. S. (1997). *Software engineering: A practitioner's approach* (4th ed.). New York: McGraw-Hill Company.

Sommerville (2001). *Software engineering.* Essex, UK: Pearson Education Ltd. / Addison Wesley Publishers.

Syntegra (1998). *Common criteria version 2.0 — An introduction.* London.

Vaughn, R., & Henning, R. (2000, June 2-5). A pragmatic applications-oriented approach to information assurance. *12th Annual Canadian Information Technology Security Symposium* (pp. 150-158). Ottawa, Canada: Department of Defence.

Whitten, J. L., Bentley, L. D., & Dittman, K. C. (2004). *Systems analysis and design methods* (6th ed.). New York: McGraw-Hill/Irwin Inc.

Chapter XII

High Assurance Products in IT Security

Rayford B. Vaughn, Mississippi State University, USA

Abstract

Corporate decisions concerning the purchase of security software and hardware appliances are often made based simply on the recommendations of the technical staff, the budget process (return on investment arguments), and/or a sales presentation and assertions. This chapter addresses the notion of trusted products and assurance in those products (i.e., confidence in the correct operation of a product) and how assurance is gained through independent review and testing. Early attempts to measure assurance in trusted products are described (some products today still refer to these procedures). Modern approaches to measuring assurance will be discussed in the context of ISO Standard 15408 (the Common Criteria *(CC)). Current U.S. federal government policy concerning the use of evaluated products is presented, as well as a discussion of why industrial organizations may wish to consider such products.*

Introduction

For a *chief information officer* (CIO), *chief security officer* (CSO), or *chief executive officer* (CEO) today, corporate oversight of *information technology* (IT) must involve significant interest in the area of computing security — to include the establishment of a robust defensive perimeter, the protection of corporate data assets (while stored, transmitted, and during processing), disaster recovery and response, and insuring that only authorized users access the system. These priorities are often offset by concerns with return on investment, cost of data recovery, liability issues associated with misuse of system resources, and the business impact of security controls imposed on users of the system. In addition, those responsible for keeping intruders out of the systems under their care must often concern themselves with monitoring the activities of authorized users to insure proper "insider" behavior, compliance with mandated procedure, and to guard against damaging accidental destructive events. Executives faced with such responsibilities often rely on their technical staff to recommend architectures, system settings, procedures, and specific hardware/software products. This reliance, while appropriate in most circumstances, must be viewed with the understanding that there is today a critical shortage of computing security expertise and that system efficiency and ease of use objectives are very often adversely impacted by corporate security strategies and risk mitigation efforts. This chapter endeavors to offer a corporate IT decision maker some insights and suggestions that may be useful in selecting proper tools (hardware and software) and making the necessary investment in those tools. Subsequent chapters in this book will discuss specific tools and techniques needed by security engineers and the security engineering process itself.

The chapter begins with an overview of the notion of assurance in systems and what constitutes that assurance (informally defined as confidence that the product operates as intended). Some discussion of U.S. government guidelines and current policy is included here for the sake of historical completeness. Suggestions for how to select products are also provided in this chapter. The initial overview is followed by a more specific treatment of trusted products (a term often associated with high-assurance products). Since the mid-eighties, attempts have been made to measure the amount of assurance that one can place in the correct operation of a software product. This area is often loosely referred to as trusted products or assured system operation. An introduction is given to the current international standard for trusted systems (ISO Standard 15408 or Common Criteria), along with an overview of the older U.S. government *Trusted Computer System Evaluation Criteria* (or TCSEC). Both of these documents allow for a qualitative measurement of assurance in security software and/or hardware products. Following the discussion of trusted product measurement schemes, a brief explanation of how assurance measurement is assigned under the ISO Standard 15408 procedure is given. Several schemes of measurement exist today — the original *Department of Defense* (DOD) standard (sometimes referred to as the Orange Book rating), some residual European rating schemes, and today's ISO Standard 15408/CC measurements (i.e., Common Criteria *evaluation assurance levels* (EAL)). These rating schemes are later explained and defined. A high-level overview of the older TCSEC rating scheme will be briefly presented, followed by a more detailed discussion of how products are evaluated today and how the EAL level is determined (process-wise). The chapter concludes with a summary and some final thoughts for the reader.

Overview

When one considers what products to purchase and to include in a security defensive perimeter, two high-level concerns should be addressed — the first is the completeness and strength of the security design architecture, while the second must be the assurance of the products used in the architecture (both hardware and software).

The completeness and strength concern is generally addressed by relying on the advice of security engineers (IT specialists with training in information security or information assurance). It should be noted here that there is a substantial body of literature on secure systems engineering and how its use can make a difference in architecting a system. This book has a separate chapter on security engineering concerns and architectures, so this subject will not be addressed in any great detail here, except to say that such engineering is today (in practice) more art than science and highly dependent on the knowledge and experience of the security engineer doing the work.

The second concern (i.e., assurance/confidence in the product's operation) is not nearly as subjective. Several methods of product correctness/assurance determination are in widespread use today but, unfortunately, often times an organization will fail to consider an assurance measurement and will purchase products based on less reliable means.

As noted by Vaughn (2003), on the defensive side of information assurance, the security engineer tries to create what is referred to as a defensive perimeter (also known as a security perimeter) around the object of protection (e.g., the system, a network, a single host, a physical facility). The objective is to create enough penetration difficulty for the attacker so that the level of effort to penetrate exceeds the value gained if the penetration is successful. This is the same concept one uses when securing a home against possible invaders — that is, to make the level of effort necessary to gain entry more difficult than the attacker is willing to exert. Just as no home is 100% secure, no useful computer system can guarantee total security. Because we cannot guarantee total security and because there is always risk present, we tend to use high-assurance products in an attempt to gain confidence in the strength of protection we have. It should be noted here that high assurance means a very strong level of confidence in terms of the correct implementation of the security protection mechanisms in a product and low assurance means that we have no proof of a correct implementation.

While, in a general and practical sense, we can often make an informal argument that we have a "stronger" system with respect to providing security — in reality we really only have more confidence in the correct operation of a product. A product that has no assurance rating might actually be stronger or perform better then one that does, but there is no proof of that in terms of third-party testing or examination. Confidence in a product can come from many sources — experience, examination of the code, testing, certification by experts, and others. Therefore, a security engineer (and management) should be concerned with information assurance (a term used within ISO Standard 15408 and the older TCSEC associated with scalable values to indicate a hierarchical assurance level) more so than "computer security" (an objective that is either present or not — and never 100% achievable). Management must also guard against a common scenario that occurs when a product choice is made — this scenario generally begins with a penetration (or near-penetration discovery) in the organization's systems. There is an immediate need perceived by management to close the vulnerability quickly, and the technical staff is advised to do so. The surrounding urgency may then drive the purchase of additional hardware or software to address the vulnerability. The decision of what to purchase is then based on what product can be delivered the fastest or on what sales claim seems most appropriate for the situation. This is sometimes referred to as a decision based on emphatic assertion and leads to a "penetrate and patch" strategy.

 Better procedures might include product selection based on past experience (variable with each security engineer), selection based on the experience of others (a testimony selection), or selection based on third-party testing and evaluation. In most circumstances, selection based on third-party evaluation would be considered the greatest indicator of assurance in a product. Even within this strategy, one can find gradations of assurance in the third-party evaluation depending on the depth of examination and assurance evidence provided in the product evaluation. At the lowest end of the assurance spectrum, for example, a third party might simply read the vendor product claims and then conduct a standard suite of tests to verify that the product does indeed work as claimed. At the higher end of trust, the third party might actually review the software code itself along with the product documentation in an effort to verify the correctness of the code, the absence of any hidden functionality, and compliance with design specifications. Clearly, this later procedure (conducted by competent examiners) would result in a greater level of assurance that the product worked properly and as claimed.

The degree of trust that we arrive at for a system (through whatever means we employ) is not a static value; that is, a highly trusted system yesterday may be reduced to a low-trusted system tomorrow through many means. This might occur because a previously undiscovered vulnerability in a specific operating system is announced, an update to the software configuration is installed with flawed code, a lapse in security procedures occurs due to a change in key personnel, or a firewall is accidentally misconfigured by a systems administrator. The lesson in this is that assurance in the individual parts of a security architecture and a system's past performance are not always indicators of future trust performance characteristics. It is incumbent on systems and/or security engineers to continuously update the security perimeter and to check on its effectiveness. There is simply no guarantee of impenetrability, and today much of our trust and reliance is on the individual skill set of those who administer the system and its protection.

The Trusted Computer Security Evaluation Criteria (TCSEC)

Third-party evaluations have been conducted for the IT community since the mid- 1980s, albeit without much industrial use until the past few years. Evaluations began as a DOD initiative to improve the trustworthiness of systems used to process sensitive and classified information. These evaluations were conducted by the government (i.e., the *National Security Agency* (NSA)) and were primarily directed toward operating systems (that part of the system that could be most reasonably expected to enforce a security policy). The foundation document for the evaluation criteria used was published by the NSA as the DOD Trusted Computer Security Evaluation Criteria in August 1983, and was later revised as DOD Standard 5200.28-STD in December 1985 (DOD, 1985). This document became known as the *Orange Book* based on the color of its cover and, for the first time, established a method for evaluating and ranking operating systems as having a specific level of assurance.

The evaluation criteria used consisted of seven hierarchical classes of assurance, which were contained within four divisions (A, B, C, and D). Divisions A, B, and C were further sub-divided into classes. Specific security mechanisms were required at each of the classes (e.g., mechanisms might include auditing of security-relevant events or identification and authentication). At the higher levels of assurance, fewer new mechanisms were added, but stronger assurance practices became necessary (e.g., security testing, covert channel analysis, and specification and verification procedures). It should be noted here that as one moved up the hierarchical class levels, requirements for assurance processes and mechanisms were cumulative; that is, every requirement for Class C2 was also necessary for Class B1 — either the same requirement or strengthened. A summary of the evaluation classes and their meaning, as partially taken from Appendix C of the trusted computer system evaluation criteria, is provided below and is presented in order of increasing assurance. The term *"trusted computing base or TCB"* is often used in the class descriptions. Informally, the TCB means those hardware and software components present in the system that provide for security functionality.

- **Class D:** *Minimal protection*

  This class is reserved for those systems that have been evaluated but that fail to meet the requirements for a higher evaluation class. (Note that the value in this category is that the product has been looked at and a report exists for examination.)

- **Class C1:** *Discretionary security protection*

  This class offers discretionary security controls providing separation of users and data. It incorporates some form of credible controls capable of enforcing access limitations on an individual basis, that is, ostensibly suitable for allowing users to be able to protect a project or private information and to keep other users from accidentally reading or destroying their data.

- **Class C2:** *Controlled access protection*

  Systems in this class enforce a more finely grained discretionary access control than C1 systems, making users individually accountable for their actions through login procedures, auditing of security-relevant events, and resource isolation.

- **Class B1:** *Labeled security protection*

  Class B1 systems require all the features required for Class C2. In addition, an informal statement of the security policy model, data labeling, and mandatory access control (i.e., implementation of a stated security policy) over named subjects and objects must be present.

- **Class B2:** *Structured protection*

  The trusted computing base is based on a clearly defined and documented formal security policy model that requires the discretionary and mandatory access control enforcement found in Class B1 systems be extended to all subjects and objects in the system. Authentication mechanisms are strengthened, trusted facility management is provided in the form of support for system administrator and operator functions, and stringent configuration management controls are imposed. The system is relatively resistant to penetration.

- **Class B3:** *Security domains*

  A reference monitor requirement must be satisfied; that is, it mediates all accesses of subjects to objects, is tamperproof, and is small enough to be subjected to analysis and tests. A security administrator is supported, audit mechanisms are expanded to signal security- relevant events, and system recovery procedures are required. The system is highly resistant to penetration.

- **Class A1:** *Verified design*

  These systems are functionally equivalent to those in Class B3 in that no additional architectural features or policy requirements are added. The distinguishing feature of systems in this class is the analysis derived from formal design specification and verification techniques and the resulting high degree of assurance that the trusted computing base is correctly implemented.

The TCSEC was in use for approximately 15 years and computing products were evaluated at each of the classes defined above. Some of these products remain on the market today and still advertise their rating under this scheme. Because of this, an agreed-upon cross-listing between the TCSEC ratings and the more recent CC has been developed and is presented later in Table 2 — but one must keep in mind that no direct mapping between the two processes is possible since the TCSEC combines requirements for mechanisms and assurance at each class level, while the Common Criteria evaluation assurance levels only relate to assurance.

The Common Criteria (CC): Evolution of the ISO Standard 15408

The TCSEC evaluation scheme was replaced in 1999 by an international standard known as ISO Standard 15408 or the CC. This newer standard is addressed in greater detail in the next section. The TCSEC ratings presented above are still valid metrics for management to use when selecting a product and should not be discounted simply because the evaluation standard has been replaced. The evaluations were rigorous under the TCSEC, and if the product has been maintained by the vendor, it should be accepted with the assurance level of its rating. The evaluation process under the TCSEC became bottlenecked due to a shortage of government evaluators and an increase in commercial products requesting evaluation. Not only was the process exceptionally time consuming, but it also required an experienced evaluation staff possessing technical skills that were in high demand in industry as well as in the federal government, and the process was expensive for both government and industry. Some evaluators were offered more lucrative positions in industry while replacement personnel became increasingly difficult to find. Over time, the TCSEC became less relevant to current security needs (e.g., networks, databases, client server applications), and other assurance evaluation approaches began to surface.

Challenges to the TCSEC approach came both nationally and internationally. In 1989, the U.S. Air Force began a program of product evaluation at its facility in San Antonio, Texas, as a service to Air Force customers. While based on TCSEC principles, this was partially a reaction to the bottlenecked process at NSA, as well as in response to a need for evaluation of products other than those submitted to NSA. At almost the same time, other countries began to publish evaluation criteria of their own that differed substantially in content and approach from the TCSEC. Other nations with evaluation interest and emerging criteria included Canada (*Canadian Trusted Computer Product Evaluation Criteria* or CTCPEC), Germany (IT — Security Criteria), the Netherlands, the United Kingdom, and France. The European efforts quickly joined together in what became know as a "harmonized criteria" in 1990, while the U.S. and Canada maintained separate approaches. The European harmonized approach became known as the *Information Technology Security Evaluation Criteria* (ITSEC) in 1991, and varied somewhat substantially from the North American approach. Whereas the TCSEC primarily addressed government systems and combined assurance and functionality into one rating, the ITSEC addressed commercial and government security and separated functionality from assurance during the rating process. Both communities, North American and European, recognized that software manufacturers could not afford to build trusted products to different standards and so began efforts to explore how they might couple the various criteria in a way that the international and commercial communities could accept them. The U.S. moved in the direction of a "federal criteria" that at the time embodied many principles later adopted by the Common Criteria. Many draft criteria involving the international community were produced for comment, and the first true version of the CC was published in January 1996. Several versions of these initial criteria were produced before CC was adopted by the *International Standards Organization* (ISO) as an international standard in 1999 (ISO Standard 15408). Today, this standard is the most widely used assurance measure of security products worldwide.

The CC is quite different from the TCSEC in several ways. First, the evaluations conducted under the CC are done so by a private laboratory certified by the appropriate government (the term appropriate government is used here since several nations have adopted the CC and its procedures and thus can certify their own national third-party laboratories). The list of certified laboratories in the United States, for example, can be found at the Web site, http://www.niap.nist.gov. Second, the CC is based on an entirely different strategy for certification than was the TCSEC. While the TCSEC was primarily used for operating system evaluations, it coupled mechanisms and assurance together into a single rating. This means that if a C2 or B3 product was purchased, the buyer was assured that specific functions were included in the product along with a specific level of trust. The CC separates mechanisms and assurance levels, which means that evaluations under the CC provide an assurance level only without any requirement for specific functions or mechanisms to exist in the product. The CC process does, however, allow for the third-party laboratory to review the product for compliance with a product specification (called a *protection profile* (PP) under CC terminology), and a report concerning this compliance to specification is provided by the evaluators (known as a *security target*). This approach is not a negative factor at all and is generally considered the more flexible and industry friendly of the two; however, it is often criticized because an assurance evaluation only of any product says very little about how it can be used to create trust in a system.

The CC evaluation scheme is hierarchical as was that of the TCSEC. At the low end is the EAL 1 rating and at the high end is EAL 7. In general, products evaluated between EAL 1 and EAL 4 are likely adequate for sensitive industrial use, while products evaluated at EAL 5 to EAL 7 are more likely to contain the assurance necessary for use in sensitive government applications. It should be noted, however, that this is a generalization based on author opinion and is not documented in the CC itself. At the time of this writing, there are no products that have been evaluated successfully at the EAL 5 or above levels — although some are in the evaluation process. More detail on this rating scheme and how it is used internationally will be addressed later in this chapter.

The Case for Evaluated Products

As suggested earlier, one could select products to be employed in an organization's defensive perimeter based solely on product literature, sales presentations, or suggestion from others with experience using the products. While each of these strategies might arguably be appropriate under certain conditions, in a general sense, this should be considered a high-risk strategy, since no evaluation of the vendor's claims has really been made by credible sources. Using such techniques to choose a product does not involve any proof of claims made concerning performance, design, functionality, or correctness. Using a third-party laboratory evaluation in the choice of products means (at the very least) that a well-defined process was used to evaluate the product's correctness and that the evaluation itself provides a quantitative measure of the product's level of trust in comparison with other similarly evaluated products. An evaluation does not guarantee the absence of error or vulnerability — no current process or technology can offer that guarantee and much depends on the competence of the evaluators themselves. Finding evaluators with a high level of competence remains as much of a problem today as it was in the mid-1980s. It does, most likely, reduce the probability of such error.

With the EAL scheme of evaluation used within ISO Standard 15408 (or CC), a product evaluated at the EAL 1 level has been "functionally tested." In software engineering terms, this might be referred to as black box tested — meaning that the code is not examined closely, but rather a series of test cases are designed with specific inputs to validate expected outputs. In other words, tests are run to see if the product performs as advertised. A successful evaluation at the EAL 1 level means only that the product performs in accordance with its documentation.

The CC EAL 2 level requires that the product under evaluation be inspected in greater detail than at EAL 1. This requires an interaction between the evaluation laboratory and the product vendor for the purpose of design document inspection, test case review, and the conduction of third-party testing. EAL 2 level products are referred to as structurally tested.

As one moves up the EAL hierarchy, more assurance is gained in the product. A description of each level as taken from the CC introductory brochure is provided in this chapter's appendix for the interested reader. In the descriptions in the appendix, the acronym TOE is used to mean "target of evaluation" — a term referring to the product that is undergoing the evaluation.

As indicated earlier, the CC represents a departure from the TCSEC approach and is more closely related to the approach developed first in the U.S. federal criteria and later adopted by the European community. This chapter presents a very brief overview at the executive summary level, but for the interested reader, a more detailed review of this document and its processes can be found at the Web sites: http://csrc.nist.gov/cc/, http://www.commoncriteria.org/, and http://niap.nist.gov/.

The CC is a very lengthy document that is divided into three volumes — known as Parts 1, 2, and 3. Part 1 provides background information on the criteria itself, an overview of its processes, and serves as a general reference. Part 2 addresses functional requirements, assists users in formulating statements of requirements for secure systems, and assists developers in interpreting those requirements. It should be noted here that Part 2 can be used by an organization in building a specification for a product or system that calls for specific functionality. Similarly, Part 3 addresses assurance requirements for a product. Note that assurance and functionality are separated and are no longer coupled as they were in the TCSEC.

The CC also introduces several new terms that are important to its prescribed processes. The first of these terms that the reader should be familiar with is that of protection profile. A protection profile is an implementation independent requirements document that specifies a need — in other words, it is a specification for a needed product or function. Theoretically, a consumer can use the information in Parts 2 and 3 of the CC to describe the functionality and assurance that he or she needs in a product. In reality, this process can be quite technical and often requires consultant help or third-party contracting. The PP also contains a concise statement of the security problem to be solved by the IT product (which may include specific assumptions that may be made concerning the operating environment, the anticipated threats, and organizational security policies). The PP, although clearly a requirements document, can be submitted for evaluation under the CC and receive a rating pertaining to the level of assurance that it calls for. Once rated, it can be placed on the list of evaluated products so that others can make use of it.

As briefly noted earlier, an IT product to be evaluated is referred to as a target of evaluation. The TOE includes the product itself and all associated documentation. In order to have a TOE evaluated under the CC process, another document known as the *security target* (ST) must be created. The ST follows the same format as the PP with the exception that the ST references a specific PP and contains a claim of how the TOE meets the requirements of a PP or where it falls short of doing so. Whereas the PP is a generic requirement — the ST is specific to a particular TOE and makes specific claims as to its

Table 1. Common Criteria product rating by year and EAL

	EAL 1	EAL 2	EAL 3	EAL 4	EAL 5	EAL 6	EAL 7	TOTAL
1998		1						1
1999	3	1	1	1				6
2000		2	1	5				8
2001		2	4	4				10
2002	3	12	3	16				34
2003	4	11	6	20				41
2004	1	26	21	19				67
TOTAL	11	55	36	65				167

assurance, its functionality, and its compliance with the PP requirements. An evaluation, therefore, under the terms of the CC, would require the ST, the set of evidence about the TOE, and the TOE itself. The result of the evaluation would be confirmation that the ST is satisfied by the TOE. More simply stated, the PP is the end-user requirement, the TOE is the product, the ST is the claim that the product meets the need, and the evaluation is the third-party review that the claim is correct (Vaughn, 2003).

Under the CC process, a government-certified private laboratory accomplishes the evaluation of the actual product. Each signatory to the CC has a government oversight body that validates laboratories as being compliant with CC standards. Evaluations conducted at any laboratory certified by a signatory to the CC are acceptable (at the first four levels of evaluation only) to all nations that participate in the CC recognition agreement. This means that an evaluation of a product, for example, at the EAL 3 level, conducted in Germany, would be considered equivalent to an evaluation of that same product in the U.S. or any other country that is a signatory to the CC standard. Evaluations are paid for by the product manufacturer, as agreed to by the vendor and the laboratory; often a laboratory is selected based on cost of evaluation and not geographical location. It should be noted that in moving away from the U.S.-controlled TCSEC evaluations, the burden of payment for evaluation has quite clearly shifted from the government to the product manufacturer. Evaluations are quite expensive — an EAL 2 product evaluation will often cost at least $250,000. This is quite prohibitive for small companies.

A complete list of certified products can be found at http://www.niap.nist.gov. The reader will note that most evaluated products lie in the EAL 1 through 4 range (see Table 1 below for a synopsis of evaluated products as of this writing). Some of the products on the evaluated products list are claimed to be in conformance with an EAL "augmented." For example, a conformance claim of EAL3 augmented means that all the requirements of EAL 3 have been met, plus some of requirements of higher level classes. In the case of augmentation, the particular additional requirements met are also specified.

There are several interesting observations concerning the data presented in Table 1. The first is that there is a marked increase in evaluated products between 2001 and 2002. Second, few product vendors are choosing to be evaluated at EAL 1. Third is that there are no ratings shown for EAL 5 and above.

The increase in evaluations occurring during the 2001-2002 timeframe is likely the result of a government directive promoting the use of evaluated products. The *National Security Telecommunications and Information Systems Security Policy* (NSTISSP) Number 11 was issued in January 2000, which required that preference be given to acquisition of *commercial off-the-shelf* (COTS) *information assurance* (IA) products and IA-enabled IT products evaluated in accordance with the CC, the *National Information Assurance Partnership* (NIAP), or NIST *Federal Information Processing Standard* (FIPS) programs. The policy further required that, as of July 1, 2002, acquisition of such products will be limited to those that have been evaluated. It is reasonable to surmise that this policy and the government's reluctance to grant waivers to it were motivating factors for vendors selling to the government and contributed to the increase in product evaluations. Notwithstanding the increase in available evaluated products, there are still not enough on the evaluated list to offer the product diversity that most engineers would prefer to see.

The second observation, that of few new EAL1 evaluations, is likely due to the cost of an EAL1 versus EAL2 evaluation not being significant; therefore, most vendors choose to obtain an evaluation of at least EAL2.

The third observation concerning the lack of products listed for EAL5 and above is more difficult to address. It is possible that such products are not yet evaluated at this higher level of assurance due to a lack of necessary software engineering tools to perform adequate formal analysis, verification, and proofs of correctness for large software-based systems, or perhaps it is an indication that vendors are not yet willing to risk the high cost of development of such systems until they are more confident of a return on investment.

As previously noted, some trusted product evaluations that were made under the old TCSEC or *Orange Book* process remain in existence today. The general equivalency between CC, TCSEC, and ITSEC (the interim European evaluation criteria) evaluations is given in Table 2, as published by the CC working group. Although commercial vendors of trusted products sometimes cite this table, one needs to be aware that many valid

Table 2. Evaluation comparisons (approximate)

Common Criteria	TCSEC	ITSEC
-	D: Minimal Protection	E0
EAL1	-	-
EAL 2	C1: Discretionary Access Protection	E1
EAL 3	C2: Controlled Access Protection	E2
EAL 4	B1: Labeled Security Protection	E3
EAL 5	B2: Structured Protection	E4
EAL 6	B3: Security Domains	E5
EAL 7	A1: Verified Design	E6

Table 3. Prevention, detection, and response/recovery mitigation strategies

Prevention & Deterrence	Detection	Response and Recovery
<ul><li>Firewalls</li><li>Public Key Infrastructure</li><li>Smart Cards for I &A</li><li>Encryption devices (hardware/software)</li><li>OS behavior monitors</li><li>Employee training</li><li>Enforcement of security policy</li><li>Use of high-assurance products</li></ul>	<ul><li>Firewalls</li><li>Malicious code scanners</li><li>Intrusion detection systems</li><li>Content filters</li><li>Audit log analysis</li><li>Employee training</li><li>Forensics tools</li><li>Procedures</li></ul>	<ul><li>Backup procedures</li><li>Forensic tools</li><li>Law enforcement</li><li>Policy</li><li>Procedure</li></ul>

arguments can be made that the mappings are not exact and that no direct comparisons can be made. It serves as a general guideline only — but one useful for those employing older products.

It remains to be seen how effective the CC scheme will be over time. At the present, it seems to be gaining acceptance and strength in both government and commercial markets. As of this writing, there are nearly 170 IT products on the evaluated list that have been certified between 1998 and 2004, with others currently undergoing evaluation. The number and diversity of such products available today are approaching the numbers necessary to construct defensive perimeters from high-assurance evaluated products. When one considers the areas of concern that a security engineer must address, those areas are generally categorized in the large as prevention, detection, and response/recovery. There are products such as those shown in Table 3 that assist in mitigating these concerns. In each case, where products are listed, those products now exist on the evaluated products list just described.

Summary and Conclusion

It has been the intent of this chapter to present an argument for commercial industry and government IT organizations to strongly consider the use of evaluated products in systems — perhaps it might even be appropriate to suggest that corporate IT managers consider a policy to that effect. For government users, such policy has been in effect since 2000 and seems to be working quite well. The alternatives to third-party testing of products are not attractive — self-assessment, experience based, or believing emphatic assertions about performance and capability. While experience with a product is most certainly a good indication of its expected performance, that experience cannot be as complete and rigorous as independent laboratory testing. Similarly, arguments that indicate such rigor is not needed for corporate assets should be dismissed by IT executives — corporate data assets do require strong protections. The gradations in ratings (e.g., EAL1 though EAL4 or 5) should be an adequate range from which products can be selected with as much or as little assurance as necessary. The problem remains, however, in how IT management determines how much assurance is really necessary. This remains a decision left to security engineers and involves subjective judgment.

References

Department of Defense (DoD). (1985). *Trusted computer system evaluation criteria (TCSEC)*. US Department of Defense, DoD 5200.28-STD. Retrieved January 10, 2005, from National Computer Security Center Web site: http://www.radium.ncsc.mil/tpep/library/rainbow/5200.28-STD.html

Vaughn, R. B. (2003). Advances in the provision of systems and software security – Thirty years of progress. In M. V. Zelkowitz (Ed.), *Advances in computers – Volume 58, Highly Dependable Software,* (pp. 287-340). San Diego, CA: Academic Press.

Appendix

Description of the seven evaluation assurance levels in Common Criteria

- **EAL 1:** *Functionally tested.*

  Used where some confidence in correct operation is required, but the threats to security are not viewed as serious. The evaluation at this level provides evidence that the target of evaluation functions in a manner consistent with its documentation and that it provides useful protection against identified threats.

- **EAL 2:** *Structurally tested.*

  Evaluation at this level involves a review of design information and test results. This level may be appropriate where developers or users require a low to moderate level of independently assured security in the absence of ready availability of the complete development record (e.g., when securing legacy systems).

- **EAL 3:** *Methodically tested and checked.*

  This level is applicable where the requirement is for a moderate level of independently assured security, with a thorough investigation of the TOE and its development. An EAL 3 evaluation provides an analysis supported by testing based on "gray box" testing, selective independent confirmation of the developer test results, and evidence of a developer search for vulnerabilities.

- **EAL 4:** *Methodically designed, tested and reviewed.*

  This is the highest level at which it is likely to be economically feasible to retrofit an existing product line with security. It is applicable to those circumstances where developers or users require a moderate to high level of independently assured security and there is willingness to incur some additional security specific engineering costs.

- **EAL 5:** *Semiformally designed and tested.*

  This is applicable where the requirement is for a high level of independently assured security in a planned development, with a rigorous development approach, but without incurring unreasonable costs for specialized security engineering techniques. Assurance is supplemented by a formal model, a semiformal presentation of the functional specification and high level design, and a semiformal demonstration of correspondence. A search for vulnerabilities that includes resistance to penetration attacks and a covert channel analysis is also required.

- **EAL 6:** *Semiformally verified design and tested.*

  This EAL is applicable to the development of specialized TOEs for application in high-risk situations where the value of the protected assets justifies the additional costs. The evaluation provides an analysis, which is supported by a modular and layered approach to design. The search for vulnerabilities must ensure resistance to penetration by attackers with high attack potential. The search for covert channels must be systematic. Development environment and configuration management controls are enhanced at this level.

- **EAL 7:** *Formally verified design and tested.*

  Applicable to the development of security TOEs for application in extremely high-risk situations and/or where the high value of the assets justifies the higher costs. For an evaluation at this level, the formal model is supplemented by a formal presentation of the functional specification and high-level design showing correspondence. Evidence of developer "white box" testing and complete independent confirmation of developer test results are required. As a practical matter, a TOE at EAL 7 must minimize design complexity and have tightly focused security functionality amenable to extensive formal analysis.

Chapter XIII

The Demilitarized Zone as an Information Protection Network

Jack J. Murphy, EDS and Dexisive Inc., USA

Abstract

This chapter presents some basic concepts for the design, implementation, and management of a network-based enterprise boundary protection mechanism. The reader should not expect to see a complete security solution from the material presented in this chapter. The concepts presented here must be combined with host and application security mechanisms, as well as procedural and administrative mechanisms. The chapter will provide an explanation of some of the security concepts involved before explaining how an information protection network *(IPN) enables collaboration and information exchange between the enterprise and external entities on the public Internet. Finally, specific technologies needed to implement an IPN will be discussed.*

Defense-in-Depth Approach

Information protection requires an in-depth risk-based approach involving network, host, and application security, which together constitute a defense-in-depth approach to information protection. Like armies defending a nation's capital, this approach has multiple layers of defense, beginning with the front line. The *demilitarized zone* (DMZ) for an enterprise corresponds to the front line of a defense-in-depth strategy, providing network-layer security from untrusted networks via an intermediary perimeter network charged with granting or denying external access to hosts and ports within the enterprise network. Hosts on the enterprise network must employ a second line of defense in the event that the network protection mechanisms are defeated or exploited for nefarious purposes while configured to permit access for legitimate use. Finally, applications on host machines protect access to enterprise information and can be thought of as the final layer of defense. Network defense mechanisms protect against attacks directed at network vulnerabilities, while host and application security mechanisms protect against host and application vulnerabilities, respectively.

The network/host/application layers can be configured in complex ways to enhance security. The network layer itself may employ diverse technologies, another dimension of defense-in-depth, to mitigate exploits against a specific technology. For example, *transmission control protocol/internet protocol* (TCP/IP) (Layer 4/3) security mechanisms may be supplemented by *virtual local area network* (VLAN) (Layer 2) security mechanisms. Diverse technologies protecting against a specific threat or vulnerability can be effective. However, redundant technologies could create a false sense of security. The subtle distinction between technological diversity and technological redundancy must be thoughtfully evaluated.

Such an approach requires an analysis of the threats to security, the vulnerabilities that may exist in networks, hosts, and applications used by the enterprise, and the value of information and processing capability to the enterprise or to threat agents outside the enterprise. Risk can be loosely modeled as the product of threat, vulnerability, and value (Risk = threat x vulnerability x value), where threat and vulnerability are real numbers in intervals (0, t) and (0, v) respectively, and value is measured in dollars, also in some interval ($0, $n). Each site must determine the risk (value of the information it is responsible for protecting, the threats, and the vulnerabilities) and the countermeasures required.

Among security professionals there is no universally agreed set of "best practices" for securing the IT components of an enterprise. However, few would argue that, at a minimum, the enterprise should have a written security policy that serves to guide the operation and evolution of the security components of the enterprise IT infrastructure. One approach that has proven successful is to establish a set of core principles. These principles should be universal (widely understood and agreeable), comprehensive (covering a broad collection of threats and vulnerabilities), and fundamental (not subject to or dependant on rapidly changing technologies or threats).

Table 1 identifies four core principles and 19 prescriptive policy statements supporting the core principles. The culture of the enterprise will determine whether this set needs modification. The information protection network referred to in several of these policy statements is the technical security component providing boundary protection. As described in greater detail in the next section, the IPN supports these four core principles.

A comprehensive enterprise security program includes technical mechanisms and operational practices, procedures, and processes. Technical mechanisms include things such as firewalls, intrusion detection, access control lists, and filtering routers. Operational practices, procedures, and processes include things such as security training, independent audits, security policies, and configuration management.

Table 1. Enterprise security core principles and supporting requirements

core principle	baseline requirements
Control outside visibility to enterprise systems	1. Each site within the enterprise will expose only that portion of the name/address space appropriate for external view. 2. DNS will be configured to permit Internet name resolution for only individual host names for which the site is authoritative. 3. Application developers will consider security requirements early in the development life cycle. 4. Only necessary host services will be enabled. 5. Publicly accessible resources will be located on a network whose access to the internal site's network(s) is under IPN control.
Control access to enterprise systems	6. The security architecture will be implemented consistent with a risk-based network, host, and application security assessment. 7. Remote access services will be under IPN management and will impose security provisions consistent with those imposed upon other "on-site" users, including protection of authentication information. 8. Source routing in IP networks will be prohibited. 9. Enterprise networks will only carry traffic whose source or destination address is associated with enterprise requirements or that is approved by the enterprise. 10. E-mail will be configured to prevent misuse of enterprise e-mail hosts (e.g., initiating spoofed e-mail). 11. Each network-attached host will be configured to require authentication before a user is granted non-anonymous access.
Control interfaces across enterprise security boundaries	12. Network access points between enterprise networks and non-enterprise networks will be subject to IPN security configuration management (e.g.. identification, change control, status accountability, and audit). 13. Any entry-point to a site that is not managed as an IPN entry point may not connect to any site network/resource protected by an IPN. 14. Access across any enterprise network boundary will be prohibited if the source address is a valid address on the destination network. 15. The IPN will permit e-mail traffic only to/from on-site mail hosts whose configuration and administrative practices and procedures are controlled or reviewed by designated site information technology security personnel. 16. Intra-site connections between campus networks with different security needs will be mediated by an IPN.
Monitor and report anomalous activity	17. Each site will implement intrusion detection and critical event logging. 18. Each site will implement vulnerability detection. 19. E-mail will be configured to allow logging of message headers for inbound and outbound e-mail.

Fundamental IPN Concepts

Figure 1 conceptually illustrates a simple, but typical, IPN separating a trusted network connecting to the internal router from below and an external network connected to the external router from the top of the figure. The dark arrows indicate visibility and access across the external router, while the light arrows indicate visibility and access across the internal router. Note from the direction of the arrows that the public access server (e.g., enterprise Web site) and *domain name service* (DNS) can be accessed and respond to requests from the external network, but they cannot initiate outbound sessions of any kind. Other servers act as proxies permitting controlled bi-directional flow across the IPN; that is, between the trusted network and the external network. Controls may involve authentication or service restrictions. Finally, some servers are needed to support IPN security functions and may be invisible and/or inaccessible to some or all network addresses. For example, the intrusion detection systems might be inaccessible (not IP addressable), but the authentication server would be invisible (not listed in the external name space) and inaccessible from the external network, but accessible from within the IPN to provide authentication services for other IPN hosts such as the application proxy server.

It is the responsibility of the external router to permit external network DNS query traffic (port 53) and nothing else to the DNS server. Likewise from the DNS server, the external router should permit DNS query responses (and nothing else) to destinations on the external network. If the DNS server is implemented on a general-purpose operating system, then the network settings on the host operating system should be configured in a similar manner to ensure that the server is used only for its intended purpose as a DNS server.

This illustrates an important enterprise security principle: never assume that another component of the IPN is completely trusted to perform its intended function with 100% reliability. It is this tenet that provides the distinction between an IPN and an archetypal

Figure 1. Basic IPN configuration

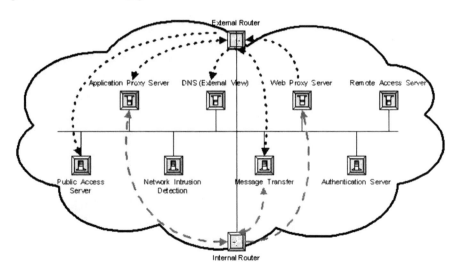

DMZ. If the network layer is compromised in a DMZ, the DMZ provides no security at all, as all hosts in the network are instantly exposed to untrusted networks. A properly designed and maintained IPN system should provide host, application, and data security even in the event of failures of individual components, whether innocently or maliciously produced. Stated differently, any single component may be compromised with minimal adverse consequences. Another implication of this principle is the need for coordination among various administrative roles. If the staff responsible for router administration is composed of a different group of individuals than those responsible for DNS host/ service administration, then there must be some coordination mechanism built into the change control process. This highlights another principle: the IPN and all its components constitute a security system, and it should be managed accordingly — as a system, not a collection of independent components.

Implementing IPNs with Complex Security

To this point, an IPN provided simple separation of a trusted network from an external network. However, a large enterprise is typically composed of several geographically distributed campus networks. These campus networks may communicate over a public Internet, private leased circuits, or some combination thereof. The IPN is the major component of the enterprise architecture with primary responsibility for access control, including remote *virtual private network* (VPN) access, to the distributed campus networks and first-level protection of information resources for the site. The IPN in this more complex environment is conceived as a comprehensive logical network consisting of an array of potential hardware and software tools that can be physically located or installed any place on a particular campus, but must be centrally configured and managed as a security information protection network; that is, the enterprise IPN is actually a system of site IPNs managed at the enterprise level.

Each site may have one or more internal networks that require boundary protection. Each may require some level of protection, but there may be differences in the degree and type of protection required. Some of these networks may be supporting projects that require only modest security, while others require greater security. The IPN provides perimeter protection commensurate with the site's risk assessments for each site network. In principle, the IPN can be used to implement an array of department-wide mandatory and recommended baseline security policies and practices, as well as those that might be site specific or used by the site to augment the department-wide direction or guidance. The IPN can be used to:

- Selectively control the flow of traffic through it;

- Selectively hide local site details;

- Facilitate protection of data in transit;

- Monitor network activity for anomalous behavior;

- Resist unauthorized use of site resources; and

- Protect the site and itself from unauthorized change.

Figure 2 illustrates a campus supporting two different business functions requiring different security policies. Network A requires enterprise standard security, while Network B requires a modified level of security.

The same physical facility and equipment are used to protect both networks. One physical router (for example, the router closest to the internal networks) may be configured as two virtual routers or just a single router with a more complex access control policy.

Another approach is to physically separate the IPNs protecting Network A and Network B. Figure 3 illustrates this approach. From an equipment and circuit perspective there are two separate IPNs for the site. However, from a systems perspective, there is one virtual IPN enforcing an enterprise and site security policy while also satisfying the special information protection needs for Network A and Network B. This approach is less efficient but may be appropriate depending on site geography and organizational structure of the enterprise at the site.

From the perspective of the enterprise, both the single-facility approach and the virtual IPN approach may appear as separate sites.

A common vulnerability, resulting from uncontrolled network connections is illustrated in Figure 4. Network A and Network B have different security policies, even though they are part of the same enterprise network. Data flow between them must be mediated by an

Figure 2. Integrated IPN

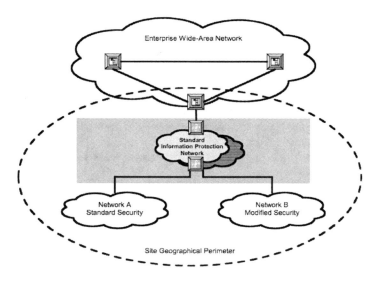

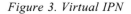

Figure 3. Virtual IPN

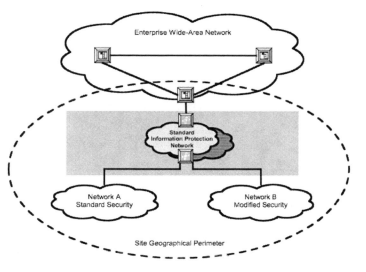

Figure 4. Connectivity policy

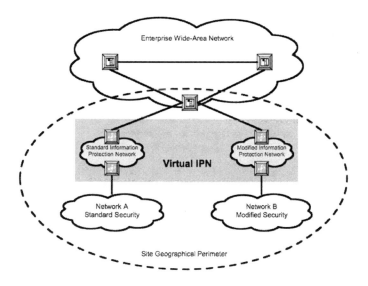

IPN. As illustrated, direct connectivity between Network A and Network B compromises the information security of both subnetworks. The correct routing policy would subject data traffic to the IPN security for both egress and ingress of both IPNs.

Network A and Network B have "different" security policies. There is no "stronger than" relationship between them. Protocol X may be acceptable and necessary for Network A,

Figure 5. Nested IPN configuration

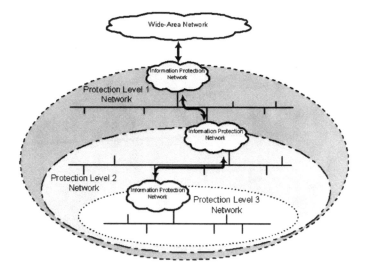

but unnecessary for Network B. On this basis alone, it appears that Network B has a stronger security policy than Network A. Consider though another protocol, say Protocol Y, that is acceptable and necessary for Network B, but unnecessary for Network A. Clearly, a direct connection as shown at the bottom of Figure 4 exposes *both* networks to vulnerabilities even though an IPN protects each according to its own needs.

As often occurs in an enterprise, there is a natural "stronger than" relationship that exists between two or more networks belonging to the enterprise or enterprise site. Figure 5 illustrates the network connectivity and IPN relationship that can be employed in such cases.

In this case, there should be clear and formal agreements between directly adjacent networks, particularly with respect to the ingress policy. Generally the egress policy is solely within the control of a single network and requires little coordination with adjacent networks. For example, the Level 2 network has no vested interest in the egress policy of the Level 3 network. However, it should ensure that traffic entering Level 2 from Level 3 actually has a source address on the Level 3 network. The Level 2 network does have an interest in both the egress and ingress policy of the Level 1 network. The egress policy must not preclude legitimate egress traffic by Level 2 hosts. More importantly, the Level 2 network assumes Level 1 enforces a certain ingress policy. Any changes to the Level 1 ingress policy may create vulnerability for Level 2 (and Level 3). Such vulnerability can be avoided by duplicating the level n ingress policy at level n+1 on top of the policy restrictions that level n+1 requires over and above that required by level n. This is a minimal trust approach. It is hardware intensive and performance inhibiting and should be considered only if it is impossible to establish and sustain formal agreements between adjacent levels. Such agreements are probably necessary anyway to preclude an inadvertent loss of service by higher level networks when a lower level adds restrictions without coordination with its subscribing community of users, including the higher level network.

Enterprise Information in the IPN

Aside from providing network-based security for the enterprise, the IPN serves another equally important role. The IPN provides a means for information and application sharing between the enterprise and its business partners and/or consumers. Until this point we have been focusing on the security aspects of an IPN without regard for how the IPN is used to facilitate collaboration and information sharing.

With the introduction of business data in the IPN, extra considerations are in play. Because IPNs are security mechanisms, they must be managed with extra diligence. This is even more important when the IPN hosts persistent, sensitive business data. Strict configuration change control procedures must be in place and trained security professionals should be an integral part of the IPN management team. Administrative accounts for IPN systems are always rigorously controlled. Some environments may even implement "two-man" rules or "split role" rules. These techniques ensure that no single person and/or role can make changes that may conflict with the enterprise security policy.

Figure 6. IPN with access zones

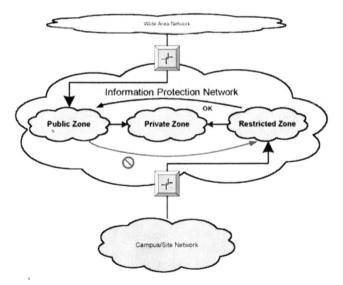

The public access server illustrated in Figure 1 presents a related operational challenge for management of IPNs. As described above, there needs to be a clear separation of roles to ensure that enterprise security isn't compromised in a misguided attempt to satisfy a single business function that could jeopardize the security of other important business functions. However, the public access servers host enterprise business information that is not within the domain of the IPN management team. There must be some way for a functional line of business people to manage the applications and data hosted on public access servers. This line of business people should not be permitted to change router configuration or other IPN security components. Similarly, the IPN system administrators should not be permitted to make changes to the public access server without the knowledge and consent of the functional business line served by the public access server.

Host and application security mechanisms are often sufficient to resolve the operational challenge presented above. However, an extra layer of network defense provides better information protection. Figure 6 shows that an IPN implementation may also include network zones. The components of the IPN shown in Figure 1 exist to implement security policy. The zones below exist to satisfy business needs. Thus, a complete IPN implementation would include all the security components shown in Figure 1, plus all the business components implemented in the various access zones. Zone separation may be enforced by routing policy or VLAN separation and may be combined with host and application security mechanisms. The separation of the IPN into separate access zones enables management of publicly accessible business applications by the business units of the enterprise rather than by the IPN staff, whose primary responsibility is infrastructure protection, not business applications.

Properly configured, zones facilitate safe and effective separation of roles while simultaneously satisfying both infrastructure security and business needs. The absence of such zones increases the risk that business systems requiring public access could be compromised. For example, access to the *restricted zone* could be limited to *campus/site* users whose role is to manage and maintain enterprise business applications. These applications may be multi-tiered architectures consisting of public facing Web applications hosted in the *public zone* with sensitive customer and/or enterprise data hosted on back-end database servers hosted in the *private zone*. Ingress to the public zone (or private zone) for purposes of management and administration services could be permitted when the source is in the restricted zone, but denied otherwise. Ingress to the restricted zone may be configured to require stronger authentication in addition to limiting access (by source network) to enterprise users at site.

Internet Connections

The concepts presented in the previous sections are applicable for an enterprise consisting of a single site with a single external connection to the Internet. They also are applicable to enterprises with multiple interconnected sites (see the enterprise *wide area network* (WAN) in Figure 4, which shows an enterprise with three interconnected sites), but there are some additional concepts that are important in such environments. For example, if an enterprise has n geographically distributed sites, how many should be established as Internet gateways for the entire enterprise and what special IPN mechanisms are necessary at these gateway sites or at the non-gateway sites?

If each site in the enterprise is also an Internet gateway for that site's users, an enterprise WAN may be unnecessary — the Internet could serve as the enterprise WAN. However, sensitive enterprise data transmitted from one site to the other must be protected by encryption (e.g., VPN technology). Furthermore, the cost of implementing and operating n independent Internet gateways with associated IPN mechanisms (see Figure 1) could be prohibitive when compared to an alternative implementation that employs a shared communication infrastructure between sites with only a small number of Internet gateways. With available MPLS technology, the enterprise can leverage the benefits of Internet connectivity, bandwidth, and resource sharing, while managing and operating its own enterprise WAN as if it were a dedicated WAN with just a few (typically 2-3) sites serving as Internet gateways.

The model enterprise WAN environment ideally consists of a single integrated enterprise network in order to take advantage of potential resource, personnel, training, management, and security efficiencies. The existence of an enterprise wide area network security architecture permits the potential future introduction of "emergency shut-off" mechanisms between the Internet gateway locations and the enterprise WAN (an enterprise IPN). Such mechanisms would normally permit the free ingress and egress of data at the Internet gateway sites and then routing to the appropriate site, which is protected by an IPN. However, there may be security situations where it is best to place access controls

Figure 7. External partner access control

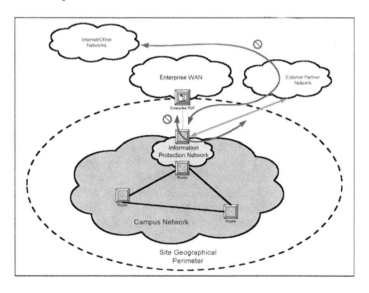

directly at the points of ingress/egress to the Internet rather than at each of the enterprise sites. First, the number of Internet connections in this architecture could be limited to as few as necessary to satisfy redundancy, connectivity, and bandwidth needs. It is much easier to respond to or monitor coordinated Internet attacks at a few locations rather than all enterprise locations. Thus, IDS systems are ideal for consolidation at such gateway sites even if a second layer of IDS is desirable at the other sites. Second, there may be some types of traffic between enterprise sites that would be permitted, but that same traffic between the Internet and the enterprise sites would be considered unsafe. Examples may include instant messaging, *peer-to-peer* (P2P) collaboration capabilities, or database transactions. Operationally, it is easier to control this access at the Internet ingress/egress points. Finally, it is economical and easy to manage services that depend on Internet connectivity at a small number of well-managed, secure Internet-attached IPNs. Such services include Internet e-mail, Web services, and DNS.

Oftentimes, an enterprise has a site whose business requires special access to/from a business partner network. Perhaps the site performing R&D for the enterprise needs direct access to a partner network. There may be bandwidth or latency issues that would be prohibitive if such traffic were routed across the enterprise Internet WAN to a gateway sites, then across the Internet to the partner network, and finally back for packet response. Also, the protocols or other aspects of such partner exchanges may place an unacceptable risk at other sites if such traffic were permitted across the Internet gateway IPN and onto the enterprise WAN backbone.

An enterprise can permit such connections if security is provided. In Figure 7, the R&D site permits direct connectivity to an external partner network (lighter, straight arrow), but the rest of the enterprise must be protected from the partner network. Traffic whose source address is not associated with the R&D site (i.e., the partner network) should be denied by routing policy from entry to the enterprise WAN. This protects the rest of the enterprise from the risk that must be accepted by the R&D site. Managers of the R&D site IPN can configure their external router to provide this protection for the enterprise WAN, but typically the organization directly responsible for managing the enterprise WAN has the ultimate responsibility for protecting the WAN from external access. This is often achieved via an enterprise point of presence (PoP) located on the R&D premises.

In most enterprise environments, the R&D site should also limit the network access to/from partner networks to only those that are required to satisfy its business needs. The partner network should not be used, for example, as an alternate path to/from the Internet. Such a "back door" could be exploited to the detriment of other sites if this implied trust is violated. Where such an implied trust cannot be tolerated, the enterprise should not relinquish management of the site IPN. Virtual routers and/or virtual firewalls are commonly available and provide an intermediate solution frequently employed by managed security service providers. In this approach, the infrastructure provider (e.g., the enterprise) retains ultimate control of the routers/firewalls and provides the sub-scriber (e.g., the R&D site) with a virtual or logical view and access. In this scenario, the enterprise PoP router and the site external IPN router (see Figure 7) may be one and the same physical device in which the external IPN router is implemented as a virtual router instance controlled and administered by the site, but wrapped by an infrastructure router controlled by the enterprise.

IPN Technology Components

Technology components required to implement an effective IPN can be categorized as connectivity components or security components. Connectivity components include all the network and application systems needed to support the primary purpose of the IPN. Security components include all of the systems designed to ensure the confidentiality, integrity, and availability of the services IPN provides.

The connectivity category includes both hardware and software components. These components provide switching and routing of the network traffic throughout the IPN environment. Components within this category usually fall between layers one through four of the *open system interconnect* (OSI) model. However, with advances in technology network, components are quickly incorporating seven-layer awareness. Multi-layer switches, routers, load balancers, IP offloaders, inline taps, and domain name service are examples of some components. Technologies such as virtual local area network, *network address translation* (NAT), *border gateway protocol* (BGP), and *open shortest path first* (OSPF) are heavily used in this category.

Security category also includes both hardware and software components. These components protect, detect, and secure all of the components of the IPN. Firewall, *intrusion detection system* (IDS), *intrusion prevention system* (IPS), honeypots, *secure socket layer* (SSL) accelerators, and *virtual private network* (VPN) devices are some examples. Technologies such as *Internet Protocol Security* (IPSec), NAT, *Secure Shell* (SSH), and *public key infrastructure* (PKI) also fall into this category.

Throughout the IPN environment, connectivity and security components should be seamlessly integrated. In most design projects, separate teams often perform these two functions. This presents challenges in effectiveness of the overall IPN. Network and security teams must also work closely with the application or service owner who depends on the IPN for business functions. The design goal should be to provide a simple and secure IPN environment.

IPN environments are often over engineered; unnecessary cost and complexity are often the result of a fragmented design effort. Consistency and forward thinking result in IPN design simplicity. Future services should be anticipated to preclude loss of conceptual integrity of the IPN design during the evolution of the enterprise. This allows for the scalability and expansion to accommodate the growth and evolution of the IPN environment. Simplicity and consistency throughout the IPN environments also simplify the operation and management of the IPN.

Performance, availability, and scalability requirements are extremely important to the successful implementation of an IPN. Network and security component selection and redundancy of components in design usually takes place based on these requirements. In large and disparate IPN implementations, provision and manageability requirements must also be considered during this component selection phase. This is crucial for the deployment and operation of the environment after the design.

Routers

A pair of redundant routers often serves as the demarcation point of an IPN environment. These routers provide routing to and from the IPN IP address space, as well as an explicit set of *access control lists* (ACLs) defining ingress and egress access control policies. These policies should always define ingress services required by the IPN, ingress host subscribing to the IPN services, and IPN hosts providing these services. The ACLs should explicitly deny all other traffic. Egress router policies are becoming more prevalent in IPN environments. IPN hosts often provide services, but almost never initiate network sessions to networks outside the IPN. This prevents propagation of malicious code and unauthorized access from a compromised IPN host. ACLs reflecting this policy should be applied on the IPN external routers. Other egress router policies to explicitly control exiting traffic from the IPN should also be implemented as standard practice. However, egress policies should be applied as a last step in the provisioning of an IPN for a new service. This will avoid complications during the implementation of the new service.

IPN routers usually provide packet filter-based ACLs because of their capability and performance. Router-based ACLs are extremely important to the IPN as the first line of defense against the unknown security threats. This is a part of an overall defense-in-depth security strategy. However, packet filter-based devices are normally unaware of the overall state of traffic flow. Stateful devices such as firewall, IDS, and IPS are necessary to further protect the IPN.

Physical routers can be virtualized to isolate and segment an IPS environment. Virtualized routers also allow delegation of the administrative functions and partitioning of high-performance network devices to be shared across multiple IPN environments with varying requirements.

Network load distribution using routing protocols such as BGP and OSPF are fairly common in typical data center environments. This provides both network path diversity and resiliency in case of a device failure. BGP can be used to enable Anycast services in a distributed IPN environment to provide quicker end-user response as well as enhanced security. Anycast is a way to virtualize an IP-enabled resource or resources across a distributed network using BGP. Critical infrastructure services such as DNS and e-mail are often virtualized using Anycast.

Network address translation (NAT) is a useful technology in IPv4 environments, but is often misapplied in an IPN environment as a security mechanism. It adds a layer of unneeded complexity resulting in an IPN environment that is difficult to manage. NAT should be used only when necessary, and the network design team should make this determination.

Switching

Today, IPN environments are heavily dependent upon layer-two switches for primary network connectivity. Switches with high-port density can be virtualized to handle logically separate environments. Typically, layer-two vulnerabilities in an IPN environment are related to human errors. This can be prevented using 802.1x and related technologies to enforce security policies. Security issues arise when a virtualized switch port is misconnected or misconfigured. Media access control level policies can prevent these types of errors. Such policies can prevent connection by unapproved devices and support more advance configuration to prevent port-to-port communication.

VLAN technology is commonly employed in an IPN environment. VLAN technology is used to provide logical separation of the IPN environment using shared security and network connectivity hardware. Human factors in the management of the VLAN are often the greatest shortfall of the VLAN implementations. This useful technology is often rejected for its perceived security risks. This perception is a legacy of the early implementation of the VLAN technology using switches with scant memory. Today, VLAN technology can be implemented consistently throughout all of the security and network devices used in an IPN environment without difficulty.

Zones in the IPN can be implemented using VLAN technology or IPSec. The IPN environment itself can be a logically or physically separated network and security area within an enterprise network environment. Even though physical separation is perceived as the most secure way to create an IPN, logically separated IPN environments can be as effective as their physical counterparts. Technology enablers such as IPSec can provide a higher level of assurance in a logically separated IPN. IPSec policies can be applied to logically separated hosts so that they can only communicate in accordance with predefined connection policies. Policies can precisely define a set of authorized services and hosts along with the optional encryption scheme. Encryption can be used to open an end-to-end assured communication channel using an authentication mechanism such as public key certificates. This provides an added layer to security in logical IPN environments.

Firewalls

Almost all the firewalls today are stateful inspection devices. Stateful inspection devices monitor the bi-directional traffic flow across the device to ensure compliance with predefined traffic control policies. They can also take specific action in response to unauthorized traffic, including session termination, redirection, logging, and alarms. Most firewalls are capable of decoding network traffic up to OSI layer 4, (transport layer), but application proxy firewalls and IPS devices can inspect traffic at all seven layers of the OSI model, permitting additional granularity in the enforcement of the IPN services security policies.

Intrusion Detection Systems

IDS devices are also capable of decoding all seven layers of the OSI model. Based on the capabilities and defined policies, an IDS can match the decoded traffic flow against known signatures of malicious traffic. Some IDS products can also detect non-compliant network activity based upon a predefined set of network protocol and traffic flow standards. IDS devices are typically placed inside the IPN perimeter, outside its perimeter, and on each host providing IPN services. Suspect events, triggered by the IDS devices are consolidated, normalized, and correlated for real-time analysis. These events are also logged for trend and post-mortem analysis. IDS policy, placement, and configuration must be carefully planned because without thoughtful deployment, an IDS can quickly become ineffective by overwhelming the operations staff with false positive events.

Intrusion Prevention Systems

An IPS device is a hybrid between a firewall and IDS. It functions primarily as an IDS, but it can be placed inline with the network devices as a firewall. Since the IPS device is capable of decoding all seven layers of the OSI model, firewall-like rules can include an additional level of precision in enforcement.

Domain Name Services

DNS provides a number of services in an IPN environment. DNS in its simplest form provides name resolution services to the host in IPN. DNS can also be used to provide local and geographical load distribution of the IPN. It can also support fail over of a host or an entire IPN environment. *Split DNS* (also called split name space) is usually implemented to hide internal host names from external view. Exposing the internal namespace can often provide useful information to those intent on exploiting vulnerabilities in the enterprise technology environment.

Web Cache and Reverse Proxy

Web cache is another component often found in an IPN environment. Reverse caching of sites hosted within IPN is also implemented for both performance and resiliency. Reverse caching in conjunction with Anycast in multiple IPN environments within an enterprise can be effective in meeting high-performance and high-availability requirements of a line of business application.

Business Continuity

During the IPN design, the business continuity and disaster recovery of an IPN must be considered. Well-conceived and implemented plans always involve seamlessly integrated rules, tools, and resources. Rules can be as simple and straightforward as the backup and restoration of a line of business application to recovering an entire IPN in a catastrophic failure. Rules are based on a set of predefined availability, reliability, performance, and survivability requirements. Manpower resources must be integrated and trained on the defined processes in order to execute effectively during the time of need. Supporting technologies fall into three categories: application, network, and storage. Enterprise line-of-business applications hosted in the IPN environment are the focal point for business continuity. Application clusters, database clusters, OS clusters, and application-specific load balancing technologies are the enablers in this category. These are often supported by network and security fail over/load-balancing hardware, routing protocols, mobile IP-related technologies, as well as tandem and clustered hardware. Today, applications often require extensive *storage area networks* (SAN) to provide required storage growth and performance. SAN hardware often has built-in resiliency. However, fail over across disparate geographical locations still requires extensive planning. Data replication is an important aspect of an enterprise storage strategy. When executing an IPN business continuity and disaster recovery plan, there is a balance between cost, downtime, and the loss of data.

Future Trends in IP

Emerging trends for IPN connectivity and security focus on data security. While a defense-in-depth approach will always apply to information protection best practices, security mechanisms are improving most rapidly in the area of data security. Field-level encryption and access control in a database and file systems are indications of what is ahead. Fundamentally, the task is to protect the data by designing and implementing sophisticated information security systems. Security technologies integrate as add-ons to protect information today will become core components of operating system, applications, and network devices. This includes technologies such as firewall, IPS, *antivirus* (AV), and admission control systems.

IPSec is being used today to provide secure virtual private network connectivity across untrusted networks such as the Internet. IPSec will be used more and more to secure and enforce network connectivity policies between hosts within and external to an IPN. IPSec is also a critical and seamless component of the next generation IPv6.

Denial- of-service (DoS) against a static host is a valid concern when implementing a secure IPN environment. As long as the destination is static, both intentional and unintentional denial-of-service situations against an IPN can arise. *Unintentional DoS* situations can be as simple as static content being linked by unknown sources. This can force your IPN environment to reach unpredictable network and processing demands. Using IPv6-based mobile IP technology, a stationary host can mimic a mobile host, preventing unwanted traffic redirection. A known host can simply locate the device using dynamic DNS. IPSec can be applied to this scenario to provide added security between two authorized hosts.

Admission control technology is mature enough today to provide policy-based access control of the IPN as well as enterprise networks. By using an admission control line of business, owners serviced by the IPN can set policies to enforce users' desktop security compliance prior to accessing the services. An example would be to scan the desktop for virus presence prior to accessing an IPN service. If the AV does not exist on the user desktop or the antivirus definition is out of date, IPN admission control components can redirect the user to a quarantine area. This area can be an IPN Zone where AV software and signature update services are available to the user.

The immune systems approach applied to the *operating system* (OS) is another emerging technology to protect the OS and the resident applications from the unknown security threats. As new security threats emerge at an increasing rate, it becomes harder to use reactive measures to protect an IPN environment. OS and application immune systems work to mitigate unknown and unauthorized use to IPN systems.

Finally, exit control technology is an emerging IPN technology. This technology is found in two main applications: smaller scale units dedicated to a single line-of-business application, and larger scale content-delivery networks. Today, this technology is commonly integrated with public key certificate infrastructure. At the low end of the spectrum, this technology is simply enforced within the business rules of an application. At the other extreme, an IPN with exit control technology signs all the content at the source host using a digital certificate, and all of the content is checked for validity and source authenticity throughout the egress path. If an unintentional modification takes place, bad content is simply discarded or replaced again with the rightful content from a secure read-only source. This is often done with large Web sites hosted within a data center IPN environment.

Chapter XIV

Software Security Engineering:
Toward Unifying Software Engineering and Security Engineering

Mohammad Zulkernine, Queen's University, Canada

Sheikh I. Ahamed, Marquette University, USA

Abstract

The rapid development and expansion of network-based applications have changed the computing world in the last decade. However, this overwhelming success has an Achilles' heel: most software-controlled systems are prone to attacks both by internal and external users of the highly connected computing systems. These software systems must be engineered with reliable protection mechanisms, while still delivering the expected value of the software to their customers within the budgeted time and cost. The principal obstacle in achieving these two different but interdependent objectives is that current software engineering processes do not provide enough support for the software developers to achieve security goals. In this chapter, we reemphasize the principal objectives of both software engineering and security engineering, and strive to identify the major steps of a software security engineering process that will be useful for building secure software systems. Both software engineering and security engineering are ever-evolving disciplines, and software security engineering is still in its infancy. This chapter proposes a unification of the process models of software engineering and security engineering in order to improve the steps of the software life cycle that would better address the underlying objectives of both engineering processes. This unification will facilitate the incorporation of the advancement of the features of one engineering process into the other. The chapter also provides a brief overview and survey of the current state-of-the-art of software engineering and security engineering with respect to computer systems.

Introduction

With the proliferation of connectivity of computer systems in the applications where the quality of service depends on data confidentiality, data integrity, and protection against denial-of-service attack, the need for secure networks is evident. In these applications, the consequences of a security breach may range from extensive financial losses to dangers to human life. Due to heavy dependence of computer network-based applications on various software and software controlled systems, software security has become an essential issue. Almost every software controlled system faces potential threats from system users, both insiders and outsiders. It is well accepted that "the root of most security problems is software that fails in unexpected ways when under attack" (McGraw, 2002, p. 101). Therefore, software systems must be engineered with reliable protection mechanisms against potential attacks while still providing the expected quality of service to their customers within the budgeted time and cost. Software should be designed with the objective not only of implementing the quality functionalities required for their users, but also of combating potential and unexpected threats. The principal obstacle in achieving these two different but interdependent objectives is that current software engineering processes do not provide enough support for the software developers to achieve security goals.

Some of the principal software engineering objectives are usability, performance, timely completion, reliability, and flexibility in software applications (Finkelstein & Kramer, 2000; IEEE, 1999; Pressman, 2001). On the other hand, some of the major objectives of security engineering are customized access control and authentication based on the privilege levels of users, traceability and detection, accountability, non-repudiation, privacy, confidentiality, and integrity (Pfleeger & Pfleeger, 2003; Viega & McGraw, 2001). Having stated that, software security engineering objectives are to design a software system that meets both security objectives and application objectives. However, software security engineering is still considered a difficult task due to inherent difficulties associated with the addressing of the security issues in the core development and maintenance of software systems. Both software engineering and security engineering are ever-evolving disciplines and software security engineering is still in its infancy. A precise and well-accepted understanding of software security engineering does not yet exist (ISSEA, 2003; Wolf, 2004).

The principal objectives of software security engineering need to be reinvestigated, and a methodology is required that can be employed for building secure software systems. Software security engineering is a practice to address software security issues in a systematic manner. We believe that the security issues must be addressed in all the stages of software system development and the maintenance life cycle, such as requirements specifications, design, testing, operation, and maintenance, to provide secure software systems. This chapter identifies some possible ways to adapt readily the current practices of security engineering into a software engineering process model. In other words, this chapter suggests a unification of the process models of software engineering and security engineering. The unification is desirable between the two processes because it removes the unnecessary differences in their corresponding steps that obscure the fundamental principles of the development and maintenance of secure software systems. This unification will help system designers to employ the techniques and tools of software engineering and security engineering in a complementary fashion. It will also help to incorporate the advancement of the features of one engineering process into the other. In our attempt, we suggest the incorporation of new, more intuitive but well-defined steps in the software security engineering process in order to build secure software systems. It may be noted here that a number of studies have already proved that "end-to-end integration" of security aspects in the software life cycle have significant benefits with respect to the quality of the end software products (Devanbu & Stubblebine, 2000; Viega & McGraw, 2001).

In this chapter, we describe a software security engineering process that is primarily based on the famous waterfall software development process model (Royce, 1987). The major steps of the proposed software security engineering process model are described in detail. The rationale for choosing the waterfall model as a basis for the description is that it contains most of the fundamental steps present in all other software process models that currently exist in the literature. Therefore, our idea of a software security engineering process that incorporates security issues in all the steps of software life cycle will work fine in other software process models. For example, the incremental model is widely used in industry with a view to reducing the delay in delivering software products. It consists of several increments or builds, where each increment follows the waterfall model. Similarly, in an incremental model-based software security engineering process, each increment may adopt the steps described in this chapter.

The rest of the chapter is organized as follows. The next section provides a brief overview of software engineering and security engineering and presents a brief synopsis of the current state-of-the-art of other related efforts towards software security engineering. The details of the proposed software security engineering process model are then provided. Finally, the chapter concludes with a summary of current research and future recommendations.

Background

A Glimpse of Software Engineering

In the IEEE Standard Glossary of Software Engineering Terminology (IEEE Std. 610.12-1990), software engineering is defined as follows: "(1) Software engineering is the application of a systematic, disciplined, quantifiable approach to the development, operation, and maintenance of software; that is, the application of engineering to software. (2) The study of approaches as in (1)" (IEEE, 1999, p. 67). It primarily focuses on applying an engineering approach to the design, implementation and maintenance of software systems. Software engineering is an engineering discipline that is concerned with all aspects of software production — from the early stages of system specification to maintenance of the system after it has been deployed for use (Finkelstein & Kramer, 2000). Software engineering is a subset of system engineering that focuses on the overall system (both software and hardware), while software engineering only focuses on the software aspects of the system development.

There are different software development life cycle models, such as the waterfall, incremental, spiral, and rapid prototyping (Pressman, 2001). Among these models, the waterfall model (Royce, 1987) is the most widely used and discussed. Most models consist of steps for requirement gathering and analysis, software architecture, implementation, and testing. Stakeholders involved in a software engineering process influence software engineers to follow certain process models to address and solve different issues of the software in an effective way. The stakeholders include analysts, designers, programmers, testers, maintenance personnel, project managers, and end-users or customers. The project manager leads the whole software development group of analysts, designers, programmers, testers, and maintenance personnel. An analyst collects and analyses the requirements, and a designer forms the architecture with a view to leading the requirements towards the implementation. A programmer implements the architecture or design provided by the designer, and testers test the software for ensuring a high-quality end-product. Maintenance personnel deploy and maintain the software so that the operators can use the software effectively.

Software engineering refers to techniques intended for making software development more orderly, systematic, and organized. It also helps to reduce the time and cost of developing software in a scientific way. In summary, low cost, high quality, and rapid software development are the key goals of software engineering. The rapid development and expansion of the software are possible with effective use of a software engineering process; however, security issues have not yet been incorporated or addressed in the software development processes.

A Glimpse of Security Engineering

The *International Federation for Information Processing* (IFIP) Working Group WG10.4 on Dependable Computing and Fault Tolerance considers security as one of the attributes of software "dependability," where dependability is defined as the "trustworthiness of a computer system such that reliance can be justifiably placed in the service it delivers" (Laprie, 1992, p. 4). The other principal attributes of dependability are reliability, availability, and safety, while security professionals usually consider safety and reliability as attributes of security. The threats to security are identified as interception, interruption, modification, and fabrication of data (Pfleeger & Pfleeger, 2003). The threats are usually defined based on some security policy of the organization, while the violations of any security policy are combated using different security mechanisms such as encryption, authentication, authorization, and auditing.

Security engineering is a discipline for "building systems to remain dependable in the face of malice, error, or mischance," where the discipline "emphasizes the tools, processes, and methods needed to design, implement, and test complete systems, and to adapt existing systems as their environment evolves" (Anderson, 2001, p. 3). Security engineering deals with a number of issues such as intrusion protection and detection. It ensures that a system is secure from both software and hardware perspectives. System security is becoming increasingly more important due to the new trend of ubiquitous/pervasive computing that has evolved during the last few years; numerous mobile or embedded devices such as PDAs and cell phones are connected via the Internet, incurring enormous security vulnerabilities.

Security engineering addresses the complete life cycle for building a secure system: requirements specification and analysis, design, development, integration, operation, maintenance and re-engineering (ISSEA, 2003). It requires expertise in interdisciplinary areas such as computer system management and development, software and hardware security, networking and cryptography, applied psychology, organizational management, and law. Without incorporating the security engineering principles derived from the relevant cross-disciplinary areas to every level of a software development process, it is nearly impossible to deliver a secure software system in its first release.

Related Effort to Address Security Issues in Software Engineering Context

We begin this section with the following question that was asked by Wolf (2004, p. 1): "Is security engineering really just good software engineering?" We also believe in Wolf's concluding observation that security engineering cannot be differentiated from software engineering if "the underlying mathematics and higher level policy and human factor issues" are not considered. Our approach to software security engineering is along the line of the following research challenges outlined in Finkelstein and Kramer (2000) and Devanbu and Stubblebine (2000): integration of security requirements with software requirements into initial development life cycle; design of adaptive software systems to handle new attacks and changing security policies of any organizations; testing security requirements of software systems; and derivation of intelligent and responsive framework for operational stage monitoring and maintenance. A number of other related efforts towards incorporating security engineering principles into software development life cycles are discussed in the following paragraphs.

In Viega and McGraw (2001), a software risk management process is proposed for assessing, quantifying, and establishing an acceptable level of risk in an organization. The proposed process is inspired by Boehm's spiral software process model (Boehm, 1988). In this process, security aspects are considered when software requirements are derived. The most severe security risks are evaluated and strategies are planned for resolving those risks. The risks are addressed through prototyping and validation that the risks of those security violations are eliminated. Then, the solution to the security risks is applied for the next version of the software requirements, design, or source code. Finally, the planning for the next phase is outlined.

In Flechals, Sasse, and Hailes (2003), a process for usable and secure software systems called *appropriate and effective guidance in information security* (AEGIS) is proposed. AEGIS involves the context in which the system is going to be used, and analyzes the potential risks to help developers handle security related issues. Similar to the risk management process proposed in Viega and McGraw (2001), AEGIS is also based on Boehm's spiral software process model. It requires communication among a system's stakeholders in the risk analysis and the selection of appropriate defense mechanisms so that the developers gain a better understanding of the security and usability requirements. AEIGS employs *Unified Modeling Language* (UML) (Jacobson, Booch, & Rumbaugh, 1999) to describe a way to perform "risk-usability-design" simultaneously.

The *Software Security Assessment Instrument* (SSAI) Project (Gilliam, Wolfe, & Sherif, 2003) identifies five important entities with respect to software security engineering: *software security checklist* (SSC), *vulnerability matrix* (Vmatrix), *flexible modeling framework* (FMF) for verification of requirements, *property-based tester* (PBT) for testing vulnerabilities, and *security assessment tools* (SATs). Similar to our objective in this chapter, the SSC incorporates "security as a formal approach in the software life cycle" (p. 243).

The *system security engineering capability maturity model* (SSE-CMM) (ISSEA, 2003) proposes a unified process of practicing security engineering in the context of software development. In the systems security engineering process, the security engineering task is divided into three interrelated but separate basic process areas: the risk process, engineering process, and assurance process. The risk process identifies and prioritizes the risks inherent to the product under development; the engineering process interfaces with the other engineering disciplines to provide solution to the identified risks; and the assurance process improves the level of confidence of the product developer and the customers with respect to the proposed security solutions. The SSE-CMM describes the characteristics of five capability levels that are inspired by the CMM used to evaluate software engineering practices.

The Unified Modeling Language (Jacobson, Booch, & Rumbaugh, 1999) has currently become the de facto standard to specify, visualize, and document models of software systems including their structure and design. More specifically, it is suitable for object-oriented analysis and design. The UML defines 12 types of diagrams of three categories. Nevertheless, the UML does not provide a framework that can address the issues with respect to developing secure software system. A number of efforts are taking place in order to enrich the UML-based software development processes. Some of them are: UMLSec (Jürjens, 2003), Misuse and Abuse cases (Sindre & Opdahl, 2000; Dermott &

Fox, 1999), Secure UML (Basin, Doser, & Lodderstedt, 2003; Lodderstedt, Basin, & Jurgen, 2002), and Security integrated rational unified process (Oikinomopoulos & Giritzails, 2004).

To address security issues in the context of software development processes, some of the elements of UML, such as use case, class, sequence, state chart, package and deployment diagrams, are extended (Jürjens, 2003). This UML extension for secure software development is called UMLSec. The extensions included in the UMLSec are based on using stereotypes and tag values, which enrich the existing UML diagrams with security-related information.

Standard use case diagrams are often useful for eliciting functional requirements, while they are not that suitable for describing security requirements (Jacobson, Booch, & Rumbaugh, 1999). The security requirements are usually related to prohibited activities. Therefore, an extension to standard UML use case notations is proposed in Sindre and Opdahl (2000) in order to include unwanted use case scenarios. A use case describes a sequence of actions that represents a service to the user. On the other hand, a misuse case in the context of security requirements is defined as a sequence of actions that results in security violations for the organization or some specific stakeholder. They also define "mis-actor" as just the opposite of an actor, and it initiates the misuse cases. In Dermott and Fox (1999), a use case-based object-oriented modeling technique is used to represent significant forms of abuses that need to be prevented. However, security issues are not addressed in every phase of the software engineering process.

SecureUML (Basin, Doser, & Lodderstedt, 2003; Lodderstedt, Basin, & Doser, 2002) describes a methodology for modeling access control policies and integrating it into a model-driven software development process. This work is inspired by the idea of using UML to model *role-based access control* (RBAC) policies. The unique feature of the SecureUML is that it also includes elements to be used in behavioral models.

A number of extensions of the UML for the purpose of security are compared and contrasted by Oikinomopoulos and Giritzails (2004). We agree with their view that most of those extensions are concerned with the presentation (notational) issues of security-related information rather than a methodology, which emphasizes the activities to be performed for software security engineering. In most of their work, Oikinomopoulos and Giritzails provide very little or no guideline about how and in what phase of the development cycle the extended UML notations will be utilized; they incorporate security engineering in the *rational unified process* (RUP). The RUP divides the software development effort into phases and major workflows. The authors extend each workflow with additional security-related activities and identify the artifacts that should be produced. To support these activities, they also introduce the role of a "security engineer" in their methodology.

Software Security Engineering

Having discussed both software engineering and security engineering, it is important to note that "while software engineering is about ensuring that certain things happen, security is about ensuring that they don't" (Anderson, 2001, p. 3). Nevertheless, following the IEEE Standard 610.12-1990 (IEEE, 1999, p. 67) definition of software engineering, software security engineering can be defined as "the application of a systematic, disciplined, quantifiable approach to the development, operation, and maintenance of" secure software; i.e., "the application of engineering" to obtain secure software (IEEE, 1999, p. 67).

In the software security engineering process, the principles and specialties of other engineering disciplines with respect to software and security are integrated to achieve the "trustworthiness" in software systems. This process will help software development to proceed in a way where it will have less chance of exposing itself to security-related loopholes. It will endorse low cost, high quality, and a rapid software development process where the security issues will be addressed in every phase of the process. Software security engineering involves the stakeholders of software engineering, while actively involving security engineers in most of its phases. Similar to both software engineering and security engineering, software security engineering incorporates expertise from several other cross-disciplinary areas such as computer system management and development, software and hardware security, computer networks, organizational management, psychology, and law.

We describe a software security engineering process that is primarily based on the famous waterfall software development process model (Boehm, 1988). The waterfall model contains most of the fundamental steps present in other software process models currently used in industry and academia. The major steps of the proposed model are: system engineering, requirements specification, software design, program implementation, and system operation. The steps are presented schematically in Figure 1. While the following paragraphs provide a brief introduction to the steps, all of the steps are further detailed in the subsections that follow.

- **System engineering:** The software concerns of a system development are separate from its hardware concerns. Then both functionality issues and security issues are identified based on the users' or stakeholders' needs and in the context of other system elements such as hardware, software, people, database, documentation, and procedure.

- **Requirements specification:** The security requirements of a software system are specified, analyzed, and integrated along with the other functional and nonfunctional requirements of the software system. It is recommended that both security requirements and the other software requirements should be specified using the same formal language.[1] The requirements are expressed as a set of scenarios.

- **Software design:** Both functionality and security issues should be considered when deciding where the application components are deployed and how they communicate with each other. A scenario-based software architecture is designed based on functional scenarios from users' perspective and attack scenarios from intruders' perspective. The architecture should be compositional so that whenever a new attack is encountered, the system architecture can easily adapt to defend against the attack.

Figure 1. A waterfall-based software security engineering process model

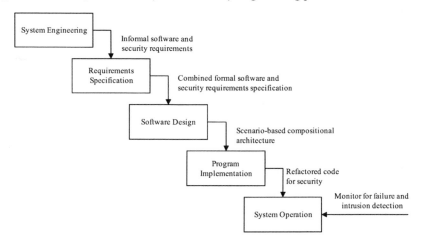

- **Program implementation:** The system is implemented to meet the specified requirements, and the correctness and effectiveness of security mechanisms, along with functional characteristics, are verified with respect to the requirements specification. When the required functionalities are implemented, the source code is refactored (changed) to control any number of vulnerabilities against threats from attackers, while still meeting all of the functional acceptance tests.

- **System operation:** The software is monitored for security violation or conformance to its functional requirements based on the specification formalized in the requirements specification phase. In other words, the software monitor is equipped with different intrusion-detection capabilities. The monitor also measures whether the operational impacts due to security vulnerabilities or residual software faults in a system are acceptable or not.

System Engineering

Software engineering deals with the software aspects of system engineering while security engineering focuses on the overall system engineering (both software and hardware). Similar to software engineering, the end-product of the software security engineering process is software. The system engineering phase of the software security engineering process identifies the software aspects of the system to be developed. Obviously, this phase focuses equally on both functionalities and security issues of the software system based on the users' or stakeholders' needs and in the context of other system elements, such as hardware, software, people, database, documentation, and procedure. Both software engineers and security engineers work closely in this phase.

Similar to IEEE Standard 1220-1998 for system engineering (Thayer, 2002), this phase of the software security engineering process involves defining the system requirements that determine the needs and constraints of the software and hardware. This is accomplished through analyzing the functional requirements and all the aspects of security related threats (see Figure 2). The outcomes of this phase are the informal functional and security requirements. These informal requirements then become the input of the requirements specification phase.

Requirements Specification

Software requirements are usually referred to as functional requirements that specify the behavior of the system; that is, the relationship between inputs and outputs. A nonfunctional software requirement describes not what the software will perform, but rather how effectively the software will perform. For example, usability, reliability, interoperability, scalability, and security are some of the nonfunctional properties of software systems. Like most other nonfunctional requirements, security is regarded as an important factor to the success of any software project, and it is usually incorporated in the system development in a subjective manner.

There are some inherent difficulties associated with security requirements specification: security requirements are often difficult to specify in the early phases of the software development life cycle, since the software model tends to be very abstract and is usually presented in an informal manner. In addition, security risks are difficult to estimate, and as the software development progresses, developers receive new information about the system security (Zhang & Zulkernine, 2004). Given that, it is often difficult to specify security measures and integrate them into the actual system from the very beginning of the software development process. In most cases, security requirements are not addressed at all during the early design phases.

Figure 2. The system engineering phase of the software security engineering process

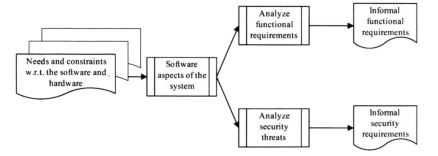

Figure 3. The requirements specification phase of the software security engineering process

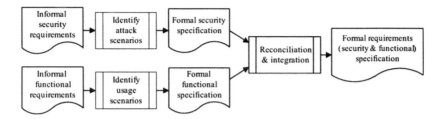

In the software security engineering process, both security and functional requirements are specified in the requirements specification phase (see Figure 3). We believe that the weaknesses of software-controlled systems with respect to the software security can be alleviated by specifying functional and security requirements using formal methods, and then by reconciling and integrating the two sets of formal specifications at an abstract level. As the software design evolves, the specifications are refined to reflect the progressive changes towards the end-product. In this way, security requirements get closely involved in the later stages of software development.

Scenarios have been widely used as a technique for elicitation, analysis, and documentation of software requirements. A scenario is a sequence of a limited number of related events or actions that represents some meaningful high-level operation in a system. The length of a scenario may vary from a single event to all the events of a system. However, all the events of a single scenario must occur during a particular run of the system. In this phase of the software security engineering process, two types of scenarios are identified based on the corresponding requirements: usage scenarios and attack scenarios. The usage scenarios are selected based on the operational profile of the intended software system. The attack scenarios can incorporate expert knowledge on security, and they may be ranked based on their importance in the system being implemented. For example, defending against a denial-of-service attack in a client machine may not be as important as it is in a server machine.

A scenario can be represented in various forms: natural language, pseudo code, data flow diagrams, state machine-based notations, communicating event-based notations, and so forth. To avoid inconsistency and redundancy, it is highly recommended that both usage scenarios and attack scenarios be defined using the same specification language. In the literature, we find a number of formal software specification languages and a relatively fewer number of attack languages to describe attack scenarios (Eckmann, 2001; Vigna, Eckmann, & Kemmerer, 2000). However, currently available software specification languages are not completely suitable for specifying the security-related aspects of software systems, nor are attack specification languages suitable in specifying functional requirements. As an initial attempt, software specification languages can be translated to attack languages and vice versa. For example, in Zhang and Zulkernine (2004), a formal software requirements specification language of Microsoft called

Abstract State Machine Language (ASML) (Barnett, Grieskamp, Gurevich, Schulte, Tillman, & Veanes, 2003) is automatically transformed to a high-level attack specification language called *State Transition Analysis Technique Language* (STATL) (Vigna, Eckmann, & Kemmerer, 2000), which can be preprogrammed and loaded into an intrusion-detection system at runtime. The translation scheme will initially help to close the gap between security requirements and functional requirements with respect to their modeling and implementation.

Software Design

A software architecture or software design defines the software components of a system and the interactions among these components. The examples of application components include user interfaces, databases, and middleware (Kazman, Carriere, & Woods, 2000). Both functionality and security issues are interconnected to where the software components are deployed and how they communicate with each other. For example, the architecture and its protection mechanisms depend on whether the system will operate as a centralized or a distributed one. The software components should be deployed based on the trustworthiness and information flow among them, following the principle: "what needs to be protected and from whom those things need to be protected, and for how long protection is needed" (Viega & McGraw, 2001, p. 34).

In the software security engineering process, a software system should be designed based on the following two principles: compositional software architecture and scenario-based software architecture. The following paragraphs discuss these two principles in the context of software security engineering.

New attacks are made to the software systems and security loopholes may be discovered at any point during the life of software. Flexible software architectures are desirable to make the design changes in those situations. A compositional software architecture is one in which the changes required for the whole system can be obtained by applying the changes to its components. As a result, whenever a new attack is encountered, the system architecture can be easily adapted to defend against the attack if a clear and clean notion of component is present. This is only possible if the principle of compositionality and the security concerns were taken into consideration in defining each software component in the software design phase. This adaptive architecture is very useful for rapidly evolving security policies in the post-deployment system administration period, and to facilitate the re-engineering of security features into legacy systems. We define the concept of compositionality with respect to software security engineering following the definition of compositional specification and verification (de Roever, 1997). Assume that a system C is composed of the components $C_1, C_2, ...,$ and C_n by employing a set of composition operators. Let the security requirements of $C_1, C_2, ...,$ and C_n be $S_1, S_2, ...,$ and S_n respectively. A compositional design implies that the whole system C satisfies the complete specification S if each component C_i satisfies S_i for $i = 1,...,n$. Therefore, any change of security requirements in any of the components can be addressed and verified without modifying the other components (in a true compositional case).

Scenarios are employed to build the software architecture of a system with a view to incorporating different features described by each scenario (Kazman, Carriere, & Woods, 2000). Scenarios are very useful to compare design alternatives and to understand a legacy system by analyzing the system responses in the context of different environments. Jacobson et al. (1999) compared scenario-based design to "making a film." However, scenario-based design of a software system is more than making a single movie, as scenarios may be composed in parallel, alternative, or iterative manner in order to build the desired composite system. Similarly, the potential attacks to a system can be specified using attack scenarios, which initially may be abstract, and are refined as the design evolves by considering all security-relevant issues.

Implementation

Security requirements define the behavior of a system that should not occur. A programmer working for a particular implementation or an intruder who somehow manages to gain access to the source code can initiate certain actions in the program that may cause target system behavior that should not be allowed. During programming, we should ensure that potential security flaws, identified as security requirements and avoided in the earlier phases of the software security engineering process, are not reintroduced in the source code. Any unexpected behavior with respect to program security is called a "security flaw," while "vulnerability" is considered as a special security flaw[2] (Pfleeger & Pfleeger, 2003). In Landwehr, Bull, McDermott, and Choi (1994), the surveyed "program security flaws" are divided into two categories: intentional and inadvertent. Intentional flaws are categorized as malicious and non-malicious, while inadvertent flaws are divided into the following six types: incomplete or inconsistent validation error, domain error, serialization or aliasing, insufficient identification or authentication, boundary condition violation, and other potential exploitable logic errors.

Given the varying and intricate nature of the above-mentioned security flaws, security engineers should participate in coding or understand the code well enough to identify potential security flaws and convey them to software developers. Security engineers may participate in formal code inspection and review processes to document any security-relevant issues present in the source code. More specifically, in the software security engineering process, we propose to follow the principle of code refactoring successfully employed in the context of extreme programming (Beck, 1999). In extreme programming, code refactoring refers to the practice of restructuring the source code without changing the intended functionalities of the system, such as removing any duplicate or unreachable code and re-organizing code for simplicity and flexibility. It is important to confirm that refactoring does not introduce any new faults or security flaws into the code. Therefore, individual refactoring steps should be small to address the above-mentioned security flaws, and each change should be tested to ensure that the implementation is as functional and self-protected as it was before the refactoring. Note that refactoring is not intended to replace testing in the software security engineering process, but rather to complement testing by increasing the confidence in the source code of security critical applications. Once the functionalities required for the system are implemented, refactoring is employed to change the program so that the software can control its vulnerabilities against attacks from intruders while still passing all of the functional requirements tests.

The software should be tested for both functional and security requirements. Based on these requirements, along with other nonfunctional requirements such as performance and quality of service identified in the early phases of the software security engineering process, the test cases for the software system are derived. Vulnerability scenarios of the software that can be exploited for intrusions or security violations are tested. A "red teaming" approach may be used where a system is tested using simulated scenarios under which it may be attacked (Viega & McGraw, 2001). We have to ensure that the system is tested in the network environment in which the system will actually run. Keeping that in mind, the testing of the software can be divided into two steps: unit testing that tests a host for security; and integration testing that tests the whole system by deploying the system in the target network configuration guided by the applicable security policies.

System Operation

A number of studies have shown that professionally written programs may contain between one and 10 faults per 1,000 lines of codes. Moreover, despite rigorous use of different "protective shields," there exist security loopholes that elude those protective efforts, and unauthorized intrusions may occur when the network is operational. The difficulty in releasing correct and secure software has resulted in a growing interest in the usefulness of operational stage monitoring of software systems. However, existing intrusion detectors cannot monitor the behavior of software systems, while the current software monitors cannot detect security violations in the target systems.

In software security engineering, a software monitor should also have the capability of detecting intrusions (see Figure 4). The monitor passively observes some of the actual events occurring in a software application at runtime and reports the occurrences of intrusions or behavioral failure. To detect any intrusion or behavioral failure in a target system, the monitor must have the knowledge of what is the ideal or normal behavior of the monitored system. This knowledge can be obtained from the system's formal (behavioral and security) specification identified in the requirements specification phase. Note that this requirements specification was originally used to design and implement the software application, as shown in Figure 4. During system operation, the behavior of the monitored system when it is under attack by the intrusions known later on can be specified. Similar to previously considered intrusions, it is also obvious that the newly discovered intrusions may change the behavioral profile of a host or a network. Therefore, new attack specifications are reconciled with the existing formal requirements specification. The monitor interprets the formal specification using the observed events of the monitored host or the network in order to generate a report on intrusive activities as well as unexpected behavior.

Figure 4. Monitoring an operational software application using a specification-based monitor

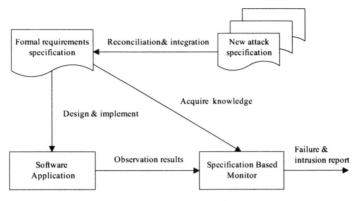

Conclusion and Recommendations

In this chapter, we have presented a software security engineering process based on the waterfall software process model. The adaptation of the proposed process into other existing software engineering process models is straightforward. It is worth mentioning here that many new engineering disciplines, such as software engineering and security engineering, have incorporated many concepts and principles from other mature engineering disciplines. Similarly, the individual concepts and techniques suggested in the proposed process are not completely new. What is new in this chapter is their systematic integration and organization into a process that will lead to secure software systems.

It is very difficult to achieve two sets of desired objectives while they "trade off against one another" (Viega & McGraw, 2001, p. 29). For example: an application software may require root-level access privileges in a system to run the application, while in some cases it may mean weakening the security of the target system. We believe that the trade-off among these goals is very application-dependent. The potential conflict between software characteristics and network defenses should be resolved early in the development phase; that is, in the requirements specification phase. In other words, security measures must not hamper the expected quality of service of a system, but at the same time any functionality should not be achieved at the cost of weakening security. Given that, a software security engineering process should be employed, where functionalities of a system must be specified and defined by considering the security concerns or requirements with respect to the system.

Currently available specification languages are not completely suitable for defining security-related aspects of software behavior. The standardized formal software specification languages used in industry should be investigated and extended (if needed) for expressing security-related features of target systems. However, it may not be always feasible to formally specify all of the suspicious activities occurring in the target system. Therefore, the formal specification may be supplemented by the statistical components of the operational profiles of the system, users, or intruders. Statistical analysis may be performed to detect any additional intrusions.

History of well-established engineering disciplines shows the key role that automatic development tools played in their advancement. Automatic tools can play a similar role in the area of software security engineering to improve the productivity and quality of the software with respect to security. Existing *computer-aided software engineering* (CASE) tools cannot be used for software security engineering, since their focus is solely on software not security. Both security and software along with productivity and quality, need to be addressed in the CASE tools. The availability of such tools is likely to provide support to further the evolution of software security engineering.

Though we have described the proposed process independent of current software development paradigms, such as procedural, object-oriented, or component-based, it is worth mentioning the issue of trustworthiness of software components. With the increase in component-based software development, the security of components has become an important issue due to the design of software systems composed of untrusted components from independent sources. It is still an open question as to the level of security one can achieve when integrating third-party components of a software system (Lindqvist & Jonsson, 1998). In component-based software development, components interact to accomplish the functionalities of software systems. In the future, a metadata-based approach can be used to address the security issues in component interactions, since metadata describes the static and dynamic aspects of the components including the accessibility by their users (Orso, Harrold, & Rosenblum, 2001).

References

Anderson, R. (2001). *Security engineering - A guide to building dependable distributed system.* New York: John Wiley & Sons.

Barnett, M., Grieskamp, W., Gurevich, Y., Schulte, W., Tillman, T., & Veanes, M. (2003, May). Scenario-oriented modeling in AsmL and its instrumentation for testing. In *Proceedings of the 2nd International Workshop on Scenarios and State Machines: Models. Algorithms, and Tools,* Portland, OR (pp. 8-14).

Basin, D., Doser, J., & Lodderstedt, T. (2003). Model-driven security for process-oriented systems. In *Proceedings of the 8thACM symposium on Access Control Models and Technologies,* Como, Italy (pp. 100-109).

Beck, K. (1999). *eXtreme programming explained: Embrace change.* Reading, MA: Addison Wesley.

Boehm, B. W. (1988). A spiral model of software development and enhancement. *IEEE Computer, 21*(5), 61-72.

Dermott, J., & Fox, C. (1999, December). Using abuse case models for security requirements analysis. In *Proceedings of the 15th Annual Computer Security Applications Conference*, Phoenix, AZ (pp. 55-66). IEEE Computer Society.

Devanbu, P. T., & Stubblebine, S. (2000, June). Software engineering for security: A roadmap. In A. Finkelstein (Ed.), *The Future of Software Engineering. Proceedings of the International Conference on Software Engineering* (pp. 227-239). Limerick, Ireland: ACM.

Eckmann, S. T. (2001, October). Translating snort rules to STATL scenarios. In *Proceedings of the 4th International Symposium on Recent Advances in Intrusion Detection (RAID 2001), Lecture Notes in Computer Science* (pp. 69-84). Germany: Springer-Verlag.

Finkelstein, A., & Kramer, J. (2000, June). Software engineering: A roadmap. In A. Finkelstein (Ed.), *The Future of Software Engineering, Proceedings of the International Conference on Software Engineering* (pp. 5-22). Limerick, Ireland: ACM.

Flechals, I., Sasse, M. A., & Hailes, S. M. V. (2003, August). Bringing security home: A process for developing secure and usable systems. In *Proceedings of the New Security Paradigms Workshop*, Ascona, Switzerland (pp. 49-57). ACM.

Gilliam, D. P., Wolfe, T. W., & Sherif, J. S. (2003, June). Software security checklist for the software life cycle. In *Proceedings of the Twelfth IEEE International Workshop on Enabling Technologies: Infrastructure for Collaborative Enterprises (WETICE '03)* (pp. 243-248). IEEE.

Institute of Electrical and Electronics Engineers, Inc. (IEEE). (1999). *Software engineering: Customer and terminology standards, Vol. 1.* New York: Institute of Electrical and Electronics Engineers, Inc.

International Systems Security Engineering Association (ISSEA). (2003). SSE-CMM: Model Description Document, Version 3.0, SSE-CMM – ISO/IEC 21827, International Systems Security Engineering Association. Retrieved November 2005, from http://www.sse-cmm.org/docs/ssecmmv3final.pdf

Jacobson, I., Booch, G., & Rumbaugh, J. (1999). *The unified software development process.* Reading, MA: Addison Wesley.

Jürjens, J. (2003). *Secure systems development with UML.* New York: Springer-Verlag.

Kazman, R., Carriere, S. J., & Woods, S. G. (2000). Toward a discipline of scenario-based architectural engineering. *Annals of Software Engineering, 9*, 5-33.

Landwehr, C. E., Bull, A. R., McDermott, J. P., & Choi, W. S. (1994). A taxonomy of computer program security flaws. *ACM Computing Surveys, 26*(3), 211-254.

Laprie, J. (1992). *Dependability: Basic concepts and terminology - In English, French, German, and Japanese.* Vienna: Springer-Verlag.

Lindqvist, U., & Jonsson, E. (1998). A map of security risks associated with using COTS. *IEEE Computer*, 60-66. Retrieved November 2005, from http://downloads. securityfocus.com/library/cots98.pdf

Lodderstedt, T., Basin, D., & Doser, J. (2002, September). SecureUML: A UML-based modeling language for model-driven security. In *Proceedings of the Fifth International Conference on the Unified Modeling Language: The Language and Its Applications*. Germany: Springer Verlag.

McGraw, G. (2002). Managing software security risks. *IEEE Computer,* 99-101.

Oikinomopoulos, S., & Giritzails, S. (2004, September). Integration of security engineering into the rational unified process –An early iteration. In *Proceedings of the Workshop on Specification and Automated Processing of Security Requirements - SAPS'04*, Linz, Austria (pp. 167-176). Austrian Computer Society.

Orso, A., Harrold, M. J., & Rosenblum, D. (2001). Component metadata for software engineering tasks. In *Proceedings of the EDO 2000, Lecture Notes in Computer Science, 1999* (pp. 129-144). Springer-Verlag.

Pfleeger, C. P., & Pfleeger, S. L. (2003). *Security in computing*. Upper Saddle River, NJ: Prentice-Hall.

Pressman, R. P. (2001). *Software engineering: A practitioner's approach*. New York: McGraw Hill.

de Roever, W. (1997). The need for compositional proof systems: A survey. In *Compositionality: The Significant Difference (COMPOS '97), Lecture Notes in Computer Science, 1536* (pp. 1-22). Berlin: Springer-Verlag.

Royce, W. W. (1987). Managing the development of large software systems: Concepts and techniques. In WESCON Technical Papers, 1970, (Reprinted), *Proceedings of the Ninth International Conference on Software Engineering* (pp. 328-338). Monterey, CA: IEEE Computer Society Press.

Sindre, G., & Opdahl, A. L. (2000, November). Eliciting security requirements by misuse cases, In *Proceedings of the 37th International Conference on Technology of Object-Oriented Languages and Systems* (pp. 174-183). Sydney, Australia: IEEE Computer Society.

Thayer, R. H. (2002). Software system engineering: A tutorial. *Computer, 35*(4), 68-73.

Viega, J., & McGraw, G. (2001). *Building secure software: How to avoid security problems the right way*. Reading, MA: Addison-Wesley.

Vigna, G., Eckmann, S. T., & Kemmerer, R. A. (2000, October). Attack languages. In *Proceedings of the IEEE Information Survivability Workshop*, Boston (pp. 63-166). IEEE.

Wolf, A. L. (2004, October). Is security engineering really just good software engineering? *Keynote Talk, ACM SIGSOFT '04/FSE-12*, Newport Beach, CA.

Zhang, Q., & Zulkernine, M. (2004, September). Applying AsmL specification for automatic intrusion detection. In *Proceedings of the Workshop on Specification and Automated Processing of Security Requirements – SAPS'04*, Linz, Austria (pp. 221-223). Austrian Computer Society.

Endnotes

[1]   For brevity, functional software requirements are mentioned as software requirements or functional requirements.

[2]   IEEE definitions (IEEE, 1999) of "fault" and "failure" are defined from a different perspective. However, Wolf (2004) views "vulnerability" as a "fault," since an attack cannot cause a security failure if no vulnerability exists.

Chapter XV

Wireless Security

Erik Graham, General Dynamics Corporation, USA

Paul John Steinbart, Arizona State University, USA

Abstract

The introduction of wireless networking provides many benefits, but it also creates new security threats and alters the organization's overall information security risk profile. Although responding to wireless security threats and vulnerabilities often involves implementation of technological solutions, wireless security is primarily a management issue. Effective management of the threats associated with wireless technology requires a sound and thorough assessment of risk given the environment and development of a plan to mitigate identified threats. This chapter presents a framework to help managers understand and assess the various threats associated with the use of wireless technology. We also discuss a number of available measures for countering those threats.

Introduction

Wireless networking provides a number of benefits. Productivity improves because of increased accessibility to information resources. Network configuration and reconfiguration is easier, faster, and less expensive. However, wireless technology also creates new threats and alters the existing information security risk profile. For example, because communications takes place "through the air" using radio frequencies, the risk of interception is greater than with wired networks. If the message is not encrypted, or encrypted with a weak algorithm, the attacker can read it, thereby compromising confidentiality. If the attacker can alter the intercepted message and then forward it to its intended destination, integrity is lost. If the attacker prevents the message from reaching its intended destination, availability is compromised. Wireless networking also alters physical security risks. For example, wireless clients (e.g., laptops, PDAs, etc.) are smaller than desktop workstations and, therefore, more easily stolen. In addition, the low cost and ease of installation of wireless access points increases the risk of unauthorized, insecure, wireless access points on the network.

Nevertheless, although wireless networking alters the risks associated with various threats to security, the overall security objectives remain the same as with wired networks: preserving confidentiality, ensuring integrity, and maintaining availability of the information and information systems. Moreover, the fundamental economic constraint on security also remains unchanged: most organizations do not have the resources to attempt to totally eliminate all risk. Consequently, wireless security involves risk management. Managers need to evaluate the likelihood that a particular threat might be successfully employed against their organization and estimate the impact of such an attack. They can then choose to invest in and deploy the set of control procedures that most cost-effectively manages risk at an acceptable level. The objective of this chapter is to assist managers in making such decisions by providing them with a basic understanding of the nature of the various threats associated with wireless networking and available countermeasures.

Wireless Threats, Vulnerabilities and Countermeasures

Figure 1 shows that wireless networks consist of four basic components:

1. The transmission of data using radio frequencies;
2. Access points that provide a connection to the organizational network and/or the Internet;
3. Client devices (laptops, PDAs, etc.); and
4. Users.

Each of these components provides an avenue for attack that can result in the compromise of one or more of the three fundamental security objectives of confidentiality, integrity, and availability. This section discusses the various security threats associated with each component and describes countermeasures that can be employed to mitigate those threats.

Figure 1. Wireless networking components

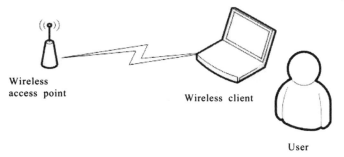

Wireless
access point

Wireless   client

User

Securing   Wireless   Transmissions

The nature of wireless communications creates three basic threats:

1.   **Interception**. Wireless communications are inherently susceptible to interception because the signals are transmitted "through the air" and so can be intercepted by anyone, thereby compromising the confidentiality of sensitive information.

2.   **Alteration**. Wireless transmissions can be intercepted and the messages altered in transit, thereby compromising the integrity of the information being transmitted.

3.   **Disruption**. Wireless transmissions can be disrupted or jammed, thereby compromising availability.

The remainder of this section discusses countermeasures that can be used to reduce these threats.

Protecting the Confidentiality of Wireless Transmissions

Two types of countermeasures exist for reducing the risk of eavesdropping on wireless transmissions. The first involves methods for making it more difficult to locate and intercept the wireless signals. The second involves the use of encryption to preserve confidentiality even if the wireless signal is intercepted.

Signal-Hiding Techniques

In order to intercept wireless transmissions, attackers first need to identify and locate wireless networks. This is not that difficult to do. Indeed, a common method for finding potential targets, called war-driving, involves nothing more than driving around with an antenna and a wireless sniffing tool. Moreover, because wireless signals travel both vertically and horizontally, it is also possible to locate access points by flying over buildings (Hopper, 2002; Slashdot, 2002). Attackers often supplement these wireless sniffing tools with a GPS to more precisely record the location of wireless access points so that they can return at a more convenient time to attempt to obtain unauthorized access.

There are, however, a number of steps that organizations can take to make it more difficult to locate their wireless access points. The easiest and least costly include the following:

- Turn off *service set identifier* (SSID) broadcasting by wireless access points. The SSID is a code used by clients to connect to wireless access points. Configuring wireless access points to broadcast their SSIDs makes it easier for users to locate and connect to the access point. However, it also makes it easy for attackers to identify potential targets. For example, in a common reconnaissance method called "war-driving," attackers use software tools like NetStumbler (http://www.netstumbler.com), Airsnarf (http://www.shmoo.com), and Kismet (http://www.kismetwireless.net) to locate wireless access points in buildings that they drive past. Configuring a wireless access point to not broadcast its SSID makes this more difficult, although other tools exist that actively attempt to connect to wireless access points (e.g., essid-jack, which is part of the Air-Jack toolkit, available at http://802.11ninja.net). Nevertheless, while not fool-proof, turning off SSID broadcasting is an important part of the defense-in-depth approach to security.

- Assign cryptic names to SSIDs. Because it is likely that attackers will be able to eventually locate wireless access points, SSIDs should be as non-informative as possible. Names like "Payroll" or "R&D" are much more likely to invite further scrutiny than are names like "access point 1." SSIDs also should not identify the access point manufacturer, as this may enable would-be attackers to identify devices for which known vulnerabilities exist. However, once an attacker locates a wireless access point, he or she will be able to determine the manufacture of the access point. Nevertheless, not providing this information in the SSID name is just another layer in the defense-in-depth approach that can be taken to make the attacker's job as hard as possible.

- Reduce signal strength to the lowest level that still provides requisite coverage. Wireless signals can propagate for several miles; reducing signal strength lessens the effective range over which they can be intercepted.

- Locate wireless access points in the interior of the building, away from windows and exterior walls. Although wireless signals do travel through glass and most building materials, such obstructions do weaken signal strength. Thus, locating wireless access points in the interior of the building forces the attacker to be closer to the source of the signals to establish and maintain a connection. Consequently, physical security of the site becomes another important part of a defense-in-depth strategy. Access to parking lots should be restricted and monitored. If someone in an unauthorized vehicle is seen loitering in the parking lot, it could be an attacker attempting to get close enough to the signal source to attack it.

More effective, but also more costly methods for reducing or hiding signals include:

- Use directional antennas to constrain signal emanations within desired areas of coverage. Omni-directional antennas broadcast wireless signals 360-degrees, which greatly increases the opportunity for interception. Directional antennas can make it more difficult for an intruder to intercept messages, particularly if combined with proper placement of wireless access points in the interior of the building. For example, in high-rise office buildings, using directional antennas to send signals horizontally virtually eliminates the risk of interception on floors above or below the one on which the antenna is located.

• Use of signal emanation-shielding techniques, sometimes referred to as TEM-PEST,[1] to block emanation of wireless signals. Metallic window tints, metallic wall paint, and the use of steel or aluminum mesh inside walls, floors, and ceilings can confine the propagation of wireless signals within enclosed areas.[2]

Organizations should regularly test the effectiveness of all these techniques for attempting to hide wireless signals by periodically scanning their site to determine how many wireless access points can be identified. Such tests should also measure the distances and locations from which wireless transmissions can be easily intercepted.

Encryption

Although the measures discussed in the preceding section may make it more difficult to intercept wireless communications, they do not totally eliminate the risk of eavesdropping. Therefore, the best method for protecting the confidentiality of information transmitted over wireless networks is to encrypt all wireless traffic. This is especially important for organizations subject to regulations, such as HIPAA and Sarbanes-Oxley (SOX), that mandate the protection of sensitive data and impose sanctions, possibly including incarceration, for failure to comply.

It is important, however, to choose a strong encryption method. Until the IEEE 802.11i standard, wireless networks were limited to using the weak *wired equivalent privacy* (WEP) encryption protocol. WEP uses a weak encryption algorithm and relies on shared secrets coupled with a limited size initialization vector, thereby making it possible for an attacker to determine the shared key by collecting sufficient traffic. In addition, WEP is a stateless protocol, so it is vulnerable to replay attacks, and it uses linear checksums, making it vulnerable to packet modification (Paladugu, Cherukuru, & Pandula, 2002). Indeed, a number of tools, such as wepcrack (http://sourceforge.net/projects/wepcrack) are readily available to attack WEP-encrypted traffic. Thus, WEP, at best, only protects data from being read by casual sniffing attacks; it does not effectively protect confidentiality.

There are two alternatives for strongly encrypting wireless communications. One is to adopt the new 802.11i protocol that supports the use of strong encryption algorithms, such as *temporary key integrity protocol* (TKIP) and *Advanced Encryption Standard* (AES), for wireless communications. The other option is to use a client-based IPSec *virtual personal network* (VPN) to create a secure connection between the client and the VPN termination point for all wireless communications.

Preventing Alteration of Intercepted Communications

Interception and alteration of wireless transmissions represents a form of "man-in-the-middle" attack. Two types of countermeasures can significantly reduce the risk of such attacks: strong encryption and strong authentication of both devices and users.

Encryption

Strong encryption of wireless transmissions reduces the risk of message alteration by providing a means to verify message integrity. For example, using TKIP with *message integrity code* (MIC) will detect if the transmission has been modified during the transmission.

Strong Authentication

To succeed, "man-in-the-middle" attacks require that the attacker be able to masquerade as a legitimate party to a conversation. Weak or non-existent authentication increases the risk that intruders will obtain unauthorized access to the wireless network and thereby succeed in executing a "man-in-the-middle" attack. Conversely, requiring strong authentication of *both* users and devices *before* allowing wireless access to the network can significantly reduce the risk that such impersonation attempts will succeed.

Device authentication should be mutual; that is, the wireless client should authenticate itself to the access point and, conversely, the access point should authenticate itself to the wireless client. A computer's *media access control* (MAC) address can be used as part of this device authentication process; however, it should not be the sole factor used to authenticate a device as it is relatively easy to spoof MAC addresses. Therefore, MAC address filtering should be supplemented with use of authentication contained in the 802.1x protocol. One attractive feature of 802.1x is that it supports the use of a wide variety of types of *extensible authentication protocols* (EAPs) to provide strong device authentication. EAP-TLS, which is based on the *transport layer security* (TLS) protocol, is considered to be the strongest method because of its use of X.509 certificates to authenticate both the client and the server, but it is also the most costly method because it requires an established *public key infrastructure* (PKI) (Kelley, 2003). EAP-TTLS is a modification of EAP-TLS. Using the tunneled TLS (TTLS) protocol means that only the server needs an X.509 certificate; the client can authenticate using a number of different methods. *Protected extensible authentication protocol* (PEAP) is similar to EAP-TTLS, except that it also supports client certificates, but its use is limited to Windows and Cisco devices. *Lightweight extensible authentication protocol* (LEAP) is Cisco's proprietary solution; it only supports the use of hashed passwords and is vulnerable to an off-line dictionary attack (Cisco, 2004). It is important to note that LEAP is not the only EAP with vulnerabilities; for example, it has been shown that improper implementations of any EAP that uses tunneled authentication are vulnerable to "man-in-the-middle" attacks (Nokia, 2003). In addition to improper implementation, another drawback with many EAPs is that they do not support credential reuse (Kelley, 2003).

There is a cost for organizations to adopt the use of 802.1x on either their wired or wireless networks, as the infrastructure needed by the 802.1x protocol must be installed and configured prior to any implementation. The cost to implement an 802.1x authentication solution will depend on the implementation of 802.1x that is chosen and the existing architecture in the organization's environment. An implementation may involve as little as installing an 802.1x client on all machines. Also, because the switches and access points can be configured to pass through authentication to a backend server, changing to another EAP involves changing only the authentication servers using the new EAP.

In many implementations the 802.1x protocol is used to authenticate only the wireless client, not the user; however, the 802.1x protocol can authenticate the user as well. This user authentication should be done using strong multifactor user authentication that uses two or more of the following methods: passwords, tokens or smart cards, and biometrics. It is also desirable to require users to re-authenticate periodically during long sessions to minimize the possibility of session hijacking or spoofing. Finally, network *intrusion detection systems* (IDS) or *intrusion prevention systems* (IPS) should be deployed and monitored to provide timely notification of attempts to obtain unauthorized access to the network.

Countermeasures to Reduce the Risk of Denial-of-Service Attacks

Wireless communications are also vulnerable to *denial-of-service* (DoS) attacks. Sometimes, this can occur unintentionally, because many devices emit radio frequency signals that may interfere with those used by the wireless network. For example, microwave ovens, many cordless phones, and Bluetooth-enabled devices all use the same 2.4 GHz frequency used by 802.11b and 802.11g wireless networks. Some newer models of cordless phones also operate at the 5 GHz frequency used by 802.11a wireless networks. Consequently, improper control over the placement and use of these other wireless devices can cause the wireless network to crash. Indeed, many readers with wireless networks at home have probably experienced the unintentional DoS when a family member uses a cordless telephone that is on the same frequency. Similar problems occur in the workplace. For example, there have been reports of incidents in which the use of an old leaky microwave oven in a cafeteria disrupted the wireless network in adjacent offices. In another case, a large manufacturer found that the wireless network it installed in a conference room was disrupted when meeting participants used Bluetooth-enabled wireless mice or keyboards.

Organizations can take several steps to reduce the risk of such unintentional DoS attacks. Careful site surveys can identify locations where signals from other devices exist; the results of such surveys should be used when deciding where to locate wireless access points. The use of directional antennas and selection of sufficient broadcast strength to maximize coverage within the desired area reduce the risk of unintentional DoS by other devices. Regular periodic audits of wireless networking activity and performance can identify problem areas; appropriate remedial actions may include removal of the offending devices or measures to increase signal strength and coverage within the problem area. If the source of the unintentional DoS cannot be eliminated, the various signal emanation-shielding techniques and products discussed earlier can be used to block the offending signals.

Not all DoS attacks on wireless networks are accidental, however. A number of attack tools exist that can be used to disrupt wireless networks. For example, a tool called macfld (http://home.jwu.edu/jwright/code/macfld.pl) floods the wireless access point with bogus MAC addresses, and a tool called Void11 (http://www.wlsec.net/void11/) floods networks with either deauthentication packets or with authentication packets that have random addresses. The countermeasures for eavesdropping discussed earlier, particularly proper placement of access points and the use of reflective wall and window coatings can reduce the risk of these attacks.

Recently, however, a professor in Australia demonstrated a wireless DoS attack method against which there is no defense. This vulnerability attacks the Clear Channel Assessment algorithm used by all 802.11 networks to determine which particular radio channel within the allowable frequency range is available for use. The attack involves overwhelming an access point with packets on the channel(s) it is configured to use, so that it shuts down (Wailgum, 2004). This attack is quite easy to execute because 802.11b and 802.11g networks can use any of 11 distinct channels. To reduce the risk of interference from adjacent channels, most access points are configured to default to channel 1, 6, or 11. Furthermore, an attacker can identify the exact channel that an access point is using (using tools like Netstumbler, Airsnarf, and Kismet). Thus, an attacker need only DoS that channel to effectively DoS a given access point. Although there is currently no known defense against this attack, the vulnerability has a limited impact because a lone attacker can only use it to disable one access point at a time.

Securing Wireless Access Points

Insecure, poorly configured wireless access points can compromise confidentiality by allowing unauthorized access to the network. Unauthorized ("rogue") wireless access points are the principal cause of this problem. This threat is ubiquitous because wireless access points are so inexpensive and easy to install that almost any employee who wants the flexibility of wireless networking can easily do so by purchasing an access point and connecting it to the wired LAN. The problem is that because such unauthorized access points are set up by end-users rather than by the IT staff, they typically have little or no security features enabled. Thus, rogue access points provide a means for intruders to obtain unauthorized access to the organization's network.

Countermeasures to Secure Wireless Access Points

Organizations can reduce the risk of unauthorized access to wireless networks by taking these three steps:

1. Eliminating rogue access points;
2. Properly configuring all authorized access points; and
3. Using 802.1x to authenticate all devices.

Eliminate Rogue Access Points

The best method for dealing with the threat of rogue access points is to use 802.1x on the wired network to authenticate all devices that are plugged into the network. Using 802.1x will prevent any unauthorized devices from connecting to the network. However, given the potential time and cost associated with upgrading to 802.1x, a more immediate and less expensive solution involves developing and deploying a security policy that prohibits the installation of unauthorized wireless access points and then regularly auditing compliance with that policy. The written security policy should explicitly prohibit the installation of wireless access points by anyone other than the IT staff responsible for computer security. That policy, and its rationale, must then be effectively communicated to all employees. The security staff needs to periodically check for compliance with this policy by regularly searching for wireless access points, using tools such as Netstumbler, Airsnarf, and Kismet. Employees are becoming ever savvier about wireless technology, so it is important to use scanning tools that can find not only access points that are actively broadcasting, but also those that have been configured to operate in more secure modes. It is also important to scan for all possible broadcast channels, not just those normally used. For example, 802.11b equipment is capable of broadcasting on 14 channels. The FCC, however, only allows channels 1-11 to be used in the United States; channels 12-14 are reserved for use in Japan and Europe. Nevertheless, security audits should check to be sure employees have not set up rogue access points to broadcast on those channels.

Any unauthorized access points discovered during these audits should be promptly disabled. It is also important to appropriately sanction the responsible employee, so that other employees learn that the organization does indeed actively enforce its written security policies.

Physical security measures are also important. Visitors should not be given unsupervised access to the office complex because they might plant a wireless access point for subsequent attempts to obtain unauthorized access to the organizational network.

Secure Configuration of Authorized Access Points

Organizations also need to ensure that all authorized wireless access points are securely configured. It is especially important to change all default settings because they are well-known and can be exploited by attackers. For example, the default SSID for Cisco wireless access points is "tsunami" (Kennedy, 2004). Checklists should be created and used to ensure that all desired security features are enabled. Physical access should be restricted to prevent visitors and employees from making changes to the device's configuration settings that compromise the effective level of security it provides. If the *simple network management protocol* (SNMP) is used to remotely manage the wireless access point, default community strings should be replaced with strong, alphanumeric community strings. Finally, it is important to deploy only those wireless access points that can be easily patched with security upgrades, and to ensure that proper patch management procedures are followed.

Use 802.1x to Authenticate all Devices

Strong authentication of all devices attempting to connect to the network can prevent rogue access points and other unauthorized devices from becoming insecure backdoors. The 802.1x protocol discussed earlier provides a means for strongly authenticating devices *prior* to assigning them IP addresses.

Securing Wireless Client Devices

Two major threats to wireless client devices are (1) loss or theft, and (2) compromise. Loss or theft of laptops and PDAs is a serious problem. Although the percentage of organizations experiencing laptop theft has been declining in recent years, it still affected 49% of respondents to the 2004 CSI/FBI Computer Crime and Security Survey (CSI, 2004). Moreover, respondents to the survey estimated the cost associated with the theft of laptop or other portable devices to be approximately $6.7 million (CSI, 2004). Replacing the lost or stolen device represents only a fraction of those cost estimates. A major vulnerability exists because users often store, or the system caches, their logon credentials on these devices. Thus, stolen devices can be used to obtain unauthorized access to the organizational network.

In addition, laptops and PDAs often store confidential and proprietary information. Consequently, loss or theft of the devices may cause the organization to be in violation of privacy regulations involving the disclosure of personal identifying information it has collected from third parties. This can result in costly remediation efforts. For example, when two laptops were stolen from a GMAC Financial Services employee's automobile, the company incurred the time and expense of notifying approximately 200,000 customers that their personal data may have been compromised (McDougall, 2004).

There are several countermeasures that organizations can employ to reduce or mitigate the risks associated with the loss or theft of a wireless client device:

- Provide employees with good quality locks to secure their laptops and train them to physically secure their laptops, even when in their own offices.

- Configuring laptops to not display the userID of the last person who logged onto the device and training employees to not have the operating system "remember" their passwords will make it harder for someone to use a stolen laptop or PDA to gain unauthorized access to other organizational resources.

- Configuring wireless clients to require the use of multifactor authentication techniques, such as the use of smart cards, tokens, or biometric data, will also reduce the risk of unauthorized access by someone who acquired a lost or stolen laptop. Multifactor authentication that requires more than just a token or similar device is important, because any such tokens may be inserted in the wireless client device at the time it is stolen.

- Provide strong encryption tools and require employees to encrypt any confidential and proprietary data stored on portable wireless clients. This reduces the risk that theft of the device will result in a breach of confidentiality, because the attacker will be unable to read the encrypted data. It may also prevent the organization from having to spend the time and money to notify third parties (e.g., customers or suppliers) whose personal information was stored on a stolen or lost device.

- Configuring laptops and other portable devices with tracking system software designed to "phone home" whenever the device attempts to connect to the Internet may aid in its recovery.

The other threat to wireless client devices is that they can be compromised so that an attacker can access sensitive information stored on the device or use it to obtain unauthorized access to other system resources. The following countermeasures can be employed to reduce the risk of attackers compromising wireless client devices:

- Establish and enforce a security policy requiring that all wireless clients must be running the most current and updated versions of antivirus and host firewall software.

- Configure wireless devices to operate only in infrastructure mode. Wireless clients can be compromised if operating in ad-hoc mode when used in public locations such as airports, hotels, or restaurants, because unless the 802.11i protocol is used, ad-hoc mode communication between devices can occur without any authentication. Such unauthenticated communications means that an attacker can access any open shares on the machine, thereby obtaining access to any confidential data stored on the device as well as being provided with the opportunity to install a backdoor to enable subsequent re-entry. Moreover, although the 802.11i protocol supports peer-to-peer authentication, not all devices and networks use it; therefore, the authors strongly believe that it is best to configure wireless devices to operate in infrastructure mode only.

- Provide users with USB-storage devices to facilitate exchange of data at meetings and conventions. This is an inexpensive way to effectively counter the urge to operate in ad-hoc mode when attending meetings in hotels, convention centers, or other public settings. Using strong encryption methods to protect the data stored on USB devices helps offset the potential threat to confidentiality should the device be lost or stolen.

- Prohibit the use of embedded wireless *network interface cards* (NICs) in wireless devices owned by the organization; instead, mandate the use of external wireless cards. The benefit of this approach is that when such external wireless NICs are removed, an "air gap" is created that ensures the device cannot be contacted. This is much more secure than disabling an embedded wireless NIC, because there is always the possibility that a computer virus or other malware could surreptitiously re-enable wireless connectivity.

- Teach users good security practices to follow when connecting to public wireless "hot spots." A wireless client may also be attacked by causing it to connect to a fake *access point* (AP) that masquerades as a legitimate one. When the user authenticates to the fake AP, the attacker captures the user's logon credentials. This attack is possible because wireless devices normally attempt to associate with the strongest nearby access point. Thus, if an attacker can sit near a public wireless "hot spot" and boost the strength of his or her device's signal so that it is stronger than that of the legitimate access point, new users will connect to the fake access point. If the intruder also performs a DoS attack against the legitimate access point, existing wireless connections will be broken; then when those users attempt to reconnect, they will also go to the fake access point. Airsnarf is just one of many tools that can be used to carry out this type of attack. The captured credentials can be used to execute a "man-in-the-middle" attack, with the attacker intercepting all communications between the compromised client and the network, or the attacker may save them in order to obtain unauthorized access to the network at a later time. Mutual authentication of both client and server can prevent this type of attack, but this requires either that both the client and server have preinstalled certificates for each other or that the client has a copy of the server's public key. Thus, mutual authentication is not always practical with public hot spots. Therefore, the best countermeasure is to train users on safe computing practices when using public hot spots. They should be shown a demonstration of how this type of attack works and be encouraged to be suspicious any time their existing connections are dropped. They should also be trained on how to spot common tell-tale signs of fake access points, such as a lack of graphics, misspelled words, or any changes to a regularly used hot spot log-in screen that just seem "odd." In addition, most browsers can be configured to warn users about invalid site certificates. However, users must be trained both to attend to such warnings and how to properly respond to them.

Training and Educating Users

Notice that Figure 1 also includes users as the fourth basic component of wireless networking. As is the case with wired security, users are the key component to wireless networking security. Indeed, the importance of training and educating users about secure wireless behavior cannot be overstated. Therefore, although previous sections discussed training and education several times, we now summarize and expand on this critically important topic.

To be effective, user training and education needs to be repeated periodically. The following are some of the most important topics that need to be covered:

1. Understanding and acceptance of the organization's wireless security policy. All employees need to be made aware of what they are expected to do and prohibited from doing. Explaining the rationale for these expectations will increase their acceptance. If possible, demonstrations of the problems resulting from failure to follow prescribed practices can improve understanding and compliance.

2. How to properly encrypt data. As noted in preceding sections, strong encryption is an important part of securing wireless networking because it can mitigate the risks of a number of threats. Users, however, need to be instructed in how to correctly use whatever encryption tools the organization chooses. Users also need to be educated in how to securely store their encryption keys.

3. How to use multifactor authentication. Strong authentication is another effective method for mitigating a number of wireless security risks. As with encryption, users

need to be trained in how to properly use the authentication methods selected by the organization. Of particular importance is training on how to create strong passwords, since they are likely to be one of the authentication used by the organization.

4.   How to identify legitimate access points, particularly when connecting to public wireless "hot spots." As discussed previously, attackers can use several tools to compromise wireless clients by enticing users in public "hot spots" to connect to the attacker's fake access point. Therefore, users need to be educated about this threat. Demonstrations of how such an attack occurs can be especially effective in training users on how to recognize this type of attack.

5.   Safe practices concerning the use of wireless NICs. Users need to understand the reasons for removing external wireless NICs whenever they are not actively connecting to a wireless network. If wireless clients contain embedded wireless NICs, users need to be trained on how to disable wireless when not in use and how to verify that the wireless NIC is in fact disabled.

6.   Procedures for secure operation in ad-hoc mode. As mentioned earlier, the authors strongly favor configuring all wireless clients to operate in infrastructure mode and to use USB tokens to exchange files with others when at meetings. Nevertheless, there may be situations in which users will need to engage in wireless networking in ad-hoc mode. Therefore, users need to be trained in how to use available methods, such as those provided by the 802.11i protocol, to authenticate peers. To be effective, such training needs to explain the reasons for requiring such authentication and, if possible, should demonstrate how easily an attacker can use an unauthenticated ad-hoc mode session to access information on the target device.

Finally, as with other aspects of computer and network security, the IT staff responsible for wireless security also needs continuing education and training. At a minimum, they should be given a budgeted amount of time each month to keep abreast of current developments by studying the information provided at various security Web sites. For example, the SANS Institute Web site (www.sans.org) contains a number of articles about wireless security in its "reading room" (http://www.sans.org/rr/whitepapers/wireless/), and CERT (www.cert.org) has a good white paper entitled "Securing Wireless Networks," available at http://www.us-cert.gov/cas/tips/ST05-003.html. In addition, a number of organizations, such as the SANS Institute, ISACA, and the MIS Training Institute, provide formal continuing education courses and conferences on wireless security issues.

Risk Management

The preceding section discussed the range of threats against wireless networks and available countermeasures. Sadly, although the risks of wireless networking have been publicized for years, many wireless networks are still not adequately secured. Indeed,

Table 1. Summary of wireless networking threats/vulnerabilities and countermeasures

Panel A - Wireless Networking Component: Transmissions	
Threat/Vulnerability	**Countermeasures**
1. Message Interception (Eavesdropping)	• Use of strong encryption during transmission • Require use of VPN for all wireless access • Disable SSID broadcasting • Use innocuous or cryptic SSIDs • Proper placement of access points • Building design (wallpaper, window coatings, etc.) • Use directional antennas • Use minimal number of access points • Reduce broadcast signal strength
2. Message alteration	• Signal hiding techniques used to increase difficulty of message interception • Strong encryption • Strong authentication of both device (using 802.1x) and user (using multifactor authentication)
3. Denial-of-Service	Unintentional DoS countermeasures: • Remove offending device • Regular site surveys • Directional antennas and proper access point placement • Shielding to stop signal emanations Intentional DoS countermeasures: • Proper location of Access Points • Building design
Panel B - Wireless Networking Component: Access Points	
1. Unauthorized ("rogue") access points	• Policy • Periodic audits • Physical access controls
2. Insecure configuration	• Turn on all available security features • Change all default settings • Disable SNMP community strings and require use of strong community strings • Purchase only Access Points that can be upgraded with security patches (e.g., APs that have "flashable" firmware)

3. Weak authentication	• Place a firewall between the wireless access point and the internal network and filter on client MAC address
	• Require both user and device authentication prior to granting IP address
	• Strong authentication including both:
	   o 802.1x to authenticate client
	   o Multi-factor authentication of user
	• Repeat authentication periodically during long sessions
	• Deploy network IDS and/or IPS

Panel C - Wireless Networking Component: Client Devices	
1. Loss or theft of device	• Physical security • Encryption of stored data • Configuration (e.g., automatic "call home" when attempt to connect to Internet) • User education and training

2. Compromise of device	• Configuration:
	   o operate in infrastructure rather than ad-hoc mode
	   o run up-to-date A-V and host firewall
	• User training and education
	• Require mutual authentication
	• Provide USB devices for file exchange at conferences and meetings, with strong encryption of USB drives
	• Use external wireless NICs
	• Employ 802.11i protocol so can do peer-to-peer authentication in ad-hoc mode

while writing this chapter, the authors conducted a 30-minute war-drive on a weekday morning in the Phoenix metropolitan area one day in January 2005 and found that almost half of the access points were not using any form of encryption. Although many of these were probably residential networks, the SSIDs suggest that a significant portion were businesses. Interestingly, virtually all of the access points found near a hospital-medical office complex were encrypted, which suggests that regulations like HIPAA are indeed effective "incentives" for improving security. Nevertheless, our war-drive results suggest that many organizations still have not taken even the basic step of using encryption to secure their wireless networks.

Table 1 summarizes the major threats and available countermeasures associated with each component of wireless networking. Notice that some countermeasures, such as using strong encryption and requiring strong authentication of both devices and users, are particularly effective because they address multiple threats.

Most organizations, however, do not have unlimited resources to address all potential wireless security threats and vulnerabilities. Therefore, management will usually need to prioritize the threats in terms of both risk and severity of impact in order to develop a wireless security policy that cost-effectively manages the risks associated with wireless networking.

The NIST Special Publication 800-30, "Risk Management Guide for Information Technology Systems" (Stoneburner, Goguen, & Feringa, 2002) provides a structured methodology to help management assess the risks associated with wireless networking.[3] The NIST framework defines risk as the product of likelihood of occurrence and impact severity. It suggests classifying likelihood as being low, medium, or high, depending upon the level motivation and skill of potential attackers and the effectiveness of existing controls. Impact severity is similarly classified as being low, medium, or high, depending upon the extent to which a successful attack would adversely affect business processes, the likely duration of such an effect, and the financial consequences. Thus, the NIST methodology uses a three (level of risk) by three (impact severity) matrix to measure the level of risk associated with a particular threat/vulnerability.

We believe that the NIST methodology can be improved by separating the estimates of impact severity into two components: operational effect on business processes and resulting economic consequences of such disruptions. Doing so enables security professionals and management to use their respective skills jointly to more accurately rank the relative importance of different threats and vulnerabilities. Security professionals can use their experience and training to estimate the likelihood of various attacks and the extent to which those attacks would disrupt operations. For example, the threat of a DoS attack against use of a warehouse wireless network might be rated as being of medium likelihood and medium operational impact, with the explanation being that picking and packing of customer orders could be significantly slowed for up to one hour. This type of information should enable management to use its knowledge about the organization's strategy and competitive environment to estimate the relative economic impact of such disruptions as being low, medium, or high and to enter a specific dollar amount in the appropriate cell. The result is a three-dimensional cube as illustrated in Figure 2. The resulting three-dimensional matrix makes it easy to visually assess the relative seriousness of various threats/vulnerabilities and prioritize which ones to attend to first.

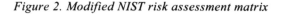

Figure 2. Modified NIST risk assessment matrix

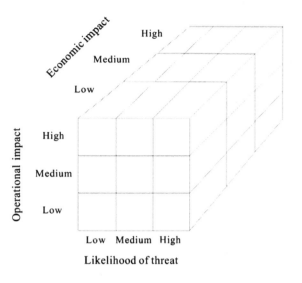

Summary and Conclusion

Wireless networking provides numerous opportunities to increase productivity and cut costs. It also alters an organization's overall computer security risk profile. Although it is impossible to totally eliminate all risks associated with wireless networking, it is possible to achieve a reasonable level of overall security by adopting a systematic approach to assessing and managing risk. This chapter discussed the threats and vulnerabilities associated with each of the three basic technology components of wireless networks (clients, access points, and the transmission medium) and described various commonly available countermeasures that could be used to mitigate those risks. It also stressed the importance of training and educating users in safe wireless networking procedures.

We then proposed a modification of the NIST risk management model as a means for helping management to assess the relative seriousness of the various threats and vulnerabilities associated with wireless networking and to evaluate the cost-effectiveness of alternative responses to those problems. As wireless networking technologies and protocols continue to evolve, old threats/vulnerabilities disappear and new ones arise. Therefore, effective risk management of wireless networks is a continual process. We believe that the methodology presented in this chapter can facilitate that endeavor.

References

Cisco. (2004). Dictionary attack on Cisco LEAP vulnerability, Revision 2.1, July 19. Retrieved November 18, 2005, from http://www.cisco.com/en/US/tech/tk722/tk809/technologies_security_notice09186a00801aa80f.html

CSI. (2004). CSI/FBI Computer Crime and Security Survey. Available at http://www.gocsi.com/forms/fbi/csi_fbi_survey.jhtml;jsessionid=BXRSPDA2R2ZOSQSNDBECKH0CJUMEKJVN (Note that you must register on the site (free) to receive the pdf document)

Hopper, D. I. (2002). Secret Service agents probe wireless networks in Washington. *Security Focus News,* September 29. Retrieved November 18, 2005, from http://www.securityfocus.com/news/899

Kelley, D. (2003). The X factor: 802.1x may be just what you need to stop intruders from accessing your network. *Information Security, 6*(8), 60-69. Also available at http://infosecuritymag.techtarget.com//ss/0,295796,sid6_iss21_art108,00.html

Kennedy, S. (2004). Best practices for wireless network security. *Information Systems Control Journal* (3). Also available at http://www.computerworld.com QuickLink No. 42642.

McDougall, P. (2004, March 25). Laptop theft puts GMAC customers' data at risk. *Information Week Security Pipeline.* Retrieved November 18, 2005, from http://www.informationweek.securitypipeline.com/news/18402599

Nokia. (2003). Man-in-the-middle attacks in tunneled authentication protocols. White paper retrieved November 18, 2005, from Nokia Research Center, Finland, http://www.saunalahti.fi/~asokan/research/tunnel_extab_final.pdf

Paladugu, V., Cherukuru, N., & Pandula, S. (2001). Comparison of security protocols for wireless communications. Retrieved November 18, 2005, from http://cnscenter.future.co.kr/resource/hot-topic/wlan/pachpa.pdf.

Slashdot. (2002, August 18). Wardriving from 1500ft Up. Retrieved November 18, 2005, from http://www.slashdot.org/articles/02/08/18/1239233.shtml

Stoneburner, G., Goguen, A., & Feringa, A. (2002, July). Risk management guide for information technology systems. *NIST Special Publication 800-30.* Available at csrc.nist.gov/publications/nistpubs/800-30/sp800-30.pdf

Wailgum, T. (2004, September 15). Living in wireless denial. *CIO Magazine.* Retrieved November 18, 2005, from http://www.cio.com/archive/091504/et_article.html

Endnotes

[1]   TEMPEST is actually a code word for a set of standards (defined in NSTISSAM TEMPEST/1-92) to limit electromagnetic radiation emanations from electronic equipment. A good Web page for this information is http://www.eskimo.com/~joelm/tempest.html.

[2]   Additional information about various forms of signal emanation-shielding techniques and products can be found at http://www.schneier.com/blog/archives/2004/12/wifi_shielding.html, http://www.forcefieldwireless.com/products.html, and http://www.lessemf.com/plastic.html.

[3]   OCTAVE® (Operationally Critical Threat, Asset, and Vulnerability Evaluation[sm]) developed by the Software Engineering Institute of Carnegie-Mellon University, is another structured methodology that can be used to assess and manage wireless networking security.

Section IV:

Security Technologies

Chapter XVI

Intrusion Detection and Response

David A. Dampier, Mississippi State University, USA

Ambareen Siraj, Mississippi State University, USA

Abstract

This chapter discusses the notion of intrusion detection and introduces concepts associated with intrusion detection and methods used to respond to intrusions. It presents information about different forms of intrusions and how they are recognized. It introduces methods for detecting intrusions and then discusses possible responses to those intrusions. It is hoped that this information will make the readers more aware of the possibility of intrusions and how they might develop a process for detecting and responding to these intrusions.

Introduction

Foremost on any executive's mind is the security, privacy, and protection of the suite of information resources within his or her scope of responsibility. Few would question the potential threat that exists to every business, government, academic, or private computing system today or dismiss this concern as unworthy of attention. CEOs, CIOs, COOs, CFOs, and CKOs[1] are all being asked to provide assurances to the corporate board, stockholders, business partners, government regulators, and other stakeholders that the information assets of the business are reasonably protected. This is not simply an issue of confidentiality — it is an issue of privacy, compliance with the law, protection of key corporate assets, and duty.

In securing one's systems, actions must be taken in three areas — prevention, detection, and response. All three are important and necessary, and no one of them will suffice completely. Simply stated, prevention involves all those actions one must take to attempt to prevent unauthorized access to a system; detection involves those actions taken to discover failures in prevention (realizing that 100% prevention is never possible); and response includes those actions taken by the enterprise after discovering an attack, attempted attack, or damage. Response is generally considered to include recovery measures, but might also include efforts to uncover what has been done to the system in the attack and how it was done. This is what is known as computer forensics. In its 2000 report titled "Enabling Technologies - Cyber Security," the Government Electronic Industry Association (Skinner & REEL, 2000) chose to illustrate these three areas, as depicted in Figure 1.

This chapter focuses on one "point solution" detection technology known as *intrusion detection systems* or IDS. We refer to this as a "technology" rather than a product, because it is a suite of different techniques that can be implemented in a host and IDS functionality exists to various degrees in many products available today from the private sector. The purpose of this chapter is to discuss, at an introductory level, the techniques and capabilities that one should expect to find in a modern intrusion detection system. We wish to make clear, however, that intrusion detection is simply part of an overall

Figure 1. Prevention, detection, and response (Source: Skinner & REEL, 2000)

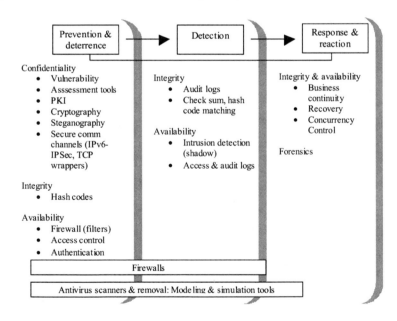

protection perimeter that one must install around any system and is not itself an adequate protection measure. It is part of an engineered security plan — one that must be periodically reviewed. We do not include any discussion in this chapter relative to honeypots, honeynets, or honeytokens. While it can be argued that such technology can be categorized as IDS, this is addressed in a separate chapter and will not be covered here.

Another part of that engineered security plan is a forensics program that enables corporate investigators to determine the nature of the activity associated with an intrusion, collect evidence that might be used to prosecute the intruders, and provide insight into how that activity might be prevented in the future. The forensic area will be discussed at the end of this chapter. Knowing that an intrusion has taken place means very little unless the organization has a response and reaction plan in place to deal with the effects of the intrusion and to attempt to prevent intrusions like it in the future.

Intrusion Detection

With the rapid development in networking technologies, the growth of the Internet, and the interconnected nature of both the commercial and public sectors, the risk and chance of malicious intrusions have also increased. It is important that the security mechanisms of a system are designed to prevent unauthorized access to system resources and data; however, completely preventing breaches of security is unlikely, in that 100% security is not an achievable objective. We can, however, try to detect these intrusion attempts so that action may be taken to defend the system, stop the intrusion, and repair the damage. This is called intrusion detection. Formally, an IDS closely monitors systems and networks for any sign of probable security violations and then reports them to an appropriate authority.

Types of Intrusions

Intrusions are attempts to access protected resources/information in an enterprise in a way that affects the expected performance of the systems and/or challenges the security policy of the systems. Intrusions may be broadly classified into three types:

1. **Physical intrusion:** This type of intrusion occurs when an intruder has physical access to a machine (i.e., use of a keyboard or access to the physical system). Several misuses of the system are possible, ranging from misusing the privileges the console provides to the ability to physically take apart the system and remove components for examination.

2. **Targeted intrusion:** This kind of intrusion occurs on a particular system (or host machine) and can be initiated by an authorized user with an account, an unauthorized user masquerading as an authorized user (e.g., with a stolen password), or an unauthorized user that has obtained illegal access in system through exploiting a flaw in the system protection perimeter (e.g., failure to install an operating system

patch to close a vulnerability). In all cases, the system is specifically targeted for the attack.

3.   **Random intrusion:** In this type of intrusion, a system is attacked simply due to the fact that a door was left open for access into the system (advertently or inadvertently) and that door was discovered by happenstance over the network when intruders were looking for access into randomly selected potential systems. This kind of attack has begun to occur in the last few years as more attack tools are posted on the Internet and integrated into automatic launch scripts. Most such attacks are random and include the following:

- Port scan attacks (mapping your system);

- Denial-of-service attacks to shut down your system;

- Spoofed attacks to hide the identity of the attacker; and

- Installation of malicious software on the target machine.

Physical intrusion must be dealt with by very common (yet extremely important) policies, procedures, audits, physical measures, and training. These methods are often an enterprise's first line of defense, but because they are low-tech, they are often overlooked. The reader should be aware, however, that all known computer security reports that the authors are aware of clearly cite the "insider" as one of the greatest threats to any enterprise, and of all reported insider damages, most incidences are due to accidental misuse (and subsequent damage) type.

Targeted and random intrusions require hardware and software solutions to detect and alert system administrators when a suspected intrusion occurs. The remainder of this chapter will outline techniques used in such solutions and provide insight into their operations.

Intrusion Detection Schemes

There are at least two approaches by which intrusion detection may be carried out, *host-based* and *network-based*. In either approach, the intrusion detection system looks for specific patterns that usually indicate malicious or suspicious intent.

Host-Based Intrusion Detection

The host-based intrusion detection approach has been used since the early 1980s, when network connectivity and implementation were relatively simple. A common approach used by host-based intrusion detection tools is to look for suspicious actions recorded in audit log files. A host-based IDS typically monitors system events and security logs (for example, Windows NT and the *syslog* file in Unix environments) for probable security violations. When any of these files change, the IDS compares the new log entry with attack signatures for potential matching or analyzes the deviation to see if it is part of normal behavior or not. For any suspicious changes, IDS generate alerts and perform other defensive actions. Recent developments in host-based IDS involve checking of key system files and executables through checksums at regular intervals to look for unexpected changes. Some host-based IDS also listen to port activity and generate alerts when specific ports are accessed. A host-based IDS is mostly suitable for an environment that has little external network connectivity. Some examples of host-based IDS are: Tripwire (http://sourceforge.net/projects/tripwire), Samhain (http://la-samhna.de/samhain), Swatch (http://swatch.sourceforge.net) and RealSecure (http://www.iss.net).[2]

Network-Based Intrusion Detection

A network-based IDS typically uses the network packet as the audit source. This is generally accomplished by placing one or more network interface cards in promiscuous mode so as to monitor and analyze all network traffic in near real time as it travels across the network. Packets are of interest to the IDS if they seem abnormal. Abnormality can be defined by anything that is uncharacteristic or out of the ordinary or anything that matches a predefined characteristic malicious signature. Three primary types of signatures are string signatures, port signatures, and header-condition signatures. String signatures look for a text string that indicates a possible attack. Port signatures simply watch for connection attempts to well-known, frequently attacked ports, and header signatures watch for dangerous or illogical combinations in packet headers. Once an attack has been detected, the IDS may send notification and alert signals that usually involve administrator notification, connection termination, and/or session logging for forensic analysis and evidence collection (ISS, 1998). A network-based IDS is mostly suitable for an environment that has large external (network) connectivity. The most widely used IDS today is a network-based IDS known as Snort (http://www.snort.org), which is an open-source IDS that uses signature detection to examine network data packets. Other examples of network IDS are: Cisco Intrusion Detection System (http://www.cisco.com), and Symantec NetProwler (http://www.tlic.com/security/netprowler.cfm).[3]

In today's distributed systems environments with heavy connectivity to the outside world via the Internet, use of both types of IDS becomes essential in establishing an

Figure 2. Block diagram of a typical anomaly detection system

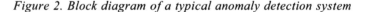

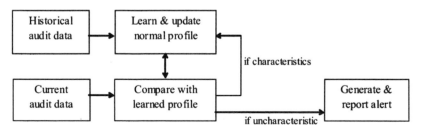

effective defense in depth strategy. An example of a Hybrid IDS, which uses both host and network based IDSs, is Prelude (http://www.prelude-ids.org).

Types of Intrusion Detection

Intrusion detection techniques (either host-based or network-based) can be divided into two main types, anomaly detection and misuse detection.

Anomaly Detection

Anomaly detection is a technique based on observation of deviations from normal system usage patterns. These behavior-based detection techniques expect intrusions to be uncharacteristic of normal user behavior. Therefore, detection consists of building a profile of the system being monitored and then detecting significant deviations from this profile. This means that if we could establish a "normal activity profile" for a system, we could, in theory, flag all system states varying from the established profile by statistically significant amounts as potential intrusion is attempted.

Anomalous intrusions are difficult to detect and such systems are computationally expensive because of the overhead needed in keeping track of and constantly updating several system profile metrics. Although a complete treatment of the techniques used in such approaches is not possible here, an example that uses a statistical approach in anomaly detection follows. In this method, initial behavior profiles for system activities and users of the system are generated and, as the system runs, the anomaly detector constantly calculates variance of the present profile from the original one. Examples of likely measures include activity measures, CPU time used, number of network connections in a certain time period, keystrokes, and time-of-day usage. Once deviations are noted, the detector flags them as suspicious and reports them to proper authority. Other approaches might include predictive pattern generation (where one tries to predict future events based on events that have already occurred); threshold monitoring (involves the setting of values on metrics by defining acceptable behavior, such as the number of failed logins in a given time period); or resource profiling (a method that monitors system-wide use of resources, such as accounts, applications, storage media, protocols, communications ports, etc., and develops a historic usage profile). There are many others. A typical anomaly-detection system approach is shown in Figure 2.

Misuse Detection

Misuse Detection, the second general approach, is characterized by well-defined attacks on known weak points of a system. They can be detected by watching for certain specific actions being performed on identified objects. Misuse detection systems (also known as *knowledge-based intrusion detection systems*) apply knowledge accumulated about specific vulnerabilities and attacks to identify similar attacks. The concept behind such schemes is that there are ways to represent attacks in the form of a pattern or a signature so that an occurrence of the same or similar attack can be detected. This means that these systems are not unlike virus-detection systems in that they can detect many or all known attack patterns, but they are of little use for yet unknown attack methods.

An engineering challenge for misuse detection systems is how to create a signature base that encompasses all possible variations of an attack and how to create signatures that do not match non-intrusive activity. The effectiveness of misuse-detection rules is dependent upon how knowledgeable developers are about vulnerabilities and how recently the patterns have been updated. Misuse detection may be implemented by developing expert system rules, model-based reasoning, state transition-analysis systems, or neural nets, to name a few. A model of a typical misuse detection system approach is shown in Figure 3.

Increased demands for "more trustworthy" systems and the fact that a single IDS cannot detect all types of misuse/anomalies have prompted most modern information systems to employ multiple, diverse IDSs. A multi-sensor environment is characterized by deployment of a homogeneous and/or heterogeneous suite of IDSs, which serve as sensors to monitor different entities in the corresponding environment. In multi-sensor environments, these sensors can collaborate with or complement each other to provide increased assurance of information. Essentially, the primary advantage of using multiple sensors is to improve detection ability and coverage within a system — whether the sensors used are homogeneous (i.e., multiple installations of the same types of sensors allowing monitoring from different points) or heterogeneous (i.e., multiple installations of different types of sensors allowing different perspectives from the same/different points).

While a homogenous suite of sensors working at different points in the network provides concrete evidence of widespread attacks, heterogeneous sensors working at a single point can provide more insight into suspicious activities in the network. Different types of sensors are more able to capture different aspects of security violations in different areas. For example, while a network-based sensor can monitor traffic to, from, and within the network, a host-level sensor can monitor unusual changes at the operating system-level of hosts. Attacks like IP spoofing can be captured only by network-based sensors such as Snort, while attacks such as unauthorized file changes can be captured only by

Figure 3. Block diagram of a typical misuse-detection system

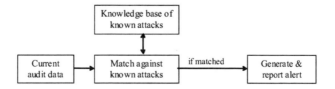

host-based sensors such as Tripwire. While misuse sensors have the advantage of detection specificity and the disadvantage of not being able to identify unknown violations, anomaly sensors have the advantage of being able to deal with novel situations and the disadvantage of prompting false alerts. Typically, anomaly sensors are able to provide earlier warning than misuse sensors because anomaly sensors can report any anomalies in progress, while misuse sensors need to wait for an entire attack signature before sending warnings (Goldman et al., 2001). Moreover, while misuse sensors can either report an alert with full confidence or cannot report at all, anomaly sensors typically can associate some confidence factor with the alerts. It is easy to see how having multiple sensors that are able to corroborate/complement/challenge each other's findings can enhance confidence in the assurance of systems. As there is no "perfect" or "one for all" sensor/IDS, it is only natural to employ a suite of different sensors to maximize trustworthiness in systems, such that an inability and/or weakness of one is compensated by capability and/or strength of another.

Procuring an Intrusion Detection System

Finding the right intrusion detection system for an organization is an engineering and a business decision. A single product cannot be recommended and, in some cases, multiple IDS might be needed. A security engineer should recommend the proper mix. There are, however, other considerations that may be a factor in the selection of a product. These include: IDS performance; the ability to benchmark a product on the organization's system prior to purchase; technical support; internal versus external help desk; software and hardware refreshment strategy; solvency of the company offering the product; third-party rating of the product; and whether the IDS is being purchased from a single vendor, multiple vendors or a third-party integrator. Each of these issues will now be discussed.

- **IDS performance:**
  - ➤ In selecting an IDS based on its performance, there are a number of factors to be considered. A powerful IDS should have the following characteristics:
  - ➤ High detection rate (which denotes the IDS's ability to identify intrusion) for known and unknown attacks. Typical IDS products are able to detect either known or unknown attacks. Hybrid IDS that can do both are still largely work-in-progress.
  - ➤ Low false positives (where an alarm is raised when it should not have been).
  - ➤ Low false negatives (where an alarm is not raised when it should have been).

It is also beneficial when the following characteristics are present in an IDS:
  - ➤ Ability to report severity of the attacks (so that the security administrator is able to prioritize the alerts and deal with them accordingly);

> ➤ Ability to indicate outcome of an attacks (so that the security administrator can filter out unsuccessful attempts from successful attacks);

> ➤ Ability to collect and store intrusion reports (so that the security administrator can go back and further investigate details.

Researchers are still working to improve IDS performance in these areas. No one IDS is commercially available today that stands out in all the above criteria. The choice of IDS should be governed by performance requirements and priorities.

- **Benchmark tests:** Many vendors will allow an organization to test a product (or some scaled down version of it) on its own system before making a purchase decision. Testing the product for ease of installation, impact on system performance, and false alarm rates is important. Generally, a 30-day test will be sufficient to know whether or not a product is a help or hindrance.

- **Technical support:** No IDS product is so user-friendly that technical support is not required. One should ask the vendor about its technical support, charges for the support, warranty, how often updates are promulgated, and whether or not a help desk is offered. If offered, is it staffed 8x5 or 24x7.

- **Internal vs. external help desk:** If the vendor offers a help desk, one should know if it is actually a help desk staffed by the vendor's employees or is it a contracted effort? A full-service help desk can be useful in determining whether or not an actual attack is or has taken place and recovery procedures that should be implemented.

- **Software and hardware refreshment strategy:** A good vendor will have a scheduled upgrade program for software and, possibly, hardware components. A less-capable vendor might only offer ad-hoc releases to fix reported problems.

- **Vendor solvency:** The authors recommend that the financial status of the vendor be reviewed as well as its past performance history. Information security businesses have multiplied in great numbers as the topic has taken on greater importance in the marketplace. A company that has been a business leader in this field and has depth and breath of experience may be more likely to deliver a capable product than an overnight startup.

- **Product ratings:** There are third-party assessments available for many products that provide the consumer with an unbiased rating of a specific product. The most well known of these today is the ISO Standard 15408 — the *Common Criteria*. This is an international rating scheme designed to offer vendors a way to measure the trust and capability in their products. Several nations have subscribed to this standard, including the United States, United Kingdom, Netherlands, Australia, New Zealand, France, Germany, and Canada. Evaluated IDS products are available for consideration (see http://www.niap.nist.gov).

- **Single vendor, multiple vendors, or third-party integrator?** : Multiple vendors can be employed to offer an IDS capability. Doing so runs the risk of integration problems and hesitation on the part of any one vendor to accept responsibility for a problem that occurs which cannot be cleanly traced to a specific product. Third-party integrators can be a good approach to use if the enterprise's internal staff assets are not capable of performing the needed engineering effort. Single-vendor purchases are certainly acceptable if the enterprise has the engineering talent to employ the product and the vendor meets other criteria listed here.

For information assurance in a protected environment, IDSs take the role of "security cameras" for the security administrator. Intelligent IDSs not only monitor for intrusion but also may take action against them. However, one should keep in mind that IDSs cannot replace firewalls, or regular security audits, or strong security policies (which are essential for preventing any intrusion in the first place). Even with these protection/prevention mechanisms, when intrusions do happen, IDSs can effectively detect and record such intrusions and report them to the proper authority. Sometimes actions are taken to stop such intrusions and also learn from them to prevent similar intrusions taking place in future. In this way, IDSs can also be used for prevention of intrusions. Remember — no technology can guarantee 100% security for a system, host, or network. Intruders may still find a weakness and get inside protected systems leading to a compromise of your assets. When this occurs it may be necessary to turn to forensic discovery.

Forensic Discovery

As shown in the *response & reaction* category of Figure 1, forensics is an important technique used in information and computer security. It is used to discover, collect, and protect evidence about an intrusion or any other criminal activity that might have been conducted on the machine. Forensics is the study of providing formal evidence that can be used in a court of law to enable the discovery, collection, and preservation of evidence that can then be used to argue a case in court. Computer forensics is defined by Kruse and Heiser (2002) as "...the preservation, identification, extraction, documentation, and interpretation of computer media for evidentiary and/or root cause analysis" (p. 1). In computer security, it is more often of interest to discover the root cause of an intrusion or attack. According to Marcella and Greenfield (2002), the sequence of network intrusions usually follows the following pattern:

- Gathering of information;
- Reconnaissance of network and system; and
- Exploitation of discovered vulnerabilities.

Forensic evidence can be gathered and analyzed after each of these stages. Forensic evidence on information gathering is limited, but may often be found in Web server or firewall logs. This evidence would likely appear as a large number of hits from a single source. Forensic evidence of reconnaissance efforts like "Ping Sweeps" will most likely be found in router logs and will appear as *Internet control message protocol* (ICMP) packets on a large range of destination addresses from the same source. Forensic evidence of exploitation activities is varied and can be discovered in system logs, temporary or hidden directories, and/or user directories (Marcella & Greenfield, 2002).

Also, if the intrusion is detected and the system is frozen fast enough, additional evidence may be discovered using typical methods for discovering evidence on computer media: searching RAM and file slack, looking at free space, and searching for recently deleted files. Key to effective forensic discovery after an intrusion is how fast a response can be mounted. Log files become so large so quickly that most evidence will be lost in a matter of days because logs will be deleted. This is especially true on servers at Internet service providers or on large networks serving many machines. The amount of traffic that can be generated in a single day can be overwhelming. For the reader interested in learning more about this area, a separate chapter in this text addresses forensics.

Conclusion

This chapter outlines some of the concerns that a manager might have in selecting an intrusion detection tool. In doing so, it becomes clear that intrusion detection is an important tool only in the sense that without it, a computer's defenses become weaker. However, with an intrusion detection tool alone, a computer system or network is still weak and very vulnerable to attack. The first order of business for any security-engineering task is to try to prevent intrusions or damaging behavior all together. There are a host of tools and techniques beyond the scope of this chapter that would need to be employed as preventative measures. They would include strong firewall architectures (normally multiple firewalls with varying capabilities), intrusion prevention tools (e.g., STAT Neutralizer, see http://www.statonline.com), monitoring tools, security policies and procedures, and employee training. Detection is only necessary because total prevention is never possible.

Response and recovery becomes important because eventually you may want to attempt to prosecute or at least reconstruct events. Damage or destruction that occurs from an intrusion can be devastating unless there is a recovery process in place that works and has been tested. A realistic defense requires a very strong protection perimeter with attention to the three areas this chapter has identified — prevention, detection, and response and recovery.

Lastly, we would add that historical success in preventing attacks in systems often says very little about predicting the ability to do so in the future. As new vulnerabilities are discovered and promulgated in the community, the astute security engineer has to make changes to the security perimeter around a protected system to insure that it remains strong in light of the new threat. This means that the suite of protection tools and procedures need to be reviewed and modified over time.

Employing an IDS as part of an enterprise's overall security strategy is recommended. Using tools that offer both host-based and network-based intrusion detection capability is a wise approach. A good IDS product should incorporate both anomaly- and misuse-detection methods. Unfortunately, many products claiming to be capable intrusion detection tools only employ the misuse technique, thus severely limiting their ability. The obvious difficulty with such an approach is that it cannot detect new attack methods. Less obvious is that such systems need a very reliable and consistent update procedure to stay current, and they can be subject to false alarms. Some newer products introduce anomaly-detection capability and try to err on the false-positive side rather than missing actual attacks. Some are using very promising artificial intelligence techniques (Florez, Bridges, & Vaughn, 2005; Forrest & Longstaff, 1999; Michael & Ghosh, 2002). Anomaly detectors are often subject to false alarms. A second vulnerability they display is that one can "train" an anomaly detector over time to accept attack behavior as a normal pattern.

Clearly, because of their complementary nature, both misuse- and anomaly-detection mechanisms are best employed together. However, there are some disadvantages associated with such multi-sensor/multi-technique systems; for example, increased workload leading to increased difficulty in analyzing alerts. Therefore, fusion of sensor data is critical in such a multi-sensor environment to provide sophisticated reasoning capabilities outside the sensors' core functions. Sensor data fusion combines alerts from both similar and diverse sensors to provide the security administrator with an overall, condensed, and intelligible view of the system. There are active research efforts in this area (e.g., Cuppens, 2001; Ning, Cui, & Reeves, 2002; Siraj, Vaughn, & Bridges, 2004). In addition to intrusion detection, collecting evidence of intrusions and attacks must also not be forgotten. The benefit of this evidence may be the difference between discovering the attacker and allowing that attacker to continue to attack you or someone else.

References

Cuppens, F. (2001, December 11-14). Managing alerts in a multi-intrusion detection environment. In *Proceedings of the 17th Annual Computer Security Applications Conference* (pp. 22-31). New Orleans, LA: IEEE Computer Society.

Florez, G., Liu, Z., Bridges, S., & Vaughn, R. (2005, September 20-23). Efficient modeling of discrete events for anomaly detection using hidden Markov models. *Proceedings of the 8th International Conference on Information Security* (pp. 506-514). Singapore: Springer.

Forrest, S., Hofmeyr, S. A., Somayaji, A., & Longstaff, T. A. (1996, May 6-8). A sense of elf for UNIX processes. In *Proceedings of the 1996 IEEE Symposium on Security and Privacy* (pp. 120-128). Los Alamitos, CA: IEEE Computer Society Press.

Goldman, R. P., Heimerdinger, W. L., Harp, S. A., Geib, C., Thomas, V., & Carter, R. L. (2001, June 12-14). Information modeling for intrusion report aggregation. In *Proceedings of the DARPA Information Survivability Conference and Exposition (DISCEX II)* (Vol. 1, pp. 329-342). Anaheim, CA: IEEE Computer Society Press.

Internet Security Systems Inc. (ISS). (1998). *Network- vs. host-based intrusion detection systems: A guide to intrusion detection technology*. Retrieved November 17, 2005, from http://www.sss.co.nz/pdfs/iss/nvh_id.pdf

Kruse, W., & Heiser, J. (2002). *Computer forensics: Incident response essentials*. New York: Addison Wesley.

Marcella, A., & Greenfield, R. (2002). *Cyber forensics: A field manual for collecting, examining, and preserving evidence of computer crimes*. Boston: Auerbach.

Michael, C., & Ghosh, A. (2002). Simple, state-based approaches to program-based anomaly detection. *ACM Transactions on Information and System Security, 5*(3). 203-237.

Ning, P., Cui, Y., & Reeves, D. S. (2002, November). Constructing attack scenarios through correlation of intrusion alerts. In *Proceedings of the ACM Conference on Computer & Communications Security*, Washington, DC (pp. 245-254).

Siraj, A., Vaughn, R., & Bridges, S. (2004). Decision making for network health assessment in an intelligent intrusion detection system architecture. *International Journal of Information Technology and Decision Making, 3*(2), 281-306.

Skinner, A., & Reel, J.S. (2000). *Enabling technologies: Cyber security*. Technical report, Government Electronics and Information Technology Association (GEIA).

Endnotes

[1]   Chief executive officer, chief information officer, chief operating officer, chief financial officer, and chief knowledge officer of a business entity.

[2]   These product names are provided for illustrative purposes only and their mention here does not constitute an endorsement by the authors.

[3]   These product names are provided for illustrative purposes only and their mention here does not constitute an endorsement by the authors.

Chapter XVII

Deploying Honeynets

Ronald C. Dodge, Jr., United States Military Academy, USA

Daniel Ragsdale, United States Military Academy, USA

Abstract

When competent computer network system administrators are faced with malicious activity on their networks, they think of the problem in terms of four distinct but related activities: detection, prevention, mitigation, and response. The greatest challenge of these four phases is detection. Typically, detection comes in the form of intrusion detection system (IDS) alerts and automated application and log monitors. These however are fraught with mischaracterized alerts that leave administrators looking for a needle in a haystack. One of the most promising emerging security tools is the honeynet Honeynets are designed to divert the malicious user or attacker to non-production systems that are carefully monitored and configured to allow detailed analysis of the attackers' actions and also protection of other network resources. Honeynets can be configured in many different ways and implemented from a full DMZ to a carefully placed file that is monitored for access.

System Administrator vs. Attacker

"All warfare is based on deception."

Sun Tzu

System administrators often consult an intrusion detection system or will manually review the event log on servers, firewalls, or hosts computers when investigating malicious activity. Unfortunately, this response to suspected malicious behavior often causes system administrators to draw erroneous conclusions. These faulty conclusions fall into two categories: mischaracterizing good traffic as malicious (known as a "false positive" or "false alarm") and failing to detect an attack (sometimes called a "false negative" or "miss"). Clearly, both types of faulty conclusions can have very serious negative consequences. Making the problem even worse is the exponentially increasing volume of legitimate traffic and system activity that IDSs must evaluate to identify malicious activity. In the present day, if an administrator were to rely solely on conventional IDSs and manual log analysis to identify malicious behavior system, it is a foregone conclusion that he or she will suffer from one or both types of errors.

Competent hackers are, of course, concerned with obscuring their malicious activity. Unfortunately for present day system administrators, hackers have developed a wide array of sophisticated tools and techniques that support their malicious intentions while minimizing the likelihood of detection. From the first stages of an attack to the final steps, skilled hackers typically work to achieve their malicious end without ever being noticed. During the reconnaissance phase, for example, skillful hackers use techniques that are specifically designed not to raise flags on conventional intrusion-detection systems while collecting as much useful information as possible about targeted systems and networks. Once a host has been compromised, hackers often retrieve powerful tools and utilities from a previously compromised computer acting as a file repository that enables them to install root kits and backdoors and conduct further stealthy penetration of the target network. They do this to allow for future access to the compromised host, while masking their activity.

Honeynets are an extremely useful security tool that can supplement conventional intrusion-detection systems and thwart hackers' attempts to avoid detection and remain anonymous. A honeynet introduces deception into the system administrators' arsenal. When implemented, a honeynet can turn a system administrator's job from finding a needle in a haystack to having a pile of needles. They do this by providing a target for hackers to attack that is designed to monitor, record, and track all of their activity while mitigating the risk exposure to the rest of the targeted network. Honeynets provide three primary functions: intrusion detection, attack understanding, and attacker attribution.

Network Deception

While network deception is not a new concept, deception is an emerging model in network operations. A common example of deception is the Allies effort to hide from Germany the nature of Operation Overlord, the invasion of France, offering false thrusts and fake equipment. A classic military definition of deception is (DOD, 2004):

> *Actions executed to deliberately mislead adversary military decision makers as to friendly military capabilities, intentions, and operations, thereby causing the adversary to take specific actions (or inactions) that will contribute to the accomplishment of the friendly mission.*

We define computer security deception as being those actions taken to deliberately mislead computer attackers and to cause them to take specific actions. The application of honeynets as part of a deception plan for network security is supported by this definition. Our general deception goal is to mislead an attacker into a predictable course of action that can be exploited (Dewar, 1989). Honeynets can be deployed in many ways — each employment should be designed to support a specific goal in the overall network deception plan. As an example, a honeynet could be deployed within the DMZ subnet of an organization providing external Web services or deployed on the inside of a network behind most firewall and intrusion detection devices. Additionally, the type of honeynet can vary from a robust network of systems designed to look like a small domain or a single record placed in a sensitive database. We will define these honeynet architectures in detail later in the chapter.

The deployment of honeynets as part of a network deception plan has proliferated in the past five years; however, we cannot cite specific deployments. At this point in the chapter, we would love to list in detail the deployments of honeynets, discuss the integration of the honeynet(s) into the security plan for an organization, and describe the attackers who have been identified — but it is impossible to get this type of sensitive information. We can cite the exponential increase in honeynet research and the frequency at which members of the Honeynet Project and others are invited to present (and consult with non-disclosure agreements). We can point to the use of honeynets by major antivirus, antispyware, and antispam organizations in search of signatures.

Honeynets in More Detail

A honeypot is a system that is placed on a network that has absolutely no production value. It often has no *domain name system* (DNS) entries and no advertised Web information. Currently, most honeynet deployments rely on tools that are signature-based to alert on specific malicious traffic. However, since a honeypot has no production use, by definition, any traffic going to that computer is at least suspicious, and, most likely, malicious. Honeypots exist in many different configurations. The design and construction of a honeypot depends greatly on the objectives and resources of the implementer. In function, a honeypot can be characterized as either low-interaction or high-interaction (Spitzner, 2004). These functions can be implemented using a combination of physical and virtual machines. A high-interaction deployment is shown in Figure 1.

A brief summary of different commercial and open-source honeypot implementations is contained in the Appendix of this chapter. This listing is current and complete at the time of this writing; however, honeypots are an active area of research and new technologies emerge continuously. Use the list as a starting point, but always use your faithful and favorite Internet search engine to find the latest technologies.

The primary difference between a low-interaction and high-interaction honeypot is the level (or depth) of interaction that a hacker can have with the target system. A low-interaction honeypot is one that uses emulated services and signatures to respond to

Figure 1. High-interaction honeynet

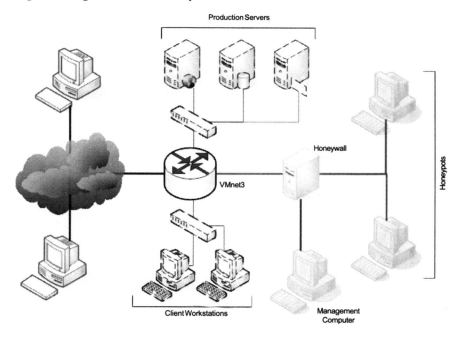

an attacker's probes. A common low-interaction honeypot is Honeyd (Provos, 2004); several other implementations can be found in the Appendix. We use Honeyd as an example because it was one of the first documented low-interaction paradigms and is still one of the most commonly used. Honeyd uses signature database to respond to scanning techniques used by hackers to fool the hackers into thinking they have found a host.

Honeyd is especially adept in identifying network scanning activity because it listens and responds to any IP addresses not claimed by another device on the subnet. This is accomplished by using the *address resolution protocol daemon* (ARPd). Using information provide by ARPd allows a device to respond to any unanswered ARP requests on a network. As shown in Figure 2, ARP requests passing through the router to Subnet 1 will be answered by Host C with its MAC address if no other host has the requested IP address.

Honeyd can respond to *Internet control message protocol* (ICMP), *user datagram protocol* (UDP), and *transmission control protocol* (TCP) packets using a simplified TCP state machine. Frequently, network scans use specially crafted packets that are configured to elicit specific responses from a given operating system, thereby giving the attacker information about the target system(s). This is the way the universally popular tool NMAP scans a host to determine its operating system. Honeyd uses a "personality engine" to generate scripted responses to standard service inquiries. For example, Honeyd can be configured to respond to a port scan that port 80 is open. In addition, if

Figure 2. ARPD process

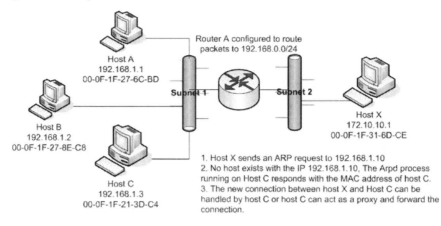

properly scripted, Honeyd can respond to an attempt to get header information from a Web server by returning a standard head request reply that includes information such as server type (Apache, IIS…). As the packet leaves the Honeyd process, the personality engine modifies the content of the packet headers to mimic the desired operating system. This is the limit of interaction that the hacker has with the system since there are no actual services to interact with — only scripts. An example interaction flow is shown in Figure 3.

In contrast to low-interaction honeypots, high-interaction honeypots provide real operating systems and services with real content with which attacker can interact. Of

Figure 3. Honeyd process (generalized)

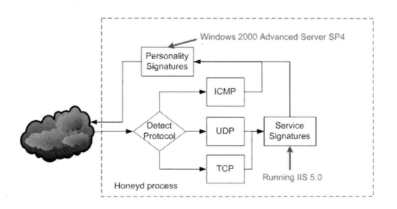

course, high-interaction honeypots have significantly higher resource, management, and risk factors. However, the information that can be gathered on a high-interaction honeypot by watching an attacker and learning about his or her techniques and tools far exceeds that of a low-interaction honeypot. It is through this extensive interaction that we gain information on threats, both external and internal to an organization. These victim systems can be any type of operating system, service, or information you want to provide. If we combine several honeypots to represent a network subnet, we call it a honeynet. Specifically, a honeynet is a collection of high-interaction honeypots designed to capture extensive information on threats.

The value of a honeynet is pretty straight forward. Since honeypots are not production systems, the honeynet itself has no production activity, no authorized services. As a result, any interaction with a honeynet implies malicious or unauthorized activity. Any inbound attempts to establish connections to a honeynet are, most likely, probes, scans, or attacks. Almost any outbound connections from a honeynet imply someone has compromised a system and has initiated outbound activity. This makes analyzing activity within a honeynet very simple. With traditional security technologies, such as firewall logs or IDS sensors, you have to sift through gigabytes of data or thousands of alerts. A great deal of time and effort is spent looking through this information, attempting to identify attacks or unauthorized activity. In many ways, it is the classic needle in the haystack problem, as you attempt to find the critical incident among volumes of information. In a honeynet, all captured activity is assumed to be unauthorized or malicious. All you are doing is capturing needles. It is then up to you to prioritize which of those needles has the greatest value and is worthy of further analysis.

Deploying honeynets is not necessarily a simple proposition. The deployment requires careful consideration of the risks associated with honeynets — after all, you are putting a computer in your network that is designed to be hacked. After a careful analysis of the risks, a deployment scheme must be defined and documented. This deployment scheme includes specific objectives of the honeynet, architectural layout of the honeynet, and policies and procedures for handling gathered data and compromises of the honeypots. Each of these steps is described in the following paragraphs.

Legal Risks of Deployment

Deploying honeynets is not risk free. Pitfalls lie in several areas that require careful planning and detailed coordination with many parties to ensure that the deployment conforms to organizational policies and does not introduce unacceptable risk. Of the areas of risk that an organization must consider, legal issues surrounding deployment of honeynets must be fully understood. These risks include both the legalities of the deployment as related to federal and state laws, as well as the handling of data that may contain personal information. An additional legal consideration is the handling of a compromise and the ramifications if your systems are used to store illicit material or are used in a subsequent attack. You should always contact your organization's legal counsel and receive written authorization before deploying any type of honeynet technologies. This section will not describe in detail the many facets of and provisions and exclusions present in the governing laws and statutes, but rather will introduce the general concepts. A very good detailed description can be found in a chapter written by Richard Salgado in Spitzner (2004, Chap.15).

In 2000, when honeynets began to receive significant attention and legitimacy as a network defense option, many concerns were raised about their constitutional legality. Cautions that were raised included concerns about entrapment and illegal data capture. These two concerns provided many long chat sessions and newsgroup threads as system administrators tried to find ways to ease the legal concerns expressed. Fortunately for those of us in charge of network security, most of the legal opinions rendered since that time have supported the legality of well-monitored honeynet systems. As a cautionary note, it is important to consider that very little case law has been developed concerning the use of honeynet. Initially, the two most common legal arguments against deploying honeynets were that the honeynets were a form of entrapment and that they were a violation a person's expected right to privacy (and related Wiretap Act/Pen Trap Act statutes).

Entrapment is defined as enticing a party to commit an act he/she was not already predisposed to do (Sherman vs. U.S., 1958). This is simply not the case for a honeynet. Providing the systems for an attacker to scan and then compromise does not constitute entrapment. If an agent contacted the attacker and lured him/her to conduct the attack, that would be looked at in a different light. Further, entrapment is purely a defensive argument for someone to use to avoid prosecution. It cannot be used in any litigation against the owners of the honeynet. The case of entrapment is pretty straight forward; the right to monitor and record someone's communications is much muddier.

We will examine the monitoring of data communications in three steps:

1.   We will examine the applicability of the Fourth Amendment (the Fourth Amendment limits the power of government agents to search for evidence without having first secured a search warrant from a judge).

2.   We will look at the Wiretap Act.

3.   We will examine the Pen Trap Act.

As before, we will only introduce the topics. For detailed analysis, read Spitzner (2004, Chap.XV).

The Fourth Amendment

The Fourth Amendment to the Constitution of the United States reads:

> *The right of the people to be secure in their persons, houses, papers, and effects, against unreasonable searches and seizures, shall not be violated, and no Warrants shall issue, but upon probable cause, supported by Oath or affirmation, and particularly describing the place to be searched, and the persons or things to be seized.*

This amendment may be used in an attempt to dismiss any evidence gathered in violation of the amendment as well as in litigation against the owner/deployer of the honeynet. This amendment hinges on a persons expectation of privacy. An individual who attacks and compromises a system on a network does not have a reasonable expectation of privacy (U.S. vs. Seidlitz, 1978). Further, the Fourth Amendment only applies to government actors, not private citizens. The Fourth Amendment significantly affects the disposition of captured data. There are significant legal considerations with honeynets when we start to examine the handling of non-attacker data. For example, consider the following scenario:

> *An attacker compromises a honeypot and sets it up as an IRC bot (a system meant to relay chat sessions between users). In that conversation, a third-party user, not knowing the bot is on a compromised system, engages in chat about some crime.*

The Wiretap Act

If a system administrator reviews the data logs from the conversation and finds the criminal discussion, is it permissible in court? This is where we move into the discussion of the Wiretap Act. The Wiretap Act was enacted to limit the ability for any individual to intercept communications. Where the Fourth Amendment may not apply, the Wiretap Act may. There are exceptions to the Wiretap Act that current legal opinions are using to support the deployment of honeynets. The exceptions that most directly apply are the "provider protection," the "consent," and the "computer trespasser" exceptions.

Provider Protection Clause

The provider protection clause of the Wiretap Act allows a service provider to intercept communications to protect the provider's rights and property. This is exactly in line with the deployment considerations of all other intrusion detection systems. The clause reads (Crimes and criminal procedure, 18 U.S.C., § 2511(2)(a)(i)):

> *It shall not be unlawful under [the Wiretap Act] for an operator of a switchboard, or an officer, employee, or agent of a provider of wire or electronic communication service, whose facilities are used in the transmission of a wire or electronic communication, to intercept, disclose, or use that communication in the normal course of his employment while engaged in any activity which is a necessary incident to the rendition of his service or to the protection of the rights or property of the provider of that service, except that a provider of wire communication service to the public shall not utilize service observing or random monitoring except for mechanical or service quality control checks.*

This exception to the Wiretap Act must be implemented within the intent of the exception. Just because you are a services provider, you must be able to draw a linkage between the monitoring being conducted and the safeguarding of your resources.

Consent Clause

The second exception to consider is that of consent. There are two ways consent may permit monitoring. First, if banners are placed such that individuals accessing resources on the target system are warned that all communications may be monitored. (Similar to the recorded message received when calling a help desk, i.e., "this call may be recorded for the purpose of..." Whether you know it or not, by continuing to hold you have consented to the recording of your conversation.) This case however is not without debate. Would an attacker necessarily see the banner ad? If you cannot prove that the attacker saw it, then you can not claim the attacker was warned. The second consideration of consent is that the honeypot can itself — as a party of the communication — consent to monitoring. There are several arguments that prove difficult to defend in this case, and it should not be considered your first claim for exception.

Computer Trespasser Exception

The final exception comes from the Patriot Act. The Patriot Act allows the government to monitor electronic communication when in conjunction with an ongoing investigation (Crimes and criminal procedure, 18 U.S.C. § 2511(2)(i)). This exception is only applicable to government use of a honeynet and is not applicable to private or commercial applications.

The Pen Trap Act

The Wiretap Act covers only the interception of content of communications between two parties. It does not cover the analysis of information stored on a honeynet (which we will cover later) or the recording of "packet header" information. However, another act, the Pen Register, Trap, and Trace Devices statute applies in this case (Crimes and criminal procedure, 18 U.S.C. §§ 3121–3127). This statute prohibits the capture of non-content related data like the information contained in the IP-packet headers. As in the case of the Wiretap Act, exceptions that closely mirror those discussed previously allow service providers to monitor this packet information.

The Computer Fraud and Abuse Act

Now that you may (or may not) be convinced that you are within your legal charter to deploy a honeynet, you must carefully consider what happens when your system is compromised. There is only one thing worse that getting a call at 3:00 a.m. that your systems have been broken into and your customer database or proprietary documents has been compromised — finding out that the attack came from one of your honeypots! What policies are in place if your honeynet is used to attack other networks or if your honeynet is used to store copyrighted or other illegal data? Honeynets must employ elements designed to mitigate the risk of contaminating your production network. One very effective method that also facilitates the second honeynet goal of data capture is to employ a gateway device that controls the data going into and out of a honeynet.

The good news is that most every computer system connected to the Internet is covered under provisions in the Computer Fraud and Abuse Act, which makes them "protected systems." The Computer Fraud and Abuse Act criminalize the act of network attacks. The provision allows for protection of any system used in interstate communication — virtually all systems connected to the Internet (Crimes and criminal procedure, 18 U.S.C. § 1030). For a detailed discussion of the applicable use cases for the provision to apply, we again refer you to Spitzner (2004, Chap.XV).

While this is good news for legal defense against your honeypot being used in malicious activity by an attacker — you still must be concerned with the disposition of illegal material. The short answer to this problem is that, prior to deployment of a honeynet, your unique situation must be discussed with your organization's legal council. Your honeynet may, in practice, become a "witness" to a crime, and the manner in which the data is handled may become very important. As part of your legal planning, developing relationships with local, state, and federal law enforcement agencies may prove valuable. As soon as illegal material is found on your honeynet, you should consult both you council and your law enforcement contacts.

Technical Details of Deployment

Once the legal and procedural concerns have been addressed — and we emphasize that this should be the very first step in deploying a honeynet — the architecture and deployment strategy must be planned. Three areas should be addressed in detail in the

Figure 4. Honeynet (Generation II) example configuration

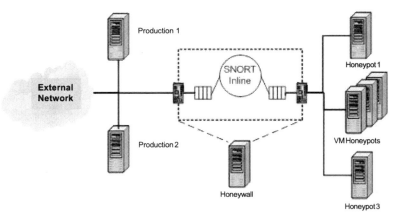

design. First, the design must include the technical means to protect your internal network from the honeynet and the means to prevent it from being used as a launching point for network intrusions against others. Second, the design must address how you will record, exfiltrate, and analyze the data associated with the activity on your honeynet. Finally, the architecture of your honeynet should be designed with a specific and well-articulated purpose. The discussion below will detail the steps developed by the consortium of researchers who participate in the Honeynet Project (www.honeynet.org).

The Honeynet Project is a not-for-profit organization that is dedicated to the advancement of honeynet technologies. The Honeynet Project has been at the forefront of development and education of honeynet technologies since 1999. An example of a honeynet configuration developed as a result of the ongoing research activities within the Honeynet Project is shown in Figure 4.

Data Control

After years of research the Honeynet Project has identified two issues that must be addressed when developing and deploying a honeynet: data control and data capture. Protecting production services and internal networks from compromise due to an attack emanating from a honeynet should be the first consideration when deploying a honeynet. This requirement of a honeynet, as defined by the Honeynet Project, is called data control. Data control is crucially important to the implementation of a honeynet. A honeynet is placed on a network in hopes that it will be attacked. This is great for getting an indication that there is malicious activity on your network, but what happens once the attacker has a foothold inside your network? Certainly you will want to avoid giving an attacker the keys to the front door. The key to protecting the rest of your network (and hosts outside your network — see *legal risks*) is to provide a mechanism for catching and mitigating all outbound packets.

The primary technical solution proposed by the Honeynet Project is the use of a proxy that operates at data link layer (Layer 2) in the network protocol stack. This proxy is a Layer-2 bridge and is referred to as a honeywall by the Honeynet Project. The software for the Honeynet Project honeywall is distributed on bootable CDs and is currently built using a Fedora Core 3 Linux kernel. (Prior versions were distributed on a bootable CD based on F.I.R.E., a forensics and security toolkit Linux distribution.) This Layer-2 proxy intercepts all out inbound and outbound packets and uses a variety of mechanisms including rate limiting, selective dropping, and "bit-flipping" to mitigate the risk of a honeynet being used to exploit or scan your own or other's networks. As shown in Figure 44, the honeywall is placed between the honeynet and the rest of the network. The honeywall uses a combination of SNORT (Roesch, 2005) and SNORT-inline to log and, where necessary, scrub incoming and outgoing packets. A detailed communication flow for a honeywall is shown in Figure 5.

In most cases, the packets coming into the honeynet through the honeywall are allowed to pass unchallenged to the honeypots. Only connection logging and payload logging are done. Outbound packets are subject to rate limiting (implemented in IP tables) and analysis by the SNORT-inline process. The rate limiting of outbound activity is based on protocol and number of packets and can be specified in the scripts that start IP tables.

Figure 5. Honeywall connection detail

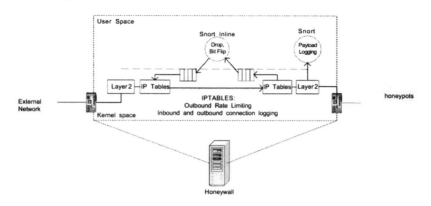

The task of protecting the internal network and external hosts from attacks originating from your honeypots is handled by the SNORT-inline process. This process receives packets from the IP table queuing feature and matches the packets against a modified SNORT rule set. If the packet matches a rule, one of three actions can be taken. First, the packet could be allowed to continue. This is a very unlikely option (why have the honeywall in the first place if you are not going to buffer traffic?). The second option is to simply drop the packet. This is certainly a viable option as it provides protection from malicious packets emanating from your honeypots. The problem with this second option is that an attacker will quickly become disenchanted with his new acquisition if bad packets are disappearing. The attacker will then, most likely, move on to more friendly networks, thereby depriving you of valuable information. A third and slightly more devious option is to have SNORT-inline slightly modify the outbound packets, thereby rendering the exploit impotent when it reaches its intended target. Using this approach, it is less likely that the attacker will become discouraged and move on.

Data Capture

Now that we have implemented features designed to control the traffic emanating from our honeypots, we need to focus on the second issue — data capture. After all, if you do not record the data and raise alerts, the honeynet will do you no good. In addition to capturing traffic for event notification, the data can be used to learn more about the attack through forensic analysis. Honeynet data can be captured at two locations: the *network* and on the *host*. We can capture data in two locations: from the honeywall and from each individual honeypot.

Data capture at the honeywall records a variety of information including network connection information, packet payload, and alerts generated from SNORT rules. By capturing this information, we are able to examine the full packet flow that caused a specific alert or action on a honeypot. Connection data is captured by IP table firewall logging. Packet payloads are captured by a SNORT process that is bound to the network interface card facing the honeypots. If the SNORT process was bound to the external interface (facing the general network), it would record a significant amount of non-honeynet data. One of the objectives of deploying honeynets is attack understanding. While the traffic captured on the honeywall is ripe with valuable data, it is none the less nothing more than could be captured by any network sniffer. Data captured at the host is much more important in leading to attack understanding.

Host-based logging must be done very surreptitiously to avoid detection by an attacker. If logging mechanisms are detected by an attacker, either the attacker will leave the host (defeating the purpose for deploying the honeynet) or, perhaps worse, disable the logging, effectively blinding us from observing the modifications and actions being taken on the honeynet. While one might fall back to the logging being done on the honeywall, any encrypted traffic, most probably in the form of *secure shell* (SSH), initiated by the attacker will not provide any valuable information if gathered at the honeywall. Host-based logging is very important. Advanced honeynets employ a form of host logging that is implemented in a manner that is similar to various root kits that are used by the hackers themselves.

The technique employed by the Honeynet Project is to trojanize the Linux operating system kernel by installing a specially modified root kit, called Sebek, to intercept specific low-level system calls at the kernel level. The original version of Sebek was based on the Adore root kit. The current version of Sebek replaces the read() function in the system call table in the 2.4 Linux kernel with a read() that is configured to copy all data that it sees into a packet and send it to a server that collects Sebek packets, as well as the normal processing handled by the read() function. (New versions of SEBEK, currently in development, greatly enhance both network functionality and host logging). Using this method, we can capture not only all activity on the honeypot, but also any data that was once encrypted between the honeypot and the attacker's SSH server. Sebek performs two additional functions to enable the data captured by the new read() function to be sent covertly out of the honeypot without being observed by the attacker. This is accomplished by bypassing the TCP/IP stack (and the corresponding raw socket interface) and sending the Sebek data packets directly to the network device driver using the transport protocol based on UDP. Since nearly all sniffers are based on the libpcap library (which relies on the raw socket interface), a user on a Sebek-modified system will not see the traffic generated by Sebek. This still presents one last problem. If the attacker has the ability to sniff network traffic from another honeypot on the same subnet, he or she would be able to see the UDP Sebek traffic, and the game is lost. To account for this, Sebek installs its own version of the raw socket interface. This new version drops all Sebek data before sending it to the user application. Detailed technical information on the Sebek implementation can be found at Honeynet.org. (2005).

While Sebek provides a tremendous opportunity to record everything an attacker does, it is not invisible. Just as we are using attacker techniques by trojanizing kernel functions for the purpose of monitoring, an attacker could determine the build of the OS on the honeynet and compare the various kernel functions known to be used by Sebek (most commonly through an MD5 checksum) and determine that he is on a honeypot. While this might be true and the attacker would probably leave, we have still gained a tremendous amount of information about the attacker — including the fact he is NOT a script kiddie. There are other detection mechanisms for honeypots and Sebek that can be found in Krawetz (2004).

Information and Physical Architecture

At this point, we have discussed the first two major tasks in deploying a honeynet: understanding the risks and the technical solution to data control and data capture. Next we must decide on the physical and logical architecture of the honeynet. This is the honeynet tuning stage. Traditionally, honeynets have simply been nothing more than default installations of commonly used operating systems, deployed on external networks. These systems have no perceived value and, as a result, this type of deployment attracts only common script kiddies or automated attacks such as worms or auto-rooters — attacks that depend on highly active and random scanning. How you deploy your honeynet will determine the type of attacker (or activity) you capture. The more perceived value your honeynet has, the more likely you will capture advanced activity. This is extremely challenging to do, and a problem that has yet to be easily solved.

Honeynets assist network defenders by reducing the amount of data that must be combed through looking for malicious activity. However, even a honeynet can become inundated by the worms and mass scans that are abundant on today's networks. To counter the massive amounts of random traffic looking for vulnerable hosts, honeynets can be "targeted" to let in only the class of attacker you are interested in tracking. The external threat to a network is the one most commonly discussed. However, the voluminous amounts of scanning and worm traffic needs to be filtered out to only let in traffic that is "interesting." Honeynets can be configured in many different ways — the architecture chosen should be designed with the intended target in mind. If a honeynet is being deployed simply to observe all malicious activity without concern for the sophistication of the attacks, then the default OS and application installations will work. If, however, a more skilled attacker is the target, the honeynet should be constructed to both filter out unwanted worm and script kiddie traffic and entice the attacker to stay.

The control of the amount of traffic a honeynet gets can happen in several places. First, just as in normal networks, a firewall can be used to block some traffic. This firewall could be a stand-alone firewall or perhaps could be implemented with an additional filter on inbound traffic at the honeywall. Another option would be to harden your honeypots. Certainly the less vulnerable a honeypot is the less likely it is to be attacked. This is a delicate balance between too much and too little traffic. A final way to control the volume of traffic your honeynet sees is to place it in an interior segment of your network. This is an especially useful deployment for finding "insider" attacks. Traditionally, most defensive measures deployed in a network focus on external threats. Using who are already inside, frequently face little or no barriers. This is a unique class of threat often overlooked in the popular press, but known by system administrators as potentially the most dangerous is the inside threat. Placing honeynets deep inside corporate networks shields them from most Internet traffic and presents inside malicious users with a mouth-watering target.

One of the remaining tasks in preparing to deploy a honeynet is to determine the physical construction of the honeynet. Honeynets can be deployed in many different ways. Each different implementation should be examined and used to meet specific security needs. The employments can range from a single computer to a remote collection of honeynets that is connected through *generic routing encapsulation* (GRE) tunnels to remote locations. A GRE tunnel is a CISCO protocol that wraps the IP header at Layer 2 and sends it to a remote location.

One of the most common and easiest deployment techniques is as a stand-alone honeynet. This is the basic configuration as described throughout the chapter. In this scenario, a collection of honeypots are placed behind a honeywall at some location in your network; typically near the DMZ. The location could be anywhere on the network and is determined by the objective of the honeynet. If an organization has more than one network location, a honeynet is deployed at each site and is usually administered by the local system administrator. For smaller scale deployments, this is a very good solution. However, as an organization grows in geographic network complexity, a honeyfarm might be considered. A honeyfarm is a collection of honeynets serving different networks, but co-located. This provides a significant savings on manpower and management costs and enhances the ability to do cross-honeynet correlation. A honeyfarm can be implemented locally using *virtual local area networks* (VLANs). A more robust solution that would allow locations anywhere in the world to access a honeyfarm is the use of GRE tunnels. The benefit of this is that the IP header does not experience and TTL decrements and the "transportation of the packet" is virtually un-noticeable.

So far, we have discussed detailed planning for the proactive deployment of a honeynet. A proactive deployment is defined as a deployment to find yet unknown malicious activity. Interestingly, the technologies used for effective and safe honeynet deployments can also be used to examine and "track" known malicious activity on your network. In this scenario, the honeynet deployment is considered reactive. If, for example, a system on your network has been compromised and it is not critical that it be repaired immediately, you can isolate the system by placing a honeywall directly in front of it. This will allow you to closely monitor and track all the activity on the compromised host from that point on. This may provide you with invaluable information that could lead to more stringent defenses on the rest of the network.

If you need to remove the compromised host instead of leaving it in place to observe, you could employ virtual machine technology to create a copy of the compromised host so that the original can be preserved for forensic analysis. So far we have only mentioned deploying honeynets using physical hardware. Now we put the previous example in a different light, where the honeypots deployed were virtual machines. If you observe an attacker on your virtual honeypot, you can simply create a copy and let a criminal investigator take the exploited system away to examine it.

A final reactive implementation doesn't wait for a system to be compromised at all — instead, honeypots are created dynamically in reaction to active scanning of your network or reports of specific exploit attempts. This system would rely on agents monitoring network traffic looking for scanning activity. Once an agent recognizes an attacker looking for a specific OS or application vulnerability, a honeypot is created using virtual machines that most closely matches the assumed target of the attacker. An example of this scenario is shown in Figure 6.

Figure 6. Dynamic honeypots using virtual machines

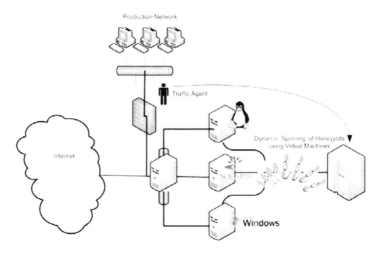

One final use for honeynet technologies does not involve the placement of physical or virtual machines on your network at all. A detailed description of virtual honeynet installation steps can be found at http://www.honeynet.org. Recall that the concept of a honeynet involves placing something on your network where no one should ever go. This objective can be applied to any resource on your network that can be monitored. For instance, a common example used to describe this particular paradigm is that of a database record in a hospital. If the database administrator enters a bogus record for a very famous person — say Elvis Presley or Bill Gates — it might very well attract users looking for valuable information in the database. If a record monitor is used in the database, an alert can be sent when the record in question is accessed, alerting the administrator of unauthorized activity. Another example of placing content where only malicious users/attackers would find is planting HTML or documents that have embedded images that don't really exist, but that have rules written by a firewall that alerts when someone opens the document and attempts to retrieve the image. Of course, this would only work if the image is cleverly designed to entice the attacker to retrieve it, for example, "secret deployment time table for military forces." These embedded images can assist greatly in attribution.

Anti-Honeynet Movements

Of course, no good deed goes unpunished. Not long after the Honeynet Project started to release its findings and other open source and commercial tools appeared, organized resistance to honeynets started to emerge. Just as IDS signatures are constantly being circumvented by modifying attack vectors, attackers are quickly learning and sharing the secrets of honeynets to avoid being discovered by a honeypot in waiting. One of the most notable groups, the Anti-honeypot Alliance has published some of its findings (and rants) in various hacker electronic journals (Cory, 2003, 2004). Commercial applications, such as honeypot-hunter (Krawetz, 2004), aimed at thwarting honeypots, while not yet very sophisticated, are starting to emerge.

While this attention is interesting and some might be alarmed, it is welcomed by the open-source development teams that are working on honeynet technologies. In fact, several developers who contribute to the open-source honeynet solutions also have published papers highlighting the vulnerabilities in existing honeynet technologies and how to exploit them (Dornseif, Holz, & Klein, 2004). This "full disclosure" assists current developers in finding and fixing shortfalls in current deployments.

Conclusion

Honeynet use is rapidly increasing. In May 2004, the Honeynet Project released a honeywall CD-ROM that was downloaded over 150,000 times in a two-week period. Honeynets are capable of capturing attack data that may otherwise go unnoticed. The deployment of honeynets should be focused on the threats that are of greatest concern to the organization in which they will be deployed. As honeynet use continues to grow, attackers will surely continue to develop ways to detect their use. Operating at Layer 2 in the network protocol stack currently provides a method of good means to mask the presence of the honeynet sensor. Unfortunately, this masking will be effective only until attackers find an easy and reliable way to detect Layer 2 bridging or begin exploiting some of the collection tools (SNORT, SNORT_inline) themselves. Quoting from [14],

When a hacker compromises a system they are on a tactically equal footing with the honeypot software. The only superiority that the honeypot software has is wholly in the strategy of honeypot deployment — in deceiving the attacker of the honeypot's presence.

This statement amplifies the fact that honeynets are tools. Tools are only effective if properly employed — a screwdriver makes a woefully inept hammer... Security professionals everywhere should constantly strive to develop new and innovative ways to outperform the attacker community.

References

Cory, J. (2003, September). *Local honeypot identification*. Retrieved July 7, 2005, from http://www.phrack.org/fakes/p62/p62-0x07.txt

Cory, J. (2004, January). *Advanced honeypot identification*. Retrieved July 7, 2005, from http://www.phrack.org/fakes/p63/p63-0x09.txt

Crimes and criminal procedure, 18 U.S.C., § 2511(2)(a)(i) (2004).

Crimes and criminal procedure, 18 U.S.C. § 2511(2)(i) (2004).

Crimes and criminal procedure, 18 U.S.C. §§ 3121–3127 (2004).

Crimes and criminal procedure, 18 U.S.C. § 1030 (2004).

Department of Defense (DOD)(2004). *Dictionary of military and associated terms.* Joint Publication 1-02, November 30. U.S.Government Department of Defense.

Dewar, M. (1989). *The art of deception in warfare.* London: David & Charles.

Dornseif, M., Holz, T., & Klein, C. (2004, June 11-12). NoSEBrEaK - Attacking honeynets. In *Proceedings of the IEEE SMC Information Assurance Workshop*, West Point, NY, June 11-12 (pp. 123-129). New York: IEEE Press.

Honeynet.org (2005, June 5). *Know your enemy: Sebek.* Retrieved   n.d. , from http://www.honeynet.org/papers/sebek.pdf

Krawetz, N., (2004). Anti-honeypot technology. *IEEE Security and Privacy, 2*(1), 76-79.

Provos, N. (2004). A virtual honeypot framework. In *Proceedings of the 13th USENIX Security Symposium,* August 11-13, San Diego, CA (pp. 1-14). Retrieved June 6, 2005, from http://www.usenix.org/events/sec04/tech/provos.html

Roesch, M. (2005). SNORT, a "lightweight" intrusion detection technology. Retrieved n.d.   from http://www.SNORT.org

Sherman vs. U.S., 356 (1958) U.S. 369, 373.

Spitzner, L. (2004). *Know your enemy* (2nd ed.). Old Tappan, NY: Prentice Hall.

U.S. vs. Seidlitz (1978) 589 F.2d 152, 160 (4th Cir.).

Appendix

The list below of commercial and open-source honeypot resources contains only a sampling of the different implementations of honeypot technology. This list was originally posted at http://www.tracking-hackers.com/solutions.

Commercial honeypots

- **PatriotBox** (http://www.alkasis.com/?fuseaction=products.info&id=20). A commercial, easy-to-use low-interaction honeypot designed for Windows.

- **KFSensor** (http://www.keyfocus.net/kfsensor/). A powerful and easy-to-use low-interaction Windows honeypot, designed primarily for detection. Extensive capabilities, including NetBIOS simulation and interoperability with Honeyd scripts. Free evaluation copies.

- **NetBait** (http://www2.netbaitinc.com:5080/). A very novel and powerful commercial solution. NetBait can be a product or service. Either way, it operates by redirecting attacks against unused IP space to "honeypot farms."

- **Decoy Server** (http://enterprisesecurity.symantec.com/products/products.cfm?ProductID=157). Previously known as ManTrap, a high-interaction honeypot sold by Symantec.

- **Specter** (http://www.specter.com/). Specter is a low-interaction honeypot designed to run on Windows. It can emulate 13 different operating systems, monitor up to 14 TCP ports, and has a variety of configuration and notification features. One of Specter's greatest strengths is its ease-of-use.

Open-source/Free honeypots

- **Bubblegum Proxypot** (http://www.proxypot.org/). An open-proxy honeypot for deceiving and detecting spammers.

- **Jackpot** (http://jackpot.uk.net/). An open-relay honeypot, also aimed at spammers.

- **BackOfficer Friendly** (http://www.nfr.com/resource/backOfficer.php). BOF is a free Windows-based honeypot designed to be used as a burglar alarm.

- **Bait-n-Switch** (http://violating.us/projects/baitnswitch/). Not really a honeypot; instead, a technology that directs all non-production or unauthorized traffic to your honeypots. Very powerful concept.

- **Bigeye** (http://violating.us/projects/bigeye/). A low-interaction honeypot that emulates several services.

- **Deception Toolkit** (http://all.net/dtk/dtk.html). DTK was the first OpenSource honeypot, released in 1997. DTK is a collection of Perl scripts and C source code that emulates a variety of listening services. Its primary purpose is to deceive human attackers.

- **LaBrea Tarpit** (http://labrea.sourceforge.net/labrea-info.html). This OpenSource honeypot is unique in that it is designed to slow down or stop attacks by acting as a sticky honeypot.

- **Honeyd** (http://www.honeyd.org/). This is a powerful, low-interaction OpenSource honeypot, released by Niels Provos in 2002. Honeyd, written in C and designed for Unix platforms, introduces a variety of new concepts, including the ability to monitor millions of unused IPs, IP stack spoofing, and simulate hundreds of operating systems, at the same time. It also monitors all UDP- and TCP-based ports.

- **Honeynets** (www.honeynet.org). These are entire networks of systems designed to be compromised. Honeynets are the most complex of honeypot solutions and have the greatest risk. However, they can also capture the most information of any honeypot.

- **Sendmail SPAM Trap** (http://www.tracking-hackers.com/solutions/sendmail.html). This honeypot identifies spammers and captures their SPAM, without relaying it to any victims. Best of all, VERY easy to setup!

- **Tiny Honeypot** (http://www.alpinista.org/thp/). Written by George Bakos, Tiny Honeypot is unique in that it always appears to be vulnerable. No matter what attack a hacker launches, it will appear successful. Great tool for collecting all sorts of information on the bad guys.

Web resources

- **The Honeynet Project**— http://www.honeynet.org

- **The Honeynet Research Alliance** is a community of organizations dedicated to researching, developing and deploying honeynets and sharing the lessons learned. Its goal is to bring together people and organizations actively involved in honeynet research. Its primary means of communication is a closed maillist.

- **Honeypots: Tracking Hackers** — http://www.tracking-hackers.com

  A Web site dedicated to honeypot technology. This Web site is run by Lance Spitzner, who is the founder of the Honeynet Project.

- **Source Forge honeypots**: http://honeypots.sourceforge.net/

- **The Honeypots: Monitoring and Forensics Project**'s purpose is to highlight cutting-edge techniques, tools, and resources for conducting Honeypot Research and Forensic Investigation.

- **Distributed Honeypot Project** — http://www.lucidic.net/

  The goal of lucidic.net is to organize dispersed honeypots across the Internet and share our findings with the security community. Focus is placed on designing and analyzing new techniques and technologies while developing methods for dispersed information sharing. For more information about honeynets in general, visit the Honeynet Project.

- **Talisker's   Network   Intrusion: Honeypot   Page** — http://www.networkintrusion.co.uk/honeypots.htm

  This site provides a complete listing of the various commercial and open source honeypot resources available.

- **Security Focus: Honeypot Mail-List** — http://www.securityfocus.com/archive/119

  The Honeypots Mail-list is a lightly moderated public mail list dedicated to developing and sharing the understanding of honeypot value, uses, deployment, and research. Its goal is to bring together people and organizations interested in the research, development, or security applications of honeypots and honeypot-related technologies.

Chapter XVIII

Steganography and Steganalysis

Merrill Warkentin, Mississippi State University, USA

Mark B. Schmidt, St. Cloud State University, USA

Ernst Bekkering, Northeastern State University, USA

Abstract

In the digital environment, steganography has increasingly received attention over the last decade. Steganography, which literally means "covered writing," includes any process that conceals data or information within other data or conceals the fact that a message is being sent. Though the focus on use of steganography for criminal and terrorist purposes detracts from the potential use for legitimate purposes, the focus in this chapter is on its role as a security threat. The history of stenography as a tool for covert purposes is addressed. Recent technical innovations in computerized steganography are presented, and selected widely available steganography tools are presented. Finally, a brief discussion of the role of steganalysis is presented.

Introduction

In the digital environment, steganography has received increasing attention over the last decade. The steganography process conceals the fact that a message is being sent, thereby preventing an observer from knowing that anything unusual is taking place. Neil F. Johnson of the Center for Secure Information Systems at George Mason University defines steganography as "the art of concealing the existence of information within seemingly innocuous carriers" (Johnson, 2003, p. 2). Much of this attention has focused on the use of steganography for illegitimate purposes by terrorists and criminals, culminating in news stories about Al Qaeda's use of the technique in its communications. The extent of actual use by terrorists remains to be seen and, so far, has never been (publicly) proven. Yet, it has been suggested by government officials in the US and elsewhere that Al Qaeda and other organizations are hiding maps and photographs of terrorist targets and are also posting instructions for terrorist activities on sports chat rooms, pornographic bulletin boards, and other Web sites.

The preoccupation with stenography as a tool for covert purposes can be explained by reviewing its history. Though the term itself is based on the Greek word for "covered writing," the term was first used in the 14th century by the German mathematician Johannes Trithemius (1606) as the title for his book *Steganographia*. On the surface, the book presents a system of angel magic, but it actually describes a highly sophisticated system of cryptography. The actual hiding of information is much older. In ancient Greece, messages might be tattooed on slaves' shaved heads and then their hair would be allowed to grow back before they were sent out as messengers. A more benign form of information hiding was inscribing messages on the wooden base of wax tablets, rather than on the surface of the wax itself (Jupitermedia Corporation, 2003). More recent forms of hiding messages were used in World War II when spies and resistance fighters used milk, fruit juice, or even urine to write invisible coded messages. Heating the source document would reveal the writing, which had turned invisible to the naked eye after the unusual form of ink had dried up. Thus, the history of steganography has long been associated with an air of secrecy, far removed from peaceful and productive purposes.

Steganography Today

More technical forms of steganography have been in existence for several years. International workshops on information hiding and steganography have been held regularly since 1996 (Moulin & O'Sullivan, 2003). However, the majority of the development and use of computerized steganography has occurred since 2000 (Cole, 2003). Modern technology and connectivity have put steganographic capabilities within the reach of the average person with a computer and an Internet connection (Bartlett, 2002). Steganography does not necessarily encrypt a message, as is the case with cryptography. Instead, the goal is to conceal the fact that a message even exists in the first place (Anderson & Petitcolas, 1998). In today's fast-paced, high-tech society, people who want to send hidden messages have very efficient methods of getting a message to its destination with the use of computerized tools that encode a message in a graphic, sound, or other type of file.

New Practices for an Ancient Technique

With the onset of the digital age, many new and innovative mechanisms became available for information hiding. Steganographic techniques and software focused on hiding information and messages in audiovisual files such as graphics files, sound files, and video files. Insignificant and unused parts of these files were replaced with the digital data for the hidden information. The information itself could be protected even further by use of cryptography, where the information was converted into a form incomprehensible without knowledge of the specific cryptographic technique and key. This highlights an important difference between steganography and cryptography. The ultimate goal of cryptography is hiding and protecting the content of information, whereas steganography hides the presence of information itself. Another difference is the mode of transmission. Cryptographic messages can be transported by themselves. In steganography, to hide information, the secret content has to be hidden in a cover message. Whereas physical covers were used to hide information in the past, both the cover and hidden content can now be in digital form. Audiovisual files are ideal covers for several reasons. First, these types of files tend to be quite large in comparison to other file types, providing more opportunity for hiding information successfully. By keeping the ratio of hidden digital data to cover data low, the probability of discovery decreases. Furthermore, audiovisual files require special software to detect the presence of hidden information. ASCII-based data can be detected with simple string comparisons, whereas detection of hidden data in pixels and waves depends on detection of statistical anomalies. In other words, an unencrypted message could be detected in a text-based message by a relatively unsophisticated search engine or spybot, requiring less processing power than for detection in the audiovisual covers.

From a technical perspective, data can easily be hidden in an image file. One such technique to hide data is called *least significant bit* (LSB) insertion (Kessler, 2001). The LSB approach allows the last bit in a byte to be altered. While one might think that this would significantly alter the colors in an image file, it does not. In fact, the change is indiscernible to the human eye. As an example, consider three adjacent pixels (nine bytes) with the following RGB encoding:

$$10010101 \ 00001101 \ 11001001$$
$$10010110 \ 00001111 \ 11001010$$
$$10011111 \ 00010000 \ 11001011$$

An LSB algorithm could be used to hide the following nine bits 101101101. The last, or least significant, bit in each byte may be adjusted. The underlined bits indicate a change (notice that it is not necessary to change some of the bits).

$$10010101 \ 0000110\underline{0} \ 11001001$$
$$1001011\underline{1} \ 0000111\underline{0} \ 1100101\underline{1}$$
$$10011111 \ 00010000 \ 11001011$$

The above example demonstrates that to hide nine bits of information, the algorithm only needed to change four of the nine least significant bits in these nine bytes. Because changing the last bit causes an extremely small change in the color of a pixel (speck of color), the change in the graphic is imperceptible to the human eye. For a more detailed description of this process, please visit http://www.garykessler.net/library/steganography.html.

A special case of steganography can be the use of watermarking, which can have beneficial applications as well. Some watermarks are prominently displayed in an attempt to discourage or prevent unauthorized copying or use, while other watermarks are hidden intentionally. When the message, identification, or graphic is an attribute of the file itself and hidden from regular users, the technique can be termed digital watermarking. In pure steganography, the content of the information added to the file has its own significance. Furthermore, steganographic content is intended to be easily separated from the cover file with the proper software tools by the intended audience. Hidden watermarks can be considered to fall within the bounds of steganography. In our discussion, we will use this expanded definition use of the term steganography, and include the use of hidden watermarks. Good watermarks should be impossible to be separated from the file in which they have been inserted. Finally, steganographic message content can lose its significance when the information becomes outdated or stale. Ideally speaking, the protection afforded by hidden watermarking would last indefinitely.

Relationship to Cryptography

Cryptography is concerned with creating electronic artifacts (typically data files) that are encoded and cannot be interpreted by an intercepting party. As such, an encrypted message often appears to be random or unintelligible. However, the goal of sending steganographically hidden messages is to appear normal — the artifact might appear to be "normal." However, steganography is often used in conjunction with cryptography to create an especially tough challenge to those responsible for enterprise security. The two technologies are completely independent, and the use of one in no way dictates the use of the other. But we ask the reader to remember that wherever steganography is used, the security of the content will be enhanced by the use of cryptography.

Steganography Tools

Steganography tools are readily available and their simplicity has made it relatively easy for terrorists and other criminals to hide data in files (Schmidt, Bekkering, & Warkentin, 2004). There are several steganography tools that are publicly available, many of which are available over the Web at no cost. The interested reader is directed to http://www.jjtc.com/Steganography/toolmatrix.htm. This site, maintained by Neil F. Johnson, currently lists and describes more than 140 examples of steganographic software publicly available.

An easy-to-use but effective steganography tool is SpamMimic. SpamMimic can be used by anyone with access to the Web without even downloading any software. To disguise a message, one can visit http://spammimic.com/ and type a message. The website will then create a message that looks like spam, but actually contains the covert message. The primary advantage for the communicating parties is that spam is typically ignored by

Table 1. Examples of steganography tools

Tool	File types	Cost	Web address
Camouflage	Several	Free	http://www.downseek.com/download/5746.asp
Invisible Secrets v4.0	JPEG, PNG, BMP, HTML, and WAV	$39.95	http://www.stegoarchive.com/
SecurEngine 2.0	BMP, JPG, and TXT	Free	http://www.freewareseek.com
Camera/Shy	GIF, and Web pages	Free	http://sourceforge.net/projects/camerashy/
Stegdetect (XSteg)	Detects the presence of steganography in JPEG	Free	http://packages.debian.org/cgi-bin/download.pl
MP3Stego	MP3	Free	http://www.petitcolas.net/fabien/software/index.html

many authorities and their systems such as Echelon and Carnivore (Clark, 2001). The recipient of the "spam" can then visit spammimic.com to decode the message. Since the message is unique and no digital signatures are generated, signature-based spam filters will not block these messages beyond the level of the normal false-positive messages blocked by filters. On inspection, the encoded SpamMimic messages also appear very innocuous and lack "red flag" words such as Viagra, porn, prescriptions, cheap, and so forth. This makes classification of encoded messages based on keywords equally unlikely.

Another user-friendly steganography tool is called S-Tools, which is also publicly available at no cost. BMP, GIF, and WAV files can be used as "host" files for steganographically embedded (hidden) messages. The *graphical user interface* (GUI) of S-Tools makes it intuitive to hide files simply by dragging them over the host image window. For an added level of protection, S-Tools can also encrypt its hidden file prior to creating the new image.

Steganalysis: The Process of Detecting Hidden Messages

How can an intercepted artifact (data file, message, video stream, etc.) be evaluated to determine if an embedded hidden message is present? Detection of steganographic content is the counterpart of hiding information through steganography. Just as cryptographers are involved in both sides of the coin — developing more secure codes and cracking adversaries' codes — and just as virus authors and antivirus software vendors are engaged in a continuous struggle for dominance, so is the field of steganography characterized by two faces. Steganography is used by those hiding messages and also by those detecting hidden messages. Research in steganography focuses on developing new steganographic techniques, but it is also focused on detection and deciphering of stenographic content.

This process is termed steganalysis and is often explained in the terms of the "Prisoner's Dilemma." In this analogy, two prisoners, Alfred and Bob, attempt to send each other secret messages. Each secret message is hidden in an innocuous message carried and inspected by the warden. Different scenarios lead to different results. One scenario is the assumption that there has been the possibility of data exchange between the prisoners before imprisonment. If Alfred and Bob can communicate and exchange a key before imprisonment, the key can be used to hide the existence of the message, and separating the hidden message from the cover is only possible if the key is known to an interceptor. Of course, the presence of hidden information can still be suspected or detected, even if the actual message cannot be obtained.

An alternative scenario relates to the role of the warden. The warden may have a passive role where he only checks the cover message for hidden content, but does not actively change the cover message. The warden will deliver the message as long as he does not notice anything unusual about the cover message and/or discovers the presence of hidden content. In this case, the safety of the hidden message relies solely on its ability to remain hidden from detection. On the other hand, if the warden actively alters the cover message, even if only slightly, then he may potentially destroy the hidden message. In this case, the safety of the hidden message relies not only on its ability to remain hidden, but also in resistance to changes in the cover. For example, writing messages in invisible ink might escape the attention of the warden, but would not survive photocopying.

The Computer Security Student gets the Bad Guy

Brokerage houses, including the fictitious Bull Run Investments, are privy to a great deal of sensitive financial information before it is publicly reported. It is illegal for employees to use "insider information" to achieve financial gain for themselves. Further, it is illegal for brokerage employees to supply such information to family, friends, or others before that information is released to the public. Any such illegal release of information would constitute a major security threat to Bull Run Investments, and could jeopardize its future.

Shady Profit was a brokerage employee with a questionable past. The U.S. *Securities and Exchange Commission* (SEC) has been on the trail of Mr. Profit for quite some time. It seemed that nearly every time there was a corporate merger where Bull Run Investments was involved, Mr. Profit's girlfriend, Imma Rich, would purchase large quantities of the acquired company prior to the announcement, thereby profiting on the sale after the price increased.

An interesting pattern emerged where Ms. Rich would purchase the stock the morning that Mr. Profit got word of the merger. The SEC knew that Mr. Profit was not telling Ms. Rich the news in person because she worked across town and she was not allowed in the Bull Run Investments office. Furthermore, the SEC had a tap on Mr. Profit's phone and no insider information was given over the phone, so it started investigating Mr. Profit's e-mail. The messages sent to Ms. Rich appeared to be innocuous. There were standard joke e-mails, several personal messages planning lunch, and a few links to Web sites. Everything seemed legitimate — the jokes were just jokes, the personal messages didn't contain any merger information, and the links were to photographs of restaurants on Mr. Profit's Web site. It was not until Kari Catchum, the fresh college graduate at the SEC who had taken a class in computer security, investigated the photographs that the SEC was able to build a case against Mr. Profit.

As it turns out, as soon as Mr. Profit received word of a merger, he edited his Web site with Microsoft FrontPage. He modified an image file of a certain restaurant by adding a ciphertext message to it using S-Tools (a program used for steganography). He would then send an e-mail to Ms. Rich asking her to join him for lunch at a restaurant and include a link to the photograph of the restaurant on his Web site. Ms. Rich would then follow the link, find the photograph, use S-Tools to obtain the ciphertext hidden in the picture, and finally decode the ciphertext to plaintext using their agreed-upon algorithm. Armed with the decoded company name, Ms. Rich would then purchase the stock before the public had access to the news. It was a brilliant scheme until Ms. Catchum investigated the photographs using steganalysis methods.

Conclusion

Stenography can be used in business environments, well beyond the prevailing image of steganography as a tool for spies, criminals, and terrorists. Though steganography offers potential for legitimate and illegitimate purposes, the focus of *chief security officers* (CSOs) and other managers of IT security is naturally on the illicit uses who may threaten organizational resources. If disloyal employees might pass trade secrets to competitors via standard e-mail protocols, without any apparent wrongdoing, the enterprise's security is threatened. If international terrorists might embed a secret message within a legitimate video broadcast or Web site display, national security is endangered. Constant vigilance must be exercised in order to ensure that the enterprise perimeter is not violated through steganographic methods. The cat-and-mouse game is likely to continue, so highly-secure environments (military, competitive industries, etc.) are advised to ensure that their staffs includes individuals with training and responsibility for such analysis.

References

Anderson, R. J., & Petitcolas, F. A. P. (1998). On the limits of steganography. *IEEE Journal on Selected Areas in Communications, 16*(4), 474-481.

Bartlett, J. (2002, March 17). The ease of steganography and camouflage. *SANS Information Security Reading Room.* Retrieved October 29, 2003, from http://www.sans.org/rr/paper.php?id=762

Clark, E. (2001). A reason to love spam. *Network Magazine, 16*(20), 1.

Cole, E. (2003). *Hiding in plain sight: Steganography and the art of covert communication.* Indianapolis, IN: Wiley Publishing, Inc.

Johnson, N. F. (2003). *Steganography.* Retrieved December 15, 2004, from http://www.jjtc.com/stegdoc/steg1995.html

Jupitermedia Corporation. (2003). *Steganography.* Retrieved Aug. 31, 2003, from http://www.webopedia.com/TERM/S/steganography.html

Kessler, G. C. (2001). Steganography: Hiding data within data. Retrieved July 21, 2005, from http://www.garykessler.net/library/steganography.html

Moulin, P., & O'Sullivan, J. A. (2003). Information-theoretic analysis of information hiding. *IEEE Transactions on Information Theory, 49*(3), 563-593.

Schmidt, M. B., Bekkering, E., & Warkentin, M. (2004, April 14-16). On the illicit use of steganography and its detection, In *Proceedings of the 2004 ISOneWorld International Conference*, Las Vegas, NV (pp. 1-10).

Trithemius, J. (1606). *Steganographia.* Retrieved November 17, 2005, from http://www.esotericarchives.com/tritheim/stegano.htm

Chapter XIX

Designing Secure Data Warehouses

Rodolfo Villarroel, Universidad Católica del Maule, Chile

Eduardo Fernández-Medina, Universidad de Castilla-La Mancha, Spain

Juan Trujillo, Universidad de Alicante, Spain

Mario Piattini, Universidad de Castilla-La Mancha, Spain

Abstract

Organizations depend increasingly on information systems, which rely upon databases and data warehouses (DWs), which need increasingly more quality and security. Generally, we have to deal with sensitive information such as the diagnosis made on a patient or even personal beliefs or other sensitive data. Therefore, a final DW solution should consider the final users that can have access to certain specific information. Unfortunately, methodologies that incorporate security are based on an operational environment and not on an analytical one. Therefore, they do not include security into the multidimensional approaches to work with DWs. In this chapter, we present a comparison of six secure-systems design methodologies. Next, an extension of the UML that allows us to specify main security aspects in the multidimensional conceptual modeling is proposed, thereby allowing us to design secure DWs. Finally, we present how the conceptual model can be implemented with Oracle Label Security (OLS10g).

Introduction

The goal of information confidentiality is to ensure that users can only access information that they are allowed. In the case of *multidimensional* (MD) models, confidentiality is crucial, because very sensitive business information can be discovered by executing a simple query. Sometimes, MD databases and *data warehouses* (DWs) also store information regarding private or personal aspects of individuals; in such cases, confidentiality is redefined as privacy. Ensuring appropriate information privacy is a pressing concern for many businesses today, given privacy legislation such as the United States' HIPAA that regulates the privacy of personal health care information, Gramm-Leach-Bliley Act, Sarbanes-Oxley Act, and the *European Union*'s (EU) Safe Harbour Law.

Generally, information systems security is taken into consideration once the system has been built, is in operation, and security problems have already arisen. This kind of approach — called "penetrate and patch" — is being replaced by methodologies that introduce security in the systems development process. This is an important advance but, unfortunately, methodologies that incorporate security are based on an operational environment and not on an analytical one. If we tried to use the operational environment to process consistent, integrated, well-defined and time-dependent information for purposes of analysis and decision making, we would notice that data available from operational systems do not fulfil these requirements. To solve this problem, we must work in an analytical environment strongly supported by the use of multidimensional models to design a DW (Inmon, 2002).

Several papers deal with the importance of security in the software development process. Ghosh, Howell, and Whittaker (2002) state that security must influence all aspects of design, implementation and software tests. Hall and Chapman (2002) put forward ideas about how to build correct systems that fulfil not only normal requirements but also those pertaining to security. These ideas are based on the use of several formal techniques of requirement representation and a strong correction analysis of each stage. Nevertheless, security in databases and data warehouses is usually focused on secure data storage and not on their design. Thus, a methodology of data warehouse design based on the *Unified Modeling Language* (UML), with the addition of security aspects, would allow us to design DWs with the syntax and power of UML and with new security characteristics ready to be used whenever the application has security requirements that demand them. We present an extension of the UML (*profile*) that allows us to represent the main security information of the data and their constraints in the MD modeling at the conceptual level. The proposed extension is based on the *profile* presented by Luján-Mora, Trujillo, and Song (2002) for the conceptual MD modeling, because it allows us to consider main MD-modeling properties and it is based on the UML. We consider the multilevel security model but focus on considering aspects regarding *read* operations, because this is the most common operation for final user applications. This model allows us to classify both information and users into security classes and enforce mandatory access control. This approach makes it possible to implement the secure MD models with any of the *database management systems* (DBMS) that are able to implement multilevel databases, such as Oracle Label Security (Levinger, 2003) and DB2 Universal Database, UDB (Cota, 2004).

The remainder of this chapter is structured as follows: first, we will briefly analyse each one of the six methodologies that incorporate security into the stages of systems development. The next section summarizes the UML extension for secure data warehouses modeling. Then, we present how the conceptual model can be implemented with a concrete product Oracle*10g* Label Security (OLS*10g*). Finally, we present the main conclusions and introduce our future work.

General Description of Methodologies Incorporating Security

The proposals that will be analysed are as follows:

- MOMT: multilevel object-modeling technique (Marks, Sell, & Thuraisingham, 1996);

- UMLSec: secure systems development methodology using UML (Jürgens, 2002);

- Secure database design methodology (Fernandez-Medina & Piattini, 2003);

- A paradigm for adding security into information systems development method (Siponen, 2002);

- A methodology for secure software design (Fernández, 2004); and

- ADAPTed UML: A pragmatic approach to conceptual modeling of OLAP security (Priebe & Pernul, 2001).

We have chosen these six methodologies because the majority of them try to solve the problem of security (mainly confidentiality) from the earliest stages of information systems development, emphasize security modeling aspects, and use modeling languages that make the security design process easier.

Multilevel Object Modeling Technique

Marks, Sell, and Thuraisingham (1996) define *multilevel object-modeling technique* (MOMT) as a methodology to develop secure databases by extending *object-modeling technique* (OMT) in order to be able to design multilevel databases providing the elements with a security level and establishing interaction rules among the elements of the model. MOMT is mainly composed of three stages: the *analysis stage*, the *system design stage*, and the *object design stage*.

UMLSec

Jürgens (2002) offers a methodology to specify requirements regarding confidentiality and integrity in analysis models based on UML. This approach considers an UML extension to develop secure systems. In order to analyse security of a subsystem specification, the behaviour of the potential attacker is modeled; hence, specific types of attackers that can attack different parts of the system in a specific way are modeled.

Secure Database Design

Fernández-Medina and Piattini (2003) propose a methodology to design multilevel databases by integrating security in each one of the stages of the database life cycle. This methodology includes the following:

- a specification language of multilevel security constraints about the conceptual and logical models;

- a technique for the early gathering of multilevel security requirements;

- a technique to represent multilevel database conceptual models;

- a logical model to specify the different multilevel relationships, the metainformation of databases and constraints;

- a methodology based upon the *unified process*, with different stages that allow us to design multilevel databases; and

- a CASE tool that helps to automate multilevel databases analysis and design process.

A Paradigm for Adding Security into IS Development Methods

Siponen (2002) proposes a new paradigm for secure information systems that will help developers use and modify their existing methods as needed. The meta-method level of abstraction offers a perspective on *information systems* (IS) secure development that is in a constant state of emergence and change. Furthermore, developers recognize regularities or patterns in the way problem settings arise and methods emerge.

The author uses the following analytical process for discovering the patterns of security design elements. First, look across information systems software development and information systems security development methodologies in order to find common core concepts (subjects and objects). Second, surface the patterns in existing secure information systems methods resulting in four additional concepts: *security constraints, security classifications, abuse subjects and abuse scenarios*, and *security policy*. Finally, consult a panel of practitioners for comments about the patterns. This process led to a pattern with six elements. Additional elements can certainly be added to the meta-notation on an ad hoc basis as required.

A Methodology for Secure Software Design

The main idea in the proposed methodology of Fernández (2004) is that security principles should be applied at every development stage and that each stage can be tested for compliance with those principles. The secure software life cycle is as follows: *requirement* stage, *analysis* stage, *design* stage, and *implementation* stage.

- **Requirements stage:** From the use cases, we can determine the needed rights for each actor and thus apply a need-to-know policy. Since actors may correspond to roles, this is now a Role-Based Access Control (RBAC) model.

- **Analysis stage:** We can build a conceptual model where repeated applications of the authorization pattern realize the rights determined from use cases. Analysis patterns can be built with predefined authorizations according to the roles in their use cases.

- **Design stage:** Interfaces can be secured again applying the authorization pattern. Secure interfaces enforce authorizations when users interact with the system.

- **Implementation stage:** This stage requires reflecting the security constraints in the code defined for the application.

ADAPTed UML: A Pragmatic Approach to Conceptual Modeling of OLAP Security

A methodology and language for conceptual modeling of *online analytical processing* (OLAP) security is presented in Priebe and Pernul (2001) by creating a UML-based notation named ADAPTed UML (which uses ADAPT symbols as stereotypes). The security model for OLAP is based on the assumption of a central (administrator-based) security policy. They base the security model on an open-world policy (i.e., access to data is allowed unless explicitly denied) with negative authorization constraints. This corresponds to the open nature of OLAP systems. Also, the authors present a *multidimensional security constraint language* (MDSCL) that is based on *multidimensional expressions* (MDX) representation of the logical OLAP model used by Microsoft.

Summary of Each Methodology's Contributions

In Table 1, a synthesis of the contributions is shown, in security terms, made by each one of the analysed methodologies. It is very difficult to develop a methodology that

Table 1. Contributions made by each one of the analysed methodologies

	Modeling/ Development standard	Technologies	Access control type	Constraints specification	CASE tool support
MOMT	OMT	Databases	MAC	NO	NO
UMLSec	UML patterns	Information systems	MAC (multinivel)	-------	NO
Fernández-Medina & Piattini	UML unified process	Databases	MAC, DAC, RBAC	OSCL (OCL based)	YES
Siponen	---------	Information systems meta-methodology	-------	NO	NO
Fernández	UML patterns	Information systems	Access Matrix RBAC	He refers to OCL as a good solution	NO
ADAPTed UML	ADAPT UML	OLAP	RBAC	MDSCL (MDX-based)	NO

fulfils all criteria and comprises all security. If that methodology was developed, its complexity would diminish its success. Therefore, the solution would be a more complete approach in which techniques and models defined by the most accepted model standards were used. And, if these techniques and models could not be directly applied, they must be extended by integrating the necessary security aspects that, at present, are not covered by the analysed methodologies.

UML Extension for Secure Multidimensional Modeling

In this section, we sketch our UML extension (*profile*) to the conceptual MD modeling of data warehouses. Basically, we have reused the previous profile defined by Lujan-Mora, Trujillo, and Song (2002), which allows us to design DWs from a conceptual perspective, and we have added the required elements that we need to specify the security aspects. Based on Conallen (2000), we define as extension a set of tagged values, stereotypes, and constraints. The tagged values we have defined are applied to certain objects that are especially particular to MD modeling, allowing us to represent them in the same model and on the same diagrams that describe the rest of the system. These tagged values will represent the sensitivity information of the different objects of the MD modeling (fact class, dimension class, base class, attributes, etc.), and they will allow us to specify security constraints depending on this security information and on the values of the attributes of the model. A set of inherent constraints are specified in order to define well-formedness rules. The correct use of our extension is assured by the definition of constraints in both natural language and *Object-Constraint Language* (OCL).

Table 2. New stereotypes: Data types

Name	Base class	Description
Level	Enumeration	The type Level will be an ordered enumeration composed by all security levels that have been considered.
Levels	Primitive	The type Levels will be an interval of levels composed by a lower level and an upper level.
Role	Primitive	The type Role will represent the hierarchy of user roles that can be defined for the organization.
Compartment	Enumeration	The type Compartment is the enumeration composed by all user compartments that have been considered for the organization.
Privilege	Enumeration	The type Privilege will be an ordered enumeration composed of all the different privileges that have been considered.
Attempt	Enumeration	The type Attempt will be an ordered enumeration composed of all the different access attempts that have been considered.

First, we need the definition of some new data types (in this case, stereotypes) to be used in our tagged values definition (see Table 2). All the information surrounding these new stereotypes has to be defined for each MD model, depending on its confidentiality properties and on the number of users and complexity of the organization in which the MD model will be operative.

Next, we define the tagged values of the class, as follows:

(a)   **SecurityLevels:** Specifies the interval of possible security level values that an instance of this class can receive. Its type is Levels.

(b)   **SecurityRoles:** Specifies a set of user roles. Each role is the root of a subtree of the general user role hierarchy defined for the organization. Its type is Set(Role).

(c)   **Security-Compartments:** Specifies a set of compartments. All instances of this class can have the same user compartments or a subset of them. Its type is Set(Compartment).

(d)   **LogType:** Specifies whether the access has to be recorded: none, all access, only denied accesses, or only successful accesses. Its type is Attempt.

(e)   **LogCond:** Specifies the condition to fulfil so that the access attempt is registered. Its type is OCLExpression.

(f)   **Involved-Classes:** Specifies the classes that have to be involved in a query to be enforced in an exception. Its type is Set(OclType).

(g)   **ExceptSign:** Specifies if an exception permits (+) or denies (-) the access to instances of this class to a user or a group of users. Its type is {+, -}.

(h)   **ExceptPrivilege:** Specifies the privileges the user can receive or remove. Its type is Set(Privilege).

(i)   **ExceptCond:** Specifies the condition that users have to fulfil to be affected by this exception. Its type is OCLExpression.

Figure 1. Example of MD model with security information and constraints

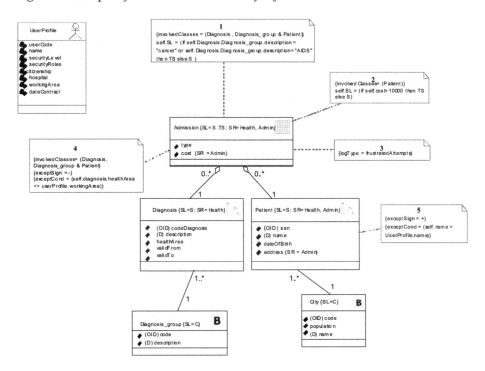

Figure 1 shows a MD model that includes a fact class (Admission) and two dimensions (Diagnosis and Patient). For example, Admission fact class — stereotype Fact — contains all individual admissions of patients in one or more hospitals and can be accessed by all users who have *secret* (S) or *top-secret* (TS) security labels — tagged-value *SecurityLevels* (SL) of classes, and play health or administrative roles — tagged-value *SecurityRoles* (SR) of classes. Note that the cost attribute can only be accessed by users who play administrative role — tagged-value SR of attributes.

Security constraints defined for stereotypes of classes (fact, dimension, and base) will be defined by using a UML note attached to the corresponding class instance. In this example:

1. The security level of each instance of *Admission* is defined by a security constraint specified in the model. If the value of the *description* attribute of the *Diagnosis_group* to which belongs the *diagnosis* that is related to the *Admission* is *cancer* or *AIDS*, the security level — tagged value *SL* — of this admission will be *top secret*, otherwise *secret*. This constraint is only applied if the user makes a query whose the information comes from the *Diagnosis* dimension or *Diagnosis_group* base classes, together with *Patient* dimension — tagged value

involvedClasses. Therefore, a user who has *secret* security level could obtain the number of patients with *cancer* for each city, but never if information of the *Patient* dimension appears in the query.

2.   The security level — tagged value *SL* — of each instance of *Admission* can also depend on the value of the *cost* attribute that indicates the price of the admission service. In this case, the constraint is only applicable for queries that contains information of the *Patient* dimension — tagged value *involvedClasses*.

3.   The tagged value *logType* has been defined for the *Admission* class, specifying the value *frustratedAttempts*. This tagged value specifies that the system has to record, for future audit, the situation in which a user tries to access information from this fact class, and the system denies it because of lack of permissions.

4.   For confidentiality reasons, we could deny access to admission information to users whose working area is different from the area of a particular admission instance. This is specified by another exception in the *Admission* fact class, considering tagged values *involvedClasses, exceptSign,* and *exceptCond.*

5.   Patients could be special users of the system. In this case, it could be possible that patients have access to their own information as patients (for instance, for querying their personal data). This constraint is specified by using the *excepSign* and *exceptCond* tagged values in the *Patient* class.

Implementing Secure DWs with OLS*10g*

In this section, we present some ideas with regard to how to implement secure DWs with OLS*10g*. We have chosen this model because it is part of one of the most important DBMSs that allows the implementation of label-based databases. Nevertheless, the match between DW conceptual model and OLS*10g* is not perfect. For instance, our general model considers security at the attribute level, and OLS*10g* only supports it at the row level (a coarser granularity access).

OLS*10g* is a component of version 10 of Oracle database management system that allows us to implement multilevel databases. OLS*10g* defines a combined access control mechanism, considering *mandatory access control* (MAC) by using the content of the labels, and *discretionary access control* (DAC), which is based on privileges. This combined access control imposes the rule that a user will only be entitled to access a particular row if he or she is authorized to do so by the DBMS, he or she has the necessary privileges, and the label of the user dominates the label of the row. Figure 2 represents this combined access control mechanism.

According to the particularities of OLS*10g*, the transformation between the conceptual DW model and this DBMS is as follows:

•   Definition of the DW schema. The structure of the DW that is composed by fact, dimension, and base classes, including fact attributes, descriptors, dimension

Figure 2. Access control mechanism

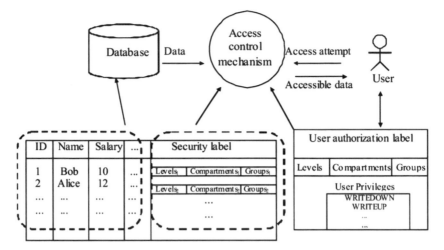

attributes, and aggregation, generalization and completeness associations, must be translated into a relational schema. This transformation is similar to the common transformation between conceptual and logical models (see Kimball, Reeves, Ross, & Thornthwaite, 1998).

- Adaptation of the new data types of the UML extension. All new data types (Level, Levels, Role, Compartment, Privilege, and Attempt) are perfectly supported by OLS10g.

- Adaptation of all tagged values that have been defined for the model. *Classes* are now represented as the set of tables of the database. *SecurityLevels, SecurityRoles,* and *SecurityCompartments* must be defined with the following sentences: CREATE_LEVEL, CREATE_GROUP, and CREATE_COMPARTMENT.

- Adaptation of all tagged values that have been defined for the classes:

  (a) *SecurityLevels, SecurityRoles,* and *SecurityCompartments* are grouped into the security label, with labeling functions. Labeling functions define the information of the security label according to the value of the columns of the row that is inserted or updated.

  (b) *LogType* and *LogCond* are grouped with auditing options.

  (c) InvolvedClasses, Except-Sign, ExceptPrivilege, and ExceptCond are grouped with SQL predicates.

- Adaptation of all tagged values that have been defined for the attributes. It is important to mention that, in this case, all security tagged values that are defined for each attribute in the conceptual model have to be discarded because OLS*10g* does not support security for attributes (only for rows). This is a limitation of OLS*10g* that has a complex solution, so if it is important to also have security for attributes, another secure DBMS should be chosen.

- Adaptation of security constraints is defined with labeling functions and SQL predicates. The application of labeling functions is very useful in order to define the security attributes of rows and to implement security constraints. Nevertheless, sometimes labeling functions are not enough, being necessary specifying more complex conditions. OLS*10g* provides the possibility of defining SQL predicates together with the security policies. Both labeling functions and SQL predicates will be especially important implementing secure DWs.

We could consider the *Admission* table. This table will have a special column that will store the security label for each instance. For each instance, this label will contain the security information that has been specified in the conceptual model in Figure 1 (Security *Level = Secret...TopSecret; SecurityRoles =Health, Admin*). But this security information depends on several security constraints that can be implemented by labeling functions. Figure 3 (a) shows an example by which we implement the security constraints. If the value of *Cost* column is greater than 10000 then the security label will be composed of *TopSecret* security level and *Health* and *Admin* user roles; otherwise, the security label will be composed of *Secret* security level and the same user roles. Figure 3 (b) shows how to link this labeling function with *Admission* table.

According to these transformation rules, the activities for building the secure DW with OLS*10g* are as follows:

- Definition of the DW scheme.
- Definition of the security policy and its default options. When we create a security policy, we have to specify the name of the policy, the name of the column that will store the labels, and finally other options of the policy. In this case, the name of the column that stores the sensitive information in each table, which is associated with the security policy, is *SecurityLabel*. The option *HIDE* indicates that the

Figure 3. Security constraints implemented by labeling functions

```
(a) CREATE FUNCTION Which_Cost (Cost: Integer) Return
     LBACSYS.LBAC_LABEL
    As MyLabel varchar2(80);
    Begin
    If Cost>10000 then MyLabel := 'TS::Health,Admin';  else MyLabel :=
       S::Health,Admin';
    end if;
    Return TO_LBAC_DATA_LABEL('MyPolicy', MyLabel);
    End;
(b) APPLY_TABLE_POLICY ('MyPolicy', 'Admission', 'Scheme', ,
    'Which_Cost')
```

column *SecurityLabel* will be hidden, so that users will not be able to see it in the tables. The option *CHECK_CONTROL* forces the system to check that the user has reading access when he or she introduces or modifies a row. The option *READ_CONTROL* causes the enforcement of the read access control algorithm for *SELECT*, *UPDATE* and *DELETE* operations. Finally, the option *WRITE_CONTROL* causes the enforcement of the write access control algorithm for *INSERT*, *DELETE* and *UPDATE* operations.

- Specification of the valid security information in the security policy.
- Creation of the authorized users and assignment of their authorization information.
- Definition of the security information for tables through labeling functions.
- Implementation of the security constraints through labeling functions.
- Implementation, if necessary, of the operations and control of their security.

Snapshots of Our Prototype from OLS*10g*

In this subsection, we provide snapshots to show how Oracle *10g* works with different secure rules that we have defined for our case study. All these snapshots are captured from the SQL Worksheet tool, a manager tool provided by Oracle to work with Oracle DBMS. Within this tool, we introduce the SQL sentences to be executed in the upper window, and in the lower window, we can see the corresponding answer provided by the server.

First, we have created the database scheme. Then, the security policy, the security information (levels and groups), the users, the labeling functions, the predicates, and the functions have been defined by means of the Oracle policy manager. Finally, in Table 3, we show some inserted rows that will allow us to show the benefits of our approach.

Although the SecurityLabel column is *hidden*, we have shown it for the Admission table, so that we can appreciate that the label for each row is correctly defined, according to the security information and constraints that have been specified in Figure 1.

For the sake of simplicity, we have defined only three users: Bob, who has a "topSecret" security level and who plays the "HospitalEmployee" role; Alice, who has a "Secret" security level and who plays an "Administrative" role; and James, who is a special user because he is a patient (so he will be able to access only his own information and nothing else).

In order to illustrate how the security specifications that we have defined in the conceptual MD modeling (Figure 1) are enforced in Oracle, we have considered two different scenarios. In the first, we have not implemented the necessary functions to enforce the security rule defined in Note 4 of Figure 1. As it can be observed in Figure 4, the first query, which is performed by Bob (who has a "topSecret" security level and "HospitalEmployee" role), shows all tuples in the database. On the other hand, the second query, performed by Alice (who has a "Secret" security level and an "Administrative" role), does not show the information of patients whose diagnosis is Cancer or AIDS (specified in Note 1 of Figure 1) or whose cost is greater than 10000 (specified in Note 2 of Figure 1).

Table 3. Rows inserted into the Admission, Patient, Diagnosis and UserProfile tables

ADMISSION				
TYPE	**COST**	**SSN**	**CODE DIAGNOSIS**	**SECURITY LABEL**
Primary	150000	12345678	S1.1	TS::HE, A
Secondary	180000	12345678	S1.2	TS::HE, A
Primary	8000	98765432	D1.1	S::HE, A
Primary	90000	98765432	C1.1	TS::HE, A
Primary	9000	12345678	D1.2	S::HE, A

PATIENT					
SSN	**NAME**	**DATE OF BIRTH**	**ADDRESS**	**CITY NAME**	**CITY POPULATION**
12345678	James Brooks	12/10/84	3956 North 46 Av.	Florida	15982378
98765432	Jane Ford	10/02/91	2005 Harrison Street	Florida	15982378

DIAGNOSIS					
CODE DIAGNOSIS	**DESCRIPTION**	**HEALTH AREA**	**VALID FROM**	**VALID TO**	**DIAGNOSIS GROUP**
C1.1	Skin Cancer	Dermatology	01/01/00	01/01/10	Cancer
C1.2	Cervical Cancer	Gynecology	12/10/04	12/10/14	Cancer
D1.1	Diabetes during pregnancy	Gynecology	07/11/03	01/11/13	Diabetes
D1.2	Other diabetes types	Endocrinology	12/12/00	12/12/10	Diabetes
S1.1	Symptomatic infection VIH	Internal medicine	10/11/00	10/11/10	AIDS
S1.2	AIDS related-complex	Internal medicine	11/11/01	11/11/11	AIDS

USERPROFILE					
USER CODE	**NAME**	**CITIZENSHIP**	**HOSPITAL**	**WORKING AREA**	**DATE CONTRACT**
P000100	James Brooks	Canadian	USA Medical Center		
H000001	Bob Harrison	United States	USA Medical Center	Gynecology	10/12/87
H000002	Alice Douglas	United States	USA Medical Center	Dermatology	11/11/80

In the second scenario, we have implemented the security rule that is defined in Note 4 of Figure 1. As we can observe in Figure 5, the first query, performed by Bob, shows all rows in which Note 4 of Figure 1 is fulfilled (that is to say, when the health area of the patient is the same than the working area of Bob). In the second query, performed by James, only his own information is shown (see Note 5 of Figure 1), hiding the patient information of other patients.

In conclusion, one of the key advantages of the overall approach presented here is that general and important secure rules for DWs that are specified by using our conceptual

Figure 4. First scenario

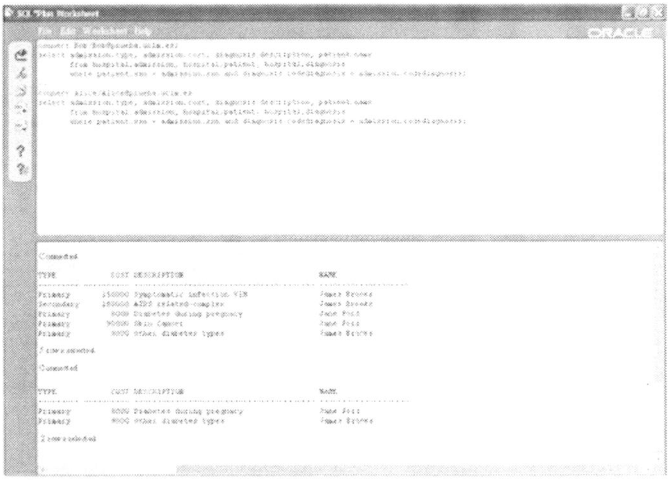

Figure 5. Second scenario

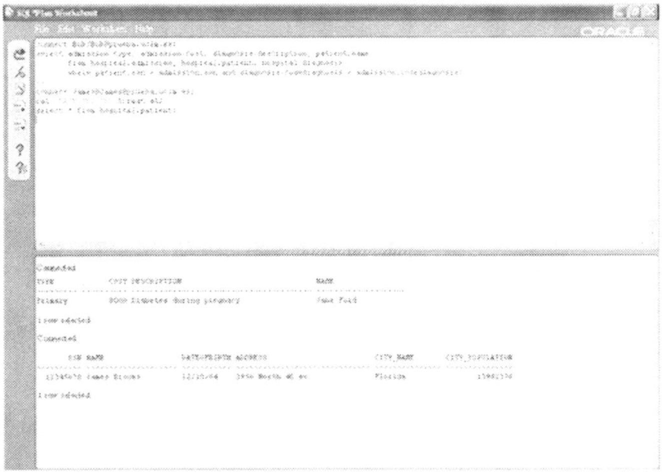

modeling approach can be directly implemented into a commercial DBMS such as Oracle *10g*. In this way, instead of having partially secure solutions for certain and specific non-authorized accesses, we deal with a complete and global approach for designing secure DWs from the first stages of a DW project. Finally, as we carry out the corresponding transformations through all stages of the design, we can be assured that the secure rules implemented into any DBMS correspond to the final user requirements captured in the conceptual modeling phase.

Conclusion

We have made a comparison of methodologies incorporating security in the development of their information systems in order to detect their limitations and to take them as a basis for the incorporation of the security in the uncovered aspects. In this way, we have put forward an extension based on UML as a solution to incorporate security in multidimensional modeling. Our approach, based on a widely accepted object-oriented modeling language, saves developers from learning a new model and its corresponding notations for specific MD modeling. Furthermore, the UML allows us to represent some MD properties that are hardly considered by other conceptual MD proposals. Considering that DWs, MD databases, and OLAP applications are used as very powerful mechanisms for discovering crucial business information in strategic decision-making processes, this provides interesting advances in improving the security of decision-support systems and protecting the sensitive information that these systems usually manage. We have also illustrated how to implement a secure MD model designed with our approach in a commercial DBMS. Our future work will focus on the development of a complete methodology based on UML and the Unified Process in order to develop secure DWs that grant information security and help us to comply with the existing legislation on data protection.

References

Conallen, J. (2000). *Building Web applications with UML*. Reading, MA: Addison-Wesley.

Cota, S. (2004). For certain eyes only. *DB2 Magazine, 9*(1), 40-45.

Fernández, E. B. (2004). A methodology for secure software design. The *2004 International Conference on Software Engineering Research and Practice (SERP'04)*, Las Vegas, Nevada.

Fernández-Medina, E., & Piattini, M. (2003, June 21-24). Designing secure database for OLS. In *Proceedings of Database and Expert Systems Applications: 14th International Conference (DEXA 2003)*, Prague, Czech Republic (pp. 130-136). Berlin: Springer-Verlag.

Ghosh, A., Howell, C., & Whittaker, J. (2002). Building software securely from the ground up. *IEEE Software, 19*(1), 14-16.

Hall, A., & Chapman, R. (2002). Correctness by construction: Developing a commercial secure system. *IEEE Software, 19*(1), 18-25.

Inmon, H. (2002). *Building the data warehouse*. New York: John Wiley & Sons.

Jürjens, J. (2002, October 4). UMLsec: Extending UML for secure systems development. In J. Jézéquel, H. Hussmann & S. Cook (Eds.), *Proceedings of UML 2002 - The Unified Modeling Language, Model Engineering, Concepts and Tools*, Dresden, Germany (pp. 412-425). Berlin: Springer-Verlag.

Kimball, R., Reeves, L., Ross, M., & Thornthwaite, W. (1998). *The data warehousing lifecycle toolkit*. New York: John Wiley & Sons.

Levinger, J. (2003). Oracle label security: Administrator's guide. Release 1 (10.1). Retrieved November 18, 2005, from http://www.oracle-10g-buch.de/oracle_10g_documentation/network.101/b10774.pdf

Luján-Mora, S., Trujillo, J., & Song, I. Y. (2002, September 30-October 4). Extending the UML for multidimensional modeling. In *Proceedings of 5th International Conference on the Unified Modeling Language (UML 2002)*, Dresden, Germany (pp. 290-304). Berlin: Springer-Verlag.

Marks, D., Sell, P., & Thuraisingham, B. (1996). MOMT: A multi-level object modeling technique for designing secure database applications. *Journal of Object-Oriented Programming, 9*(4), 22-29.

Priebe, T., & Pernul, G. (2001, November 27-30). A pragmatic approach to conceptual modeling of OLAP security. In *Proceedings of 20th International Conference on Conceptual Modeling (ER 2001),* Yokohama, Japan (pp. 311-324). Berlin: Springer-Verlag.

Siponen, M. (2002). Designing secure information systems and software (Academic Dissertation). Department of Information Processing Science. University of Oulo, Oulo, Finland.

Chapter XX

Digital Forensics

David A. Dampier, Mississippi State University, USA

A. Chris Bogen, United States Army Corps of Engineers,
Engineering Research & Development Center, USA

Abstract

This chapter introduces the field of digital forensics. It is intended as an overview to permit the reader to understand the concepts and to be able to procure the appropriate assistance should the need for digital forensics expertise arise. Digital forensics is the application of scientific techniques of discovery and exploitation to the problem of finding, verifying, preserving, and exploiting digital evidence for use in a court of law. It involves the use of hardware and software for finding evidence of criminal activity on digital media, either in a computer or in a network device, and attributing that evidence to a suspect for the purposes of conviction. Digital forensics can also be used for non-law enforcement purposes. Data recovery is a form of computer forensics used outside of the legal arena. The authors hope that the reader will understand some of the intricacies of digital forensics and be able to intelligently respond to incidents requiring a digital forensic response.

Introduction

While violent crimes such as armed robbery and murder are decreasing in the US, computer crime[1] is becoming more prevalent worldwide (Anderson, 2000; Householder, Houle, & Dougherty, 2002; Noblett, Pollit, & Presley, 2000; Wolfe, 2003). The growth of the Internet has contributed to an increase in cyber crimes such as child pornography, gambling, money laundering, financial scams, extortion, and sabotage (Bequai, 2002; Kessler & Schirling, 2002; Wolfe, 2003). From teenage network hackers (Gibson, 2002) and corporate executives to child pornographers and terrorists (Gordon, 2002; Quayle & Taylor, 2002), the computer has attracted a potpourri of potential offenders with various skills, motives, experiences, and nationalities.

In addition to using a computer in the commission of a crime, computer criminals share another similarity: the chances of their being caught, prosecuted, reported, and/or detected are relatively small (Householder, Houle, & Dougherty, 2002). In one example, a sheriff's department investigator working exclusively on computer crimes full-time for five years made only five arrests, none of which led to convictions (Thompson, 1999). Though the FBI has attempted to encourage businesses to report computer crimes against their infrastructures, law enforcement often seems to respond apathetically towards relatively small business victims (Gibson, 2002; Schultz, 2002). This may be due to a heavy backlog of computer forensics cases and the need to prioritize efforts to catch the higher profile criminals. Large businesses, on the other hand, are more likely to become victims of computer crime but may be reluctant to report computer crimes for fear that it would result in a lack of confidence among customers or stockholders. Many businesses are more interested in getting their systems running again than in determining who the culprit is or perhaps prosecuting the root cause of the problem (May, 2002).

While computer crime continues to increase, computer forensics analysts and technicians remain scarce (Kessler & Schirling, 2002). A shortage of qualified digital forensics personnel is an obvious cause of backlogs in handling digital forensics cases. However, there are also secondary contributing factors that are important to consider: the constant growth of digital storage media capacity (Alameda County, 2000; Anderson, 2000; Shannon, 2004), and the lack of standard technical methodologies for digital forensics (Carney & Rogers, 2004; Palmer, 2001). When searching for evidence on a 100 GB (or bigger) hard drive, it is going to take a large amount of time to do the analysis. It is no longer sufficient to rely upon ad hoc, best-guess keyword search techniques for finding evidence (Anderson, 2000). More intelligent and efficient ways to structure searches are needed to reduce the time necessary to conduct analyses.

The inexperience of local law enforcement agencies (with respect to digital forensics), lack of standard digital forensics methodologies, constantly increasing digital storage capacity, and the "hidden"[2] nature of computer crimes all contribute to what may be referred to as an emerging e-crime crisis.

Digital forensic science is an emerging scientific discipline defined by the First Annual Digital Forensics Research Workshop as (Palmer, 2001):

> *The use of scientifically derived and proven methods toward the preservation, collection, validation, identification, analysis, interpretation,*

documentation, and presentation of digital evidence derived from digital sources for the purposes of facilitating or furthering the reconstruction of events found to be criminal, or helping to anticipate unauthorized actions shown to be disruptive to planned operations.

Compared to traditional forms of forensic science, digital forensic science is not yet a mature scientific discipline. It is growing in maturity, but it does not yet exhibit all of the required characteristics of a scientific discipline: theory, abstractions and models, elements of practice, corpus of literature and professional practice, and confidence/trust in results (Palmer, 2001). This has caused some courts to question the validity of digital evidence. They do not allow what they do not understand and what cannot be backed up by scientific method. The theory behind digital forensic science can be categorized in scientific method. In digital forensic science, an investigator needs to define a hypothesis based on evidence gathered at the "scene" of the crime and other facts of the case. He or she then needs to develop research questions based on that hypothesis, and then search for answers to those questions in the evidence available. The answers will hopefully provide evidence that the hypothesis is correct. If methods and tools designed for digital forensics follow this scientific method, they will be more widely accepted in court cases. Some models of digital forensics have been developed and will be discussed in more detail later in this chapter, but these models are not yet sufficient to cover all aspects of the discipline. We will discuss the current state of practice in the next section, so will not discuss it here. As far as a corpus of literature and professional practice, efforts are underway to create these in the digital forensic science discipline but are not yet completed. A new *International Federation for Information Processing* (IFIP) Working Group on Digital Forensics was started in the last year and enjoyed its first annual conference in February 2005. Smaller, more focused committees were formed at this meeting that will begin to lay the foundations for the professional practice needed of this emerging discipline. The last area of concern in this list is that of confidence and trust in the discipline. This, we believe, relates to the ability for an expert witness to appear before a judge and jury and testify on digital forensics matters and have the testimony well understood. This is a matter of training. Judges need to be familiarized with the technology underlying digital forensic science — like mathematical hashing for authenticating images — and then they will begin to believe that the testimony of experts is based on true science. It is also a matter of experience. More and more cases are going to trial involving digital forensics matters, and this continued exposure will make the courts more comfortable with technology.

Digital forensics can be further divided into three major areas. Although these areas are not necessarily all-inclusive, they are sufficient to provide a foundation from which to discuss current technology. They are:

1. **Computer forensics:** Collecting, analyzing, and preserving evidence from digital storage media;

2. **Network forensics:** Collecting, analyzing, and preserving evidence that is spread throughout a network of computers; and

3. **Software forensics:** Determining the identity of the original author of a piece of software, malware, virus, malicious code, or the like.

This classification is not necessarily orthogonal. Much of the work done in network forensics and software forensics requires the use of techniques that might be classified as computer forensics. Computer forensics is the core of digital forensics, and any digital forensics investigation is likely to require finding evidence on digital media of some kind.

The remainder of this chapter discusses the current state of digital forensics practice, open research problems in digital forensics, current research in digital forensics, and future opportunities for computer forensics research. The chapter concludes with a summary and a listing of referenced materials.

Current State of Practice

Digital forensics started with investigators needing to find evidence of criminal activity on computers seized from drug dealers, embezzlers, counterfeiters, and other criminals. Computer crimes, such as child pornography and identity theft, were not yet widely practiced using computers, as most computers were very expensive and very large. The sophistication of personal computers 25 years ago was minimal and not many people had them. As a result, most investigators working in the area of digital forensics were paving new ground and did not have formal education in computer-related disciplines. They were, in fact, seasoned criminal investigators with a novice level of understanding of computers, at best. Investigators with little or no knowledge of how computers were constructed had to develop methods on their own to enable them to find evidence. Most of the existing tools and methods used in practice employ techniques developed by these investigators. Until less than 10 years ago, there was not a lot of sharing among these investigators, so the techniques currently in use are sometimes very different from one another. For example, tools developed and marketed by New Technologies, Inc. are all DOS-Based and are typically used in conjunction with a boot disk. Other tools like Encase[3] and Forensic Toolkit[4] are Windows-based and are not restricted to use with a boot disk. Additionally, there is a bevy of open-source toolkits available on the Internet for free download and use. Even with these available tools, there has been no real standardization of techniques employed. Only recently has the academic community become involved in the development of tools and technologies. Searching for literature today in digital forensics will confirm that the available literature is very new and very sparse. In 2000, the federal government sponsored the first Digital Forensics Research Workshop (Palmer, 2001), and in 2004, the first IFIP Working Group on Digital Forensics was formed. There are currently only two international journals dedicated to digital forensics, and they are both less than three years old. *Digital Investigation: The International Journal of Digital Evidence & Incident Response* is published by Elsevier, and released its first issue in February 2004. *The International Journal of Digital Evidence* is published in the United States and is currently in its second year of publication. This relative lack of published material provides evidence that the "home-grown" techniques developed by investigators in the field are still widely used by investigators today.

Catching Intruders

Discovering evidence that someone has broken in to your network or computer is not a difficult task. There are techniques readily available for detecting intrusions (Dampier & Vaughn, 2002). The difficult task is finding sufficient evidence to tie a particular criminal to those intrusions. Any intruders worth catching are likely to be intelligent enough not to leave evidence behind, at least not that is easily discovered. In 2004, Eoghan Casey discussed the need to install tools that will collect evidence of intrusions and better facilitate the prosecution of intruders (Casey, 2004). Unfortunately, there is not a problem in digital forensics that is more troublesome than network forensics and gathering enough evidence to support a conviction.

Encryption/Decryption

The exact extent of encryption use in computer crime is likely not known, but with the ready availability of encryption and decryption technology today, it should not be unexpected. Eric Freyssinet and Zeno Geradts (2004) state that the integration of encryption into Windows file systems will result in the wider use of encryption. Hank Wolfe (2004) discusses methodologies for penetrating encrypted evidence, and the first choice is still to get the suspect to give up the key. When the key is not available, the likelihood of retrieving the evidence decreases considerably. As encryption technology advances, this will only get worse.

Data Hiding

Data hiding is a technique used by individuals to make information inaccessible. In criminal investigations, data hiding would be used to make the evidence an investigator is searching for hard to find. Data hiding is not a new idea, however; it has been used for centuries and is as old as war. One of the first recorded examples, according to the Greek historian Herodotus, involves Demaratus, an exiled Greek living in Persia during the 5th century BCE. Demaratus warned the Greek city-states of an attack by melting the wax on a writing tablet, then carving his message into the wood of the tablet and restoring the wax. More details from this and other instances of ancient data hiding can be found in Singh (1999).

Data hiding is even more prevalent today because computers have made it easier. Now, vast amounts of data can be hidden electronically and carried in the palm of a hand. There are many techniques available for hiding data, and these techniques have become easy to obtain for anyone with a Web browser and a little understanding of the subject. One example can be found in Eric Cole's book (2001), *Hiding Data in Plain Sight*. Cole ran an experiment to determine how widespread hiding data in images — or "steganography" — had become. Out of 500 randomly downloaded images from eBay, he discovered 150 that contained hidden data. Data hiding has gained in popularity and is actually in use, so data hiding poses a serious challenge to anyone examining media for evidence.

In order to defeat data hiding, an investigator must be able to recognize the "symptoms" of a technique. An investigator must know the symptoms because the methods themselves have become too numerous and increasingly sophisticated as technology advances. Data can be hidden in almost any form. Techniques have been shown for hiding data in image files, sound files, or even executable files (Cole, 2001; Donovan, 2001; Petitcolas, 2003). Therefore, even if no evidence is immediately obvious, as long as files are visible on the disk, evidence could be hidden, and sometimes even when files are not visible. With so many techniques available to hide data, some classification is needed. Warren Kruse and Jay Heiser (2002) in their book *Computer Forensics: Incident Response Essentials* break down data hiding into three categories.

- **Obfuscating data** — Data is easily visible but not in a format that is readily readable. Encryption and compression are examples of obfuscation.

- **Hiding data** — Data is not visible, but the carrier file that contains it is. Steganography is an example of hiding data.

- **Blinding the investigator** — The data is not visible at all because the operating system has been modified to not display it.

When data is obfuscated, the data is easily seen, but it is obvious that data access is being restricted. One example of this would be where data is present and it is obviously visible, but it has been encrypted and cannot be easily read. Encryption has become very widespread, but most encryption technologies available today can be overcome in a very reasonable amount of time. Data that is hidden using a technique like steganography is not readily apparent, but the hider has left clues to its existence. It has already been shown that hiding data in pictures is an example of this technique. Hiding data in audio files is another example (Petitcolas, 2003). Eric Cole even describes a way to automatically hide data in executables (Cole, 2001). So, the presence of files on the computer can give clues to what hiding techniques are being used and what searching method to apply.

Blinding the investigator is a technique employed by rewriting operating system tools that would normally be used to view files. If, for example, the "My Computer" application in most Windows implementations were rewritten to not show any files with a particular character at the beginning of the filename, then, the person trying to hide the data would be able to hide their files by naming them something starting with that character. Although this discussion of data hiding is not extensive, the area of data or information hiding is a field of research that is very popular. A survey of current forensics literature will yield much more information about it. Unfortunately, space will not permit a more extensive discussion here.

Current Research

Process Frameworks

Process frameworks are popular in current digital forensics research. Digital forensics process frameworks have been proposed by members of the law enforcement community (AOPO, 2003; DOJ, 2001, 2002; SWDGE, 2000), the academic community (Ahmad, 2002; Carrier & Spafford, 2003; Reith, Carr, & Gunsch, 2002; Stephenson 2002), and the industrial community (Anderson, 2000). Collaborations between all of these digital forensics communities have also produced process frameworks such as that proposed at the *Digital Forensics Research Workshop* (DFRWS) (Palmer, 2001).

Process frameworks prescribe a sequence of tasks/activities that, when conducted, will yield a desired digital forensics goal or product. The features of a process framework should be determined by the goals of the investigation. Such goals may include identifying evidence for a legal proceeding, identifying and preventing network attacks, or gathering intelligence from digital sources in a combat zone.

The DFRWS process framework contains tasks and activities that are typical of most process frameworks: identification, preservation, collection, examination, analysis, presentation, and decision. Figure 1 provides an illustration of the process framework that resulted from the First Annual DFRWS (Palmer, 2001). Participants in the DFRWS continue to present enhancements to the DFRWS process model (Baryamureeba & Tushabe, 2004; Beebe & Clark, 2004), and the topic still sparks lively debate among the attendees at the workshop.

Readers who are interested in building digital forensics process frameworks could investigate the evolution of software engineering process frameworks starting with Roger Pressman's (2005) or Ian Sommerville's (2004) popular software engineering textbooks. Software engineering process frameworks continue to evolve as the needs of software projects continue to evolve. It is the opinion of the authors that software

Figure 1. Process framework that resulted from the First Annual DFRWS

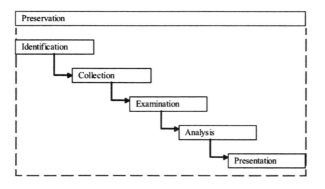

engineering provides a relevant source of lessons learned and inspiration for digital forensics process frameworks and for the general subject of digital forensics maturity; software engineering is still an emerging scientific discipline, and digital forensics is an even newer emerging scientific discipline.

Evidence and Investigation Modeling

Evidence and investigation modeling has the potential to provide the digital investigator with methods for expressing information and artifacts such as adversary strategy, a chain of events, experience/lessons learned, and investigation plans. Thus far, there has been very little published research in digital forensics evidence or investigation modeling. The motivation behind such research is to make the investigation more efficient and perhaps to provide a more formalized approach to digital investigations. The following paragraphs in this section provide highlights of research in evidence and investigation modeling.

Schneier's attack tree (1999) is perhaps the earliest digital forensics modeling technique published in the context of computer security/information assurance. Attack trees allow the investigator to model an adversary's potential attack methods. Figure 2 presents an illustration of the authors' application of Schneier's attack tree to computer forensics. Moore, Ellison, and Linger (2001) and Lowry, Rico, and Wood (2004) have also contributed novel techniques for modeling attacks and adversary resources and motivations.

Figure 3. An illustration of the authors' application of Schneier's attack tree to computer forensics

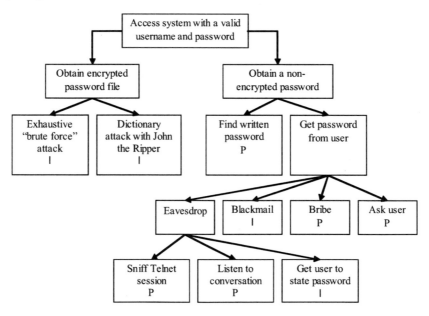

Figure 3. DIPL example

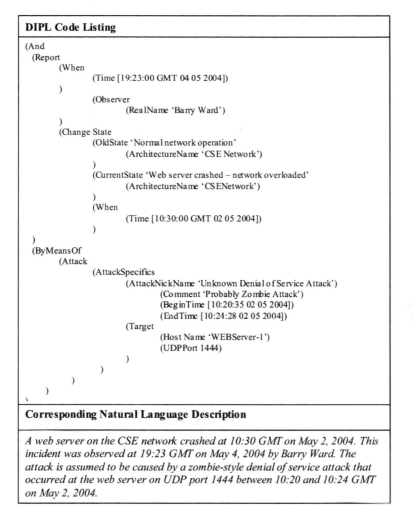

DIPL Code Listing

```
(And
  (Report
       (When
              (Time [19:23:00 GMT 04 05 2004])
       )
              (Observer
                     (RealName 'Barry Ward')
       )
       (Change State
              (OldState 'Normal network operation'
                     (ArchitectureName 'CSE Network')
              )
              (CurrentState 'Web server crashed – network overloaded'
                     (ArchitectureName 'CSENetwork')
              )
              (When
                     (Time [10:30:00 GMT 02 05 2004])
              )
  )
  (ByMeansOf
       (Attack
              (AttackSpecifics
                     (AttackNickName 'Unknown Denial of Service Attack')
                            (Comment 'Probably Zombie Attack')
                            (BeginTime [10:20:35 02 05 2004])
                            (EndTime [10:24:28 02 05 2004])
                     (Target
                            (Host Name 'WEBServer-1')
                            (UDPPort 1444)
                     )
              )
       )
  )
`
```

Corresponding Natural Language Description

A web server on the CSE network crashed at 10:30 GMT on May 2, 2004. This incident was observed at 19:23 GMT on May 4, 2004 by Barry Ward. The attack is assumed to be caused by a zombie-style denial of service attack that occurred at the web server on UDP port 1444 between 10:20 and 10:24 GMT on May 2, 2004.

Due to space constraints, the details of these modeling techniques are left to the reader to investigate. Peter Stephenson's proposed *digital investigation process language* (DIPL) promises to be a powerful but practical tool for expressing the chain of events that occur in a digital investigation (Stephenson 2003a, 2003b). Figure 3 presents an example of DIPL code with the corresponding natural language description.

Carney and Rogers (2004) have developed a statistical model for event reconstruction. Carney and Rogers' ultimate goal is to provide a standardized event reconstruction method that has measurable accuracy and significance. For example, if such a method existed, an expert witness may be able to claim that he/she is 99% sure that a suspect intentionally placed an illicit file on his/her suspect hard drive. Carney and Rogers illustrate how their preliminary statistical model works in the context of the preliminary scenario.

Bruschi and Monga (2004) propose a methodology for "archiving, retrieving, and reasoning about computer forensics knowledge." Bruschi and Monga's work is based on the assumption that common patterns exist in crimes that can be exploited to ease the work of investigators. They propose a hypothesis framework that accompanies the following investigative process followed by detectives:

> *Formulate a hypothesis on the state of the world that caused the case, collect evidence on the basis of these hypotheses, correlate actual evidence with hypotheses, and adjust hypotheses, and repeat the process until the consistency state of the knowledge about the case is sensibly high.*

Their framework is formalized by a mathematical definition.

The authors of this chapter (Dampier and Bogen) are also currently involved in computer forensics modeling research. First, they published their preliminary research goals (2004). Then, they published a paper describing case domain modeling (2005a), and most recently they published a paper describing a unified computer forensics modeling methodology (2005b). In the future, Bogen and Dampier will publish the results of experiments that will report on the utility of case domain modeling for planning and executing computer forensics examinations.

Software Forensics

Software forensics is typically concerned with identifying the author of a piece of computer software, a Web site, and even e-mail. Software forensics not only seeks to identify an author, but software forensics may also attempt to perform author discrimination, characterization, and intent analysis (Gray, Sallis, & MacDonnell, 1997).

Current software forensics research is limited, but this paragraph provides a couple of examples of significant research highlights. Gray et al. illustrate how document authorship analysis techniques may be applied to software forensics (1997). De Vel (2000) and de Vel, Anderson, Corney, and Mohay (2001) illustrate an application of data mining techniques for identifying and discriminating between e-mail authors.

Future Opportunities

The field of digital forensics is wide open for exploration. This field of research is new and immature and the potential for innovative new technology is great. The area of network forensics is likely the area with the most potential. If a technology were developed or discovered that enabled the efficient capture of potential evidence of unlawful intrusions, this technology would be extremely valuable.

Another area of great potential is the classification of images when searching for graphics files. The problem with current methods of matching hash values is that any change, even small, will change the hash value. If a technology were developed to enable matching images by their content as opposed to their hash values, this would likely increase the ability of prosecutors to introduce evidence in child pornography cases.

The introduction of the encrypted file system also poses additional new problems. Ways to overcome the encryption must be found, or hiding evidence will be as simple as deleting the key to the data, making prosecution of computer criminals very difficult.

Lastly, methods for very quickly making accurate images of digital media would also be very useful. Making images is very time consuming and likely contributes the major amount of time in the current backlog in criminal investigation and analysis of digital media.

Summary and Conclusion

Digital forensics is a relatively new tool in the investigator's arsenal of tools to deal with computer crime. Interest in this field has grown tremendously in the last couple of years, but there are still many areas worth investigating. Computer criminals are still very difficult to prosecute, and unless technologies are developed to allow more efficient investigation and analysis of digital evidence, the backlog of digital evidence will continue to grow. New groups like the IFIP Working Group on Digital Forensics and the Digital Forensics Research Workshop are beginning to tackle difficult-to-solve problems, and their solutions will significantly improve digital forensics practice.

References

Ahmad, A. (2002, September 2-4). The forensic chain-of-evidence model: Improving the process of evidence collection in incident handling procedures. Paper presented at the *Sixth Pacific Asia Conference on Information Systems*, Tokyo, Japan.

Alameda County (CA) District Attorney's Office. (2000). *Computer searches.* Retrieved July 1, 2004, from http://www.acgov.org/da/pov/documents/web.htm

Anderson, M. (2000). *Electronic fingerprints: Computer evidence comes of age.* Retrieved July 1, 2004, from http://www.forensics-intl.com/art2.html

Anderson, M. (2001). *Hard disk drives — Bigger is not better, increasing storage capacities, the computer forensics dilemma.* Retrieved July 1, 2004, from http://www.forensics-intl.com/art14.html

Association of Chief Police Officers (AOPO). (2003). *Good practice guide for computer-based electronic evidence.* Retrieved May 31, 2004, from http://www.acpo.police.uk/asp/policies/data/gpg_computer_based_evidence_v3.pdf

Baryamureeba, V., & Tushabe, F. (2004). *The enhanced digital investigation process model.* Retrieved January 11, 2005, from http://www.dfrws.org/2004/bios/day1/tushabe_EIDIP.pdf

Beebe, N. L., & Clark, J. G. (2004). *A hierarchical, objectives-based framework for the digital investigations process.* Retrieved January 11, 2005, from http://www.dfrws.org/2004/bios/day1/Beebe_Obj_Framework_for_DI.pdf

Bequai, A. (2002). Syndicated crime and international terrorism. *Computers and Security, 21*(4), 333-337.

Bogen, A. C., & Dampier, D. A. (2004, June 16-18). Knowledge discovery and experience modeling in computer forensics media analysis. Paper presented at the *International Symposium on Information and Communication Technologies*, Las Vegas, NV.

Bogen, A. C., & Dampier, D. A. (2005a, August 16-19). *Preparing for large-scale investigations with case domain modeling.* Presented at the Digital Forensics Workshop, New Orleans, LA. Retrieved from http://www.dfrws.org/2005/proceedings/bogen_domainmodel.pdf

Bogen, A. C., & Dampier, D. A. (2005b, November 7-9). Unifying computer forensics modeling approaches: A software engineering perspective. Presented at the *First International Workshop on Systematic Approaches to Digital Forensic Engineering,* Taipei, Taiwan (pp. 27-39).

Bruschi, D., & Monga, M. (2004, August 10-13). How to reuse knowledge about forensic investigations. Paper presented at the *Digital Forensics Research Workshop*, Linthicum, MD.

Carney, M., & Rogers, M. (2004, Spring). The Trojan made me do it: A first step in statistical-based computer forensics event reconstruction. *International Journal of Digital Evidence, 2*(4). Retrieved from http://www.ijde.org/docs/03_fall_carrier_spa.pdf

Carrier, B., & Spafford, E. (2003, Fall). Getting physical with the digital investigation process, *The International Journal of Digital Evidence, 2*(2). Retrieved from http://www.ijde.org/docs/03_fall_carrier_spa.pdf

Casey, E. (2004). Network traffic as a source of evidence: Tool strengths, weaknesses, and future needs. *Digital Investigation, 1*(1), 28-29.

Cole, E. (2001). *Hiding in plain sight: Steganography and the art of covert communication.* Indianapolis, IN: Wiley Publishing.

Dampier, D., & Vaughn, R. (2002, July). The use of intrusion detection in securing information assets. *World Market Series Business Briefing - Global Information Security,* 38-43.

de Vel, O. (2000, August 20-23). *Mining e-mail authorship.* Paper presented at the ACM International Conference on Knowledge Discovery and Data Mining, Text Mining Workshop, Boston.

de Vel, O., Anderson, A., Corney, M., & Mohay, G. (2001). Mining e-mail content for author identification forensics. *ACM SIGMOD Record, 30*(4), 55-64.

Donovan, A. (2001). Digital steganography: Hiding data within data. *IEEE Internet Computing, 5*(3), 75-80.

Freyssinet, E., & Geradts, Z. (2004). Future issues in forensic computing and an introduction to ENSFI. *Digital Investigation, 1*(2), 112-113.

Gibson, S. (2002). *The strange tale of the denial of service attacks against GRC.COM.* Retrieved May 31, 2004, from http://grc.com/dos/grcdos.htm

Gordon, S., & Ford, R. (2002). Cyberterrorism? *Computers and Security, 21*(7), 636-647.

Gray, A., Sallis, P., & MacDonell, S. (1997, September 4-7). *Software forensics: Extending authorship analysis techniques to computer programs.* Paper presented at the 3rd Biannual Conference of the International Association of Forensic Linguists, Durham, NC.

Householder, A., Houle, K., & Dougherty, C. (2002). Computer attack trends challenge Internet security. *Computer, 35*(4), 5-7.

Kessler, G., & Schirling, M. (2002). Computer forensics: Cracking the books, cracking the case. *Information Security*, 68-81.

Kruse, W., & Heiser, J. (2002). *Computer forensics: Incident response essentials.* Boston: Addison Wesley.

Lowry, J., Rico, V., & Wood, B. (2004, August 10-13). *Adversary modeling to develop forensic observables.* Paper presented at the Digital Forensics Research Workshop, Linthicum, MD.

May, C. (2002). Computer forensics: The Morse or Clouseau approach. *Computer Fraud and Security*, (11), 14-17.

Moore, A., Ellison, R., & Linger, R. (2001). *Attack modeling for information security and survivability.* Technical Note No. CMU/SEI-2001-TN-001. Pittsburgh, PA: Carnegie Mellon University.

Noblett, M., Pollit, M., & Presley, L. (2000). Recovering and examining computer forensic evidence. *Forensic Science Communications, 2*(4). Retrieved from http://www.fbi.gov/hq/lab/fsc/backissu/oct2000/computer.htm

Palmer, G. (Ed.). (2001, August 7-8). A road map for digital forensic research. *Proceedings of the First Digital Forensic Research Workshop,* Utica, NY. Technical Report No. DTR-T001-01. Retrieved from http://www.dfrws.org/2001/dfrws-rm-final.pdf

Petitcolas, F. (2003). *The information hiding homepage, digital watermarking and steganography.* Retrieved November 4, 2003, from http://www.cl.cam.ac.uk/~fapp2/steganography

Pressman, R. (2005). *Software engineering A practitioner's approach* (6th ed.). New York: McGraw Hill.

Quayle, E., & Taylor, M. (2002). Child pornography and the Internet: Perpetuating a cycle of abuse. *Deviant Behavior: An Interdisciplinary Journal, 23*, 331-361.

Reith, M., Carr, C., & Gunsch, G. (2002). An examination of digital forensics models. *International Journal of Digital Evidence, 1*(3). Retrieved from http://www.ijde.org/archives/02_fall_art2.html

Schneier, B. (1999). Attack trees. *Dr. Dobb's Journal, 24*(12), 21-29.

Schultz, E. (2002). The sorry state of law enforcement. *Computers and Security, 24*(4), 290-292.

Scientific Workgroup on Digital Evidence. (2000). Digital evidence: Standards and principles. *Forensic Science Communications, 2*(2). Retrieved from http://www.fbi.gov/hq/lab/fsc/backissu/april2000/swgde/htm

Shannon, M. (2004, Spring). Forensic relative strength scoring: ASCII and entropy scoring. *International Journal of Digital Evidence, 2*(4). Retrieved from http://www.ijde.org/docs/04_spring_shannon.pdf

Singh, S. (1999). *The code book: The evolution of secrecy from Mary, Queen of Scots to quantum cryptography.* New York: Doubleday.

Sommerville, I. (2004). *Software engineering* (7th ed.). New York: Addison Wesley.

Stephenson, P. (2002). End-to-end digital forensics. *Computer Fraud and Security,* (9), 17-19.

Stephenson, P. (2003a). Applying DIPL to an incident post-mortem. *Computer Fraud and Security,* (8), 17-20.

Stephenson, P. (Ed.). (2003b). *Using a formalized approach to digital investigation* (Vol. 1). New York: International Institute for Digital Forensic Studies & Elsvier Advanced Technology.

Thompson, R. (1999). Chasing after "petty" computer crime. *IEEE Potentials, 18*(1), 20-22.

United States Department of Justice, Office of Justice Programs.(DOJ)(2001). *Electronic crime scene investigation: A guide for first responders.* Washington, DC: U.S. Department of Justice.

United States Department of Justice, Office of Justice Programs, Computer Crime and Intellectual Property Section. (DOJ) (2002). *Search and seizure manual: Searching and seizing computers and obtaining electronic evidence in criminal investigations* (1.0 ed.). Washington, DC: U.S. Department of Justice.

Wolfe, H. (2003). Computer forensics. *Computers and Security, 22*(1), 26-28.

Wolfe, H. (2004). Penetrating encrypted evidence. *Digital Investigation, 1*(2), 102-105.

Endnotes

[1]   Encase is a registered trademark of Guidance Software, Inc.

[2]   Forensic Toolkit is a registered trademark of Access Data, Inc.

[3]   Computer crime is generally defined as a crime involving the use of a computer to commit a crime or a crime in which a computer is the victim of a crime.

[4]   Computer crime is hidden because a law enforcement officer is less likely to intercept a computer crime that is in progress. Conversely, other more visible crimes such as traffic violations, robbery, and assault are more likely to be intercepted by law enforcement officers.

Section V:

Authentication Issues

Chapter XXI

A Comparison of Authentication, Authorization and Auditing in Windows and Linux

Art Taylor, Rider University, USA

Lauren Eder, Rider University, USA

Abstract

With the rise of the Internet, computer systems appear to be more vulnerable than ever from security attacks. Much attention has been focused on the role of the network in security attacks, but it is ultimately the computer operating system that is compromised as a result of these attacks. The computer operating system represents the last line of defense in our security chain. This final layer of defense and its core defense mechanisms of authentication, authorization, and auditing deserve closer scrutiny and review. This chapter will provide an exploratory, descriptive, and evaluative discussion of these security features in the widely used Windows and Linux operating systems.

The Last Line of Defense:
The Operating System

The number of computer security incidents reported from various forms of attacks has increased significantly since the introduction of the Internet (CERT, 2005; Staniford, Paxson, & Weaver, 2002). Though it is clear that the introduction of the Internet coupled with the decreased cost of networking has helped to pave the way for attackers, the end result of most malicious attacks is the alteration of the host operating system. This alteration is often with the intent of propagating the malicious program and continuing the attack (virus, Trojan horse) or potentially damaging, stealing, or altering some content on the host machine (Yegneswaran, Barford, & Ullrich, 2003). While this type of attack may be aided by the ubiquitous network and security weaknesses therein, the attack could not be successful without ultimately compromising the host operating system. These threats cannot be addressed without concentrating on the security weaknesses in the operating system (Loscocco et al., 1998). Security weaknesses in host operating systems are, therefore, a major concern for the IT practitioner. If unwanted modification of the host system can be prevented, then the attack may be thwarted despite any weaknesses in the network that allows the attacker to contact the host machine.

There has been a distinction drawn in research between application security and operating system security. It has become increasingly clear, however, that such as distinction is academic and that, in practice, malicious programs and the individuals who create them make no such distinction. Malware such as Code Red exploited weaknesses in both application security and operating system security (Staniford, Paxson, & Weaver, 2002). What is required is an end-to-end solution, one that considers not only the distributed nature of the current computing environment and the network, but also the close relationship between the application program and the operating system (Howell & Kotz, 2000; Saltzer, Reed, & Clark, 1981; Thompson, 1984).

This chapter will examine the principles of security for the host operating system in a descriptive and exploratory manner. By understanding the security controls available at the operating system level and the security weaknesses in those systems, it is possible to understand how to better prevent attacks on these systems.

Operating systems and their underlying security mechanisms are clearly a varied landscape which, over time, can be quite fluid. For purposes of this discussion, the focus will be on two server operating systems: Microsoft Windows Server 2003 and Red Hat Linux ES Version 3. (These server operating systems are increasingly being deployed on desktops so this discussion also has some relevance for the desktop computing environment.) Rather than refer to specific versions of these operating systems, this chapter will use the terms Windows and Linux to refer to Windows Server 2003 and Red Hat Linux ES Version 3, respectively.

Operating System Security Architecture

Historically, the development of the electronic computer required the development of software to manage the operations of the computer. Over time, these programs matured into software that not only managed the jobs running on the computer, but also managed all of the resources on that computer. The resources managed included not only the memory and CPU, but also the disk, printers, and tape drives attached to the computer. Early computers operated in closed environments running single tasks executed in sequence. The introduction of time-sharing operating systems with multiple executing tasks sharing resources required the consideration of how to manage the resources of the computer relative to the processes using the computer. Butler Lampson (1974) detailed some of the basic principles of operating system protection. Initial computer security concerns had focused on protecting executing tasks or processes from each other. Lampson expanded on that with a broad definition of protection that involved all resources under control of the operating system: memory, CPU registers, files (disk resources), and password security. Lampson proposed protections to define access rights and objects and associated object-access lists. Under this paradigm, access to objects is enforced in relation to the protection domain of the user.

By definition, the purpose of the operating system is to control the resources available to the computer — disk, memory, and peripherals. The implementation of operating system protection occurs in both user-space (the code executed directly by the user) and the operating system kernel-space (the core components of the operating system). Both Linux and Windows implement final mediation of resource allocation in kernel-space

Table 1. Standard design for security systems

Principle	Description
least privilege	A user's security permissions should only be adequate for the task being performed.
economy of mechanism	The system must be sufficiently small and simple to allow verification and implementation.
complete mediation	Access to each object in the system must be checked by the operating system.
open design	The design of the system must be open to scrutiny by the community.
separation of privilege	A process that requires multiple security conditions to be satisfied is more reliable than a process that only requires one condition to be satisfied.
least common mechanism	The amount of security mechanism in use by more than one task should be minimized.
psychological acceptability	The human interface should be designed for ease-of-use so that excessive complexity does not hinder user acceptance of the security mechanism.
fail-safe defaults	System defaults should be restrictive such that the default is lack of access.

(Viega & Voas, 2000). Note that while the ultimate actual protection of resources is implemented in kernel-space, the applications requesting access to system resources are operating in user-space and are most likely implementing some protection mechanisms in their code. Thus, protection is implemented, either successfully or unsuccessfully, in both user-space and kernel-space. This implies that both user applications and operating system kernel design have an impact on the security of an operating system. Currently, there is some debate over whether it is best to implement security in application-space or kernel-space (Loscocco et al., 1998).

In order to be able to evaluate operating system security, some standard is needed. The standard for the design of secure systems was established by Saltzer and Schroeder (1975) in 1975 and remains relevant today. These basic principles are described in Table 1.

In modern operating systems, it is difficult to discern exactly where the operating system ends and application software begins. This is true for both the Windows and Linux operating systems. This becomes problematic for any discussion comparing the security features of these two operating systems (not the applications that run under them). For this reason, this discussion will focus on specific operating system functionality that pertains to security. This discussion will use a specific theoretical framework as identified by Lampson (2004). In this paper, Lampson discussed operating system security using a specific set of protective security features present in most modern operating systems: authentication, authorization, and auditing (termed the "gold standard" since they begin with *au*, the chemical symbol for gold) (see Figure 1). The definitions used by Lampson in his 2004 paper are provided below and will be the definitions used for the discussion presented in this chapter:

- **authentication** is the process of determining which security principal made a request;

- **authorizing** access is the process of determining who is trusted to perform specific operations on an operating system object; and

- **auditing** is the process of tracking system activity to determine which specific events occurred on the system as well as when they occurred.

Figure 1. Protective security features

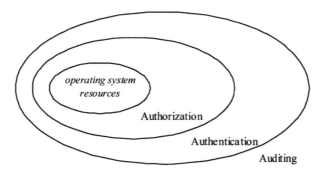

Apples to Oranges

Any assessment of Windows and Linux must take into account the institutional and developmental background of these two operating systems. The Windows operating system is a product of a business entity with specific organizational goals. Historically, Microsoft has used a business model that emphasized easy-to-use, feature-rich software that does not require a high level of technical skills to use. This composition of the Windows operating system is a direct result of the Microsoft business model. Windows server distributions bundle many software products together so that users do not have to deal with the technical issues of finding and installing compatible software (Microsoft, 2005a). The inclusion of *Active Directory* for network authentication is an example of this.

The composition of the Linux operating system reflects a different approach. Linux is a UNIX variant, a version of original UNIX developed at Bell Labs in New Jersey in 1971 for academic and research work (Ritchie, 1979). Linux was developed about 20 years after the original UNIX and is not a product owned by a single company. Its design is purposely sparse and modular. The core operating system component is the Linux kernel, and it is this kernel that is packaged with numerous open-source operating system utilities and programs to create the various Linux distributions available today. There is no overarching business strategy that influences the development of Linux distributions. This, combined with the fact that the business model under which Linux distribution vendors operate is new and volatile, has led to a varied landscape of Linux distributions. Though some Linux distributions are marketed as complete solutions, most Linux administrators will add a variety of additional software solutions to suit their environment.

This difference in the composition of operating system features has a direct bearing on making a valid "apples-to-apples" comparison of Windows and Linux security. Administrators for Windows installations often elect to use the security features packaged with the operating system (for example, Active Directory for network authentication), whereas Linux administrators will commonly piece together a comparable solution by installing separate programs (for example, installing Kerberos, a *lightweight directory access protocol* (LDAP) server and the MySQL database for a network authentication solution). Any assessment of authentication, authorization, and auditing security features between these two operating systems must consider this and discuss the security components commonly installed with Windows and commonly added to Linux installations in order to make a reasonable comparison. That is the approach used in this chapter.

Authentication

Authentication on both Windows and Linux commonly use password authentication. Though biometric devices are available that will easily integrate with both operating systems, the issues involved with using these applications and the simplicity and availability of password authentication make it the most widely used authentication method on both operating systems (Luis-Garcia, Alberola, Aghzout, & Ruiz-Alzola, 2003).

Windows Authentication

Authentication on Windows allows a user to login to either a local workstation or an NT domain that provides access to the resource of one or more Windows NT hosts. The login process involves the interaction of several operating system components. A login process requests the user name and password and interacts with the local security authority to request a security access token that contains the *security identifier* (SID) for the user. The *security account manager* (SAM) database contains user and group names, security identifiers, and passwords stored in encrypted form. The SAM database is stored in the Windows registry, but unlike other entries in the registry, it is not accessible by system users. When a user logs on to the local workstation, the local host registry is used. When a user logs on to a Windows network domain, the registry of the domain server contains the SAM file to be used for authentication.

The logon process and local security authority are processes that run in user-space. A security reference monitor is executed in kernel-space and is used to determine whether a user has permission to access a system object (WindowSecurity.com, 2002).

Authentication is started using a trusted path (Loscocco et al., 1998; Yee, 2002), a trusted communication channel between the user and the secure system that can only be initiated by the user. A user name and password prompt are displayed using the *graphical identification and authentication* (GINA) facility that can be substituted to provide a different form of authentication (for example, smartcards or fingerprint readers). The user then enters a user name and password, and the local security authority invokes the authentication package provided with Windows or may invoke a custom package to provide authentication.

The password provided by the user is converted to a cryptographic hash. The plain-text version of password entered by the user is discarded, and this cryptographic hash is compared to the cryptographic hash stored in the SAM database for the user being authenticated. If the entries match, then the security access token for that user is returned containing the security identifier for the user. The Windows security identifier uniquely recognizes every user and group on the local host or in the domain and determines authorization privileges throughout the system.

Logging in to a Windows domain uses a slightly different approach to the authentication process. Since a domain logon will most likely be performed over a network, a nonce (a unique number generated only once) is used to reduce the possibility of a replay attack to gain passwords for a system. This nonce is used to encrypt the password before sending it from the client to the domain server. As with the local login, if the encrypted password matches, the user is considered authenticated and the security access token for the user is returned (WindowSecurity.com, 2002).

An alternative network login facility known as *LAN manager* (LM) is supported in Windows for backwards compatibility. This login facility has a number of well-known weaknesses, and its use is not recommended. For the purposes of comparison, the more secure authentication method as described previously will be used.

Windows provides a runas utility that allows a user within a session to run a program as another user. The user using the runas utility must provide the user name and password of the user identity under which the program will run. Once the program is executed by the runas utility, it assumes the identify of the user name and password passed to the runas program and any programs executed by runas are run under the account (Microsoft, 2005b).

Linux Authentication

User authentication in the UNIX world has traditionally varied from implementation to implementation with a core set of authentication services usually available. This assessment will examine the basic authentication services provided with Linux and then examine the features and functionality provided through the facilities that are commonly used to extend basic UNIX authentication.

Linux basic authentication is performed using a login process that authenticates a user and provides a "shell" in which the user can then operate. The login process checks to see that logins are allowed and prompts for the user name. If the user is attempting to login as root, the login process restricts the login to specific terminals or locations. If the user is allowed to continue the process, the plain-text password entered and the salt value (a 12-bit random number) retrieved from the password file are added together, and the result is encrypted with DES or MD5 encryption (depending on how the system is configured). This encrypted value is then checked against the password file that stores the encrypted password. If a match is found, the user id and group id of the user are returned. Once the user has logged in, a user id and group id are associated with the user and are later used to determine accessibility rights for objects on the system (Bacic, 1991; Morris & Thompson, 1979).

Earlier Linux versions used a one-way DES encryption algorithm and stored the result along with a user name, user ID and group ID in a file readable by all users (/etc/passwd). It is still possible to do this in Linux, but an option to use a more secure MD5 encryption algorithm and store the results in a file readable only by the administrator (/etc/shadow) is available during installation and is recommended (Red Hat Linux, 2003b).

While early versions of Linux used the basic authentication services described in previous paragraphs, current installations commonly use the *pluggable authentication module* (PAM). PAM is a product of efforts by the former Open Software Foundation (currently the Open Group) to address shortcomings and variations in authentication, account management, and session management across UNIX variants. When PAM is installed, Linux uses an abstraction layer to communicate an authentication request to the PAM subsystem. The PAM subsystem then chooses one or more modules to perform the authentication (Samar & Schemers, 1995). A PAM module could be used to perform the work of the login process and also be used to encrypt and store user passwords. The substitution of these two modules in the standard version of Red Hat Linux allows the MD5 encryption algorithm to be substituted for the standard DES encryption (Red Hat Linux, 2003a).

The use of a PAM login module that supports lightweight directory access protocol is used in many Linux installations to allow network authentication to be performed using an LDAP server. The LDAP server is used to store the user names and passwords for an entire enterprise. This is an authentication approach similar to that of the Windows domain registration.

The Kerberos utility is commonly used with Linux to provide network domain authentication (http://www.web.mit.edu/Kerberos/www/). Using Kerberos, authentication realms can be established and inter-realm trust relationships can be configured.

Linux provides a utility named su that allows a user in a particular session to authenticate as a new user. This utility requires all users other than the root user to enter the password for the user identity they are trying to assume. A root user (the super-user or administrator of the Linux system) can use su to assume the identity of any user on the system without providing a password for that user. A user who has switched identities can then execute programs using the new identity.

Alternatively, a program can run with a set of privileges different from the set of privileges associated with the user without performing authentication as the user. This can be done by setting a specific file system identifier for the program being executed with the setuid bit. This feature has the effect of allowing a user executing a program to assume the identity of another user (the owner of the executable file that is the program) without authentication.

By default, non-root users — users who do not have super-user privileges — may shutdown the system. Configuration parameters in Linux can be changed to restrict this capability to a specific set of users.

Integration of Windows and Linux Authentication

It is not uncommon for large computer installations to use a combination of operating systems running several servers across a number of different hardware platforms. In these larger computing environments, there is a desire and a need to consolidate the large number of user ids and passwords into a central location. Users do not want to re-authenticate each time they need to access a different server. A *single-sign-on solution* (SSO) is desired, one that allows users to authenticate once and then use that authentication to access all the servers they need to access in a single session. At large sites with multiple platforms, this requires cross-platform authentication for Windows and Linux machines.

Network authentication for the two environments is commonly shared. A complete discussion of SSO and cross-platform authentication is beyond the scope of this chapter; however, a more in-depth discussion can found in Vacca (1994).

Windows provides domain authentication using Active Directory for storage of user information and Kerberos for the authentication protocol. Active directory is an LDAP implementation that has a modified schema to support additional information used in the Windows authentication process.

There are a variety of integration solutions for Windows and Linux authentication. Windows client applications can authenticate to a directory server other than Active Directory using the pGina replacement for GINA, or a Linux client can authenticate to an Active Directory server using a PAM module. These are common but not trivial solutions.

Software must be installed, configuration steps must be performed, and user account information must then be loaded to complete the integration (PGINA).

Authorization

Windows Authorization

Windows authorization involves a set of user and group identifiers for each user and group on the system. Objects on the system (files, directories, peripherals) have associated *access-control lists* (ACLs) that identify which users and groups can access an object. Actions permitted are reading, executing, writing, and deleting.

Authorization in Windows is enforced by the security reference monitor running in kernel-space. An access-control list identifies the users or groups that can access an object. The security reference monitor manages the request for the object by the program (on behalf of the user). First, the access denied entries in the list are checked and if any match the SID of the user requesting the resource, no other access-control list entries are checked and access is denied. Next, the access allowed entries are checked until enough entries are found to grant access to the object. If there are not enough entries found to grant access to the object, or there are no entries found then object access is denied (WindowSecurity.com, 2002).

An administrator account exists in Windows that provides a supreme (super-user) set of privileges. An administrator can set and change access-control lists, grant or deny user privileges, and access any object on the Windows system regardless of the access-control list entries for the object. Windows supports a number of different administrator accounts, each with different levels of authorization.

Windows also provides access-control facilities to perform certain system actions such as system shutdown or backup. These are referred to as user rights and can be assigned to specific users (Microsoft, 2005b).

Multiple Security Domains

Within Windows, domain-security models from multiple domains can be combined to provide a scalable, flexible solution to managing security across multiple servers and organizational departments. In many cases, users who have been authenticated in one domain need to use resources in another domain. This requires one domain to trust another domain's users with what is known as inter-domain trust. This trust relationship can optionally be transitive or intransitive. It can also be one-way or reciprocal, and hierarchies of trust can be established (WindowSecurity.com, 2002).

Linux Authorization

By default, Linux uses a discretionary access control approach to authorization. Authorization privileges can be read, write, execute. The objects under the control of the operating system are files, directories, and special files that provide access to device drivers (Bacic, 1991; Ritchie, 1979).

When a program attempts to access an object in Linux, a system call is made that requests that the kernel return a handle (reference) to the object. The request specifies an operation as read, write or execute for the object. The ability to delete an object is implied by the write permission.

When an object-access request has been made, the kernel first checks to determine whether the user has permissions to use the object (which in this case would mean the user owned the file). If user permissions on the file match the user permissions of the program requesting the object, then the kernel will move to the next step. In this step, the privilege type for the user is evaluated. If the privilege type on the object is suitable for the operation being requested, the object handle is returned to the object. If no user permissions on the file are found to match the user requesting the object, then group permissions are checked. If the group identifier for the user matches that of the file, then the next step is to determine which access privilege will be used. If no suitable access privileges are found that satisfy the access being requested, the program is not permitted to use the object.

If the user permissions are not found, then the kernel checks to see that the privilege permissions on the object are suitable for the operation being requested. At that point, the group permissions are checked. If no match is found for group permissions or user permissions, the program or user is denied access to the file (Bacic, 1991).

Linux Security Modules

In response to heightened security concerns and a Linux user-base that is expanding to larger mission-critical operations, there has been an effort to provide extensible and flexible security features in Linux without having the operating system kernel source code fracture into numerous variants. The Linux security module was designed to provide a lightweight, general purpose, access-control framework that supports kernel-space mediation of object access (Wright, Cowan, Morris, & Kroah-Hartman, 2002). *Linux security modules* (LSM) provide a pluggable architecture for the enforcement of security authorization by the kernel. A strict, finely grained authorization model can be substituted using an LSM module, or a less-restrictive, discretionary access model could be used instead by using a different LSM module.

Security-enhanced Linux (SELinux), which will be available in the next version of Red Hat Linux, provides *mandatory access control* (MAC) and role-based access control using LSM. MAC allows a finely grained set of permissions to be defined for subjects (users, programs, and processes) and objects (files, devices). This allows an administrator to grant an application with only the permissions needed to perform its task (Karsten, 2004).

Auditing

Windows Auditing

Windows optionally maintains an audit trail of a number of events that occur on the system. This logging can include both successful and unsuccessful attempts that concern the resources of the system. Events logged can be system logon and logoff, object access, changes to account policies, and system startup and shutdown. Finely grained access of disk resources is also possible.

Linux Auditing

Linux provides logging for various programs running on the system. Failed login attempts and other pertinent security events are logged, but the administration and configuration of the audit trail for these events is not completely centralized and is dependent on the program being used.

Assessment and Comparison of Security Features

Based on the previous evaluative discussion, the following section provides an assessment of the two operating systems presented in this chapter. The principles identified by Saltzer and Schroeder (1975) will be used as a framework for this evaluation in combination with other relevant security principles which apply.

Authentication

In terms of the principle of economy of design, both Windows and Linux provide adequate approaches to authentication. Both Windows and Linux depend primarily on user accounts and passwords to authenticate system users. Both provide the means to substitute an alternative authentication method, Linux using PAM modules and Windows allowing PGINA substitution. Windows does provide a trusted path to authentication. Currently, Linux does not provide a similar feature.

In evaluating the default password authentication methods of Linus and Windows, the use of password encryption does differ between the two. Linux uses a password salt, a random value generated and added to the user's password before encryption. This increases the difficulty of guessing the password with a brute force attack. Windows does not use a password encryption salt, which, combined with other weaknesses, has led to some well-publicized concerns about the ease of cracking Windows passwords (Lemos, 2003).

Considering the principle of psychological acceptability of the authentication process, using Active Directory, the Windows network authentication scheme is more robust and flexible, making administration easier. Though there are incompatibility issues with using Linux and Windows network authentication together, these incompatibilities are not insurmountable and are not severe enough to change this assessment.

With regard to fail-safe defaults, both Windows and Linux provide installation default accounts but, unlike previous versions of both operating systems, they no longer use default passwords. Passwords are chosen during installation, and if password best practices are followed, an acceptable level of authentication security should be maintained. Altogether, this provides an acceptable level of fail-safe defaults for authentication.

It is important to note that accountability should be managed appropriately under authentication and authorization. For example, general shared user accounts should be limited and discouraged since a user account shared among multiple users does not provide accountability for the actions performed by a particular user account on the system (since it could be one of many users). In Windows, the "guest" account is commonly used as a shared account and is now disabled by default. In Linux, the "nobody" account is commonly used by a number of programs, but login is disabled by default.

Authorization

By default, the security authorization (access) facilities of Windows are more robust and finely grained. Windows allows access-control lists to be established for objects in the system based on user accounts or groups. Linux default authorization uses discretionary access control that can limit access to objects to a single user ID. Groups of user IDs cannot be added to an ACL to allow or prohibit access as can be done with Windows. Users could be added to groups and groups' permissions set on the objects to achieve a similar result in Linux. The introduction of SELinux with MAC provides an access-control facility that is more flexible than that provided currently in Linux or Windows. However, MAC is a double-edged sword — the level of administration required to effectively manage MAC could have a detrimental impact on the psychological acceptability of this security feature.

Regarding the principle of complete mediation, both Windows and Linux check the permissions of objects in kernel-space. Mediation is thorough and complete in both operating systems.

An evaluation of the principle of least privilege raises concern with both operating systems. According to Saltzer and Schroeder (1975, p. 7), "Every program and every user of the system should operate using the least set of privileges to complete the job." Compliance with this principle is troublesome in a large part because of the history of each operating system.

Windows legacy environment (DOS, Windows 95) is that of a single-user computer not necessarily connected to the network, where any security that existed was implemented largely through physical security mechanisms (a lock on the computer, the computer in a locked office, etc.). No authentication or authorization facilities existed in the basic operating system. If an individual had access to the computer, the user had access to all components of the computer. Thus, programs operating in this environment had complete and unfettered access to virtually all objects under control of the operating system. By nature of this design, programs running in this legacy Windows environment violated the principle of least privilege.

For business policy reasons, Microsoft has long been committed to providing backwards compatibility with legacy applications. Consequently, in order to run some legacy applications in a Windows environment that supports access privileges, programs must operate with administration privileges, privileges in excess of "what is needed to complete the job" (Saltzer and Schroeder, 1975, p. 6).

Linux provides the ability for a program to assume rights in excess of what the user running the program has available. Whether or not using this feature is required would need to be evaluated for each application. In cases where such a change in application permissions is merely a matter of administrative convenience, the security principal of separation of privilege is being compromised.

Linux provides a super-user account known as the root account, which has access rights and control over all objects on the operating system. The existence of this account violates the principle of least privilege since the actions performed using this account rarely require complete and unfettered access to operating system resources. For example, administration of the printer queue does not require the ability to delete all files on the system as the root account allows.

Windows provides a similar set of capabilities with the administrator account but provides the ability to create other accounts that have some but not all of the administrator account privileges. Using this capability, administrative accounts could be established with various gradations of security required for administrative tasks (for example, a backup account to perform backups, a network account to perform network maintenance, etc.). The use of these limited administrative accounts is more aligned with the principal of least privilege.

Both the Linux root account and the Windows administrator account exist largely for convenience reasons. The Linux operating system is derived from the UNIX operating system that began in an academic research environment where access security was not a major concern. As UNIX matured, however, it quickly became a "best practices" standard to severely limit the use of the root account when running UNIX. For this reason, few legacy applications running on Linux use root account privileges, and it continues to be widely discouraged.

The ubiquitous buffer overflow attack has been used extensively on Windows platforms over the past five years (Microsoft, 2003; Yegneswarean et al., 2003). This attack involves exploiting memory bounds within a program (usually a network program) and loading the overrun memory with a different program (Bates, 2004). Once the new program is loaded, the program that has been exploited executes the new program code that has been loaded into the overrun buffer. That these exploits are possible is due in part to programming flaws in the application being exploited, but that these exploits are able to perform malicious activities on the operating system being attacked is due to an inadequate least privilege implementation on the host operating system. Installation of software should be an administrative function on any operating system. In most cases, a Windows application that is able to install software on the host operating system is the result of an exploited program that should have been limited from installing such software (CERT, 2001). Such exploits are rare on Linux and even when they do occur, the exploit does not always achieve root access permissions and are thus limited in the amount of malicious activity that can be performed on the system (CERT, 2003).

Auditing

According to Lampson (2004, p. 45), security depends "more on punishment than on locks." This implies that our security environments must enable us to catch the attackers and ultimately punish them. To make this happen, good audit techniques must be in place. Logging is the foundation of good auditing. Both Windows and Linux have good logging capabilities, though user-friendly centralized administration makes the Windows version more psychologically acceptable.

More sophisticated audit-support features are not part of either operating system. Given that most attacks occur via the network interface, an optional network logging capability would be useful but is not currently part of the basic Windows or Linux operating system. A host-based *intrusion detection system* (IDS) would provide monitoring of critical system files (libraries, logs, etc.), logging of the network activity in the event a network attack is detected and monitoring and logging of network port activity.

Summary and Conclusion

Both Windows and Linux have advantages and disadvantages in relation to their authentication, authorization, and auditing capabilities. Neither has any significant disadvantage and both provide an acceptable level of security for these protection mechanisms. Nevertheless, it is still worth identifying the more significant security issues that exist in both operating systems and how they might be mitigated.

Password protection is currently the primary source of authentication in both Windows and Linux though it is known to have limitations (Weirich & Sasse, 2001). The Linux password encryption scheme is more effective than Windows but is still not completely resistant to discovery. Both authentication models are modular and provide for substitution of an alternative authentication scheme. For example, a biometric scheme based on iris scans or fingerprints could be used to improve security (see Luis-Garcia et al., 2003).

The Windows Active Directory has become the prevalent form of enterprise-level authentication. Though the trust scheme is robust and flexible, the password authentication issues at the domain-authentication server remain. Linux with Kerberos, LDAP, and Samba offers an alternative, though the flexibility and non-trivial installation and configuration represent issues. The breadth and depth of Microsoft product usage in the current computing environment means that integration with Active Directory for network authentication must be managed across a variety of operating system desktops.

Malicious software running in user-space is the most common cause of security exploits. Despite efforts to improve application software security, failures continue to plague the computing environment. Mandatory access controls provide a higher level of security that could mitigate weaknesses in application security that exist and will likely continue to exist in the near term (Loscocco et al., 1998).

This chapter has highlighted and contrasted the implementation of key operating system security features against a framework of essential security principles. Operating system developers must constantly balance the development and improvement of these security features with other software development issues such as usability and legacy compatibility. Over time, these efforts should lead to increasingly more secure computing environments to meet the demands of our connected computing environment.

References

Bacic, E. M. (1991). *UNIX & Security* [Online]. Canadian System Security Centre, Communications Security Establishment. Retrieved January 7, 2005, from http://andercheran.aiind.upv.es/toni/UNIX/UNIX_and_Security.ps.gz

Bates, R. (2004). Buffer overrun madness. *ACM Queue, 2*(3), 12-14.

CERT (2001). *Incident Note IN-2001-09, Code Red II: Another worm exploiting buffer overflow in IIS indexing service DLL*. Retrieved December 20, 2004, from http://www.cert.org/incident_notes/IN-2001-09.html

CERT. (2003). Vulnerability Note VU#596387, Icecast vulnerable to buffer overflow via long GET request. *US-CERT Vulnerability Notes Database*. Retrieved January 4, 2005, from http://www.kb.cert.org/vuls/id/596387

CERT. (2005). CERT/CC Statistics 1988-2005. CERT® Coordination Center, Carnegie Mellon University. Retrieved January 7, 2005, from http://www.cert.org/stats/cert_stats.html

Howell, J., & Kotz, D. (2000, October 22-25). End-to-end authorization. In *Proceedings of the 4th Symposium on Operating Systems Design and Implementation,* San Diego (pp. 151-164).

Karsten, W. (2004). *Fedora Core 2, SELinux FAQ*. Retrieved January 5, 2005, from http://fedora.redhat.com/docs/selinux-faq-fc2/index.html#id3176332

Lampson, B. W. (1974). Protection. *SIGOPS Operating System Review, 8,* 18-24.

Lampson, B. W. (2004). Computer security in the real world. *IEEE Computer, 37,* 37-46.

Lemos, R. (2003). Cracking Windows passwords in seconds. ZDNET News.com., July 22, 2003. Retrieved July 22, 2003, from http://news.zdnet.com/2100-1009_22-5053063.html

Loscocco, P. A., Smalley, S. D., Mucklebauer, P. A., Taylor, R. C., Turner, S. J., & Farrell, J. F. (1998, October 6-9). The inevitability of failure: The flawed assumption of security in modern computing environments. In *Proceedings of the 21ˢᵗ National Information Systems,* Crystal City, VA. Gaithersburg, MD: NIST.

Luis-Garcia, R., Alberola, C., Aghzout, O., & Ruiz-Alzola, J. (2003). Biometric identification systems. *Signal Process, 83*, 2539-2557.

Marson, I. (2004, October 26). Munich's Linux plans attract international attention. *ZDNet.* Retrieved January 7, 2005, from http://news.zdnet.co.uk/software/applications/0,39020384,39171380,00.htm

Microsoft. (2003). *Security Bulletin MS03-026, Buffer overrun in RPC interface could allow code execution (823980).* September 10 revision. Retrieved January 7, 2005, from http://www.microsoft.com/technet/security/bulletin/MS03-026.mspx

Microsoft. (2005a). *Product Information: Windows Server 2003.* Retrieved April 22, 2005, from http://www.microsoft.com/windowsserver2003/evaluation/features/default.mspx

Microsoft. (2005b). Windows Server 2003 TechNet: Using runas. Retrieved March 22, 2005, from http://www.microsoft.com/resources/documentation/WindowsServ/2003/standard/proddocs/en-us/Default.asp?url=/resources/documentation/windowsserv/2003/standard/proddocs/en-us/AD_runas.asp

Morris, R., & Thompson, K. (1979). Password security: A case history. *Communications of the ACM, 2*, 594-597.

Red Hat Linux. (2003a). *Red Hat Linux reference guide,* Chapter 15, Pluggable authentication modules (PAM). Retrieved January 6, 2005, from http://www.redhat.com/docs/manuals/enterprise/RHEL-3-Manual/ref-guide/ch-pam.html

Red Hat Linux. (2003b). *Red Hat Linux reference guide,* Chapter 6, Users & Groups, 6.5: Shadow Passwords. Retrieved January 6, 2005, from http://www.redhat.com/docs/manuals/linux/RHL-9-Manual/ref-guide/s1-users-groups-shadow-utilities.html

Ritchie, D. M. (1979). On the security of UNIX. *UNIX Documents, 2.* Bell Laboratories.

Ritchie, D. M., & Thompson, K. (1978). The UNIX time-sharing system. *The Bell System Technical Journal, 57*, 1905-1920.

Saltzer, J. H., Reed, D. P., & Clark, D. D. (1984). End-to-end arguments in system design. *ACM Transactions on Computer Systems, 2*, 277-288.

Saltzer, J. H., & Schroeder, M. D. (1975). The protection of information in computer systems. In *Proceedings of the IEEE, 63*, 1278-1308.

Samar, V., & Schemers, R. (1995, March 14-16). *Unified login with pluggable authentication modules (PAM).* The 3rd Annual ACM Conference on Communications Security. New Delhi, India: ACM.

Staniford, S., Paxson, V., & Weaver, N. (2002, August 5-9). How to own the Internet in your spare time. In *Proceedings of the 11ᵗʰ Usenix Security Symposium,* San Francisco (pp. 149-167).

Thompson, K. (1984). Reflections on trusting trust. *Communications of the ACM, 27*, 761-763.

Vacca, J. R. (1994). Sign on to streamlined security. *Datamation, 40, 18, 65-6.*

Viega, J., & Voas, J. (2000). The pros and cons of UNIX and Windows security policies. *IT Professional, 2,* 40-45.

Weirich, D., & Sasse, M. A. (2001). Pretty good persuasion: A first step towards effective password security in the real world . In *Proceedings of the 2001 Workshop on New Security Paradigms* (pp.137-143). Cloudcroft, NM: ACM Press.

WindowSecurity.com. (2002, October 16). Network strategy report: Windows NT security. Retrieved on January 5, 2005, from http://www.secinf.net/windows_security/Network_Strategy_Report_Windows_NT_Security.html

Wright, C., Cowan, C., Morris, J., Smalley, S., & Kroah-Hartman, G. (2002, August 5-9). Linux security modules: General security support for the Linux kernel. In *Proceedings of Usenix 2002,* Berkeley, CA (pp. 17-31).

Yee, K. (2002, December 9-12). User interaction design for secure systems. *Proceedings of the 4th International Conference on Communication Security* (pp. 278-290).

Yegneswaran, V., Barford, P., & Ullrich, J. (2003). Internet intrusions: Global characteristics and prevalence. In *Proceedings of ACM SIGMETRICS* (pp.138-147). New York: ACM Press.

Chapter XXII

Taxonomies of User-Authentication Methods in Computer Networks

Göran Pulkkis, Arcada Polytechnic, Finland

Kaj J. Grahn, Arcada Polytechnic, Finland

Jonny Karlsson, Arcada Polytechnic, Finland

Abstract

This chapter outlines classifications of user-authentication methods based on five different taxonomies. The outlined taxonomies are: user identification-based taxonomy, authentication methodology-based taxonomy, authentication quality-based taxonomy, authentication complexity-based taxonomy, and authentication scope-based taxonomy. Administration of user authentication is briefly discussed. A technical survey of different user-authentication methods and elements of a user-authentication method is also given. User-identification methods such as passwords, tokens, and biometric methods are described. Proposed and implemented user-authentication protocols to overcome security weaknesses of the basic password authentication are surveyed. New user-authentication protocols such as PANA and SOLA are also included. Protocols and software for user registration as well as centralized user authentication are presented and compared.

Introduction

User authentication is a process where a computer, computer program, or another user attempts to confirm that a user trying to set up a communication, is the person he or she claims to be. The definition of authentication is often mixed with the closely related definitions for identification and authorization. Identification is a way of providing a user with a unique identifier for an automated system. During the authentication process, the system validates the authenticity of the claimed user identity by comparing identification data with data stored in a user registry. Authorization is a process of assigning rights to an authenticated user to perform certain actions in the system.

Implementation of secure user-authentication mechanisms is essential when designing computer networks. In a local computer network, such as a corporate *local area network* (LAN) containing highly confidential data, it is important that only authorized users have access to the network. If the user-authentication mechanisms are incomplete, an intruder can steal an authorized user's identity and obtain confidential company information. User authentication is a particularly critical issue in *wireless LANs* (WLANs) where data is transmitted through the air across *radio frequency* (RF) communication channels. In WLANs, physical security measures, such as door locks, identity cards, and security personnel, are ineffective since the connectivity is hard to limit to a certain room or building. User authentication is also very important in public network service systems, such as e-commerce systems and Internet bank systems. If an intruder could access another person's bank account over the Internet, the consequences would be disastrous.

Abbreviations used in this chapter are listed in the Appendix.

Authentication Taxonomy Options

A taxonomy defines a hierarchical structure for an object set. Many taxonomies can be defined for the same object set. A taxonomy is most useful for the management of an object. The classical example of a generally acknowledged and widely used scientific taxonomy is the taxonomy defined by Carolus Linnaeus for classification of living organisms.

User authentication is a very import network security issue. The set of proposed, used, developed, and possible user-authentication methods is already quite large and rich in features. Much benefit would be gained from well-defined taxonomies in network security design and administration. A taxonomy of some current authentication and/or authorization systems is presented in Lopez Montenegro, Oppliger, and Pernul (2004). This taxonomy establishes four categories:

- **General scope solutions** for all network scenarios. These solutions are based on the Kerberos authentication protocol and/or on certificate authentication schemes.

- **Web scope solutions** for single sign-on to a set of Web services. Such solutions are:
  - ➤ Microsoft.Net Passports and with these authentication passports competing solutions,
  - ➤ http protocol-based solutions, and
  - ➤ authentication middleware like Shibboleth.
- **Framework-based solutions**. These solutions are *public key infrastructure* (PKI) based.
- **Authentication/authorizations languages and protocols**. The languages are *Extensible Markup Language* (XML) based. The protocols *Simple Object Access Protocol* (SOAP) and *Simple Policy Control Project* SPOCP) based.

In this chapter, other taxonomies of user-authentication methods are described and assessed.

User Identification-Based Taxonomy

The usual taxonomy of user authentication is based on how a user identifies himself or herself. This classification has four main branches, as shown in Figure 1. The three first branches represent well-known user identification methods:

- "something you know" — knowledge-based user authentication
- "something you have" — token-based user authentication
- "something you are" — biometric-user authentication

The fourth branch, recognition-based user authentication, is a method in which the user makes appropriate responses to several items shown by the network-authentication system to the user (Matsuura, 2001) or in which the network authentication system discovers a unique user feature like the *message authentication code* (MAC) address of the user computer. MAC address discovery must, however, be considered as an insecure authentication method. MAC adddresses are, in principle, unique but still quite easy to spoof.

The user identification-based taxonomy of user authentication is the most useful for overview purposes. The survey of user authenticaton methods in this chapter is structured by this taxonomy.

Authentication Methodology-Based Taxonomy

The taxonomy of user authencation based on the authentication methodology (see Figure 2) has branches for:

Figure 1. User identification-based taxonomy of user-authentication methods

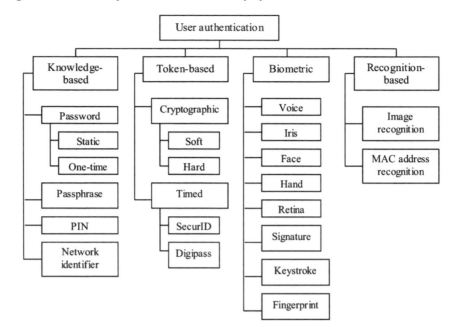

- cryptographic authentication,
- non-cryptographic authentication, and
- open access.

Authentication Quality-Based Taxonomy

From the quality point-of-view, user authentication can be classified in the following categories:

- **Insecure authentication** — unacceptable security risks
- **Weak authentication** — significant security risks
- **Strong authentication** — small security risks.

A taxonomy graph is shown in Figure 3. This taxonomy supports user-authentication method choices when networks and network services are designed.

Figure 2. Methodology-based taxonomy of user-authentication methods

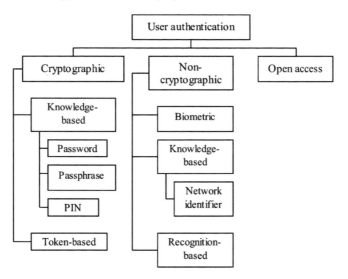

Authentication Complexity-Based Taxonomy

An authentication complexity based taxonomy classifies authentication methods as:

- single-factor authentication, or

- multiple-factor authentication.

Multiple-factor authentication means that a user is identified by more than one method. *Token-based authentication* is the best-known example of two-factor authentication, since token use is authorized by a PIN or by a passphrase or even biometrically. Another common example of two-factor authentication is biometric voice-based authentication, in which a user speaks a pre-registered passphrase.

Multiple-factor authentication is usually strong. A software-implemented cryptographic token provides, however, only weak authentication, since significant risks are associated with a filed token that must be used in the main memory, even if the token file is stored encrypted with a good passphrase.

Authentication Scope-Based Taxonomy

An authentication scope-based taxonomy classifies authentication methods in service-bound methods and *single sign-on* (SSO) methods. Service-bound authentication gives a legitimate user access to one service or to one computer or to one network. A SSO

348   Pulkkis, Grahn & Karlsson

Figure 3. Quality-based taxonomy of user-authentication methods

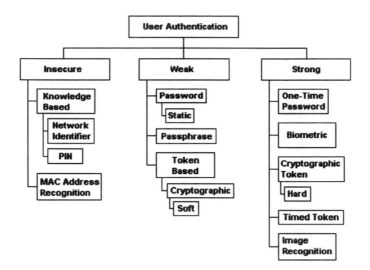

authentication opens user access to a set of services and/or computers and/or networks in which this user has been registered. A taxonomy of SSO systems presented in Pashalidis and Mitchell (2003) defines four SSO authentication categories:

- Local pseudo-SSO authentication,
- Proxy-based pseudo-SSO authentication,
- Local true SSO authentication, and
- Proxy-based true SSO authentication.

Pseudo-SSO means authentication to a component, in which passwords and/or access tokens to a set of services and/or computers and/or networks are used. True SSO means that one authentication method (password-based, token-based, or other) opens access to a set of services and/or computers and/or networks. Proxy-based SSO means that authentication occurs in an authentication server that is external both to the local host and to the set of services and/or computers and/or networks to which SSO opens access (Pashalidis & Mitchell, 2003).

Administration of User Authentication

Administrative procedures are aimed to limit information access to chosen parties and guard information from all others. Typical areas in which general policies and procedures must be implemented and maintained include (Gue, 2005):

- **Certification** — technical evaluation of the network based on security requirements;

- **Chain of trust partner agreements** — an agreement between information-sharing partners;

- **Contingency Plan** — a plan to maintain continuity of operations;

- **Formal mechanism for processing records** — a policy for processing data;

- **Information access control** — a policy for different access levels to information;

- **Internal audit** — regular inspection of access patterns;

- **Personnel security** — a staff security policy;

- **Security configuration management** — a policy to coordinate overall security;

- **Security incident procedures** — a policy for responding to security incidents;

- **Security management process** — a policy to handle security breaches;

- **Termination procedures** — a policy to prevent continuing access; and

- **Training** — security awareness for the personnel.

Intrusion management is the attempt to prevent unauthorized access to system resources and data, and to detect inappropriate, incorrect, or anomalous activity for damage repair later. Intrusion detection provides an extra layer of protection compared to more conventional access prevention methods. Proper choice and implementation of user authentication methods is an essential and proactive intrusion-management issue.

Authentication and authorization need to be considered together in management of user access. Authentication confirms the identity of a user within the network system, while authorization determines whether an identity is permitted to perform some action. On a general level, the following methodologies may be applied to control user access (Lynch, 1998):

- **IP source address filtering:** IP filtering is the most common authentication and authorization mechanism employed by vendors. It is assumed that all traffic coming from a range of IP addresses is valid. This method can be combined with other methodologies for remote authentication.

- **Proxies:** A proxy server is often used together with IP filtering. Proxies act as an intermediary between the remote user and the resource provider. A proxy may operate by utilizing an internal authentication system to validate the remote user.

- **Credential-based access:** The user interacts directly with the resource provider. Many forms of credentials are possible, such as userIDs, passwords, or X.509 certificates. The credential-based approach involves authentication and authorization.

Taxonomies described in this chapter support overview, availability estimation, comparison, choice, and implementation effort estimation of different user authentication methods.

Survey of User Authentication Methods

Elements of an User-Authentication Method

A user authentication method consists of three key elements:

*   User identification,
*   Authentication protocol, and
*   Registration of legitimate users.

Four fundamental methods to identify a user are shown in the classification tree in Figure 1. User identification is necessary but not sufficient for user authentication. A legitimate user must also be registered. An authentication protocol is a procedure that verifies the identity and the registration of a user. The same authentication protocol usually supports different user identification and/or user registration methods. Authentication protocol examples are basic *password authentication protocol* (PAP), challenge-response protocols like *challenge-handshake authentication protocol* (CHAP) and *Microsoft CHAP* (MCHAP), Kerberos, *extensible authentication protocol* (EAP), and the like. Some authentication protocols and/or user-registration methods require dedicated servers.

Knowledge-based, biometric and recognition-based user identification usually requires user registration. A password, a passphrase, a PIN, or image recognition responses cannot be verified without a direct or indirect user registration. However, cryptographic token-based user identification is possible without any user registration, since a public key with or without certification is usually attached to an authentication request, and the user identity can be verified with this public key.

User Identification

User Passwords

A user password is a character string known only by the user. Security risks are related to password quality and password privacy. Improved password security is achieved by password renewal policies. Best password security is achieved by *one-time passwords*.

Exclusive User Ownership of a Token

Exclusive user ownership of a token means exclusive access to a private key in public key cryptography or exclusive access to a generator of successive access codes (timed token or authenticator). Timed-token technology examples are SecurID (RSA, 2005) and Digipass (Vasco, 2005).

Exclusive user ownership of a token is software based, when, for example, a private key can be stored in an encrypted file and an authenticator can be software based. Exclusive user control of a token is hardware based, when, for example:

- a private key is stored in a *Subscriber Identity Module* (SIM) card chip, in some other smart card chip, in an *Universal Serial Bus* (USB) token chip, or the like, or

- successive access codes are generated by a piece of unique hardware

Security risks with private key tokens are related to:

- trust in the corresponding public keys,

- key strength,

- access privacy,

- key capture, and

- advances in algorithms for breaking public-kcy cryptographic systems in future computer systems.

Security risks with tokens generating access-code sequences are related to secrecy of the seed of generation algorithms.

Biometric User Identification

Biometric user identification can be based on unique human characteristics like (Huopio, 1998):

- **Fingerprint**. No fingers have identical prints, even from the same person or from identical twins. Traditional fingerprint technology systems rely on small unique marks of the finger image known as minutiae. The minutiae points classify the ridge and valley patterns of the fingerprint. The relative position of minutiae is then used for comparison.

- **Hand**. A three-dimensional image of the hand is taken and the shape and length of fingers and knuckles are measured to verify an individual's identity. This optical technology is user-friendly but does not achieve the highest level of accuracy.

- **Voice**. Speaker identification determines which speaker is present. This process is based on the speaker's utterance. The input is compared to models stored in a data base to determine the speaker's identity. Voice verification is accomplished by comparing a PIN or a password with a stored voiceprint.

- **Face**. The unique shape, pattern, and positioning of facial characteristics, and their relationship to each other, are analyzed. Face recognition technology is complex and software based. Artificial intelligence and machine learning are applied. There are two main methods of capture: video or thermal imaging.

- **Iris**. Visually, the iris is the coloured ring of textured tissue surrounding the pupil of the eye. Each iris has a unique and complex structure that is stable and unchanged throughout life. Iris scanning can be done from a distance of a few meters and the results are very accurate.

- **Retina**. Optical technology is used to map the capillary pattern (fovea) of the retina of the eye. Retina scanning is thought to be the most accurate of all biometrics. A severe drawback is the inconvenience for end users. The eye must be positioned approximately three inches from an eyepiece, the head must be in a stabilized position, and the eye must focus on a green dot.

- **Signature**. *Dynamic Signature Verification* (DSV) extracts a number of characteristics from the physical signing process. Such characteristics are the angle of the pen, velocity and acceleration of the tip of the pen, number of times the pen is lifted, and the time taken to sign.

- **Keystroke**. Keystroke verification (typing rhythms) analyzes the way we type by monitoring the keyboard input 1000 times per second. Studies have been established that typing patterns are unique (Leggett et al., 1991). The verification occurs seamlessly while the person is doing his or her job.

Security risks — such as insufficient recognition accuracy, faked biometric features, or the existence of an unknown identical twin — are considerably lower than for other user-identification methods.

Authentication Protocols

Several user-authentication protocols have been proposed and implemented in order to overcome security weaknesses of the basic PAP with encrypted password comparison. Presently, new user authentication protocols like *Protocol for Carrying Authentication for Network Access* (PANA) and *Statistical One-Bit Lightweight Authentication* (SOLA) are also being developed.

Strong Password-Based Authentication Protocols

In strong password-authentication protocols, passwords are verified by public-key cryptography, usually the Diffie-Hellman key agreement protocol. The *Secure Remote Password Protocol* (SRP), first published in Wu (1998) and later adopted as an *Internet Engineering Task Force* (IETF) Request For Comments (RFC) standard (Wu, 2000), is the most widely used authentication protocol in this protocol category. In SRP, password verifiers obtained by hashing and modular exponentiation are stored in the server-user data base. A user password is integrated in a Diffie-Hellman-like protocol for key agreement. The user is authenticated after the obtained session key has been mutually verified. A standard — Institute of Electrical and Electronics Engineers (IEEE) P1363.2 for Password-Based Public-Key Cryptography — is presently being developed. Further developed SRP versions and other strong password-authentication protocol proposals have been submitted to the IEEE Working Group developing the P1363.2 standard (IEEE, 2005).

Challenge-Response Authentication Protocols

CHAP is a classic *challenge-response protocol*. A challenge is typically a unique random number combined with a counter value. A response is a return value created by applying a mutually agreed-upon hash function to a concatenation of the received value and a shared secret. The response is verified if the receiving side can calculate the same hash value. A challenge-response protocol protects the communication between a user and the IT context, where a user is registered. User passwords must usually be explicitly accessible, also in the IT context.

MS-CHAP is a challenge-response protocol for mutual authentication of the user and the authentication server. This means that the user also challenges the authentication server. The user is authenticated only if the responses to both challenges are verified.

The Kerberos challenge-response authentication protocol was developed in Project Athena at *Massachusetts Institute of Technology* (MIT) in the U.S. and first published in 1988. Kerberos is based on traditional symmetric cryptography. The components of Kerberos are an *Authentication Server* (AS) with a password data base and a *Ticket-Granting Server* (TGS). A key distribution service is assumed to be available. Kerberos supports True SSO, since tickets can be granted from the TGS to a set of services to an authenticated user. An improved Kerberos version (v5) is presently an adopted IETF RFC standard (Kohl & Neuman, 1993).

RSA Authentication and Certificate Authentication use public-key cryptography-based challenge-response protocols. The random challenge is encrypted with a public key, and the response is hashed and can be signed by the corresponding private key.

Image recognition-based user authentication can be regarded as a challenge-response extension to knowledge-based user authentication. Image recognition-based authentication is quite secure from the human point-of-view, when the items are randomly generated images that are difficult to write down or tell to other persons. A typical recognition protocol is based on a user choice of about 10 pass objects from a set N of hundreds of images. A challenge is a screen with all N objects randomly scattered shown to the user. The user must respond by mouse-clicking in a triangle defined by tree pass objects. The challenge is repeated about 10 times. A user giving correct responses to all challenges is authenticated. The probability of clicking in a correct region for every challenge is very low for a user who doesn't know the pass objects (see, for example, Dhamija & Perrig, 2000; Sobrado & Birget, 2002).

Extensible Authentication Protocol (EAP)

EAP, specified in the IETF standard RFC 2284 (Blunk & Vollbrecht, 1998), is a universal authentication protocol used in point-to-point connections, wired LANs, and wireless LANs. Currently, EAP is most often used in WLANs invoked by the 802.1X standard. EAP handles the transportation of authentication messages between a client and an *Authentication, Authorization, and Accounting* (AAA) server over the link layer. A typical EAP authentication conversation between a client and an AAA server in a WLAN is illustrated in Figure 4.

EAP supports a number of authentication protocols, usually called EAP types. Examples of EAP types are:

- **MD5** (Message Digest 5),

- **LEAP** (Lightweight EAP),

- **TLS** (Transport Layer Security),

- **TTLS** (Tunneled Transport Layer Security),

- **PEAP** (Protected EAP), and

- **SIM** (Subscriber Identity Module).

EAP-MD5 and EAP-LEAP provide username/password-based user authentication between the supplicant and the authentication server. EAP-MD5 is the least secure version of EAP due to the lack of support for mutual authentication and session key creation. EAP-LEAP supports mutual authentication and uses a challenge-response exchange.

EAP-TLS, EAP-TTLS, and EAP-PEAP are based on PKI authentication. EAP-TTLS and EAP-PEAP, however, only use certificate authentication for authenticating the network to the user. User authentication is performed using less complex methods, such as user

Figure 4. EAP authentication exchange messages

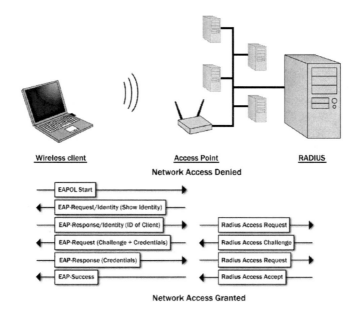

name and password. EAP-TLS provides mutual certificate-based authentication between wireless clients and authentication servers. This means that a X.509-based certificate is required both on the client and authentication server for user and server authentication (Domenech, 2003).

EAP-SIM is an emerging standard, allowing users to authenticate to a network using mobile phone SIM cards and the *Global System for Mobile Communications* (GSM) mobile phone authentication network (Open System Consultants, 2003). An EAP-SIM-supported network needs a *Radius Authentication Dial in User Service* (RADIUS) server with a GSM/Mobile Application Part/Signaling System 7 (GSM/MAP/SS7) gateway implemented. During authentication, the RADIUS server establishes a connection with the user's GSM operator through the GSM/MAP/SS7 gateway and retrieves the GSM triplets, which are then used to authenticate the user.

Protocol for Carrying Authentication for Network Access (PANA)

PANA is a client/server network layer protocol, where:

- the client implementation is called PANA Client (PaC);

- the server implementation is called the *PANA Agent* (PAA), which is communicating with an *authentication server* (AS), for example, a RADIUS server; and

- the access control is implemented by an *enforcement point* (EP).

PANA is a carrier of existing authentication protocols like EAP. No new authentication protocol is introduced by PANA.

PANA is presently an Internet draft level IETF protocol. An open source implementation of PANA is already available (Jayaraman et al., 2005; Fajardo, 2004).

Lightweight Security for Access Control (SOLA)

The principle of SOLA is simple. A WLAN client and an access point use the encryption key of a successful key agreement to generate the same random bit sequence. The sending side adds the next bit in the generated bit sequence to the MAC header of each transmitted data frame. The communication overhead of SOLA is very low, since only one bit is added to each data frame. The probability for an intruder to guess a sequence of n bits correctly is 2^{-n}. (Johnson, 2002)

A SOLA implementation also requires a synchronization algorithm for advancing the bit choice from the generated sequence for the next data frame, since data frames and acknowledgement frames can be lost in the data link level communication between a WLAN client and an access point (Johnson et al., 2002; Wu, Johnson, & Nilsson, 2004).

The security and robustness of SOLA, as well as the functionality of a synchronization algorithm has been proved by simulation. In the WLAN research community, it has been proposed to include SOLA in the IEEE 802.11 standard (Wu, Johnson, & Nilsson, 2004).

Registration of Legitimate Users

Registration in a File System

Basic user registration is a sequential file of records representing users, for example, the /etc/passwd file in UNIX computers. In the /etc/passwd file, the user passwords are stored in encrypted form. The encryption type is one-way, which means that it is impossible to recover a password from the encrypted version. However, this method is still vulnerable since the /etc/passwd file is readable by anyone on the UNIX system. This means that "bad" passwords can easily be cracked using a password-cracking utility. A more secure solution is using shadow passwords. By using shadow passwords, the encrypted passwords in the /etc/passwd file are moved to another file, /etc/shadow, that is not readable by ordinary users on the system (Toth, 1999).

Authentication files needed for user authentication to a LAN can be replicated to several computers as in *network information system* (NIS). The benefit of this is that user credentials don't need to be administrated on every single host in a LAN, only on a centralized NIS server. The NIS server distributes password, group, and *network file system* (NFS) information to every host in a LAN. To the user, the network appears as one single system with the same user account on all hosts (Stern, Eisler, & Labiaga, 2001).

In network protocols, such as 802.1X requiring an AAA server, user registration information can be stored as records in local flat files in the AAA server's file system. AAA servers can also obtain user credentials from the UNIX system's password file in case of a UNIX-based AAA server, or from the local Windows user data base in case of a Windows-based AAA server.

For certificate authentication, user registration can also be implicit. Legitimate users are defined by configuration file directives based on certificate information.

Registration in a Directory System

Users of current local area networks are usually registered in a directory structure, which can be replicated to several servers. Examples of such directory systems are *Novell Directory Services* (NDS) in Novell networks and *Active Directory* in Windows networks. Such a directory system can also have an external extension based on the *lightweight directory access protocol* (LDAP).

LDAP is a software protocol for enabling anyone to locate resources in a directory structure, such as organizations and individuals. As NIS, this protocol can be used for managing user accounts and centralizing user authentication in computer networks. There are, however, a number of advantages with LDAP compared to NIS. NIS is only designed for UNIX platforms, while LDAP is supported by many operating systems, including Microsoft Windows, UNIX/Linux, and Novell. User information data in NIS is stored in simple text files. This makes it difficult to handle large amounts of data. An LDAP directory maintains user data bases in a hierarchical tree structure. Another benefit with LDAP is the network security. NIS has no security model, and the user passwords are sent over the network in clear. Any client can bind to a NIS server without authentication, and all clients are granted same permissions. Clients need to authenticate to an LDAP server with a bind operation. A connection between the client and the LDAP server is not established before the bind operation is successful. Supported authentication methods between LDAP clients and LDAP servers include simple username/password and certificate authentication using SSL (Bialaski, 2000; Falcone, 2003; Novell, Inc., n.d.).

Due to the wide support for LDAP in applications and security protocols, a user register in a LDAP directory can be used for validating users in several network login services. In addition to LANs, such services may be remote login services such as *Secure Shell* (SSH) and *virtual private networks* (VPNs). AAA servers like RADIUS can also be configured to use external LDAP services for user registration.

Registration in a Data Base

As an alternative to directory services, data base servers such as MySQL and Oracle can also be used for user registration. AAA servers like RADIUS can be configured to validate user information against such a data base server.

Authentication Protocols

RADIUS

RADIUS, specified in Rigney et al. (2000), is a client/server-based protocol defining central remote access user authentication, authorization, and accounting. The protocol was developed in the mid-1990s by Livingstone Enterprises and is a system of distributed security for securing remote network access and protecting unauthorized network service access. The RADIUS model, shown in Figure 5, consists of three components (Cisco, 2004):

- a protocol with a frame format using *User Datagram Protocol/Internet Protocol* (UDP/IP),

- a server, and

- a client.

The RADIUS protocol provides two main functions: authentication, authorization, and configuration; and accounting.

1. **Authentication, authorization, and configuration** — The RADIUS client operates on a *Network Access Server* (NAS), which can be a wireless access point or a network switch. It passes user information from a client to the RADIUS server and then acts on the returned response. The RADIUS server receives user-connection requests, and validates the user's identity against a local user data base or an external user data base/directory such as LDAP prior to permitting a user network access. The RADIUS server also performs authorization that defines what network services are allowed for the user once network access is granted. Additionally, all configuration information necessary for the client to deliver service to the user is sent by the RADIUS server to the client. RADIUS servers support a number of user-authentication methods based on usernames and passwords, such as PPP, PAP,

Figure 5. The RADIUS client/server model

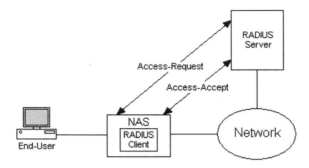

CHAP, and MS-CHAP. Most RADIUS servers also include support for EAP, which provides a number of additional user-authentication methods (Cisco, 2004).

2.   **Accounting** — RADIUS accounting is a method for collecting information about the user's network use. This is needed for billing, auditing, and capacity-planning purposes.

The RADIUS server and RADIUS client authenticate each other using a shared secret. This shared-secret string is never transmitted over the network. Authentication information messages sent by users are encrypted through the use of the shared secret before they are transmitted between the client and the RADIUS server. This prevents attackers from determining user login information (Cisco, 2004).

TACACS (RFC 1492)

Terminal Access Controller Access Control System (TACACS) forwards username and password information to a centralized server. This server is either a TACACS data base or a data base like the UNIX password file with TACACS protocol support (Cisco, 2004).

XTACACS

XTACAS is an extension added by Cisco. XTACAS is a multiprotocol that can authorize connections with *Serial Line Internet Protocol* (SLIP) and enable PPP, IP, or *Internetwork Packet Exchange* (IPX), and Telnet. Multiple TACACS servers and syslog for sending accounting information to a UNIX host are supported (Cisco, 2004).

TACACS+ (IETF draft proposal)

A TACACS+ server provides services of AAA independently. Each service can be tied to its own database or can be used with the other services available on the server or on the network. The following features are included (Cisco, 2004):

- TCP (Transmission Control Protocol);
- AAA support;
- Encrypted link;
- LAN and *Wide Area Network* (WAN) security;
- SLIP, PPP, *AppleTalk Remote Access* (ARA), *Network Asynchronous Services Interface* (NASI);
- PAP, CHAP, and MS-CHAP support;
- Auto-command support;
- Call-back; and
- Per-user access lists.

Password-Based Authentication

Basic Password Authentication

In basic password authentication with PAP, encrypted passwords are stored in the IT context. The user presents a password to the IT context, where the password is encrypted and compared to stored encrypted passwords. A match authenticates the user.

Security weaknesses are absence of control that presents the password and password catching when the password is presented to the IT context.

Pre-Shared Secret

A pre-shared secret is a manually configured ASCII or hexadecimal password string known by a network server and all authorized clients in a network environment. A pre-shared secret is used as a client-authentication method in small office and home network environments by standards such as IEEE 802.11, IEEE 802.11i, or IPSec.

Challenge-Response-Based Password Authentication

Challenge-Handshake Authentication Protocol (CHAP)

When using the CHAP protocol, the user and the authentication server share a predefined secret. The user asks for a challenge, for example, with the user name. The authentication server sends a challenge consisting of nonce (a unique random number) and a counter value. The user calculates a MD5 hash (see Rivest, 1992) of a concatenation of the received challenge and the shared secret. The user sends the calculated hash to the authentication server. The response is verified, and the user is authenticated if the authentication server can calculate the same hash value. The counter value is increased for each CHAP dialogue for protection against replay attacks (Simpson, 1996).

MS-CHAP

MS-CHAP was proposed by Microsoft for remote user authentication over a serial connection based on the *point-to-point protocol* (PPP) but is presently used also for authentication of WLAN users. Present MS-CHAP Version 2 is supported by several Windows environments (Microsoft, 2005).

Kerberos

The AS of Kerberos responds to a user-authentication request with an encrypted challenge. The user password is needed to decrypt the challenge. Kerberos is presently used for user authentication in Windows 2000/XP, as well as in Linux and in other UNIX-based networks. Kerberos can be used also in the Mac OS operating system environment (MIT Kerberos Team, 2005).

S/Key

S/Key challenge-response protocol is based on an unencrypted challenge and a hashed response. S/Key is a one-time password system, first presented in Haller (1994), adopted by IETF (Haller, 1995) and developed as a RFC standard (Haller & Metz, 1996; Haller, Metz, Nesser & Straw, 1998).

In S/Key, a sequence of one-time passwords is generated by multiple hashing. A one-time password is user generated by applying a hash function N times to a private user secret concatenated with a seed S. S and N are given as a challenge to the user by the authentication server. The next challenge to the same user is S and N-1. The user responds with the calculated hash as a one-time password. The authentication server only stores the preceding one-time password from the user. A one-time password is verified by applying the hash function. If the hash of the received one-time password matches with the stored one-time password, then the user is authenticated and the stored one-time password is overwritten with the verified one-time password. S/Key must be re-initialized after N challenge/responses if the first one-time password is generated by hashing N times. S/Key security is based on the practical impossibility to reverse a hash function.

Token-Based Authentication

Cryptographic Authentication

RSA Authentication

RSA authentication is an optional challenge-response user-authentication protocol in SSH. The challenge of the SSH Server is encrypted with the public key of the user. The protocol communication proceeds as shown in Figure 6.

Figure 6. RSA authentication

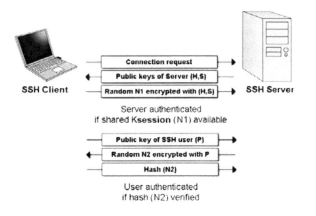

Certificate Authentication

Certificate authentication is a challenge-response and digital signature based authentication method using X.509 certified public/private key pairs. PKI is a system of digital certificates, *certificate authorities* (CAs), and optional registration authorities used to verify and authenticate parties in an Internet transaction. This provides secure user and server authentication methods in large network environments.

An X.509-based digital certificate consists of a public key and identity information of a user issued by a trusted third party, CA. A certificate also includes a validity period that defines the time period for which the certificate is valid for use. An important part of the PKI system is also certificate revocation. A certificate may need to be revoked before the expiration date if:

- the private key is assumed to be compromised,

- the user is no longer certified by the CA, or

- the CA certificate is assumed to be compromised.

The certificate is signed by the private key of the CA. Any user/entity in a network to whom the corresponding CA public key is known and the CA is trusted can thus verify the validity of a certified public key. The X.509 certificate structure and authentication protocols are defined in a variety of contexts, such as *Secure Multi-Purpose Internet Mail Extensions* (S/MIME), *Internet Protocol Security* (IPSec), *Secure Electronic Transactions* (SET), and *Secure Socket Layer/Transport Layer Security* (SSL/TLS) (Stallings, 2002).

Certificate authentication is also supported by a proposed extension to the Kerberos Version 5 protocol (Tung & Zhu, 2005).

Timed Token-Based Authentication

A one-time password with a short validity time (typically 30 … 60 s), combined with a protecting PIN code known only by the owner of the one-time password generator, is submitted to an authentication device for authentication with software that has been custom-designed for the used one-time password generator.

SecurID

The components of SecurID-based timed-token authentication are:

- Hardware- and software-based SecurID authenticators;
- RSA Agent software for identification of SecurID-based authentication requests; and
- RSA Authentication Manager software for registration of users and their SecurID tokens.

SecurID-timed tokens create new single-use access codes every 60 seconds. The current assess code is issued with a secret PIN code by the timed-token owner. Authentication of a user — for example, for LAN access — is based on user name and the access code combined with the PIN code. LAN access is guarded by built-in RSA agent software, which initiates an authentication session over a preconfigured connection to a RSA Authentication Manager. The user is authenticated by the RSA Authentication Manager if the PIN code matches and if the access code matches the correct access for the current, the preceding, or the following minute. RSA Authentication Manager can run on most Windows and UNIX platforms. TACACS+ and RADIUS authentication sessions are also supported by the RSA Authentication Manager software. The user-account data base in a RADIUS server can thus serve both RADIUS and SecurID authentication (RSA, 2005).

SecurID is also one of the authentication methods that are recommended by the IETF (Nystrom, 2000).

Digipass

Digipass is a PIN code-protected hardware device for generation of one-time passwords, that are valid for 30 seconds after creation. Digipass one-time passwords are verified by Vacman Middleware or by Vacman Controller software. Vacman software is integrated in the application, to which the user tries to authenticate. Vacman Middleware can also be integrated in the authentication software of a RADIUS server.

Recognition-Based Authentication

Image recognition-based user authentication requires strong security from the authentication server. User pass object choices cannot be stored hashed as user passwords, since they must be accessible for challenges to authenticating users. Image recognition is single-factor authentication but still provides strong authentication when properly implemented because of the practical impossibility to eavesdrop an authentication sequence.

Biometric Authentication

Biometric authentication as such is usually single factor but is still strong, since it is based on unique and irreproducible human characteristics. Biometric authentication is also used to further improve the security features of multiple-factor authentication, for example, by replacing PIN authorization of a token with fingerprint authorization in token-based user authentication.

Digital Signature-Based Authentication

Three digital signature-based authentication methods are included in the X.509 certificate specification: one-way authentication, two-way authentication, and three-way authentication.

X.509 certificates with public keys needed for signature verification are assumed to be available. B authenticates A by verification of a signed data in one-way authentication. For two-way authentication, two signed data packets are needed, and for three-way authentication, three signed data packets are needed.

802.1X-Based Authentication

IEEE 802.1X is a standard defining client-server-based access control and user-authentication mechanisms to prevent unauthorized network access through publicly accessible network ports (IEEE, 2001). 802.1X, adopted as a standard by IEEE in August 2001, was originally designed for LANs. Later, the standard was also utilized in WLANs. Initially, 802.1X was used in conjunction with the original WLAN security standard *Wired Equivalent Privacy* (WEP), and was later integrated in the recently ratified standards *Wi-Fi Protected Access* (WPA) and WPA2. Services of an unprotected LAN supporting *Dynamic Host Configuration Protocol* (DHCP) are easily accessed by connecting a computer to a network switch port. WLANs are, by nature, even more easily accessed since they are based on open-air connections. IEEE 802.1X prevents network access until successful authentication between the client and the network is successfully performed. 802.1X is based on a three-element configuration. These elements are:

- a supplicant (station, client),
- an authenticator (network switch/wireless access point), and
- a AAA server (typically RADIUS).

Figure 7. 802.1X authentication in unauthorized state

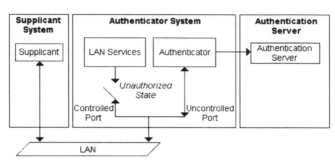

Figure 8. 802.1X authentication in authorized state

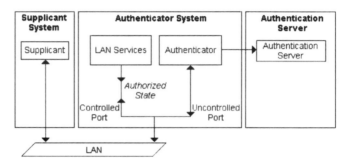

During the authentication process, the authenticator works as an intermediary between the supplicant and the authentication server, passing authentication information messages between these entities. Until the supplicant is successfully authenticated on the authentication server, only authentication messages are permitted between the supplicant and the authentication server through the authenticator's controlled port. The uncontrolled port, through which a supplicant can access the network services, remains in unauthorized state (see Figure 7). As a result of successful authentication, the uncontrolled port switches to authorized state, and the supplicant is permitted access to the network services (see Figure 8).

Authentication Middleware

Middleware is a software layer between the network and the applications for providing services like identification, authentication, authorization, directories, and security (Internet2, 2004). Shibboleth (2005) is an example of open-source authentication and authorization middleware.

The two major components of Shibboleth middleware are the Shibboleth *identity provider* (IdP) and the Shibboleth *service provider* (SP). These two components communicate to provide secure access to protected Web-based resources. SP software is installed in resource provider Web site, and IdP software is installed in the user's home site (Morgan, 2004).

With Shibboleth, a user trying to browse a protected Web resource is redirected by the SP software to a "navigation" page, where the user must select his/her home site from a list of organizations, whose users have access right to the Web resource. The user will then execute a login dialogue controlled by the IdP software in his/her home site. After a successful login, the user is redirected by the IdP software to the original Web resource site. User sign-on is proved and registration information about the user is sent to the Web resource site in data communication between the Shibboleth software modules IdP and SP. User access to the protected Web resource is granted as users with retrieved registration information are accepted according to the access policy of the Web resource site.

However, the authentication protocol is often simpler. The "navigation" page can insert a cookie in the user's browser. The user will then not see the "navigation" page in the next browsing attempt. If the Web authentication service in the user's site uses single sign-on and the user is already sign on, the user will not see the login page. In many cases, a user can thus access the protected Web resource without seeing any intermediate Web pages at all (Morgan, 2004).

Pluggable Authentication Module (PAM)-Based Authentication

The PAM framework consists of the authentication library *Application Programming Interface* (API) and the authentication protocol specific modules (for example, PAP module, S/Key Module, and Kerberos module).

PAM supports integration of different authentication protocols. Authentication protocols are application specific and more than one authentication protocol can be configured for some applications. For example, in a UNIX server, Telnet could be configured for S/Key authentication while login is configured for both PAP and Kerberos authentication. User authentication requests generate calls to the PAM API, which loads authentication modules defined in a configuration file. After this, the authentication protocols of the modules are applied (Samar & Lai, 2005).

Conclusions

Secure user-authentication mechanisms are cornerstones in the design and implementation of computer networks or network services containing important and confidential information. User-authentication needs are dependent on several factors, such as the size of the network, number of users, and the needed security level.

Classifications of user-authentication methods based on five different taxonomies have been outlined. The outlined taxonomies are:

- user identification-based taxonomy,

- authentication methodology-based taxonomy,

- authentication quality-based taxonomy,

- authentication complexity-based taxonomy, and

- authentication scope-based taxonomy.

The outlined taxonomies provide structures for describing and categorizing user-authentication methods in computer networks. Flexible and representative taxonomies of authentication methods are essential for the improvement of information retrieval security. When planning a taxonomy, it is important to consider user perspectives, expectations, sources of information, and uses of information. The technological emphasis is on user identification, user-authentication protocols, authentication servers, and user registration. An overview of the concepts, technologies, and products was presented.

References

AIT Documents (2005). Retrieved January 16, 2005, from http://www.afmc.wpafb.af.mil/organizations/HQ-AFMC/LG/LSO/LOA/aitdocs.htm

Bialaski, T. (2000). Directory server security. *Sun BluePrints™ OnLine*. Retrieved January 17, 2005, from http://www.sun.com/blueprints/1200/ldap-security.pdf

Blunk, L., & Vollbrecht, J. (1998). *PPP extensible authentication protocol (EAP)*. The Internet Engineering Task Force (IETF), Network Working Group, Request for Comments (RFC) 2284. Retrieved January 20, 2005, from http://www.ietf.org/rfc/rfc2284.txt?number-2284

Cisco Systems, Inc. Cisco Networking Academy Program. (2004). *Fundamentals of network security companion guide*. San Jose, CA: Cisco Press. ISBN 1-58713-122-6.

Dhamija, R., & Perrig, A. (2000, August 14-17). Déjà vu: A user study using images for authentication. In *Proceedings of the 9th USENIX Security Symposium,* Denver, CO (pp. 44-58).

Domenech, A. L. (2003). Port-based authentication for wireless LAN access control. Report of Graduation Degree. Faculty of Electrical Engineering. Eindhoven University, The Netherlands.

Fajardo, V. I. (2004). *PANA functional architecture, version 1.0.0*. Retrieved August 31, 2004, from http://diameter.sourceforge.net/pana/

Falcone, K. (2003, July 7-11). LDAP: Integrating authentication across operating systems and applications. In *Embracing and Extending Proprietary Software*, O'Reilly Open Source Convention, Applications Track, Portland, OR. Retrieved from http://conferences.oreillynet.com/cs/os2003/view/e_sess/4166

Gue, D. G. (2005). The HIPAA security rule (NPRM): Overview. *The HIPAAdvisory.com, Phoenix Health Systems*. Retrieved June 5, 2005, from http://www.hipaadvisory.com/regs/securityoverview.htm

Haller, N. (1994, February). The S/KEY one-time password system. In *Proceedings of the ISOC Symposium on Network and Distributed System Security,* San Diego, CA (pp. 151-157).

Haller, N. (1995). *The S/KEY one-time password system.* The Internet Engineering Task Force (IETF), Network Working Group, Request for Comments (RFC) 1760. Retrieved January 13, 2005, from http://www.ietf.org/rfc/rfc1760

Haller, N., & Metz, C. (1996). *A one-time password system.* The Internet Engineering Task Force (IETF), Network Working Group, Request for Comments (RFC) 1938. Retrieved January 13, 2005, from http://www.ietf.org/rfc/rfc1938

Haller, N., Metz, C, Nesser, P., & Straw, M. (1998). *A one-time password system.* The Internet Engineering Task Force (IETF), Network Working Group, Request for Comments (RFC) 2289. Retrieved January 13, 2005, from http://www.ietf.org/rfc/rfc2289

Huopio, S. (1998, Fall). Biometric identification. In *Proceedings of the Seminar on Network Security: Authorization and access control in open network environments.* Helsinki University of Technology, Espoo, Finland. Retrieved January 15, 2005 from www.tml.hut.fi/Opinnot/Tik-110.501/ 1998/papers/12biometric/biometric.htm

IEEE (2005). *IEEE P1363.2: Password-based public-key cryptology.* Retrieved January 20, 2005, from http://grouper.ieee.org/groups/1363/passwdPK

Institute of Electrical and Electronics Engineers, Inc. (IEEE). (2001, July 13). *Standard for local and metropolitan area networks: Port-based network access control.* IEEE.

Internet2 (2004). Middleware initiative (I2-MI) portal. Retrieved March 27, 2004, from http://middleware.internet2.edu/

Jayaraman, P., Lopez, R., Ohba, Y., Parthasarathy, M., & Yegin, A. (2005). PANA framework. Retrieved January 20, 2005, http://www.ietf.org/internet-drafts/draft-ietf-pana-framework-05.txt

Johnson, H., Nilsson, A., Fu, J., Wu, S. F., Chen, A., & Huang, H. (2002, November) SOLA: A one-bit identity authentication protocol for access control in IEEE 802.11. In *Proceedings of GLOBECOM 2002 - IEEE Global Telecommunications Conference, 21*(1), 777-781.

Kohl, J., & Neuman, C. (1993). *The Kerberos Network Authentication Service (V5).* The Internet Engineering Task Force (IETF), Network Working Group, Request for Comments (RFC) 1510. Retrieved January 16, 2005, from http://www.ietf.org/rfc/rfc1510

Leggett, J., Williams, G., Usnick, M., & Longnecker, M. (1991). Dynamic identity verification via keystroke characteristics. *International Journal of Man-Machine Studies, 35*(6), 859-870.

Lopez, L, Montenegro, J.A., Oppliger, R., & Pernul, G. (2004, June 7-10). On a taxonomy of systems for authentication and/or authorization services. In *Proceedings of the TERENA Networking Conference*, Greece. Retrieved January 17, 2005, from http://www.terena.nl/conferences/tnc2004/programme/presentations/show.php?pres_id=69

Lynch, C. (1998). Authentication and access management issues in cross-organizational use of networked information resources. *Coalition for Networked Information White Paper*. Retrieved June 5, 2005, from http://www.educause.edu/LibraryDetailPage/666?ID=CSD1340

Massachusetts Institute of Technology (MIT). Kerberos Team. (2005). *Kerberos: The network authentication protocol*. Retrieved June 15, 2005 from http://web.mit.edu/kerberos/

Matsuura, K. (2001, September 26-28). Echo back in implementation of passphrase authentication. In R. J. Hwang & C. K. Wu (Eds.), *Proceedings of the 2001 International Workshop on Cryptology and Network Security*, Taipei, Taiwan (pp. 238-245).

Microsoft Corporation. (2005). *Microscoft Challenge-handshake authentication protocol version 2 (MS-CHAP v2)*. Retrieved January 16, 2005, from http://www.microsoft.com/technet/prodtechnol/windowsserver2003/library/ServerHelp/ffb29197-9e0f-4639-a891-3f47735c8751.mspx

Morgan, R. L., Cantor, S., Carmody, S., Hoehn, W., & Klingenstein, K. (2004). Federated security: The Shibboleth approach. *Educause Quarterly, 27*(4). Retrieved January 16, 2005, from http://www.educause.edu/apps/eq/eqm04/eqm0442.asp?bhcp=1

Novell, Inc. (2005). *SUSE LINUX - Administration guide*, Chapter 14. Linux in the Network / 14.7. LDAP - A directory service. Retrieved January 17, 2005, from http://www.novell.com/documentation/suse91/suselinux-adminguide/html/ch14s07.html

Nystrom, M. (2000). *The SecurID(r) SASL mechanism*. The Internet Engineering Task Force (IETF), Network Working Group, Request for Comments (RFC) 2808. Retrieved January 16, 2005, from http://www.ietf.org/rfc/rfc2808

Open System Consultants (2003). *Radiator EAP-SIM support*. Retrieved, January 14, 2005, from http://www.open.com.au/radiator/eap-sim-whitepaper.pdf

Pashalidis, A. & Mitchell, C. J. (2003). A taxonomy of single sign-on systems. In R. Saravi-Naini, and J. Seberry (Eds.), *Information Security and Privacy – 8th Australasian Conference, ACISP 2003*, Wollongong, Australia, July 9-11 (LNCS 2727) (pp. 249-264). Berlin: Springer-Verlag.

Rigney, C., Livingston, S. W., Merit, A. R., & Simpson, W. (2000). *Remote authentication dial in user service (RADIUS)*. The Internet Engineering Task Force (IETF), Network Working Group, Request for Comments (RFC) 2865. Retrieved January 16, 2005, from http://www.ietf.org/rfc/rfc2865.txt

Rivest, R. (1992). *The MD5 message digest algorithm.* The Internet Engineering Task Force (IETF), Network Working Group, Request for Comments (RFC) 1321. Retrieved January 13, 2005, from http://www.ietf.org/rfc/rfc1321

RSA Security (2005). *RSA SecurID Authentication.* Retrieved January 20, 2005, from http://www.rsasecurity.com/node.asp?id=1156

Samar, V., & Lai, C. (2005). *Making Login Services Independent of Authentication Technologies.* White Paper, Sunsoft, Inc. Retrieved January 16, 2005, from http://www.sun.com/software/solaris/pam/pam.external.pdf

Shibboleth (2005). *Shibboleth Project.* Retrieved November 30, 2005, from http://shibboleth.internet2.edu/

Simpson, W. (1996). *PPP Challenge Handshake Authentication Protocol (CHAP).* The Internet Engineering Task Force (IETF), Network Working Group, Request for Comments (RFC) 1510. Retrieved January 16, 2005, from http://www.ietf.org/rfc/rfc1510

Sobrado, L., & Birget J.-C. (2002). Graphical Passwords. *The Rutgers Scholar*, Vol. 4. Retrieved June 13, 2005, from http://rutgersscholar.rutgers.edu/volume04/sobrbirg/sobrbirg.htm

Stallings, W. (2002). *Cryptography and network security: Principles and practice.* Upper Saddle River, NJ: Prentice Hall.

Stern, H., Eisler, M., & Labiaga, R. (2001). *Managing NFS and NIS.* Sebastopol, CA: O'Reilly.

Toth, T. V. (1999). *Linux: A network solution for your office.* Indianapolis, IN: Sams Publishing.

Tung, B., & Zhu, L. (2005, May 23). Public key cryptography for initial authentication in Kerberos. *Internet-Draft.* Retrieved June 15, 2005, from http://www.ietf.org/internet-drafts/draft-ietf-cat-kerberos-pk-init-26.txt

VASCO (2005). *Digipass.* Retrieved January 20, 2005, from http://www.vasco.com/products/range.html

Wu, T. (1998, March). The secure remote password protocol. In *Proceedings of the 1998 Internet Society Network and Distributed System Security Symposium*, San Diego, CA (pp. 97-111).

Wu, T. (2000). *The SRP authentication and key exchange system.* The Internet Engineering Task Force (IETF), Network Working Group, Request for Comments (RFC) 2945. Retrieved January 16, 2005, from http://www.ietf.org/rfc/rfc2945

Wu, F., Johnson, H., & Nilsson, A. (2004). SOLA: Lightweight security for access control in IEEE 802.11. *IT Professional, 6*(3), 10-16.

Appendix: List of Abbreviations

AAA	Authentication Authorization and Accounting
API	Application Programming Interface
ARA	AppleTalk Remote Access
AS	Authentication Server
CA	Certificate Authority
CHAP	Challenge-Handshake Authentication Protocol
DHCP	Dynamic Host Configuration Protocol
DSV	Dynamic Signature Verification
EAP	Extensible Authentication Protocol
EP	Enforcement Point
GSM	Global System for Mobile Communications
IdP	Identity Provider
IEEE	Institute of Electrical and Electronics Engineers
IETF	Internet Engineering Task Force
IP	Internet Protocol
IPSec	IP Security
LAN	Local Area Network
LDAP	Lightweight Directory Access Protocol
MAC	Message Authenticaiton Code
MIT	Massachusetts Institute of Technology
NAS	Network Access Server
NASI	Network Asynchronous Services Interface
NDS	Novell Directory Services
NFS	Network File System
NIS	Network Information System
PAA	PANA Agent
PAM	Pluggable Authentication Module
PANA	Protocol for Carrying Authentication for Network Access
PAP	Password Authentication Protocol
PKI	Public Key Infrastructure
PPP	Point-to-Point Protocol
PIN	Personal Identification Number
RADIUS	Radius Authentication Dial In User Service

RF	Radio Frequency
RFC	Request For Comments
S/MIME	Secure Multi-Purpose Internet Mail Extensions
SET	Secure eElectronic Transactions
SIM	Subscriber Identity Module
SLIP	Serial Line Internet Protocol
SOAP	Simple Object Access Protocol
SOLA	Statistical One-Bit Lightweight Authentication
SP	Service Provider
SPOCP	Simple Policy Control Project
SRP	Secure Remote Password Protocol
SSH	Secure Shell
SSL	Secure Socket Layer
SSO	Single Sign-On
TACACS	Terminal Access Controller Access Control System
TCP	Transmission Control Protocol
TGS	Ticket-Granting Server
TLS	Transport Layer Security
XML	Extensible Markup Language

Chapter XXIII

Identity Management:
A Comprehensive Approach to Ensuring a Secure Network Infrastructure

Katherine M. Hollis, Electronic Data Systems, USA

David M. Hollis, United States Army, USA

Abstract

This chapter provides an introductory overview of identity management *as it relates to data networking and enterprise information management systems. It looks at the strategic value of identity management in corporate and government environments. It defines the terms, concepts, and technologies associated with identity management. This chapter is a capstone to other chapters that deal with the specific technologies (strong identification and authentication, PKI, encryption, LDAP, etc...).* Federated identity management *is a strategic concept that encapsulates and integrates these disparate technologies into a coordinated, comprehensive strategy to accomplish enterprise-wide goals. This chapter introduces some practical business case concepts to assists the reader in putting together their own identity management strategies using ROI and* success criteria.

Identity Management

Identity management (IdM) provides a combination of processes and technologies to securely manage and access the information and resources of an organization. IdM both protects and secures the organization and its information. It is a comprehensive approach that requires the integration of the entire network architecture — inherently providing an end-to-end solution.

With the widespread use of the Internet as a business-enabling platform, enterprises are seeing unprecedented opportunities to grow revenue, strengthen partnerships, achieve efficiencies, and win customer loyalty. The widespread use and openness of the Internet, which makes such communication in business relationships possible, also exposes core resources to corruption and inadvertent disruptions. An IdM strategy gives businesses a framework for protecting their infrastructure and incrementally addressing vulnerabilities while remaining open to new opportunities.

IdM is comprised of and supported by the full spectrum of network security technologies. IdM is the system of technologies and policies/procedures that allows the:

- identification,
- authentication,
- authorization,
- access control, and
- provisioning (secure repository)

of individuals, subsystems, objects, information, and data. It is intrinsic to the validation and secure manipulation of information and the control of individual users.

The integrity of an IdM system relics fundamentally on the validity and thoroughness of initial vetting procedures, to include identity management validity and strong authentication. This is intrinsic and provides the secure foundation for the entire infrastructure.

IdM systems technology consists of directory services, user provisioning and management, access management systems, and agents that monitor requests for resources and service. The foundation for a robust IdM system is the user data that typically resides in, preferably, a central store such as a directory server. Clean user data and well-defined business processes reduce the potential for data integrity issues and ensure that identity data across the enterprise is from an authoritative source. On this foundation is built the framework of rights and privileges that support IdM.

IdM, as noted above, is the amalgamation of business processes and technology that enable businesses, organizations, or government agencies to function as a single, secure, integrated entity with efficient, standardized processes for the management and maintenance of user rights and privileges. In an ideal world, each user possesses a single identity that can be leveraged across both the entire enterprise and an infrastructure that allows central management of users and access rights in an integrated, efficient and cost-effective way (EDS SPPS, 2004).

IdM has often been defined in different ways to support various technology trends. One such definition of identity management is the ability of a user to sign-on to a desktop once and have seamless access to *all* his or her applications (often used in conjunction with *single sign-on* (SSO) technology). This definition has historically tended to include script-based or proprietary solutions. Another definition is the ability of a user to sign-on to a desktop once and have seamless access to *many* of his or her applications. This is viewed as "reduced sign-on" that is targeted at "high-value" applications and addresses both business and security issues simultaneously. Technology companies would lead one to believe these functions are IdM. In truth, and as explained earlier, this definition is limited and doesn't fully illustrate the comprehensive solution set that IdM coherently provides.

IdM is the comprehensive strategy of managing identities (logins, profile information, etc.) across many data sources, and maintaining the relationship between those identities. Many technologies and products claim to be identity management systems but, in most cases, they are only a component and rarely address the processes and policies required for successful implementation. Identity management is *established* through company strategies, policies and processes, then *enabled* through education and technology

An important and related concept is that of federated identity. Federated identity is a means by which — through the use of a common trust model — organizations can overcome the constraints of the enterprise and facilitate business between disparate entities. Information is exchanged and accessed securely following accepted rules and policies outlined in the trust model. There are several organizations that are actively assisting in standards efforts to define and reconcile business and technical hurdles towards this vision of facilitating business between disparate organizations.

Technical Fundamentals and Functional Components

IdM is strategic, and its approach requires and encompasses several security technologies. It integrates these often disparate technologies into a comprehensive whole in order to meet defined operational and regulatory requirements in an effective and efficient manner. The following are some of the technologies that may (but do not necessarily) constitute an IdM solution:

- **Strong identification and authentication (I&A)** — this requirement is predicated by and requires strong vetting procedures to insure adequate security. It can be implemented through the use of Biometrics or time/event-based card tokens.

- **Public key infrastructure (PKI)** — inherent in secure infrastructure and generally thought of as "public," in this case we also consider "private" key exchange. For example, VPN servers, firewalls, and bulk-encryption devices often exchange private keys in order to authenticate data traffic between them that is organizationally internal but physically transmitted over the Internet.

- **Virtual private network (VPN)** — the necessary use of encryption to ensure confidentiality throughout the system network.
- **Access management** — the managed control of resources and their access, both from external and internal sources. This is generally managed from a central location within the infrastructure.

IdM is a holistic approach that encapsulates the functionalities of specific technologies and wraps them into a more comprehensive strategy with practical application for the business environment. Consequently, it is important to recognize that the scope of IdM within a secure architecture is comprehensive and necessitates the cohesive application and incorporation of the following:

- **Information**
  - ➢ Attributes, credentials, entitlements, work product, and so forth
  - ➢ Trusted sources of authority and sources of information
- **Lifecycle**
  - ➢ Creation and active management of identity and profile info
  - ➢ Deactivation (removal of entitlements)
  - ➢ Alumni and Retiree (for re-instatement, benefits, etc.)
  - ➢ Removal of expired data related to the individual
- **Context / Role**
  - ➢ B2E, B2B, B2C
  - ➢ Employee, Client, Supplier, Partner
  - ➢ Platforms (type and ownership)
  - ➢ Locale (geography and environment)

In considering an IdM solution, an organization must consider what features are necessary to support its requirements then incorporate the relevant technologies. These features must enhance the conduct of operations and provide the following functionalities:

- Uniformly manage and enforce business policies;
- Leverage existing authoritative information sources;
- Automate administration by using workflows and approval routing;
- Reconcile and correlate account and identity information;
- Reduce security risks via identification of errant accounts;
- Provide for immediate revocation of access;
- Provide self-service of account info and password reset;
- Allow application owner a stake in the approval process;

Figure 1. The five functional components of identity management (Adapted from RSA 2001)

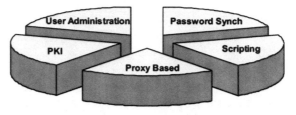

Figure 2. Further discussion of components (Adapted from RSA, 2001)

Component	Pros	Cons
Password Synchronization	Simplifies end-user experience	Still requires manual password entry, and Varying password policies prohibit scope
Scripting	Well understood and easy to create	Some implementations can be difficult to scale, and Not very secure
Proxy-based	Adds security layer	Can be difficult to include some applications
PKI	Based on standards and PKI-enabled apps increasing	Not widely deployed yet
User Administration	Simplifies administrator's work	Problem of too many passwords still exists

- Ensure security within a delegated control model;
- Facilitate business by reducing time to complete requests;
- Reduce costs by gaining efficiencies in effort and operations;
- Improve service levels, productivity, and end-user experience;
- Ensure regulatory compliance and privacy of information; and
- Manage inventory, assigned resources as well as system access.

These functionalities can be divided into five basic components once adequate vetting and authentication have been ensured.

When considering the components and their incorporation, the following comparison is beneficial (Figure 2).

IdM Strategic Focus and Direction

From a comprehensive perspective, one can readily ascertain the various components required to build an IdM solution. The following considerations must be addressed:

- **Policies, procedures, and processes** — Identity management, comprehensively is a process, supported by policy/procedures and enabled through technology, whose purpose is to efficiently, accurately, and securely manage the entire lifecycle, scope, and context of identity and entitlement information across the enterprise. Critical components include the following:

  - *Password policies* — passwords are one of the weakest links in an organization's network security system and typically require considerable attention.

  - *Approval routing/Process and required signatures* — an important but often overlooked part of the business process.

  - *Purchasing processes*

  - *Naming convention process*

  - *Security and privacy policies* — IdM is a critical part of an organization's overall security and privacy policy, which should encompass network perimeter security, incident handling, prevention of social engineering attacks, and other concerns.

  - *Employee management processes* (hiring/exit/retirement)

- **Legal and regulatory requirements** — Much of the notoriety gained by IdM in the last few years is the direct result of the many legal and regulatory statutes put in place to support information protection. HIPAA, Gramm-Leach-Bliley, FDA 21 CFR (Part 11), E-SIGN, and Sarbanes-Oxley are just a sample of the legal and regulatory requirements that impact the fielding of IdM. The aforementioned laws and regulations have one thing in common: they create new compliance pressures on CIOs and CSOs, placing new demands on an organization's security infrastructure. Fortunately, IdM solutions provide a strong, reliable technology foundation for meeting compliance requirements by tightly controlling access to resources and providing reporting tools that demonstrate compliance (EDS SPPS, 2004).

In addition to the immediate issues to be resolved, there are longer-term considerations. Life cycle management of IdM plays a key role in the successful implementation of IdM. Figure 3 illustrates the full life cycle approach to comprehensive IdM.

Each of the IdM phases is supported by the following relevant technologies:

- Directory and data base services

- Identification, vetting, and validation

- Strong authentication

- Provisioning processes

Figure 3. IdM life cycle phases (Adapted from EDS SPPS, 2004, and Hollis, 2005)

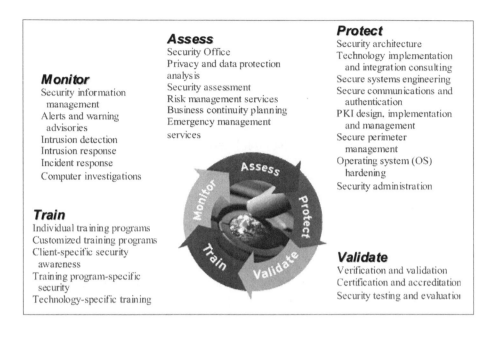

- Information sharing (meta)
- Workflow management
- Collaboration and messaging
- Delegated administration
- Self-service applications

Given the distinct advantages to comprehensive IdM implementation, there are a number of compelling reasons to deploy comprehensive IdM. Some are self-explanatory, such as associated cost reductions. Others are not so obvious, such as the extremely important security and regulatory compliance area. The ability to ensure adherence to company security policies and procedures across business organizations, as well as identification of existing exposures, is key to managing the risk security breaches. Legislation is forcing enterprises to properly maintain their environments, assigning access on a need-to-know basis to ensure the privacy and integrity of information. Automation and self-service of an individual's identity, coupled with pervasive sharing rather than duplication of valued information, will assist with the control and reduction of overhead and operational costs. Integrating existing business processes and information systems into a uniform workflow will further reduce cost by eliminating redundant efforts and duplicate data. By elimina-

Figure 4. IdM advantages (Adapted from Forrester Research, Inc., 2001)

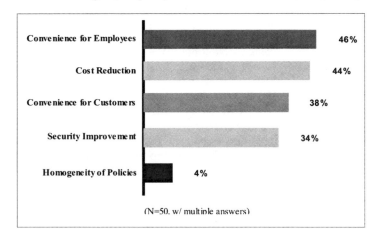

Figure 5. Phased implementation approach to identity management (Adapted from EDS SPPS, 2004)

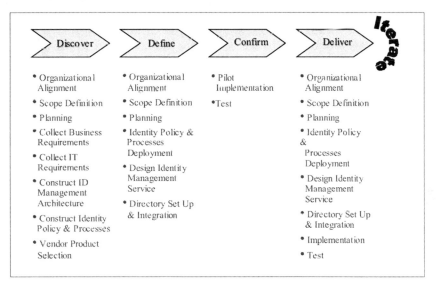

tion of human error and reducing the time to complete a request, service-level agreements can be exceeded. Improving the end-user experience and reducing idle time on redundant tasks raises productivity in the environment.

Precise, timely management of user data and access policies is required for identity management functions. This includes access management and strong, two-factor identification/authentication. There are many commercially available solutions with features such as delegated administration, approval workflow, and user self-service that further enhance user management. There are solutions that streamline user-management tasks, enhance data accuracy and reduce technical help desk and administrative costs. Among the many benefits of IdM is its ability to improve user productivity by reducing the number of account/password combinations by providing single sign-on (SSO), password synchronization, or federated identity solutions. By eliminating the annoyance of multiple logins and passwords, IdM enhances the user experience, reduces vulnerabilities caused by lax password practices, and reduces password-related administrative and help desk costs. Additional benefits of IdM can be experienced with features such as self-service, delegated administration, portal aggregation of content/data, and the ability to remotely access systems. Finally, IdM will facilitate business. Enterprises need to provide their target audience with the ability to self-register for available services in order to easily and quickly establish new business and conduct existing transactions.

Successful IdM Implementation

An IdM strategy must be developed and deployed pervasively throughout an environment and accommodate the entire lifecycle of the identity. There must be top-to-bottom organizational buy-in and support. The approach needs to be phased in to ensure a measurable deployment and positive acceptance throughout the organization (see Figure 5 for an example of a phased approach). It must ensure accountability for identity information, adhere to local laws and government regulations, support commercial best-practices for security and privacy, and be an essential component for non-repudiation. From a business point-of-view, it must provide flexibility and process improvement and show a *return on investment* (ROI) or other defined strategic benefit.

An important first step is to identify the common processes within the enterprise. These processes will be improved during deployment by identifying the technology components within the enterprise and bridge component gaps by introducing the new technology that meets the enterprise view needs, not the point-solution problem. The phases of deployment must be planned by determining the high value-added /immediate impact items that can be implemented in the shortest timeframe. This provides for early "wins" to facilitate the fielding of the IdM system.

Business Case for IdM

Although often viewed as difficult to develop, it is necessary to recognize the compelling business case in support of IdM. It is immediately recognized that, from an operations perspective, the ease of systems use is vastly improved. For example, the enhanced security provided through strong identification and authentication and limited password requirements allows system administrators to enforce password policies across Web, client/server, thin client, and mainframe applications and reduces the possibility of the single authentication point being compromised. But a business case for IdM is generally a requirement of any acquisition and implementation. The foundation of that business case is the return on investment, which is often expressed in terms of the benefit/cost ratio, break-even point, and the comparison of the return from an IdM investment compared to the return from alternative business operations investments. The following discussion illustrates some of the specific items (success factors) that can be used in a typical ROI analysis.

There are four specific areas of improvement that can be used to develop metrics to define an ROI business case for IdM. In addition, success criteria can be developed, and used to baseline and justify the level of success for the IdM business case. These success factors must be defined at the beginning of the process, and progress should be measured against realistic values.

- **Users are no longer required to juggle dozens of usernames and passwords.** This eliminates the need for users to manage changing passwords and allows users to launch critical applications faster.

- **Immediate cost savings are inherent, as many help desks may be spending 40% or more of their time on password resets.** IdM frees up IT resources for more strategic work.

- **Administrators and users spend more time on productive tasks and repetitive data entry for users is eliminated.**

- **There is a quantifiable aspect to enhanced security.** The cost of a managed security service, the cost of maintaining firewalls and IDSs, and the like. Security is considerably enhanced as IdM could eliminate the requirement for passwords through the use of strong authentication (i.e., biometrics). Should passwords continue to be required, IdM eliminates user tendency to keep passwords on sticky notes, keyboards, and rolodexes. Policies are enforced that eliminate poor password management:

  ➤ Easy to remember = "easy to guess."

  ➤ Strong authentication mechanisms can protect the "keys to the kingdom."

  These factors play a strong role in defeating social engineering attacks. The cost associated with successful attacks against corporate IdM is quickly becoming astronomical (Roth, Mehta, Boorstin, & Levinstein, 2005).

Success criteria are immediately self-evident and compelling. For example, the enhanced security provided through strong authentication and limited password requirements allows administrators to enforce password policies across Web, client/server, and mainframe applications and reduces the possibility of the single access point being compromised.

A comprehensive IdM deployment ensures continuous investment protection through managed access and the use of technologies that are reusable across multiple applications. It is also important that the technologies that are deployed adhere to published standards in order to make components modular so they can be added as needed. This ensures maximum interoperability and re-use. In this way, cost savings will be consistently realized.

In conclusion, it is imperative that we recognize the three strategic values that an IdM implementation must provide in an overall ROI business case:

*   Enforcement of business and security policies;

*   Foundation for IT infrastructure strategy; and

*   Compliance with regulatory requirements.

Conclusion

In today's collaborative and interconnected e-business world, federated IdM provides a secure and effective way to share trusted user information across business boundaries —inside and outside the organization. Authenticated, portable identities improve user productivity and enable organizations to seize new business opportunities. Several early adopters in diverse industries are attempting to implement real-world capabilities for federated IdM as they lessen the need to manage accounts for external users and reduce associated administrative costs.

IdM is a security, legal, and regulatory requirement for all organizations' current and future operational frameworks, even if it is not specifically identified. In an increasingly competitive business environment, leading government agencies and industries are building new Web-based infrastructures. These organizations are seeking to gain the strategic advantages of secure collaborative networking. For those organizations that are able to build a collaborative IdM e-Business model, the door opens to a wealth of measurable benefits. IdM provides the security infrastructure necessary to ensure the appropriate authentication, resulting in secure, prescribed access and consequent strong information security.

References

Electronic Data Systems SPPS. (2004). *Identity and Access Management: Concepts and Components*. Retrieved November 16, 2004, from http://www.eds.com

Forrester Research, Inc. (2001). *Build unified access control*. Retrieved March 15, 2001, from http://www.forrester.com/my/1,,1-0,FF.html

Hollis, K. M. (2005). *Identity management briefing*. Retrieved from http://www.eds.com

Roth, D., Mehta, S., Boorstin, J., & Levinstein, J. (2005). The great data heist. *Fortune, 151*(10), 66-72.

RSA. (2001). *RSA security briefing on identity management and single sign on (SSO)*. Retrieved June 25, 2001, from http://www.rsasecurity.com/solutionsTertiary. asp?id=1093

About the Authors

Merrill Warkentin is professor of MIS at Mississippi State University, USA. He has published over 125 research manuscripts, primarily in e-commerce, computer security management, and virtual teams, in books, proceedings, and journals such as *MIS Quarterly*, *Decision Sciences*, *Decision Support Systems*, *Communications of the ACM*, *Communications of the AIS*, *Information Systems Journal*, *Journal of End User Computing*, *Journal of Global Information Management*, and others. Professor Warkentin is the co-author or editor of four books and is currently an associate editor of *Information Resources Management Journal* and the *Journal of Information Systems Security*. Dr. Warkentin has served as a consultant to numerous organizations and has served as national distinguished lecturer for the Association for Computing Machinery (ACM). Previously, Dr. Warkentin held the Reisman Research Professorship at Northeastern University in Boston, where he was also the director of MIS and e-commerce programs. Professor Warkentin holds BA, MA, and PhD degrees from the University of Nebraska-Lincoln. He can be reached at mwarkentin@acm.org and www.MISProfessor.com.

Rayford B. Vaughn received his PhD from Kansas State University in 1988. He is a professor of computer science and teaches and conducts research in the areas of software engineering and information security. Prior to joining the university, he completed a 26-year career in the Army, where he commanded the Army's largest software development organization and created the Pentagon agency that today centrally manages all Pentagon IT support. While on active duty with the Army, he served a three-year assignment with the National Security Agency's National Computer Security Center, where he authored national-level computer security guidance and conducted computer security research. After retiring as a full colonel in June 1995, he accepted a position as vice president of DISA Integration Services, EDS Government Systems, where he was responsible for a wide variety of technical service contracts. Dr. Vaughn has over 70 publications to his credit and is an active contributor to software engineering and information security conferences and journals. In 2004, Dr. Vaughn was named a Mississippi State University, USA, eminent scholar. He holds the Billy J. Ball Endowed Professorship of Computer Science and Engineering.

* * *

Sheikh I. Ahamed is an assistant professor in the Department of Mathematics, Statistics, and Computer Science at Marquette University in Milwaukee, Wisconsinm, USA. He is a member of the IEEE, ACM, and the IEEE Computer Society. Dr. Ahamed received a BSc in computer science and engineering from the Bangladesh University of Engineering and Technology, Bangladesh in 1995. He completed his PhD in computer science from Arizona State University in Tempe, Arizona in 2003. His research interests are security in ad hoc networks, middleware for ubiquitous/pervasive computing, sensor networks, and component-based software development. He serves regularly on program committees of international conferences in software engineering and pervasive computing, such as COMPSAC 04, COMPSAC 05, and ITCC 05. Dr. Ahamed can be contacted at iq@mscs.mu.edu; http://www.mscs.mu.edu/~iq.

Richard Baskerville is professor and chairman of the CIS Department in Georgia State University, USA. His research and authored works regard security of information systems, methods of information systems design and development, and the interaction of information systems and organizations. Baskerville is the author of *Designing Information Systems Security* (J. Wiley) and more than 100 articles in scholarly journals, practitioner magazines, and edited books. He is a chartered engineer, holds a BS summa cum laude from The University of Maryland, and MS and PhD degrees from The London School of Economics.

Ernst Bekkering is an assistant professor in management information systems at Northeastern State University in Tahlequah, OK, USA. Dr. Bekkering received both his MS and PhD degrees at Mississippi State University. In his dissertation, he demonstrated how trust in video communication can be negatively influenced by an artificial effect of gaze avoidance created by camera positioning. His current research interests include adoption of new technologies, security, and telecommunications. He has published in *Communications of the ACM*, *Journal of Organizational and End User Computing*, the *Journal for the Advancement of Marketing Education*, and several conference proceedings.

A. Chris Bogen earned his BS and MS in computer science from Mississippi State University (MSU) where, at the time of this publication, he is a PhD candidate. His current research evaluates the utility of domain modeling in planning computer forensics examinations. From 1999-2004, Mr. Bogen assisted and taught software engineering courses at MSU. He also served three-month internships at the Mississippi Attorney General's Cyber Crime Unit and the National Defense University in Washington, D.C. Mr. Bogen is currently a software engineer for the U.S. Army Corps of Engineers, Engineering Research and Development Center, Information Technology Lab, Vicksburg, MS.

Mark W. S. Chun is an assistant professor of information systems at the Graziadio School of Business and Management at Pepperdine University, USA. He earned a PhD in information systems from the University of Colorado at Boulder and received an MBA from the University of California, Irvine, in the area of international business and strategy. He holds a Bachelor of business administration degree with an emphasis in management information systems from the University of Hawaii. Dr. Chun's research focuses on the use of information technology to create value and to transform organizations. His research interests also include the integration of information systems and the management of knowledge in corporate merger environments. He can be contacted at mark.chun@pepperdine.edu.

David A. Dampier is assistant professor and undergraduate coordinator in the Department of Computer Science and Engineering at Mississippi State University (MSU), USA. He received his BS in mathematics from the University of Texas at El Paso in 1984, and MS and PhD in computer science from the Naval Postgraduate School in 1990 and 1994, respectively. Dave Dampier is a retired U.S. Army officer with 23 years of military service. He currently leads the computer forensics effort for the Center for Computer Security Research and teaches computer forensics and software engineering classes in the Department of Computer Science and Engineering at MSU. His research interests include computer forensics and software evolution. He has had papers published in the *Annals of Software Engineering*, *Journal of Systems Integration*, and *Transactions of the Society for Design and Process Science*. He is a member of the ACM, IEEE, SDPS, and IFIP WG 11.9 on Digital Forensics.

Gurpreet Dhillon is a professor of IS in the School of Business, Virginia Commonwealth University, Richmond, USA. He holds a PhD from the London School of Economics and Political Science, UK. His research interests include management of information security, and ethical and legal implications of information technology. His research has been published in several journals including *Information Systems Research, Information & Management, Communications of the ACM, Computers & Security, European Journal of Information Systems, Information Systems Journal, and International Journal of Information Management* among others. Dr. Gurpreet has just finished his sixth book *Principles of Information System Security: Text and Cases* (John Wiley). He is also the editor-in-chief of the *Journal of Information System Security*, the North American regional editor of the *International Journal of Information Management,* and sits on the editorial board of *MISQ Executive*.

Lieutenant Colonel **Ronald C. Dodge, Jr.**, PhD is an assistant professor and director of the Information Technology and Operations Center at the United States Military

Academy. He has served for over 17 years as an aviation officer and is a member of the Army Acquisition Corps in the U.S. Army. Ron received his PhD in computer science from George Mason University, Fairfax, Virginia. He has published over 20 research manuscripts, addressing a variety of information security and information technology topics, and is a frequent guest speaker. His publications have appeared in books, journals, and proceedings. Additionally, he serves on the boards and chairs several national and international organizations. His current research focuses are information warfare, network deception, security protocols, Internet technologies, and performance planning and capacity management. Lieutenant Colonel Dodge can be reached at ronald.dodge@usma.edu; www.itoc.usma.edu/dodge.

Martin Dortschy is studying electronic business at the University of Arts, Berlin, and is in his final semester. He holds a bachelor's degree in computer science and business studies and participated the Master of Electronic Business program as a study-abroad student at Edith Cowan University in Western Australia. While studying, he worked for three years in the Project Quality Assurance Department at IBM Germany and in the IT Consulting Department of Siemens Business Services.

Jun Du is associate professor of information systems at the School of Management, Tianjin University, China. He received his bachelor's, master's and PhD degrees, all from Tianjin University. His research interests include management information systems, industrial management, engineering economics, and operations management.

Lauren Eder is associate professor and chair of the Department of Computer Information Systems at Rider University, Princeton, New Jersey, USA. She received her PhD and MBA in management information systems from Drexel University and a BS in business education from Boston University. Prior to her career in academia, Dr. Eder worked as a marketing representative for both IBM and for Digital Equipment Corporation (not at the same time). Her current research interests include the adoption, diffusion, and infusion of Internet technology, and the deployment of enterprise resource planning systems. Her work has been published in *Omega, Communications of the ACM, Computer Personnel,* the *Journal of Information Systems Education,* and the *Information Resources Management Journal,* among others. She is editor of *Managing Healthcare Information Systems with Web-Enabled Technologies,* Idea Group Publishing, Hershey, PA (2000). Most recently Dr. Eder completed the Advanced Wine Certificate program at the Wine School of Philadelphia and her research interests have expanded to include the history and development of New World wines.

Eduardo Fernández-Medina has a PhD and an MSc in computer science from the University of Sevilla. He is assistant professor at the Escuela Superior de Informática of the Universidad de Castilla-La Mancha at Ciudad Real (Spain). His research activity is on security in databases, data warehouses, Web services and information systems, and also security metrics. He is co-editor of several books and chapters of books on these subjects, and has had several dozens of papers presented at national and international conferences (DEXA, CAISE, UML, ER, etc.). He is author of several manuscripts on national and international journals (including *Information Software Technology, Computers and Security, Information Systems Security*, and others). He participates in the ALARCOS research group of the Department of Computer Science at the University of Castilla-La Mancha, in Ciudad Real, Spain. He belongs to various professional and research associations (ATI, AEC, ISO, IFIP WG11.3, and others). His e-mail is eduardo.fdezmedina@uclm.es

Dieter Fink is an associate professor in the School of Management Information Systems at Edith Cowan University in Western Australia. Prior to joining academe, he worked as a systems engineer for IBM and as manager, information systems consulting for Arthur Young (now Ernst & Young). He has been a visiting academic at various universities, including the Australian National University, Canterbury University and Free University of Berlin. His interests, published in a wide range of international journals, cover information technology value and benefit realization and minimizing the risk of e-commerce and e-business applications.

Steven Furnell is the head of the Network Research Group at the University of Plymouth in the United Kingdom, and an associate professor with Edith Cowan University in Western Australia. He specializes in computer security and has been actively researching in the area for 13 years. Dr. Furnell is a fellow and branch chair of the British Computer Society (BCS), a senior member of the Institute of Electrical and Electronics Engineers (IEEE), and a UK representative in the International Federation for Information Processing (IFIP) working groups relating to information security management, network security and information security education. He is the author of over 140 papers in refereed international journals and conference proceedings, as well as the books *Cybercrime: Vandalizing the Information Society* (2001) and *Computer Insecurity: Risking the System* (2005).

Arif Ghafoor is currently a professor in the School of Electrical and Computer Engineering, at Purdue University, West Lafayette, Indiana, USA, and is the director of the Distributed Multimedia Systems Laboratory and the Information Infrastructure Security Research Laboratory. He has been actively engaged in research areas related to database security, parallel and distributed computing, and multimedia information systems. He has served on the editorial boards of various IEEE and ACM journals. He has co-edited a book entitled *Multimedia Document Systems in Perspectives* and has co-authored a book entitled *Semantic Models for Multimedia Database Searching and Browsing* (Kluwer Academic Publishers, 2000). He is a fellow of the IEEE. He has received the IEEE Computer Society 2000 Technical Achievement Award for his research contributions in the area of multimedia systems. He can be contacted at ghafoor@ecn.purdue.edu.

Erik Graham, CISSP, is the chief information security officer for General Dynamics C4 Systems, USA, where he is responsible for protecting the confidentiality, integrity, and availability of General Dynamics' digital assets from a wide range of threats. Erik earned a BS from the University of Phoenix and holds multiple industry certifications, including:

Microsoft certified systems engineer, master certified novell engineer, and certified information systems security professional. Erik is an active member in a number of professional organizations and has taught continuing education classes about wireless security issues to the Phoenix Chapter of the Information Systems Audit and Control Association (ISACA). Erik has also been a guest speaker addressing issues about wireless security to classes at Arizona State University.

Kaj J. Grahn, Dr Tech, is presently senior lecturer in telecommunications at the Department of Business Administration, Media, and Technology at Arcada Polytechnic, Helsinki, Finland.

Charla Griffy-Brown, PhD, is an associate professor of information systems at Pepperdine University's, USA, Graziadio School of Business and Management and has served as an associate professor at Tokyo Institute of Technology. In 2004, she received a research award from the International Association for the Management of Technology in which she was recognized as one of the most prolific researchers in the technology management and innovation field. Dr. Griffy-Brown's research examining information systems in Japan and China is currently funded by an SAP University Alliance Grant. She also holds research funding from the Pepperdine Voyager/Lilly Foundation and the Rothschild Research Endowment for international projects exploring information systems security and ethics. Dr. Griffy-Brown graduated from Harvard University, is a former Fulbright scholar, and holds a PhD in technology management from Griffith University in Queensland, Australia. Her e-mail address is charla.griffy-brown@pepperdine.edu

Ronda R. Henning, CISSP-ISSAP, ISSMP, CISM, is a senior scientist at Harris Corporation (USA), a Melbourne, Florida-based international communications company. Ms. Henning is the network security manager for the FAA Telecommunication Infrastructure (FTI) Program. Prior to this assignment, she led the Harris Information Assurance Center of Excellence. Prior to her employment at Harris, Ms. Henning worked in information security research and development at the National Security Agency. Ms. Henning holds an MBA from the Florida Institute of Technology, an MS in computer science from Johns Hopkins University, and a BA from the University of Pittsburgh.

David M. Hollis (LTC, MI, USAR) is currently on extended active duty as the senior operations planner for the U.S. Army Computer Emergency Response Team (ACERT), 1st Information Operations Command. He was previously the ACERT S-2/intelligence branch chief, where he created the branch and led a team of Internet intelligence analysts, and developed innovative methods of visualization graphics for Internet attack/defense analysis. He was also an information operations vulnerability assessment team chief (Red Team), leading a team of military/contractor network penetration attack specialists. Prior to his mobilization, he was senior vice president at Cryptek Secure Communications, and director of federal operations/sales at Secure Computing Corporation. He has a BS in interdisciplinary studies (engineering management) from Old Dominion University and an MBA from Strayer University. He is a graduate of the National Defense

University's information-based warfare course and the Army's Command and General Staff College.

Katherine M. Hollis has over 20 years of experience in the government, military, and private enterprise. She has made significant contributions toward introducing security and identity management information systems into U.S. Government agencies and private industry on a global basis. She is an experienced director, program manager, operations manager, and senior information assurance professional. Currently, she is the Electronic Data Systems (EDS), USA, director for security and privacy professional services security architecture and is the recognized global lead in secure identity management. In these roles, she supports government and industry clients on a worldwide basis. Ms. Hollis is a noted speaker and has supported conferences and seminars in government and industry venues, to include speaking engagements in Hong Kong, Singapore, and London. She is a member of the AFCEA Technical Board, a member of the Federation for Identity and Cross-Credentialing Systems Board, and is a prominent member of the Electronic Authentication Partnership (EAP), Industry Advisory Board (IAB) and FiXs Federation. She has also been active in the International Collaborative Identity Management Forum. Ms. Hollis provides senior leadership to multiple leads and program managers for information assurance (IA) support to multiple government agencies, industry, and European Union member countries. Ms. Hollis also has extensive government PM experience as PM for DoD Electronic Commerce and the Installation Support Module (ISM) programs.

Tobias Huegle is studying electronic business at the University of Arts, Berlin, while currently writing his final thesis in collaboration with Siemens Business Services. He was on a study-abroad program at Edith Cowan University in Western Australia, where he participated in lectures in the Master of Electronic Business program. Before working with Siemens, he worked on a number of consulting and research projects for major German companies and government agencies at the Institute of Electronic Business in Berlin. His academic and professional interests concentrate on information and knowledge management and IT governance.

Jianxin (Roger) Jiao is associate professor of systems and engineering management, School of Mechanical and Aerospace Engineering, Nanyang Technological University, Singapore. He received his PhD in industrial engineering from Hong Kong University of Science & Technology. He holds a BS in mechanical engineering from Tianjin University of Science & Technology in China, and an MS in mechanical engineering from Tianjin University, China. His research interests include mass customization, design theory and methodology, reconfigurable manufacturing systems, engineering logistics, and intelligent systems. His publications have appeared in *IIE transactions, Computer-Aided Design, CIRP Annals, Journal of Intelligent Manufacturing, Concurrent Engineering: Research and Application, AIEDAM, International Journal of Advanced Manufacturing Technology*, and *International Journal of Production Research*. He is a member of IEEE, ASME, and IIE.

Yuan-Yuan Jiao is associate professor of business management at the School of International Business, Nankai University, China. She received her bachelor's degree in textile engineering from Wuhan Textile Engineering Institute, a master's degree in industrial engineering from Tianjin University, and a PhD in systems engineering from Tianjin University, China. Her research interests include industrial management, project management, and international business.

Allen C. Johnston is an assistant professor and the entergy endowed professor of CIS at the University of Louisiana-Monroe, USA, and a doctoral candidate in business information systems at Mississippi State University. He holds a BS from Louisiana State University in electrical engineering, as well as an MSIS from Mississippi State University. He has works published in the *Proceedings of the National Decision Sciences Institute*, *Proceedings of the Americas Conference on Information Systems*, *Proceedings of the Information Resources Management Association*, *Proceedings of the Security Conference*, and in the *Proceedings of the ISOneWorld International Conference*. His current research interests include risk analysis and behavioral aspects of computer security management.

Jonny Karlsson, BSc (Eng), is presently working as a research assistant in the field of network security at the Department of Business Administration, Media, and Technology at Arcada Polytechnic, Helsinki, Finland.

Markus Klemen holds an MA in international business administration and currently is working on his dissertation in the field of SME-specific IT security. He is reading various lectures on IT security at the Vienna University of Technology, Australia, and is employed at the Institute of Software Technology and Interactive Systems, where he is responsible for the IT management of the institute, as well as for various scientific projects concerning IT security. He was self-employed for more than 10 years, specializing in IT security management and administration.

K. Pramod Krishna has several years of work experience as an IT consultant. His experience includes working in the capacity of a program manager with Wipro Ltd, one of India's largest software companies. He has worked on several projects related to the design and development of IT infrastructure including system integration and network design. He holds a Bachelor's of technology degree in electronics and communication engineering. Pramod is a Cisco-certified network administrator, as well as a Sun certified system administrator.v

Ammar Masood received a BS degree in aeronautical engineering from the College of Aeronautical Engineering, NED Engineering University, Pakistan, in 1991, and an MS in electrical and computer engineering from Purdue University, West Lafayette, Indiana, in 2003. He is currently working toward a PhD degree at the School of Electrical and Computer Engineering at Purdue University. His research interests include software security testing and information infrastructure security. His e-mail address is ammar@ecn.purdue.edu.

Sushma Mishra is a doctoral student at Virginia Commonwealth University, Richmond, USA. She has a MBA degree from New Delhi, India. Her research interests lies in the areas of corporate governance practices and its implications on information technology, knowledge management and information security.

Jack J. Murphy is president and CEO of Dexisive Inc., an information technology system integrator focusing on information assurance, network solutions, and enterprise infrastructure applications. Before founding Dexisive Inc., Jack was the CTO for EDS U.S. Government Solutions Group, USA. Jack is an EDS fellow emeritus and remains actively involved with EDS thought leaders. Jack received his PhD in computer science from the University of Maryland in 1986. Dr. Murphy retired as a lieutenant colonel from the Air Force where he spent much of his career on the faculty of the Air Force Academy teaching math, operations research, and computer science.

Mario Piattini has an MSc and a PhD in computer science from the Politechnical University of Madrid; is a certified information system auditor by ISACA (Information System Audit and Control Association); an associate professor at the Escuela Superior de Informática of the Castilla-La Mancha University (Spain); and the author of several books and papers on databases, software engineering, and information systems. He leads the ALARCOS research group of the Department of Computer Science at the Universidad de Castilla-La Mancha, in Ciudad Real, Spain. His research interests are: advanced database design, database quality, software metrics, object-oriented metrics, and software maintenance. His e-mail address is Mario.piattini@uclm.es.

Göran Pulkkis, Dr Tech, is presently senior lecturer in computer science and engineering at the Department of Business Administration, Media, and Technology at Arcada Polytechnic, Helsinki, Finland.

Colonel **Daniel Ragsdale**, PhD is associate professor and director of the information technology program in the Department of Electrical Engineering and Computer Science at the U.S. Military Academy. An Army officer with over 24 years of active service, he has published over 50 research manuscripts, addressing a variety of information security and information technology topics. His publications have appeared in books, journals, and proceedings such as *IEEE Security and Privacy*, *IEEE Computer*, the *Journal of Information Security*, and the *Journal of Information Warfare*. Colonel Ragsdale serves on the board of several national and international organizations. He holds a BA from the U.S. Military Academy, an MS from the Naval Postgraduate School, and a PhD from Texas A&M University. Colonel Ragsdale can be reached at daniel.ragsdale@usma.edu and www.itoc.usma.edu/ragsdale.

H. Raghov Rao is a professor in the School of Management at State University of New York at Buffalo, USA. His interests are in the areas of management information systems, decision-support systems, and expert systems and information assurance. He has chaired sessions at international conferences and presented numerous papers. He has authored or co-authored more than 100 technical papers, of which more than 60 are published in archival journals. His work has received best paper and best paper runner-up awards at AMCIS and ICIS. Dr. Rao has received funding for his research from the National Science Foundation, the Department of Defense, and the Canadian Embassy, and he has received the University's prestigious teaching fellowship. He has also received the Fulbright fellowship in 2004. He is a co-editor of a special issue of *The Annals of Operations Research*, the *Communications of the ACM*, and the associate editor of *Decision Support Systems*, *Information Systems Research,* and *IEEE Transactions in Systems, Man and Cybernetics*, and co-editor in chief of *Information Systems Frontiers*

Mark B. Schmidt, MBA, MSIS, is an assistant professor of BCIS at St. Cloud State University in St. Cloud, MN, USA, and a doctoral candidate in business information systems at Mississippi State University. He has works published in the *Communications of the ACM, Journal of Computer Information Systems, Mountain Plains Journal of Business and Economics, Journal of End User Computing, Proceedings of the National Decision Sciences Institute, Proceedings of the Americas Conference on Information Systems, Proceedings of the Information Resources Management Association, Proceedings of the Security Conference,* and in the *Proceedings of the IS OneWorld International Conference*. His current research interests include computer security and wireless computing.

Sahra Sedigh-Ali received a BS from Sharif University of Technology and MS and PhD degrees from Purdue University, all in electrical engineering, in 1995, 1998, and 2003, respectively. She is currently an assistant professor with the Departments of Electrical and Computer Engineering and Information Science and Technology at the University of Missouri-Rolla, USA. She worked for Cisco Systems from May 1997 to May 2000. Dr. Sedigh-Ali held a Purdue Research Foundation fellowship from 1996 to 2000, and is a member of Eta Kappa Nu, IEEE, ACM, and ASEE. Her research interests include software quality, intelligent infrastructures, and safety-critical software. She can be contacted at sedighs@umr.edu.

Raj Sharman is an assistant professor in the School of Management at State University of New York at Buffalo, USA. His research interests are primarily in the field of information assurance, medical informatics, conceptual modeling and ontology, and data mining. His current projects in the area of information systems security include developing biologically inspired computer security models, as well as developing architectures for critical incident management systems. He is a recipient of several grants, both internal and external. These include grants in the areas of information security from NSF and AFSOR. His publications appear in peer-reviewed journals and international conferences in both the information systems and the computer science disciplines. He also serves as an associate editor for *Journal of Information Systems Security*. His past work experience includes developing and managing hospital information systems. Raj Sharman has served on several PhD and Master's thesis committees. He is currently guiding several projects in the area of information assurance. Raj Sharman received his Bachelor of technology in engineering and Master of Technology in industrial management from the Indian Institute of Technology Bombay, India. He received his MSc in industrial engineering and his PhD in computer science from Louisiana State University, Baton Rouge.

Ambareen Siraj is a PhD candidate in the Computer Science and Engineering Department at the Mississippi State University, USA. She is working under the direction of Dr. Rayford B. Vaughn. Her research is in the area of information assurance.

Andrew P. Snow received his BS and MS degrees in engineering (electrical) from Old Dominion University, and his PhD in information science from the University of Pittsburgh. His publications appear in *IEEE Transactions on Reliability, IEEE Transactions on Engineering Management, Journal of Networks and Systems Management, Telecommunications Policy, ACM/Baltzer Journal on Mobile Networks and Applications,* and *IEEE Computer.* Prior to returning to university for an academic career, he held positions as electronics engineer, member of the technical staff, manager, director, vice president, general manager, and chairman in telecommunications carrier, systems integration, and consulting firms.

Detmar Straub is the J. Mack Robinson distinguished professor of information systems at Georgia State University, USA. Detmar has conducted research in the areas of Net-enhanced organizations (e-commerce), computer security, technological innovation, and international IT studies. He holds a DBA (Doctor of Business Administration) in MIS from Indiana, and a PhD in English from the Pennsylvania State University. He has published over 120 papers in journals such as *Management Science, Information Systems Research, MIS Quarterly, Organization Science, Communications of the ACM, Journal of MIS, Journal of AIS, Information & Management, Communications of the AIS, IEEE Transactions on Engineering Management, OMEGA, Academy of Management Executive,* and *Sloan Management Review.*

Paul John Steinbart is a professor in the Department of Information Systems at Arizona State University, Tempe. He has developed and taught graduate courses on computer and information security and also teaches an undergraduate course on accounting information systems. Professor Steinbart's research has been published in leading academic journals including *MIS Quarterly, Decision Sciences,* and *The Accounting Review.* He is also co-author of the textbook *Accounting Information Systems* published by Prentice-Hall. Professor Steinbart also serves as associate editor for the *Journal of Information Systems* (published by the American Accounting Association) and is a member of the editorial board for the *International Journal of Accounting Information Systems.*

Carl Stucke is a member of the Computer Information Systems faculty within the Robinson College of Business at Georgia State University, USA, and serves as coordinator of the Security SIG. Carl's interests include security, privacy, business continuity, object-oriented systems analysis, and advanced technology-based business solutions. Before GSU, Stucke held senior technical and management positions at Equifax including chief scientist (VP R&D). Topics he addressed ranged from PKI, consumer identity verification, consumer products, and Equifax's first Internet presence, to machine learning, expert systems, and supercomputing as applied to Equifax's processes. Carl holds a PhD degree in mathematics from Emory University and initially taught mathematics and computer science.

Art Taylor has over 17 years' experience as a practitioner in information systems and has published numerous books and articles on a variety of technical topics. As a practitioner, he was the technical lead on a number of projects where data security was a major concern. He is currently a lecturer at Rider University, Princeton, New Jersey, USA, where he teaches computer programming, network security, and other courses in the Computer Information Systems Department.

Juan Trujillo is a professor at the Computer Science School at the Universidad de Alicante, Spain. Trujillo received a PhD in computer science from the University of Alicante in 2001. His research interests include database modeling, conceptual design of data warehouses, multidimensional databases, OLAP, and object-oriented analysis and design with UML. He has published papers in international conferences and journals, such as ER, UML, ADBIS, CAiSE, WAIM, *Journal of Database Management (JDM)*, and *IEEE Computer*. He served as a member of the Program Committees of several workshops and conferences, such as ER, DOLAP, DSS, and SCI. He also served as a reviewer of several journals such as *JDM, KAIS, ISOFT*, and *JODS*. He can be contacted at jtrujillo@dlsi.ua.es.

Shambhu Upadhyaya is an associate professor of computer science and engineering at the State University of New York at Buffalo, USA. He is currently PI on a DARPA Seedling grant on intrusion detection and, more recently, he received a DARPA contract (jointly with Telcordia and Carnegie Mellon University) in the area of insider threat mitigation using high-dimensional search and modeling. He is also PI on an ARDA effort in the area of insider-threat mitigation in electronic documents. His research interests are information assurance, security in distributed systems, fault diagnosis and fault-tolerant computing. He has authored or co-authored more than 130 refereed articles in these areas. He was an NRC Summer research fellow in 2001 and 2002. He has held visiting research faculty positions at University of Illinois, Urbana-Champaign, Intel Corporation, AFRL, and NRL. He was guest editor of a special issue on reliable distributed systems in *IEEE Transactions on Computers,* for which he also serves as an associate editor. He has served as the program co-chair of IEEE Symposium on Reliable Distributed Systems, 2000. He was a principal organizer of the 1st New York State Cyber Security Symposium in 2003, and the Secure Knowledge Management Workshop in 2004. He is currently on the program committee of three security-related IEEE workshops and conferences. He is a senior member of IEEE and is a member of IEEE Computer Society.

Rodolfo Villarroel has an MSc in computer science from the Universidad Técnica Federico Santa María (Chile), and is a PhD student at the Escuela Superior de Informática of the Universidad de Castilla-La Mancha at Ciudad Real (Spain). He is an assistant professor at the Computer Science Department of the Universidad Católica del Maule (Chile). His research activity focus is security in data warehouses and information systems, and software process improvement. He is the author of several papers on data warehouses security and improvement of software configuration management process, and is a member of the Chilean Computer Science Society (SCCC) and the Software Process Improvement Network (SPIN-Chile). His e-mail address is rvillarr@spock.ucm.cl.

Edgar R. Weippl was project manager of large industry projects for two years. Customers included Deutsche Bank in Frankfurt and BlueCross/BlueShield insurance in New York. He has considerable experience with applied IT security. Weippl has taught many tutorials, including "Security in E-Learning," at ED-MEDIA 2003, 2004, and 2005. Currently, Weippl is assistant professor at the Vienna University of Technology, Austria. He holds an MSc and a PhD in computer science, and an MA in business administration. He taught courses on computer security at the University of Linz, Austria, the Polytechnic University, Hagenberg, Austria, and Beloit College, WI, USA. Previously, he worked for three years in a non-profit research organization focusing on security.

Mohammad Zulkernine is a faculty member of the School of Computing of Queen's University, Canada, where he is leading the Queen's Reliable Software Technology (QRST) research group. He received his BSc in computer science and engineering from Bangladesh University of Engineering and Technology in 1993; an M Eng in computer science and systems engineering from Muroran Institute of Technology, Japan in 1998; and his PhD from the Department of Electrical and Computer Engineering of the University of Waterloo, Canada in 2003, where he belonged to the university's Bell Canada Software Reliability Laboratory. Dr. Zulkernine's research focuses on software engineering (software reliability and security), specification-based automatic intrusion detection, and software behavior monitoring. His research work has been funded by a number of provincial and federal research organizations of Canada, and he has an industry research partnership with Bell Canada. He is a member of the IEEE, ACM, and the IEEE Computer Society. Dr. Zulkernine is also cross-appointed in the Department of Electrical and Computer Engineering of Queen's University, and a licensed professional engineer of the province of Ontario, Canada. He can be reached at mzulker@cs.queensu.ca; http://www.cs.queensu.ca/~mzulker/.

Index

mandatory access control (MAC)
  99, 127, 235, 303,345
Massachusetts Institute of Technology
  (MIT) 353
MCHAP (Microsoft CHAP) 350
MD5 (Message Digest 5) 140
MDSCL (multidimensional security
  constraint language) 299
MDX (multidimensional expressions) 299
media access control (MAC) 239
merchants 132
message authentication codes (MACs) 141
Message Digest 5 (MD5) 140
message integrity code (MIC) 239
Microsoft CHAP (MCHAP) 350
middleware 364
misuse detection, *see also knowledge-
  based intrusion detection system* 258
MIT (Massachusetts Institute of Technology) 353
MNC (multi-national corporations) 93
MOMT (multilevel object-modeling
  technique) 297
multi-national corporations (MNC) 93
multidimensional (MD) models 296
multidimensional expressions (MDX) 299
multidimensional security constraint
  language (MDSL) 299
multilevel object-modeling technique
  (MOMT) 297
multiple-factor authentication 347
MySQL 357

N

NAS (network access server) 357
NAS (network-attached storage) 48
NAT (network address translation) 209,
  210
National Cyber Security Partnership
  (NCSP) 6
National Information Assurance Partner-
  ship (NIAP) 192
National Security Agency (NSA) 185
National Security Telecommunications and
  Information Systems Security Policy
  (NSTISSP) 192

NCSP (National Cyber Security Partnership) 6
network 277
network access server (NAS) 357
network address translation (NAT) 209,
  210
network deception 267
network file system (NFS) 356
network forensics 313
network information system (NIS) 356
network interface cards (NICs) 244
network-attached storage (NAS) 48
networking 234
NFS (network file system) 356
NIAP (National Information Assurance
  Partnership) 192
NICs (network interface cards) 244
NIS (network information system) 356
NSA (National Security Agency) 185
NSTISSP (National Security Telecommunications and Information Systems
  Security Policy) 192

O

Object-Constraint Language (OCL) 300
object-modeling technique (OMT) 297
OCL (Object-Constraint Language) 300
OECD (Organisation for Economic Co-
  operation and Development) 3, 63
OLAP (online analytical processing) 299
OMT (object-modeling technique) 297
one-time passwords 350
online analytical processing (OLAP) 299
open shortest path first (OSPF) 209
operating system (OS) 214
operations FU (OFU) 102
Oracle 357
Oracle Label Security (OLS10g) 295
Orange Book 192
Orange Book rating, 183
Organisation for Economic Co-operation
  and Development (OECD) 3, 63
OS (operating system) 214
OSPF (open shortest path first) 209

V

verification management 171
VeriSign 142, 145
virtual local area network (VLAN) 198, 280
virtual machines 280
virtual personal network (VPN) 238
virtual private network (VPN) 48, 88,
      201, 209, 357, 375
virus
        32-bit viruses 53
        encrypted 54
        -detection database 58
        lifecycle 46
        polymorphic 54
        encrypted 54
        retrovirus 55
vulnerability management 171

W

WAN (wide area network) 206
war-driving 236
Web cache 212
Web site defacement 135
Web-based portal 26
WEP (wired equivalent privacy) 238, 363
Wi-Fi Protected Access (WPA) 363
wide area network (WAN) 206
wired equivalent privacy (WEP) 238, 363
wireless
         access points 235
        LANs (WLANs) 344
        networking 234
        security 235
        transmissions 236
Wiretap Act 272
WLANs (wireless LANs) 34
World Trade Center (WTC) 152
WPA (Wi-Fi Protected Access) 363
WPA2 363
WTC (World Trade Center) 152

X

XTACACS 358
XML (Extensible Markup Language) 345

CPSIA information can be obtained at www.ICGtesting.com
Printed in the USA
BVOW040755050412

286899BV00006B/4/P